A HISTORY OF THE WORLD

Atlas, the Greek deity and war-leader of the Titans, bearing the world on his shoulders, a punishment inflicted on him by Zeus and the Gods.

A HISTORY OF THE WORLD

R. J. Unstead

Adam & Charles Black · London

First published 1983
by A & C Black (Publishers) Ltd
35 Bedford Row, London WC1 4JH

© 1983 R. J. Unstead Publications Ltd
Maps by Roger Gorringe

Unstead, R. J.
  A history of the world.
  1. World history
  I. Title
  909   D21

  ISBN 0-7136-2241-5

ISBN 0-7136-2241-5

Typeset in Hong Kong by Graphicraft Typesetters Limited
Printed in Great Britain
by Biddles Ltd, Guildford, Surrey

Contents

Contents

Photographs

Photographs

Photographs

Photographs

Maps

Maps on this scale can indicate only relative positions and distances. For more detail, the interested reader should refer to a good historical or general atlas.
Names and boundaries of modern states are shown in a grey tint.

Maps

Foreword

My aim in writing this book was to present a straightforward history of the world telling of the rise and achievements of early civilizations, the emergence of nation-states, the course of events and the personalities of those who directed them. Also, I wanted to say something about social conditions and about the period of European dominance in the world and to show how, during the last two hundred years, countries and continents have lost their separateness. As a result, all are now likely to be affected by some momentous event - such as the storming of an old fortress in Paris, the invention of a steam-engine or the assassination of an archduke in a dusty little town in the Balkans.

As I write these words there is, on my desk, a copy of a masterly study of a period of thirty years in the seventeenth century. (To its author, as to a great many others, I am deeply indebted.) The book is almost exactly the same length as this one of mine - yet I have attempted to deal with some 5000 years. It will not be surprising then, if I have over-simplified some issues and failed to present a balanced account of others.

I have, however, tried to tell in broad outlines what has happened in history, showing how the world has come to be what it is. I hope that at least some of my readers will be stirred to burrow more deeply.

Finally, I should like to record my thanks to my indefatigable editor, Anne Watts, and to my wife, without whose help the book would never have been written.

R.J.U.

PART ONE

The Ancient World

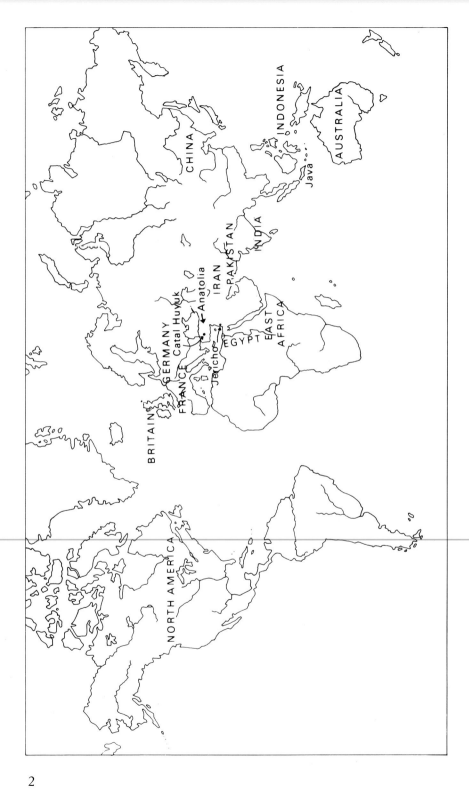

1 Before Civilization

The earth on which we live is very old – perhaps six thousand million years old – and after it came into existence, an immense period of time went by before the first living things appeared. These were ferns, grasses, sponges and trees. Animal life first developed as one-celled creatures, then kinds of jelly-fish and worms. Next came fishes and amphibians, and these were followed by giant reptiles – the dinosaurs and pterodactyls of 180 to 70 million years ago.

These huge creatures were succeeded by birds and mammals, such as rodents, horses, sheep, elephants and flesh-eaters like lions and tigers and bears. Last of all appeared the ancestors of Man, members of ape-like groups of mammals called primates. The first of these groups probably appeared in East Africa about three-quarters of a million years ago, though some experts place them much farther back in time. This type, called *Australopithecus*, which means 'Southern Ape', had a small brain and was not quite human, but a second type, *Homo habilis* ('Skilful Man'), a small creature about four feet tall, used stone tools and was probably our direct ancestor.

By the time of the first Ice Age, some 500 000 years ago, Man's ancestors had spread from Africa as far as Indonesia, China and Europe. Fossilized remains of a type called *Pithecanthropus erectus* ('Upright Man') have been found in widely-separated places, so that they have been called Java Man, Peking Man and Heidelberg Man. All were about five feet tall, with a low forehead, a bony ridge above the eyes, massive teeth and strong jaws. They lived by gathering food and hunting, knew how to use fire and made an all-purpose stone tool, the hand-axe.

The next type of developing man is known as *Neanderthal Man*, because remains of him were found in the Neander Valley in Germany. From about 80 000 BC, he was using a variety of stone tools and scrapers, was making clothes out of skins and burying his dead with food and implements beside the body. By about 25 000 BC he had died out, driven from his hunting-grounds by a stronger, more intelligent being, *Cromagnon Man*, who, in the Old Stone Age, made tremendous advances. His name comes from a place in France where skeletons were found in a cave in 1868.

The Cromagnons, or 'Advanced Hunters', still lived by hunting wild animals, catching fish and gathering berries, fruits, roots and shell-fish, but

Cave painting of a bison at Altamira, Spain.

Cave paintings at Brandberg, south-west Africa.

they learned how to store food and cook their meat They made tools and weapons of bone, flint, stone and wood - axes, spears, harpoons, knives, eyed needles, bows and arrows, and fat-burning lamps. Dwelling in family groups in caves and huts, they sewed skins together to make clothes and ornamented themselves with bracelets and necklaces made of shells, ivory and coloured stones.

Some of them, especially a group called Magdalenians, who lived between 15 000 and 10 000 BC, painted marvellous pictures of animals and hunting-scenes on the inner walls of caves, particularly in the Dordogne region of France, and they also carved small figures of animals and women out of stone, ivory and bone. Carvings of women with huge breasts, belly and thighs may indicate that they believed in a Mother Goddess, giver of life, whether to children or young creatures.

During the Middle Stone Age, a short period lasting from about 10 000 BC for two or three thousand years, people in parts of Asia and the Near East were gathering the ears of wild wheat and barley and using querns (hand-mills) to grind the ripe seeds into flour. They were only a step away from farming, a way of obtaining a regular food supply by growing crops and keeping animals to provide milk and meat. True farming began in the New Stone Age, from about 8000 BC, in southern Anatolia (Turkey) where the wild ancestors of wheat, barley, sheep and goats flourished naturally in the fertile valleys. Here, and presently in other parts of the Near East, people were able to live settled lives and to build villages and even towns like Jericho and Catal Huyuk. They cultivated fields and developed skills in pottery, metal work, spinning and weaving.

This new style of living spread to some of the Mediterranean shores and islands, to Egypt, Mesopotamia, Iran and Pakistan and northern India. But outside these areas, people went on living by hunting and food-gathering; it was not until about 3000 BC, for instance, that New Stone Age people reached Britain, bringing with them their pots and ploughs. Yet by this time splendid civilizations had arisen in Egypt and Mesopotamia. The North American Indians and the aborigines of Australia followed an Old Stone Age way of life for centuries and, even today, there are still nomads in the world who hunt with bows and arrows.

Farming led to the rise of the first civilizations. What do we mean by 'civilization' and how did it happen? These are not easy questions to answer.

We generally say that people became civilized when they lived together in an organised way, obeying laws and following a variety of occupations; they built towns and cities, usually (though not always) made use of wheels for pottery, vehicles and machinery, and possessed some form of writing. Most frequently, civilizations arose where a warm climate, fertile soil and an ample water supply enabled the farmers to produce so much food that there was no need for everyone to work on the land. Some men could design buildings or act as rulers, lawyers and priests; others could work as sculptors, painters, scribes, jewellers, potters, carpenters and so on. This certainly happened in the first civilizations of which we know anything, where people were unaware of the world outside their own valley or region. Later, as races moved from the deserts and mountains into the fertile lands, and as people began to travel and conquer, the idea of civilization spread more and more widely.

2 Mesopotamia
c. 3500 – 2000 BC

A great crescent of land curves north of Palestine, through Syria and south through Mesopotamia to the Persian Gulf. This land, between the mountains of the north and the deserts of the south, is known as the Fertile Crescent. In Mesopotamia (now called Iraq), in the eastern part of this crescent, arose one of the first civilizations in the world.

Mesopotamia means 'between the two rivers', the Tigris and the Euphrates, which rise in Turkey and flow south-east into the Persian Gulf. (6000 years ago, they had separate mouths about 100 miles north of where they now enter the Gulf as one river.) These rivers regularly overflowed their banks and covered the plain with a deep layer of rich mud, excellent for crops. The inhabitants of the southern part, called Sumer, became farmers from about 5000 BC or even earlier, keeping sheep and cattle, and growing grain crops such as barley, millet and a kind of wheat called *emmer*.

They learned by experience how to irrigate their fields. They became expert potters, who used a wheel and decorated their pots with artistic designs. They also learned how to work copper and make razor-sharp tools from stones brought in from the desert.

By about 3500 BC, the Sumerians were living in cities such as Eridu, Ur, Lagash and Kish. There was no building stone on the plain, so they made bricks from river mud and dried them in the hot sun. Not only houses, but town walls and temples called *ziggurats* were built of sun-dried mud-bricks. A ziggurat was a vast edifice, often built on top of the ruins of earlier temples, which rose in terraces to a small shrine that was sacred to a particular god. Anu was father of the gods, who included Enil, god of the air; Enki, god of wisdom and water; Nannar, the moon, and Shamash, the sun. The temple stood in a large walled *timenos* or courtyard which contained the priests' houses, lesser temples, a royal palace and storerooms filled with the 'god's treasures'.

Priests formed the highest and most important class of citizens, for they served the gods who were held to control the lives of all Sumerians. It was the priests who looked after the 'gods' lands' outside the city, collected the offerings and conducted trade with neighbouring peoples, exchanging surplus food for timber, stone, gold and silver which their own country lacked.

In the early days of Sumer, the ruler of the city-state (ie. a city and an area of land round about) was the High-Priest but, in time, he became the King or King-Priest who took charge of everyday matters like law and order, upkeep of canals, and military training. It was his duty to lead the army in its frequent wars with other cities.

Besides potters, Sumerian craftsmen included skilled workers in bronze and precious stones. Others made furniture, built river boats from wicker-work covered with hides and pitch, carved statues and depicted people and animals in metal and stone with realistic skill. By 3000 BC, they were making carts and rather clumsy four-wheeled chariots.

Sumerian writing is probably the oldest in the world. It began with little pictures on cylinders which were rolled on to damp clay; scribes then began to make symbols by pressing the wedge-shaped end of a cut reed into wet clay which was afterwards baked hard. This kind of writing is called *cuneiform*, from the Latin word *cuneus*, meaning a wedge.

In the cities, houses fronting on to narrow winding streets revealed only a door and one or two small windows set high up in the wall but, inside, the main rooms were built round an open courtyard, often with a verandah leading into rooms on the upper floor. Underneath each house was a deep pit or soakaway for waste water from washing and the lavatory. Both men and women dressed in a kind of skirt or kilt made of sheepskin and belted or fastened over one shoulder. The nobles loved elaborate head-dresses, wigs and gowns covered with costly beads. Some of the men grew luxuriant spade-shaped beards, but shaved off the rest of the hair on their heads.

Sumerians believed in a rather gloomy sort of life after death and they

The code of Hammurabi. (Louvre)

buried their dead in brick-lined shafts dug beneath their houses. At Ur, a king and queen were buried in a deep pit, accompanied by courtiers, servants and soldiers who had drunk poison so that they could serve the dead sovereigns in the next world.

North of Sumer and in the same plain lay a region called Akkad which.was occupied by Semites who had come in from the Arabian desert. These people were originally nomadic shepherds belonging to many tribes and groups - the Arabs and Hebrews are two of the best known - who moved about with their flocks along the margin of the Fertile Crescent. They traded with the people of the towns and villages and, from time to time, some would decide to give up their wandering way of life and settle down in a town or district which they seized by force of arms.

This they had done in Akkad and, in about 2500 BC, a great Semitic king, Sargon I, conquered all the Sumerian cities to the south and made himself lord of the entire plain. This Akkadian empire, as it might be called, lasted for some 200 years, after which Ur rose again to power under King Ur-Nammu. He and his successors ruled many provinces but, in about 2000 BC, Ur was conquered by the Elamites, a people who moved into the plain from the highlands lying east of Mesopotamia. Meanwhile, other peoples were entering the Fertile Crescent, such as the Amorites, another Semitic people, who established themselves in Akkad and Assur, to the north, occupying Babylon, Damascus and Jericho, three of the oldest cities in the world. Pressing in from the north came the Hittites, a warlike people who moved from the steppes of Central Asia and occupied much of northern Syria and Asia Minor (modern Turkey).

The Amorites founded a new empire round Babylon where, in about 1800 BC, a great King named Hammurabi drove out the Elamites and won possession of the whole of Mesopotamia. A wise and energetic ruler, he issued a Code of Laws which were inscribed on stone pillars set up in the temples for the public to see.

Hammurabi's Laws give us a good idea of the society which he ruled; there were three classes of people - nobles (including warriors and officials), commoners (merchants, craftsmen, farmers) and slaves. Though by no means equal, all had rights, even the slaves. Women could own property and divorce their husbands; freeborn children had to go to school; there were laws governing trade, property, medical treatment and punishment of bad workmen, thieves and dishonest merchants. For its time, the Code was remarkably humane, even if many of the laws were based on the rule of an 'eye for eye, tooth for tooth'. For example, if a house collapsed and the owner was killed, the builder was put to death and 'if a man has made the tooth of another fall out, one of his own teeth shall be knocked out'.

Babylon declined after Hammurabi's death, when the Hittites and, after them, a rough uncivilized Indo-European people called the Kassites, from the mountains north-east of Mesopotamia, occupied the plain for several centuries.

3 Egypt
c. 3200 – 663 BC

The River Nile rises in the mountains of central Africa and for the last 1000 kilometres of its course runs across a practically rainless desert to the Mediterranean Sea. Its valley, seldom more than three or four kilometres wide, is in effect an immensely long oasis, Here, a little later than in Mesopotamia, arose the richest of the ancient civilizations. The Nile brought life to Egypt, overflowing its banks every year and depositing a layer of rich mud in the fields which, from Stone Age times, produced abundant crops of vegetables, barley and emmer.

From 5000 BC or earlier, various peoples had settled in the valley, growing crops, hunting and fishing in the marshes and building papyrus boats to get about on the river. It seems likely that in about 3500 BC Semitic people entered the country from Mesopotamia, bringing with them knowledge of bronze, pottery and writing.

Two kingdoms gradually emerged, those of Upper (i.e. Southern) Egypt and Lower Egypt. In about 3200 BC Menes, King of Upper Egypt, conquered the north and united the country. He founded the First Dynasty or family of rulers who retained power for several centuries, but we know little of his successors until we come to Zoser, who lived some 500 years later. Zoser's architect, Imhotep, built the Step Pyramid, the world's oldest building of stone, in which to house the King's dead body.

The Egyptians looked on their king (the word Pharaoh was not yet used) as a god who, after death, would join all the gods in another world. Therefore his body had to be embalmed and placed in a massive tomb, with food, drink, weapons, jewellery and other possessions that he would need in the after-life. Later, the nobles and eventually all classes came to believe in a life after death and went to enormous trouble to decorate, furnish and conceal their tombs. Alas, almost every one was robbed of its treasures.

Like Sumer, Egypt had unlimited supplies of river mud to make sun-dried bricks, which were used for every kind of building except the pyramids and temples. Being the homes of the gods, the temples had to last for ever and, fortunately, Egypt had plenty of limestone and granite in cliffs and hills not far from the river.

With tools of bronze and stone, immense blocks, pillars and obelisks were shaped in the quarries and, by means of levers, rollers and huge labour

11

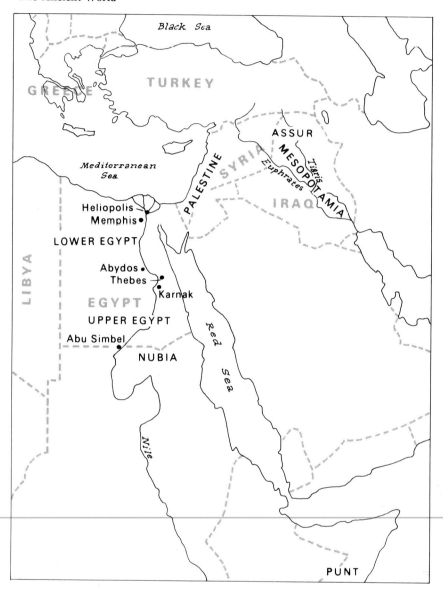

gangs, were manoeuvred on to rafts and taken to the building site by canal or across the flooded countryside. At the site, the great stones were hauled up earth ramps by muscle power, for the Egyptians never invented pulleys. Thus, on completion, a temple was filled with sand that was gradually removed as the painters and sculptors decorated it from the roof downwards.

Scores of pyramids were built on the western bank of the Nile, the mightiest being the Great Pyramid of Pharaoh Khufu (or Cheops) which was erected in about 2500 BC. It is so vast that it may have taken 100 000 men 20 years to build. In addition to the pyramids, centres like Karnak, Thebes, Heliopolis, Memphis, Abydos and Abu Simbel were filled with the most massive temples and statues that have ever been erected by Man. How were such feats achieved so many centuries ago?

Egypt was rich. The silt left behind by the annual flood was so fertile that the land produced food in abundance. There was enough to feed the peasants who grew it and a vast surplus to pay the builders, craftsmen and scribes (wages always took the form of food, drink and cloth, for the Egyptians never invented money) and to support everyone else from the king and his nobles to the labourers and slaves. The Egyptians were docile people, obeying their god-king's orders without question; and during the Inundation, or annual flood, when there was little for the peasants to do for several weeks, the officials would enrol labour battalions for royal building projects. The peasants might also be called up at harvest time or for some big irrigation work such as digging a canal.

The majority of Egyptians did not live in cities as the Sumerians did, but in villages and small towns above flood level. The few great cities like Memphis and Thebes were centres of religion and government, inhabited mainly by priests and officials, temple workers of every kind and possibly by the King himself, with his Court and all its ministers, soldiers and attendants.

To carry out the business of governing the country, to make calculations to build pyramids and temples, to record numbers of cattle and the size of harvest, to set down laws, religious beliefs, legends and stories, the Egyptians developed writing at an early stage. They began with picture signs and improved these with pictures that stood for a sound instead of a thing. This kind of writing is called *hieroglyphic*. The scribes later used a more rapid kind of writing called *hieratic*, which had signs that another scribe would recognise. They wrote on sheets made by laying strips of papyrus reed side by side and then placing more strips across them at a right-angle and pressing the two layers together while they were damp and tacky.

In addition to writing, educated Egyptians understood mathematics and knew a good deal about astromomy and medicine. They were the first people to work out a calendar of 365 days, divided into 12 months, each with 10-day 'weeks' and 5 extra days at the end of the year. As artists and craftsmen, they were superb decorators and painters, skilful carpenters, weavers and jewellers, who excelled in making exquisite ornaments as well as graceful furniture and chariots. Cheerful, affectionate people, they set great store by family life and loved feasting, merriment, music and domestic pets.

As in Sumer, women were better treated than in later periods of history. They could own property; they excelled as musicians and dancers, and some were able to read; there was even a word for a female scribe. In the royal family, the throne descended as a rule through a woman, the heiress giving her husband the right of succession. As a result, a brother might marry his sister and some Pharaohs married their daughters.

Egyptian religion was extremely complicated but, in simple terms, the greatest of the gods was Ra or Re, the sun-god, giver of life, whose children were Geb, the earth god, Nut, the sky-goddess, Shu (air) and Tefnut (water). The offspring of Geb and Nut were Osiris, Seth and Isis. Seth killed his brother Osiris and cut him in pieces but Isis found them and brought Osiris back to life. He then became god of the dead and his son, Horus, defeated Seth and reigned on earth in his father's stead. Every Pharaoh was Horus in life and Osiris after death.

In addition, there were hundreds of other gods and goddesses who presided over the fortunes of towns and villages, of various workers, of music, love, crops, writing and mummification. Many had the bodies of human beings and the heads of birds or animals, such as Anubis, the jackal-headed god of mummification, Sobek, the crocodile-god, Bast, the cat goddess and Thoth, the ibis-headed god of wisdom and writing. Horus is shown in pictures with the head of a falcon, while Hathor, goddess of happiness and love, has a cow's head.

Life in Egypt was so good that people believed that the after-life would simply be a continuation of it for ever. That was why a man wanted his preserved body to be buried with his best possessions in a tomb covered with scenes of his life and good deeds. It was as well to be kind and just in this life because when the dead man reached the Hall of Osiris, his good deeds (his heart) would be weighed against the bad, while a terrible creature called the Devourer waited for those who failed the test!

Roughly speaking, Egyptian civilization began in about 3200 BC, reached its peak during the period known as the New Kingdom (1554-1085 BC) and was in decline from about 1000 BC. During this time, there were many ups and downs and, for long after 1000 BC, Egyptian art, architecture and knowledge continued to amaze all who came into contact with them, including the Greeks and Romans and we ourselves today.

The Pyramid Age occurred during the time of the Old Kingdom (c. 2664-2155 BC) and then, after a period of disorder, the country became united again as the Middle Kingdom (2052-1786 BC) with its capital at Thebes, whose local god, Amun or Amen, was to become so rich and powerful that he was to be linked to the sun-god as Amen-Ra. This was a time of strong government, when Nubia, the land to the south, was conquered and Syria invaded, when wealth increased and vast temples were built.

Suddenly, in about 1785 BC, this orderly society was overthrown by the Hyksos, possibly a Semitic people from Palestine, who invaded Egypt and defeated Pharaoh's armies chiefly by means of horse-drawn chariots which were quite new to the Egyptians. The Hyksos may also have had iron weapons which the Egyptians lacked, for the country had no iron-ore. For some 200 years, they allowed the pharaohs to occupy the throne until, in about 1567 BC, Ahmose I, founder of the Eighteenth Dynasty, raised an army and drove the Hyksos clean out of Egypt.

This victory was the start of the New Kingdom, when Egyptian conquests created an empire that stretched from Nubia in the south, through Palestine and Syria to the River Euphrates in Mesopotamia. Thotmes I, a great warrior and builder, who campaigned as far as the Euphrates and added to Amen-Ra's temple at Karnak, was succeeded by his daughter, Queen Hatshepsut who, after her husband's death, became sole ruler. More interested in peaceful pursuits than in further conquests, she used the enormous riches amassed through war to beautify the country with palaces, temples and monuments, to improve irrigation and foster trade. She sent a fleet to the land of Punt (Somaliland) to bring back rare goods such as ebony, ivory, myrrh, cinnamon and other spices (for making the incense, perfumes and scented body oils so dearly prized by the Egyptians).

Hatshepsut's architect built her a magnificent temple which was (and still is) set into the cliffs on the west side of the Nile opposite Thebes. Further inland, in the desolate Valley of the Kings, the pharaohs were now buried in superbly decorated underground tombs, whose entrances were carefully concealed in the vain hope of outwitting grave-robbers.

The next pharaoh, Thotmes III, resumed the policy of foreign conquest, campaigning far into Syria, and exercising a certain amount of power over Crete and the Greek islands, but even he was unable to subdue a warlike horse-rearing people called the Mitanni, whose kingdom lay along the Euphrates in north-western Mesopotamia. During his reign and that of Amenhotep III, Egypt and its capital, Thebes, reached their peak of power and prosperity, but a dramatic change took place in the next reign.

Amenhotep IV, who succeeded his father in 1379 BC, changed the state religion by commanding his people to abandon all the old gods in favour of one god, Aten, the Disk of the Sun. He changed his name to Akhen-aten and left Thebes for a new capital which he had built at a place now called Amarna. But while he worshipped the new god in open-air temples and wrote poetry in the god's honour, the empire was under attack from the Hittites who, armed with iron weapons, defeated the Mitanni, and overran many Egyptian outposts in northern Syria.

After Akhen-aten's death, the priests of Amen-Ra soon recovered their power and brought back to Thebes the new Pharaoh, a young man whose name has become the most famous of all the Egyptian kings. He was Tutenkhamen, whose sumptuous burial may have been his reward for

The back panel of Tutankhamen's wooden throne, showing the young King being anointed by his wife. A very minor pharaoh, he was only 19 when he died (c. 1350 BC).

agreeing to the return of the old religion. Egypt's empire recovered somewhat under pharaohs of the Nineteenth Dynasty, such as Seti I and Rameses II, who fought the Hittites in Palestine. Rameses, sometimes called 'the Great', reigned for 67 years, during which he filled the land with temples and monuments, inscribed with boastful accounts of his triumphs, including his debatable 'victory' over the Hittites at Kadesh. But he had to come to terms with the enemy and cement the treaty by marrying a Hittite princess.

When he died (c. 1225 BC), the New Kingdom still had two centuries of life ahead, but the empire was now in decline and the pharaohs gradually lost their power to the priests. The country suffered attacks from Libyans and from the so-called Sea Peoples, who were repulsed with difficulty. Meanwhile, the whole of the Middle East was in ferment, as uncivilized invaders, known as Indo-Europeans, pushed in from behind the Balkan mountains and the Black Sea to penetrate Asia Minor (Turkey) and the Fertile Crescent.

The newcomers forced the inhabitants of the coasts and islands of the central Mediterranean to take to their ships in search of new homes and, as did the Sea Peoples, to try to win a footing in Egypt. Rameses III, the last of the great military pharaohs, drove them out, but Egypt's decline could not be halted for long and, by the end of the New Kingdom in 1085 BC, her days of glory were almost over.

The kingdom lost its unity, for the north (Lower Egypt) came to be ruled by merchant princes from a city called Tanis, while the priests of Amen held sway from Thebes in Upper Egypt. There was a brief recovery around 950 BC under a Libyan ruler called Sheshouk, but by 730 BC Egypt was torn by civil war and Nubians (or Kushites) from the south took control of much of the country.

Their rule lasted for only 70 years, for, in 663 BC, they were driven away by an Assyrian army which invaded Egypt and captured Thebes.

A key reason for the Egyptians' failure to repel their enemies was that they were a Bronze Age people and when iron weapons came into use, their own armaments became obsolete. Egypt had no iron-ore and her soldiers could not withstand attacks by men equipped with sharper weapons and superior armour.

4 Minoa and Mycenae
c. 3000 – 1000 BC

Crete is the largest of the Greek islands. In about 3000 BC Indo-Europeans crossed there from the mainland of Greece. The climate was warm and the soil in the valleys fertile, so that grain crops and vines flourished. The new-comers (later to be called Minoans) cultivated olive trees and probably raised large flocks of sheep.

The name Minoan comes from Minos, a legendary king whose wife, daughter of the sun, was supposed to have given birth to a bull-headed monster, the Minotaur, who lived in a labyrinth where he devoured youths and maidens sent from Greece, until slain by the hero Theseus. By 2500 BC, the Minoans were living in towns built of brick and stone. They knew how to work bronze and make weapons, tools and ornaments of great beauty. They were marvellous potters whose exquisite pots, bowls and vases have been found by archaeologists all over the Middle East, for the Minoans

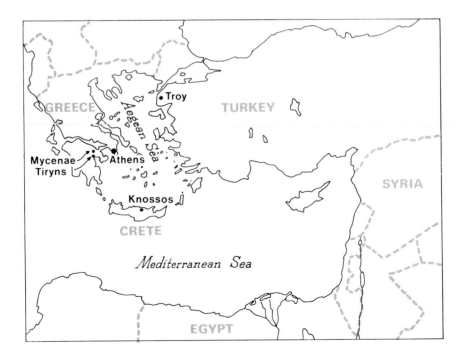

A relief fresco of the Young Prince, also called the Priest-King, in the Palace of Minos, Knossos, Crete (c. 1550 BC).

built up a thriving sea-trade with the Aegean islands, Egypt and neighbouring countries.

From about 2000 BC, they took a sudden leap forward, devising a written script which is still not fully understood, and building large cities with great palaces and public buildings. The main city, Knossos, stood on a hill not far from the sea, with palatial buildings grouped round a grand courtyard. Bathrooms, lavatories and kitchens were connected to an efficient drainage system and there were numerous storerooms, workshops and offices for the palace servants and craftsmen. The walls of the royal apartments were decorated with colourful scenes of Cretan life, besides birds, plants and sea-creatures. Everywhere could be seen evidence of bull worship, which probably went back to the legend of the Minotaur and, at festivals, gymnasts performed startling acrobatics from the horns and backs of wild bulls released into an arena.

The peak of this lively civilization was reached in about 1600 BC; then, suddenly, about a century later, the Minoan cities were destroyed, possibly by an earthquake. There was partial recovery from this disaster and the cities had been rebuilt when invaders from the Greek mainland captured Knossos and reduced it to ruins. This time it was not rebuilt and Minoan civilization came to an end in about 1400 BC.

The invaders, known as Achaeans (the name usually given to these early Greek-speakers) were little better than barbarians. On the mainland, they lived in small towns such as Mycenae, Tiryns, Argos, Athens and Pylos, each protected by a hillfortress or *acropolis* with colossal walls made of rough-hewn stone blocks. In this Bronze Age society, petty kings ruled an aristocracy of warriors whose lands around each city were worked for them by tenants and slaves. These kings must have combined forces for the invasion of Crete, where they soon learned a great deal, adapting Minoan writing and taking over the Mediterranean sea-trade. Hittite kings respected the Achaeans and probably made a pact with them to join in attacks on Egypt.

The Achaeans, or Mycenaeans, as they came to be called, also made raids on the coasts of Asia Minor and, in about 1200 BC, under King Agamemnon, laid siege to the ancient city of Troy, which they eventually captured and destroyed.

However, the power of these seafaring warlords came to an end towards the end of the 12th century BC, when fierce invaders from the north, migrating from the Danube valley and called Dorians, entered Greece and sacked the fortress towns. They cared nothing for art, fine buildings or trade, and for several centuries all trace of Minoan and Mycenaean culture seemed to have disappeared. Yet, from this crude violent society, the Greek civilization was to arise.

5 India
c. 2500 BC–AD 400

THE INDUS VALLEY CIVILIZATION

On the western side of the Indian sub-continent, in what is now Pakistan, flows the River Indus. Its valley, far larger than the Nile valley, was similarly flooded every year and, from about 3000 BC, men were growing crops in the rich soil and keeping domestic animals.

They undoubtedly came into contact with Sumer and must have learnt about the more advanced ways of life in Mesopotamia. At all events, a civilization arose which some historians call the Indus Valley civilization and others the Harappan Culture, after Harappa, one of its two principal cities. It flourished for a thousand years, from about 2500 to 1500 BC and then mysteriously disappeared. Although it did not last as long as the other two great river civilizations of Egypt and Mesopotamia, and its culture had a less widespread influence, it actually covered a larger area, for its towns and cities not only stood on the valley plain, but were built along the coast on either side of the delta.

Archaeologists have unearthed the remains of more than 50 towns and villages on the river plain, as well as seaports and two large cities - twin capitals perhaps - Mohenjo-Daro, on the main Indus river, and Harappa, on a tributary some 400 kilometres to the north-east. A lesser city was called Kalibangan and the largest port was Lothal, with a splendid dock at the head of the Gulf of Cambay.

Mohenjo-Daro and Harappa were rectangular in shape, with sides about a kilometre in length. Unlike the Sumerian cities, with their narrow streets, these had fine broad streets, running straight north and south and cut at right-angles by others running east and west, like many modern American cities built on the grid system.

The houses which lined these regular streets were built of bricks baked in kilns and not merely dried in the sun, as in Egypt and Sumer. Many of the houses were two storeys high and all had flat roofs; as is common in the East, blank walls faced onto the street but, inside, the rooms were arranged round a courtyard.

Sanitation was very advanced, for nearly every house had its own bathroom and indoor lavatory connected to sewers running under the

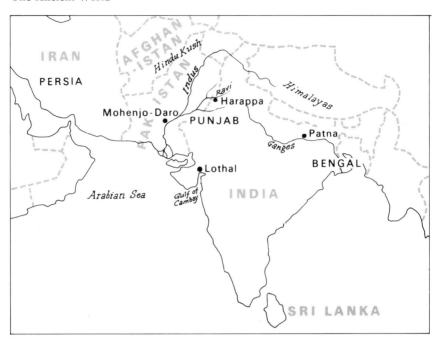

streets. There were openings to the drains for official sanitary inspection.

Each city was dominated by a tall fortress or citadel containing a huge granary, from which, presumably, the people received corn brought in from the surrounding countryside. There were also a large assembly hall and a public bath, which may have been used for religious cleansing.

At Mohenjo-Daro, a city of some 20 000 people, the great public bath, about 12 metres long and over 2 metres deep, was lined with bitumen to make it waterproof. The water, supplied by a well, was emptied away through a vaulted drain two metres high. These brick buildings were useful and solid, but lacking in beauty or in the grandeur of Egyptian temples.

We know little about the people of this Harappan society or their religion or how they were governed. Some of the excavated houses in the two capitals were much bigger than others, which suggests a class of nobles or rich merchants, but there were no temples or palaces like those of the Egyptian kings. Yet the orderly layout of cities, the building of irrigation canals, the sewerage system and the public granaries make it certain that there must have been firm government. Perhaps it was a dictatorship or a kind of totalitarian state run by a superior class of officials.

The irrigated fields produced wheat, barley, fruits, vegetables and the earliest known cotton crops in the world. Rice was grown along the west coast, cattle and pigs were reared and the Indus people invented the bullock-cart for transport. Men wore a toga-like garment that went over one

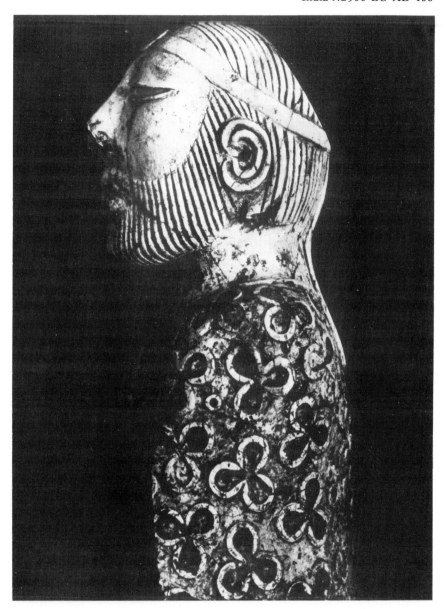

The 'Priest-King' from Mohenjo-Daro, Sind, Pakistan.

shoulder, while women dressed in gaily-coloured short gowns. As craftsmen, the Indians were skilful but not outstanding. They produced decorated pottery, as well as figurines of animals, gods, goddesses and dancing girls; they modelled sacred bulls, worked copper and bronze and were expert jewellers. From ports like Lothal, with its shipping dock over 200 metres long, their ships sailed up the Persian Gulf to trade with the Sumerian cities

23

in gold, timber, cotton, grain, copper and jewellery. They seem to have set up trading colonies in Ur, Bahrein and other cities of Sumer and Akkad. Hundreds of soapstone seals about 25 mm square have been found, exquisitely carved with figures of animals, some of them as far away as Mesopotamia. These were probably fixed to bales of merchandise as owners' marks, and they bear a kind of writing which is quite different from Egyptian hieroglyphics or Mesopotamian cuneiform. Unfortunately, no-one has yet been able to decipher these inscriptions.

The people probably worshipped a Mother Goddess. Female figurines have been found, and figures of a three-headed god with horns. The bull seems to have been regarded as a sacred creature, as well as the elephant and rhinoceros.

From about 1500 BC the Indus Valley civilization vanished. A slow decline had set in at Mohenjo-Daro but, at Harappa, the life of the city seems to have stopped suddenly. Disastrous floods may have occurred; the land, too heavily cropped and stripped of its timber, may have become infertile or the sea may have retreated, leaving seaports far inland. The final blow may have been dealt by the invasion of Indo-European peoples.

THE ARYANS

From the steppes of Asia, invaders called Aryans entered India and, with the help of swift horse-drawn chariots, easily defeated the Indus people. The newcomers were related to the Indo-Europeans who settled in Asia Minor, Persia and Greece. Originally, they were nomadic herdsmen living in tribes that were often at war with one another but apt to form alliances to conquer new lands. Such a people could not understand city life and they left no towns, buildings, statues or pottery.

What they did leave was a remarkable collection of religious literature - hymns, poems and beliefs which were committed to memory by the Aryan priests and passed on for a thousand years, from 1500 to 500 BC. Later, these hymns and prayers were written down in four books known as *Vedas*, so this period is called the Vedic Age. In it, the principles of the Hindu religion were formed and laid down.

The most important of the Vedic books, the *Rig Veda*, consists of over a thousand hymns, prayers and poems to Aryan gods, such as Veruna, the stern sky god, Indra, god of heroes and war, and Agri, god of fire. The Vedas give us a picture of a society divided into four classes - the Brahmans who were educated priests and scholars, the nobles who chose one of their number as *raja* or king, the ordinary tribesmen and, lowest of all, the 'unclean' non-Aryans, the despised conquered people. These early classes developed into the caste system of India whereby the people came to be divided into hundreds of castes, all with their own rules relating to food, marriage and occupations.

The Brahmans set down their thoughts about the meaning of life in books known as *Upanishads*, which show that they believed in reincarnation: that is, that after death people reappeared on earth as animals, insects, plants or perhaps as human beings. Only a man who had lived a good life would be reborn in a human body, but the best future of all was to reach *nirvana*, a state where the soul was utterly at peace.

As the centuries passed, the Aryans settled down to agriculture and trade; they penetrated far into India, built cities and founded kingdoms that took the place of the old tribal families. Religion still played a great part in their lives and they continued to discuss the meaning of life and even to oppose the ideas of the Brahmans. The greatest of the new religious thinkers was Siddhartha Gautama, known to his followers as the Buddha, which means 'the Enlightened One'. A prince of the warrior class, he was born in about 560 BC in what is now Nepal; when about 29 years of age, he abandoned his life of leisure to devote himself to meditation and preaching. His message was simple and sensible: enjoy all things in moderation, be kind to all human beings and creatures, help people less fortunate than yourself. Although the Buddha won many followers, the Hindu religion and the caste system proved too strong to be overthrown in India itself, and it was in other parts of Asia that Buddhism was to spread and become one of the most potent religions in world history.

THE MAURYAN EMPIRE

In Buddha's time, (*c*. 500 BC) most of India reached a high stage of civilization, as towns and cities were built, iron came into general use and merchants traded with China, Mesopotamia and Persia.

The Persians, an Aryan people who had occupied the land of the Elamites lying east of Mesopotamia, had only recently risen to power, thanks to the conquests of Cyrus and of Darius the Great (521–485 BC), who, with his almost invincible army of archers and cavalry, advanced into the Indus Valley.

North-west India became a province or satrap of the Persian Empire and for nearly 200 years the Persians ruled this area, introducing Persian art, trade and religious ideas. However, Persian rule was ended in 327 BC, when Alexander the Great led his army of Greeks and Macedonians through Afghanistan and down to the plains, across the Indus and into the Punjab. There, having defeated a local ruler named Porus, he continued his march eastwards, hoping to reach the Ganges, but his weary troops refused to go any further and Alexander reluctantly agreed to return to Babylon. He left

Porus and some Macedonian governors to rule in his absence, but he never returned and the garrisons were too weak to hold on to the territory which he had briefly conquered.

Within a few years, a prince from north-east India, named Chandragupta Maurya, made himself master of the Mauryan Empire, a huge area, which eventually included north and central India and Afghanistan. From his capital, Pataliputra (now Patna), the emperor ruled his vast realm with an iron hand, controlling commerce, mining of copper and iron, agriculture, public works and all the towns and villages by means of officials, spies, and army units. Nevertheless, Chandragupta cared about the people's welfare; the country became prosperous; commerce flourished, roads were built and irrigation systems founded, so that his reign came to be looked upon as the beginning of a golden age.

His grandson, the Emperor Ashoka fulfilled that promise, for, during his reign (275-232 BC) he devoted himself to the Buddhist religion and, through his personal goodness, encouraged his subjects to treat one another with gentleness, to avoid violence and to care for the poor. He sent missionaries to preach Buddhism in Ceylon (now Sri Lanka), Syria and even Egypt, and he had carved on rocks, in caves and on pillars set up in various parts of the kingdom, edicts or messages of advice for his subjects and for those who would come after them.

Ashoka has been described as the greatest and noblest ruler India has ever known and indeed one of the great kings of the world. He died in 232 BC and, less than 50 years later, the Mauryan Empire fell to pieces. While Ashoka's successors quarrelled, provincial governors rebelled, so that a number of small kingdoms emerged and, in place of Buddhist ideals, the Brahman priests recovered their influence and re-introduced the separation of peoples - the caste system.

A feature of the Mauryan Age was the opulence of the imperial court. The emperors built luxurious palaces of stone and marvellously carved timber, and surrounded themselves with hundreds of courtiers, servants and bejewelled dancing-girls. They toured the realm in ceremonial processions, riding on elephants or in gilded carriages drawn by horses decked out with plumes and jewelled harness; as they went, they gave alms to the poor, for, at this time, India was so rich that the royal store-rooms were crammed with gold, silver, diamonds, rubies and sapphires.

THE GUPTAS

The collapse of the Mauryan Empire was followed by several centuries of disunity and unrest, during which several groups of invaders entered the country and established themselves on lands which they wrested from the native peoples. First, in the 2nd century BC, came the Greeks from central Asia, north of the Hindu Kush mountains, where Alexander the Great had left garrisons, and they were followed by people called Scythians, from the same region, and Parthians from Iran. In about 100 BC, a horde of semi-civilized people called Kushans moved in from Afghanistan, occupied lands in the Punjab and established a kingdom in the north-west which lasted for 200 years. Their greatest king, Kaniska, accepted Buddhism and helped to spread that faith to central Asia and China.

The invaders, especially the Greeks, brought new ideas and knowledge into India and after the Kushan kingdom collapsed for some obscure reason, a new empire arose in much the same way as the Mauryan Empire had done. A prince from north-east India, again called Chandragupta (*c*. AD 320-335), defeated many of the local rulers and forced them to pay homage. His son, Samudra, and grandson, Chandragupta II, continued to expand their dominions, until the Gupta Empire stretched right across northern India, from Bengal to the Arabian Sea.

Under the Guptas, India enjoyed a second - and last - golden age. The emperors, especially Chandragupta II, created a state that was prosperous, peaceful and so orderly that people could travel safely from one end of the country to another. Indian craftsmen produced excellent implements made of iron and steel, as well as cotton, calico and cashmere cloth finely woven and dyed in brilliant colours; in universities that attracted students from all over Asia, Indian scholars made great advances in science, astronomy and mathematics. They knew, for example, that the earth is round and rotates on its axis and they developed the symbol for zero and the numerals, later called Arabic numerals, which did not reach the West until centuries later.

Art and literature reached perhaps their highest levels in Indian history. The principal art was sculpture, from tiny carved figures to statues of the Hindu gods and intricately carved gateways and furnishings of Buddhist temples. Using the Sanskrit language, Indian writers, of whom the greatest was Kalidasa, created poems, stories and fairy-tales which were later to become known to writers of the West.

The Gupta dynasty was eventually overthrown by barbarians from central Asia, who pressed into India and destroyed a wonderful civilization. By the end of the 5th century AD, the White Huns, who were probably related to the Huns who devastated Europe, poured into northern India, sacking the palaces and temples and massacring whole populations. The country fell into a state of anarchy in which petty rulers of small kingdoms warred perpetually with one another. Fortunately, there were periods of recovery, and art, literature and science did not entirely perish, but the serenity of the Gupta Age vanished for ever.

6 China
c. 2200 BC – AD 220

As in Sumer, Egypt and India, Chinese civilization grew up in the valley of a great river, the Hwang-ho or Yellow River of modern China. There, during the New Stone Age in about 5000-4000 BC, people were growing crops in the rich soil, raising cattle, sheep and pigs, making pottery and keeping silkworms to make silk cloth.

THE HSIA DYNASTY *c.* 2200-1760 BC

Chinese history is said to begin with the Hsia dynasty, a family which ruled the Yellow River area from about 2200-1760 BC. Our knowledge of this period is shadowy, and the Hsia dynasty may be only a legend, but it seems likely that the Chinese were influenced by the more highly developed civilizations in the ancient Middle East. In this period, they were using bronze and living in large villages, surrounded by fortified walls as protection against nomadic raiders. They knew how to train horses to pull chariots and, in order to control the annual floods and to water the crops, they built dykes and irrigation canals. Even so, the Yellow River sometimes burst its banks and flooded vast areas, destroying villages, fields and irrigation systems; from time to time, the country was afflicted by droughts, dust-storms, freezing winters and burning summers and, to cope with these disasters, the Chinese became obedient to harsh rulers and bureaucratic officials.

THE SHANG DYNASTY *c.* 1760-1000 BC

In about 1760 BC, the Hsia dynasty was overthrown by a chief named T'ang who founded the Shang dynasty which lasted for over 700 years. Under the Shangs, many towns were built, the kingdom was extended as far south as the Yangtze River and various outlying states were made to pay tribute.

Near present-day An-yang, Chinese archaeologists have discovered the city of Yin, the Shang capital of around 1300 BC. Not as large as Ur or Babylon, it was protected by mud-brick walls and had a palace area with temples and royal dwellings set upon platforms of beaten earth. The roofs were upheld by wooden pillars on stone bases and the interiors were divided into rooms by plaster partitions. Craftsmen and slaves had their own quarters and the common people lived in pit houses covered by thatched roofs.

In the ruins of An-yang were found beautiful white pottery and many urns and vessels made of bronze and marvellously decorated with dragons, bulls, rams and tigers. Bronze was also used for weapons, helmets, armour and chariot parts. Shang craftsmen carved marble into the shape of animals and monsters, as well as making daggers, cups, beads and ornaments out of jade, which the Chinese regarded as a magical stone. Their astronomers worked out a calendar of 365 days and the merchants developed a decimal monetary system based on the exchange of cowrie shells, metals and salt.

The Shang people did not leave behind great stone temples and monuments like the Egyptians but, at An-yang and in many other sites, tens of thousands of bones have been found which tell us something of life in those times. The Oracle Bones, as they were called, are the flat shoulder blades of oxen and other animals (turtle shells were also used) and on the bones the priests and scribes scratched a question. It might, for instance, ask whether the king should build a new town or make war on the northern

29

tribes. Then the diviner applied a hot metal implement to the bone to cause cracks which he read or interpreted to get the answer to the question, which he then wrote below the cracks.

The Oracle Bones show that the Shang scribes used a written language in which there were some 3000 picture-signs, each representing a thing or an idea. Many of the signs are similar to those used today, for the foundations of modern Chinese writing were created by the Shang people.

The king and the nobles consulted their ancestors through the oracles and, in addition to ancestor-worship, the common people worshipped natural gods of harvest, rain, birth and fertility. The father god was Shang Ti, while the earth was the mother goddess of all forms of life. Human sacrifices had to be made to the gods, especially in spring at the time of sowing; bodies were cast into the water from boats to appease the river god.

Kings were buried in deep underground tombs, in which they were accompanied to the next world by chariots, horses, servants and even wives. Often a beautiful piece of pottery or a bronze vessel was placed on a shrine in the grave.

The Shangs were constantly at war with their neighbours and it was one of these tribes, called the Chous, who eventually overthrew the Shang dynasty in about 1125 BC and ruled a great part of China for the next 900 years.

THE CHOU DYNASTY *c*. 1125-256 BC

The Chous, who came from the south-west, made their capital at Sian (Ch'ang-an) in the west for several centuries but, in 771 BC, the hostility of nomadic or semi-nomadic peoples like the Turks, Mongols and Tibetans, as well as an uprising of feudal lords who killed the Emperor, forced them to move to a new capital further east at Loyang on another tributary of the Yellow River. Hence, the dynasty is divided into two periods, Western Chou and Eastern Chou.

During the Western Chou, the kingdom became too big for one ruler to control, so he put relatives, nobles and some of the defeated Shang family in charge of large districts. These great landowners parcelled land to the peasants to farm for them, creating a feudal system in which the lords paid tribute to the Chou king and were supposed to obey his orders. As centuries passed, the lords became more powerful and independent; big estates swallowed up the smaller ones so that, by the time of the Eastern Chou, quarrelling states were constantly at war with each other. The Chou king became merely a figure-head. Standing armies came into existence, with foot-soldiers, armed with cross-bows and commanded by officers riding in four-horse chariots. In one battle, a state is said to have put 4900 chariots and 100 000 soldiers into the field.

Nevertheless, China made great progress under the Chou. Iron came into use (from about 500 BC) and farming improved with better irrigation and the introduction of the ox-plough. Grain and merchandise could be sent from one part of the country to another along new roads and canals; trade increased and people began to use copper coins.

Many words were added to the written language and, in books made of bamboo or wooden tablets fastened together with thongs, scribes wrote down poems, hymns, philosophy and historical records. A whole new class of educated civil servants appeared who held government posts and from them emerged a group of gifted men known as the Scholars, who were held in great respect.

The most famous man in Chinese history was a Scholar named Confucius, who was born in 551 BC at Lu, in Eastern Chou. A minor government official, he travelled widely and, as he grew older, gathered about himself a group of followers to whom he explained his ideas about life and society. Confucius did not found a religion but put forward a plan for right living at a time of strife and confusion. He taught that people should behave with kindness and respect towards one another; there had to be loyalty between father and son, husband and wife, brother and brother, friend and friend, emperor and subject. This meant obedience by an inferior person to a superior, ancestor-worship, respect of children for their elders. The family was all important and the ruler should set a good example and rule as a wise father of his people. Confucius himself did not write down many of his ideas, apart from some poetry, but his sayings were collected by his disciples and published in a book called *The Analects* (Conversations), which influenced the Chinese people for many centuries.

The Chou era produced other Scholars, such as Mencius, who held that men are naturally good, and a group called the Legalists who took the opposite view, believing that men needed to be ruled by a powerful state that dealt out severe punishments. Lao Yzu, who thought men should ignore government and return to the ways of nature, inspired his followers to create beautiful paintings and poetry.

Respect for education led to a mania for examinations. Schools were set up to teach Confucianism and prepare students for civil service examinations. The more examinations a student could pass, the higher would be his position, so hundreds of young men spent years doing nothing but preparing for examinations.

THE CH'IN DYNASTY 256-206 BC

As the power of the Chou declined, China went through troubled times known as the period of Warring States, which lasted from 473-256 BC.

Tomb figure of a kneeling soldier found at Sian (or Ch'ang-an) in Shensi province, capital city of the Chou, Ch'in, Han and T'ang dynasties. Archaeological excavation continues at Sian, where the modern city's walls are, in part, of T'ang construction.

Eventually one state defeated all the others; this was the Ch'in, whose people came from the west and who treated their enemies with ruthless cruelty. Their prince changed his name from Cheng to Ch'in Shih Huang Ti, which meant First Emperor of the Ch'in, and, with tremendous energy, he set about restoring order and founding the Chinese Empire. With the aid of an able minister named Li Ssu, Huang Ti divided the country into forty provinces, each ruled by a military governor and officials, all directly responsible to the emperor. To prevent the feudal lords giving trouble, he ordered them to live in Sian, the capital, which, with their wealth, they made into a rich and artistic city.

Over the years, different ways of writing and speaking had developed in the separate states and Huang Ti, seeing that there could be no unity without a common language, gave orders that only one style of writing was to be allowed. He also insisted on the whole country using the same system of weights and measures and money. Other reforms included the building of fine new roads, draining swamp-lands, improving irrigation and constructing a magnificent palace at Sian. Harsh punishment was dealt out to anyone who questioned the emperor's authority; he himself had no time for the teachings of Confucius or the ideas of poets and scholars and, in 213 BC, he ordered the destruction of all the volumes of sayings and philosophy, and of the laws and records of various states. This was called the Burning of the Books and came to be looked on as one of the worst acts of tyranny in Chinese history, for a great many ideas, poems and writings were lost for ever. However, some of the classics survived because they were hidden or committed to memory.

The emperor next turned his attention to extending China's borders far to the south, to the west and north-west. Then, to protect its borders from nomadic tribesmen, he built the Great Wall of China, a colossal fortification, linking older sections of wall until it stretched for more than 2500 kilometres across northern China. The thousands of slaves and convicts who were forced to build this mighty barrier were treated with merciless cruelty.

Huang Ti died in 210 BC and, within three years, the Ch'in dynasty was ended, the empire broken apart and the beautiful capital plundered and burnt. The emperor's rule had been so oppressive that the people had come to hate him and after his death they rose in rebellion against his son. But Huang Ti had given his country an idea of unity which it never lost; the very name of Ch'in caused it to become known as China, for the fame of the empire, its wealth, achievements and victorious armies had spread to India and further to the west.

THE HAN DYNASTY 206 BC - AD 220

Out of the turmoil which followed Huang Ti's death, a new leader emerged, a peasant of great ability named Liu Pang, who founded the great Han dynasty and, as Emperor, ruled China from 206-195 BC.

The Han dynasty, which lasted for 400 years, was as important to the Eastern world as the Roman Empire was to the West, for, in many ways, this was China's greatest period of achievement, when so many of the developments and inventions occurred which have amazed Western historians.

The Han quickly restored the Ch'in system of an organised central government which, from the rebuilt capital, Ch'ang-an (Sian), directed the governors, officials and civil servants who controlled affairs in the thirteen provinces into which China was divided. Confucius had stressed the importance of education for rulers and, under the Han, officials were chosen for their knowledge of Confucian writings, and for their own literary skill, tested in examinations that were held regularly throughout the country. High officials, therefore, had to be scholars and, although the sons of rich families had the best chance of obtaining the necessary education, clever boys from peasant homes could also rise to high rank.

With good government and prosperity, the population increased - in AD 2, for example, there were 60 million people in China - farming methods improved, more rice was produced and new crops, such as grapes, oranges, apricots and tea were grown. The government controlled the mining of iron ore, lead, silver and tin, issued bronze coins and collected the taxes which as usual fell heavily upon the peasants, though not as oppressively as in the past.

Writing, on paper made from bark and hemp, was done with brush pens and ink by scholars who composed poems and essays, produced the world's first dictionaries and recorded China's past in a great work called *Historical Memoirs*, which continued to be written until the end of the last Chinese dynasty in 1911.

The Chinese made many discoveries and inventions during this period, for they observed sunspots, predicted eclipses, produced an accurate calendar, invented a compass, a seismograph to record earthquakes and lacquer as a coloured waterproof coating for all kinds of things from house walls to carved boxes.

The Han cities have all disappeared but, from paintings, we know that rich court officials, merchants and aristocrats lived leisurely lives in elegant timber houses, adorned with sculptures and jade ornaments. Waited upon by slaves, they dressed in silk garments, rode in horse-drawn carriages and, when not engaged in official business, enjoyed music, tea-drinking, games like draughts and hunting in the country. The great mass of the population were of course peasants who toiled in the fields, served in the armies and on government projects like road- and canal-building. It was a society in which scholars were respected more highly than the rich merchants.

Like the Romans, who reached greatness at the same time, the Han expanded their territory. The emperor Wu Ti (140-87 BC), who ruled for over 50 years, conquered Manchuria, Korea and southern China, opening up new areas to Chinese influence, including Indo-China (now Vietnam,

Cambodia and Laos). His armies travelled far to the west, beyond the mountains and deserts which isolated China from the rest of the world, and they brought back information about India and goods from Greece and Rome, which, in exchange for silk, were carried along the immensely long caravan route known as the Silk Road. At its peak, the Han Empire was even larger than the Roman Empire and, although there was no direct contact between the two governments, trade went on for many years.

Later emperors enlarged the empire further by advancing into Mongolia to defeat the ferocious tribesmen who lived on the grasslands beyond the Great Wall. By preventing them from breaking into China, they probably caused the Huns to move westwards and menace the Roman World.

As with the Chous, the Han dynasty eventually went into decline, as emperors left business of government to their generals and ministers and as the landlord class recovered its power and oppressed the peasants into serfdom. In AD 220, the last of the Han emperors was overthrown by a general named Tsao, and the period of disunity that followed lasted until the 7th century, when the T'ang dynasty restored China's greatness.

Carthaginian mask used by actors.

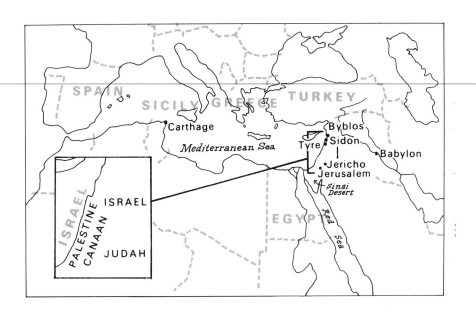

7   Phoenicians and Hebrews
c. 1200 – 587 BC

Around 1200 BC, that is, a thousand years before Huang Ti built the Great Wall of China, Indo-European peoples from the north brought about the overthrow of the Hittite and Mycenaean civilizations and the destruction of prosperous cities in Syria. Attacks also fell upon Egypt which was now beginning to decline and had already lost most of its empire.

However, these upheavals did not prevent - indeed, they may have helped - the advance of the Phoenicians, a Semitic people who lived along a narrow strip of coast at the eastern end of the Mediterranean Sea having first settled there between 3000 and 2500 BC. From their sea-ports, Byblos, Tyre and Sidon, they became the greatest merchant seamen of the ancient world, trading with Egypt, Cyprus and the Greek islands, as well as taking over the Minoans' role as sea-carriers. So successful were they that they expanded westwards, founding colonies (*c.* 1000 BC) on the coasts of Sicily, Spain and north-west Africa, where one Phoenician colony, Carthage, was later to engage in an epic struggle with Rome.

Phoenician galley carved on a sarcophagus from Sidon, Lebanon.

The Phoenicians developed from Egyptian hieroglyphics an alphabet of 22 characters that was simpler to use than the complicated writing which had been the special skill of scribes and priests. This alphabet passed to the Greeks and from them it became the basis of all Western alphabets.

Another Semitic people, the Hebrews, are supposed to have been led by their ancestor, Abraham, into Palestine - then called Canaan - from Ur in Mesopotamia in about 1900 BC. Eventually, to escape famine, one group moved to the Nile delta and, later, probably welcomed their kinsmen, the invading Hyksos. But, after Pharaoh Ahmose had expelled the Hyksos, the Hebrews were enslaved for 300 years or more, until Moses led them out of captivity into the Sinai desert. This great leader gave his people a set of laws called the Ten Commandments, which he said were dictated to him by the Hebrew god, Yahweh or Jehovah, who, he insisted, was the *only* god.

Moses died before reaching Canaan but his successor, Joshua, invaded the country, captured some towns, including Jericho, and enabled the Hebrews to settle down somewhat uneasily with the Canaanites. Their principal enemies were the Philistines, kinsmen of the Phoenicians, and in their need for a war leader, they chose Saul to be king in about 1030 BC. His successor, David, a warrior-prophet, defeated the Philistines and made Jerusalem the capital of an enlarged Hebrew kingdom called Israel.

This country had no natural riches but through it ran the overland trade route from the Red Sea to the Phoenician seaports. David's son, King Solomon, made a treaty with Hiram, ruler of Tyre, which brought in such wealth that he was able to embark on a vast programme to improve Jerusalem and to build a magnificent temple to the Hebrew God. He also made war on neighbouring tribes, expanded Israel's borders and built a navy.

Solomon prospered partly through his own ability, but mostly because great powers like Egypt and the Hittites were in eclipse and their successors, Assyria and Persia, had not yet arisen. After Solomon's death in 935 BC, his kingdom split up, ten tribes of the northern part keeping the name of Israel, with its capital at Samaria, while in the south, the tribes of Benjamin and Judah held Jerusalem as capital of the kingdom of Judah.

Guided by popular preachers known as prophets, Judah remained faithful to Yahweh, but Israel leaned towards the Phoenicians and their god Baal. Led by King Ahab, the Israelites twice defeated an invading army of Assyrians but, in 722 BC, the kingdom was wiped out by the Assyrians and the ten tribes, deported to the east, vanished from history.

Judah lasted until 587 BC, when Nebuchadnezzar, the Chaldean king of Babylon, destroyed Jerusalem and carried its people into captivity at Babylon. There they remained until 539 BC when Cyrus, king of Persia, took the city and allowed them (now known as the Jews) to return home.

8 The Assyrians
c. 900 – 539 BC

Among the peoples who survived the coming of the Indo-Europeans were the Assyrians, Semitic inhabitants of a district called Assur, in the north of the Tigris valley in Mesopotamia, where they settled in about 2250 BC. Fierce, cruel and toughened by centuries of warfare against their neighbours, they eventually built up an army which transformed a small kingdom into the most powerful empire the world had yet known.

In a series of campaigns led, first by King Ashurnasirpal II (883-859 BC), they swept across the Middle East, overwhelming kingdoms, seizing their wealth and deporting thousands of captives to toil in the towns and fields of Assur. Their invincible armies captured Babylon from the Kassites in 729 BC; next they destroyed Israel and occupied Damascus and the Phoenician seaports. Pressing on into Egypt, they annexed most of the country, while the cities and kingdoms of Syria submitted and paid tribute to the conquerors. When they overran the land of Elam, lying to the east of Mesopotamia, its defeated kings were said to have been made to drag the

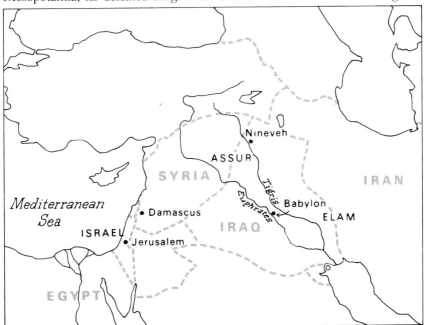

Assyrian monarch's chariot through the streets of Nineveh, which, like Nimrud ('Calah' in the Old Testament) was one of the principal Assyrian cities.

These astounding conquests were made possible by the best disciplined and most ruthless army seen until that time. The infantry, armed with iron-tipped spears and shields, were supported by masses of archers and squadrons of chariots used as shock forces.

Tiglath-Pileser III (745-727 BC), one of the greatest warrior-kings, is said never to have lost a battle. Siege-artillery moved with the armies, for the Assyrians invented battering rams and siege towers to make short work of cities defended by mud-brick walls.

With plundered riches, the Assyrian kings set up a splendid court; Sennacherib (c. 705-680 BC) employed slave labour to rebuild Nineveh as a walled city filled with palaces and tower-temples made of stone and brick. He built the world's first aqueduct to bring water to the new capital and had the palaces faced with glazed tiles of gorgeous colours. Gigantic figures of winged bulls with human heads guarded gateways and halls, while court-yards and temples were adorned by huge carved friezes stretching along the walls for hundreds of metres. These stone reliefs depict the kings' triumphs in war and in the hunting field, where lions, horses and dogs were carved with wonderful skill. Some of the carvings illustrate the hideous cruelty of war, when captives were hanged in batches, impaled on stakes, flayed alive or made to grovel on all fours before their conquerors.

The last of the great kings, Ashurbanipal (670-625 BC), seems to have been more civilized and humane; at least he was a scholar whose library of more than 20 000 clay tablets contained stories, legends and hymns of ancient Mesopotamia, as well as all that was known about the stars, medicine, plants, science and mathematics.

Perhaps the Assyrians were too few in number to hold together so vast an empire. At all events, their power suddenly collapsed when, soon after Ashurbanipal's death, the Babylonians, supported by desert tribesmen called the Chaldeans, raised a rebellion. A neighbouring people, the Medes, joined in and launched a direct attack on Nineveh itself. The great city was sacked in 612 BC, and, like the Assyrian Empire, it never rose again.

NEW BABYLON

This dramatic collapse was not quite the end of the story, for Babylon enjoyed a last brief period of grandeur when the Chaldean king, Nebuchadnezzar (c. 605-560 BC), imposed his rule over most of the lands which the Assyrians had conquered. It was he who destroyed Jerusalem and carried the Jews away into captivity. Nebuchadnezzar is also remembered for

King Ashurbanipal (c. 650 BC) in the hunting field: a wall relief which shows the marvellous skill of Assyrian artists in depicting animals.

the Hanging Gardens or terraces of his palace that came to be known to the Greeks as one of the Seven Wonders of the World. Babylon, built on both sides of the Euphrates, was said to have been over 20 kilometres square, with a wall so massive that a chariot could be driven along its top. Among the marvels of the city were the huge Ishtar Gate, faced with brilliantly coloured tiles and sacred to Ishtar, the goddess of love, and the Temple of Marduk, the principal Babylonian god; it was so vast that it seemed to the exiled Jews to reach the sky.

But Babylon was soon to belong to another master. Not long after Nebuchadnezzar's death, new conquerors appeared from the east; they were the Persians, who invaded the country and captured Babylon in 539 BC. Their king did not destroy the city, for he wanted its wealth for the empire he was about to create.

9 Persians
c. 560 – 330 BC

Some time around 1000 BC, Aryan tribes from the north settled in the country now called Iran. Among them were the Medes and the Persians, of whom the Medes were to overthrow Assyria in the 6th century BC. The Persians settled in the south, eventually occupying the old kingdom of Elam and, in about 560 BC, there arose to power a remarkable young ruler called Kyrash, later known as Cyrus the Great.

The mass of the Persian army was made up of archers; the kingdom was rich in iron and horses, which provided its soldiers with iron weapons and matchless cavalry support. With these advantages and his own gifts of leadership, Cyrus overcame the Medes, captured Babylon and advanced across Turkey and down through Syria to the borders of Egypt. He established his capital at Pasargadae in Persia, but, on an eastern campaign, he was killed fighting the Scythians far away on the borders of Afghanistan. By that time, the Persian Empire was bigger than that of the Assyrians, and his son, Cambyses, added to it by conquering Egypt in 525 BC.

Darius I, 'the Great', (521-485 BC) continued the work of expansion by campaigning as far east as the River Indus in India, north to the borders of Russia, and west to Macedonia. It was here that he made up his mind to crush the troublesome, pugnacious Greeks who had been helping their

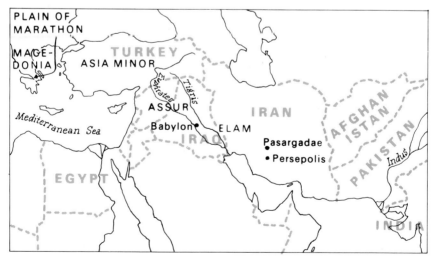

The cylinder seal of Darius the Great (c. 521-485 BC). Above the king in his hunting chariot is the emblem of the Persian god Ahuramajola.

kinsfolk to resist Persian overlordship in Asia Minor. Against all the odds, his invasion army was beaten by the Athenians at Marathon and, after his death, his son Xerxes suffered severe defeats at sea and on land. The Persians therefore gave up their attempts to expand into Europe and concentrated instead on ruling their territories in Asia from their new capital, Persepolis. They remained a major power in Asia for another 150 years, until Alexander the Great added Persia to the Macedonian Empire in 330 BC.

The Persian Empire was far kinder and more efficient than that of the Assyrians. Cyrus and his successors divided their huge territories into twenty provinces, each under a *satrap* who was a prince or nobleman. A remarkable system of roads linked these provinces to the central government, together with a common language, called Aramaic, which had derived from the Assyrians and was written, not in cuneiform, but in the Phoenician alphabet.

At the heart of Persian religion was respect for good conduct. A prophet named Zoroaster taught that life was a struggle between Good and Evil and that man ought to choose to support Mazda, 'the Lord of Wisdom' and his helper Mithras, the god of Light, against Ahriman, the god of Darkness and Evil. After death, those who had lived good lives in this world would be judged worthy of resurrection and life everlasting. These teachings spread through western Asia and came to have a direct influence upon Christianity; they survive in Iran and with the Parsees (i.e. 'Persians') of Bombay, India.

In later years, the god Mithras became especially popular with the soldiers of the Roman army, who built temples in his honour, including one in the City of London.

43

10 Greece
800 – 31 BC

The Dorians who defeated the Achaeans in the 12th century BC, overran the southern part of Greece, occupying cities at Sparta, Corinth, Megara and Argos. At Sparta, in particular, they oppressed the native inhabitants, forcing them to work the land for them as serfs. Some Dorians made their way to Crete and Asia Minor.

Another race of newcomers from lands lying west of the Black Sea, the Ionians, settled mainly in Attica, where Athens became their chief city. Others went to live on the Aegean islands or to found cities along the coast of Asia Minor which became known as Ionia.

These invaders, Dorians and Ionians, lived in 'city states', which at first were no more than small fortified towns surrounded by farmlands. Cut off from one another by mountains and sea, the states, quarrelsome and fiercely independent, were constantly at war. Yet they came to think of themselves

as one people, the Greeks or *Hellenes*, who spoke the same language, followed the same customs and feared the same gods.

From about 800 BC, as the cities became crowded and the land proved to be too poor to support a growing population, parties of Greeks left their homes to found 'colonies' in southern Italy, Sicily and along the coasts of Asia Minor, North Africa and the Black Sea. Each colony modelled itself upon its mother-city and followed the same ways of life but, as time went by, although they still kept in touch, the colonies developed their own trade and industries.

In the Greek world, each locality had its own minor gods and spirits, but all Greeks believed in the great family of gods and goddesses who were said to dwell on Mount Olympus in northern Greece. The king was Zeus, lord of thunder and lightning, whose brothers Poseidon, god of the sea, and Hades, god of the underworld, sometimes disputed his authority. Zeus had several wives, of whom Hera was the chief, and many children including Apollo, the sun-god, who was god of prophecy, youth, law and order; Athena, goddess of wisdom; Dionysus, god of wine; and Hermes, the messenger. There were also Aphrodite, goddess of love, Ares, the war god, Artemis, the huntress and Hephaestos, the gods' blacksmith.

Apollo came to be reverenced above all other gods, so that his temple at Delphi became the religious centre of Greece. Before a city founded a colony, went to war or made a treaty, its leading citizens would consult Apollo's priestess, the Delphic oracle, who, in a trance, made utterances which her priests claimed to understand. They gave her reply in verse to the questioners who often had difficulty in working out what she meant. However, the oracle must have given much good advice, for Delphi kept its importance for centuries.

A second place that was regarded with reverence was Olympia where, from 776 BC, athletic games were held in honour of the gods. Every four years, a month's truce was declared, so that city-states at war with one another would send their best athletes to compete in the various contests – running races, long jump, wrestling, boxing, throwing the discus, chariot- and horse-racing. A victor's only prize was a crown of olive leaves but, when he got home, he might receive great rewards; at Athens, for instance, he would be given a large sum of money and free dinners for life.

In the early days, petty kings ruled the city-states but, except in Sparta, the kings were replaced by councils of rich landowners, known as *aristocrats*, who governed, in some cases, for life. Merchants, artists and craftsmen had some privileges but the peasants and slaves possessed no citizens' rights at all. Trade was increasing, greatly helped by the introduction of coins, in about the 6th century BC, so that a class of rich men emerged, one of whom would gain power and become the sole ruler or *tyrant*.

These tyrants were not always bad men. Having to win support from the poor, they often curbed the rich and introduced reforms; Pisistratus of Athens (560-527 BC), for instance, ruled the city well, but his sons were unable to keep the power which he had seized and, in most cases, the tyrants did not last very long. They were replaced by the old aristocratic councils or by a new kind of government called *democracy*. Democracy, which means 'rule of the people', was introduced into Athens in 508 BC by a noble called Cleisthenes, who encouraged the citizens to meet together as the Assembly to discuss the city's affairs and elect the Council of Five Hundred which formed the government. Citizens who served as jurors in the law-courts, elected leaders called *archons*, chose generals for the army and had the power to banish anyone whose conduct displeased them.

Yet it must not be thought that all the people living in Athens at that time had a share in its government. Women, foreigners, immigrants from other Greek cities and slaves had no vote and few citizens' rights.

Sparta, standing on the plain of Laconia, did not develop like most other city-states. The Spartans, descended from the fierce Dorian invaders, lived as overlords of a population of serfs or *helots* who outnumbered them by seven to one. Therefore every Spartan had to be ready at a moment's notice to suppress an uprising or defend his city against enemies. Subjected to iron discipline, he lived as a soldier, permanently under military training which, from time to time, included killing off some of the helots to prevent them becoming too numerous.

Sparta itself was no more than a collection of straggling villages, without any fine houses, temples or public buildings. It even lacked a defensive wall, for the Spartans believed they would fight more bravely without such a protection. The state was governed by two kings, who commanded the army in the field, but otherwise had limited power, and a Council of Elders, twenty-eight citizens, all over sixty, who held office for life. The Assembly included all male citizens but had little power, apart from the right to elect annually five officials called *ephors* who supervised the affairs of state in peace and war.

The Spartan way of life aroused the awe and admiration of most Greeks, even if they did not follow it themselves. With the best-trained soldiers and the only standing army in Greece, Sparta naturally dominated its neighbours. By 500 BC, almost every city in the Peloponnese (the southern part of Greece) belonged to a league which acknowledged Sparta as its head.

Athens, situated not far away to the east, was never likely to join the Spartan alliance, for the inhabitants of the two cities were completely opposed to one another in outlook and methods of government. The Athenians, quick-witted, artistic and argumentative, loved freedom and money-making infinitely more than Spartan discipline. They naturally took to trade, for which Attica, although not rich, had certain advantages. The district produced wine and olives in abundance, some corn and pasturage, with a reddish clay for pottery, while the mountains yielded silver, lead and marble. More important, there were good harbours from which Athenian merchant ships could trade with the Greek islands and the seaports of the eastern Mediterranean.

Under the tyrant, Pisistratus, Athenian trade flourished and the city was beautified with some fine buildings. He died in 527 BC and then, after a few more years of prosperity, there came the clash with Persia.

When Cyrus the Great, the Persian conqueror, advanced into Asia Minor, he defeated Croesus, the fabulously rich king of a state called Lydia. Along its coast stood numerous Greek or Ionian cities which now became subject to Persia and were forced to pay tribute. This they resented, so, after the death of Cyrus, they raised a revolt and sent to their kinsmen in Greece for assistance. Thus it was that an Athenian force helped to burn the Persian-held city of Sardis in Lydia.

The revolt was crushed and Darius I, King of Persia, made up his mind to punish the Athenians for their interference. In 490 BC, his fleet crossed the Aegean Sea and landed an army on the plain of Marathon, about 26 miles from Athens. Outnumbered, but more heavily armed, the Athenians charged their enemy with such fury that the Persians broke and fled back to their ships. Darius died, leaving the task of taking revenge for Marathon to his son, Xerxes, who, in 480 BC, assembled a vast army drawn from all parts of the Persian empire. It marched through Lydia, crossed the Hellespont (the narrow channel that separates Asia from Europe) by a bridge of boats and came south through Macedonia into Greece. Skirting the coast, a powerful fleet accompanied the advancing host of cavalry, archers and spearmen. Realising that Athens was doomed, Themistocles, the Athenian leader, evacuated the women, children and old people to nearby islands, while the men went aboard the Athenian fleet in the Bay of Salamis. From the ships, they watched Athens go up in flames and then turned to meet the Persians who, thinking they had the Greeks trapped, sailed boldly into the bay.

However, in the narrow waters, the Greek ships, lighter, more manoeuvrable and better-manned, had the advantage, so that, after a day-long battle, the Persian fleet was almost totally destroyed.

Xerxes now retired to Asia Minor, leaving part of his forces to continue the war on land, but when they were defeated at Plataea in the following year, the Persians left the mainland of Greece for ever. However, the Aegean islands and the Ionian cities were still threatened, so the Greek states, except Sparta, agreed to unite under the leadership of Athens. An alliance was formed, called the Delian League, after the island of Delos, where a treasury was set up to hold the money paid in to support the fleet.

By this time, the First Citizen of Athens was a brilliant young man named Pericles who, over a period of more than 30 years (461-429 BC), ruled the city and filled it with splendid temples, public buildings, baths, statues, athletic fields and gymnasia. Under his leadership, trade, art, learning and drama flourished; the Athenians were better-off than ever before and much of their new-found prosperity was based on money from the Delian League.

By removing the treasury from Delos to Athens and sending the fleet to overawe any city that did not obey orders, Pericles turned the League into an Athenian empire. Although peace was made with Persia in 447 BC, the League was not dissolved and the states were made to go on paying ship-money. In truth, it had become tribute and the allies were now the subjects of Athens. Not liking this state of affairs, some of the cities looked towards Sparta which, with her ally, Corinth, had become alarmed at Athenian power and wealth. A quarrel over a Corinthian colony led to the outbreak of the long struggle between Sparta and Athens which is known as the Peloponnesian War (431-405 BC).

With the Athenians supreme at sea and the Spartans invincible on land, neither side could gain the upper hand. Each spring, the Spartans would march into Attica and devastate the countryside, but they were too cautious to besiege Athens itself. In reply, the Athenians would send a fleet to the Peloponnese to raid the coast and plunder the farms of Sparta's allies. In 429 BC, a fearful plague killed thousands of Athenians, including Pericles himself, but the war dragged on, with the leadership falling to a bombastic tanner, called Cleon, until he was killed. Peace was made in 421 BC.

This did not last long and when war broke out again, the Athenians, led now by Alcibiades, the clever, unscrupulous nephew of Pericles, decided to attack Syracuse in Sicily, a wealthy colony of Corinth. Disaster followed, for Alcibiades, having fallen out with his own side, fled to Sparta and advised the Spartans to send an expedition to Syracuse. There, the Athenian fleet was trapped in the harbour and destroyed, along with most of the army (413 BC.)

Athens never really recovered from this defeat. The Spartans, still advised by Alcibiades, built a stronghold in Attica and, by staying there throughout the year, made farming impossible and cut the supply routes into Athens. With Persian help, the Spartans obtained a fleet which enabled their general Lysander to destroy the last Athenian fleet. The city of Athens was starved into surrender in 404 BC. Through greed, treachery and incompetence, Athens lost everything - her wealth, overseas possessions and the leadership of the Greek World.

Nevertheless, in spite of their mistakes and follies, the Athenians made an enormous contribution to civilization, with ideas and values which the world still admires. The period of Pericles' rule is generally taken to be the Golden Age of Athens, for it was then that the city, especially the Acropolis, was

A Greek vase of about 530 BC, with black figures, showing maidens drawing water and gossiping at the Fountain of Callirrhoë. Pisistratus, tyrant of Athens, increased the city's water-supply by providing a number of reservoirs and fountains from the Spring Callirrhoë.

filled with statues and buildings of exceptional grace. Phidias, the greatest sculptor of his time, and his pupils carved the figures which decorated the great temple of Athena called the Parthenon; other artists, like Myron and Polyclitus, created statues of exquisite beauty. Athenian potters turned out an enormous quantity of pots, urns, bowls, vases and ornaments whose shapes and decoration have never been surpassed.

Like most Greeks, the Athenians loved drama so passionately that the theatre of Dionysus could seat 20 000 spectators. Three Athenian

49

playwrights, Sophocles, Aeschylus and Euripides, wrote some of the world's most moving tragedies, whose plots, based on Greek legends, often show men and women as the victims of fate. There were comic writers, too, notably Aristophanes, who poked fun at the follies of his fellow-citizens during the disasters of the war with Sparta.

Athens also produced a number of great philosophers. Socrates, who lived in Pericles' time, left no writings, but we know that he taught the young to think clearly by asking difficult questions about man's conduct and the purpose of life. His pupil, Plato, founded an Academy in Athens, where he taught for 40 years; in his *Republic*, he described an ideal state whose government was in many ways different from Athenian democracy. His own pupil, Aristotle, was the most gifted man of his time and the tutor of the young Alexander of Macedon.

These and other Greek scholars generated an astounding amount of knowledge and original thought for so small a country - in science, astronomy, poetry, music and mathematics. Herodotus and Thucydides wrote masterly histories; Hippocrates of Cos put forward new ideas about diseases and the practice of medicine; Homer, Pindar and the dramatists gave the world some of its greatest poetry.

Through her victory, Sparta had become the greatest power in Greece but she was soon hated more than Athens had been, especially when it was seen that, as the price for her help, Persia regained the Ionian cities. The mainland states began to resist Spartan tyranny, as Athens revived sufficiently to win a naval victory and to make an alliance with Thebes. In Epaminondas, this small city found a soldier of genius who astonished everyone by defeating the Spartans at Leuctra (371 BC) and invading the Peloponnese. However, Thebes was not strong enough to take control of a divided and exhausted country which soon fell victim to an energetic conqueror from the north.

He was Philip of Macedon, a country adjoining Greece and, by Greek standards, semi-barbaric. But its sturdy peasants were natural warriors and Philip, the best general of his day, trained them to fight as disciplined soldiers. The infantry, armed with long heavy pikes, fought shoulder to shoulder in dense formations, each known as a *phalanx*. Supported by light skirmishing troops and by well-mounted cavalry on either wing, the Macedonian phalanx proved irresistible, so that when Philip met the Greek armies at Chaeronea in 338 BC, he won a victory so complete that the whole of Greece was his.

By forming the League of Corinth, Philip intended to impose order in Greece and to raise a national army, which he would command for an invasion of Persia. But he was murdered in 336 BC and was succeeded by his 20-year-old son, Alexander.

ALEXANDER THE GREAT

If the Greeks thought that they could easily throw off the rule of this untried youth, they were speedily disillusioned. When Thebes revolted, Alexander captured the city and razed it to the ground, sparing only the temples and the house of Pindar, the poet.

In this way, he demonstrated his ruthlessness and, at the same time, his respect for Greek culture. As a boy, Alexander had been taught by Aristotle who had been summoned to the Macedonian court by Philip; from his teacher, Alexander learned to love Greek ideas and literature to such an extent that he came to believe that he was descended from the gods and destined to win fame as a heroic conqueror.

With little delay, he raised an army of Macedonians and Greeks to carry out his father's plan of invading Persia and in the spring of 334 BC he crossed into Asia. He was never to return, but in the next five years he conquered the entire Persian empire and extended his possessions as far as Russian Turkistan and India.

First, he defeated a Persian army, strengthened by Greek mercenaries, at Granicus on the Dardanelles where he showed reckless courage in battle and only escaped death through the timely action of his friend Clitus. In the following year, he won a greater victory at Issus where he put to flight the main Persian army and its king, Darius III. Contemptuously dismissing offers of peace, he turned south to free the Ionian cities and to take the Phoenician seaports, Syria and Jerusalem. Egypt itself fell into his hands without resistance, and he stayed there long enough to found at the mouth of the Nile the greatest of the many Alexandrias which he named after himself.

Back on campaign, Alexander struck at the heart of Persia, crossing the Euphrates to defeat a host said to number more than a million men at Arbela in 331 BC. Darius again escaped but was later murdered. Meanwhile

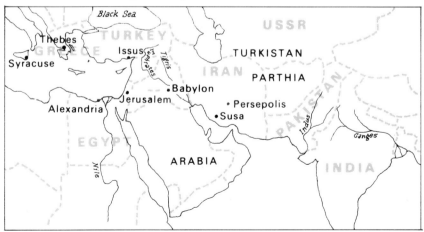

Alexander had seized all the treasures of Babylon, Susa and Persepolis. In search of fresh conquests, he led his army farther and farther east, until they crossed the mountainous border of India and came down into the Indus valley, where he defeated a local ruler named Porus. He planned to go on to the River Ganges and perhaps even to China, but at long last his weary soldiers refused to march any further.

Reluctantly, he embarked his troops and sailed down the Indus to its mouth where he founded yet another Alexandria. Then, having despatched his admiral Nearchus to explore the coast of India, he set out on the long march homewards across the parched deserts of southern Persia. His army suffered terrible hardships but the survivors eventually reached Babylon where Alexander set up his court as an eastern potentate. By now, he had become a merciless tyrant. His restless mind, as brilliant as ever, was filled with plans for his colossal empire. Intending it to be a partnership between Greeks and Persians, he married a Persian princess and encouraged his men to wed eastern women.

He was planning a marine expedition to open a sea-route from Babylon to Egypt round the coast of Arabia when, after a two-day drinking bout, he died of fever. He was only 32 years old, a man of such extraordinary gifts that it is impossible to guess what he might have achieved had he lived longer.

After Alexander's death, his empire split up and, following forty years of warfare, three principal kingdoms emerged: Egypt, seized by Ptolemy Soter, one of Alexander's generals, whose descendants ruled the country well for the next 300 years; the Seleucid Empire, stretching from Afghanistan to Syria, named after Seleucus, another Macedonian general; and Macedon, ruled by the Antigonid dynasty, which managed to keep control of the Greek states.

Throughout this vast area, the Greek language, Greek culture and the founding of many Greek cities spread Greek civilization to the east. In addition, the release of Persian gold brought a certain amount of inflation but also a marked increase in trade and wealth. In Egypt, for example, Alexandria grew enormously in wealth and importance, so that it soon rivalled Athens as the centre of learning and culture in the Mediterranean world.

In Persia, the Seleucids encouraged Greek culture for many years but, from 187 BC, most of the empire came to be dominated by the Parthians, warriors from the province of Parthia, who overcame their former masters and built themselves a new capital at Seleucia, near Babylon. Their other chief cities were Ecbatana and Ctesiphon. Less advanced than the Greeks, Macedonians and Persians, the Parthians achieved little in the way of art, literature or building. But, in later years, as fighters, they matched and even

Alexander at the Battle of Granicus. Statue found at Herculaneum.

excelled the Roman legions, for their mounted archers were the deadliest troops in the world and the Parthians only met defeat twice in their long series of wars with Rome.

Bronze figure of a Celtic warrior whose right hand probably held a spear. Wearing only helmet, torque (collar) and belt, he fights naked to proclaim his courage and contempt for death. Celts held sway in central and western Europe for several centuries, until their power was fragmented by the rise of Rome and the influx of Germanic tribes.

11   Other Cultures

As we have seen, the first civilizations arose in Mesopotamia, Egypt, India, China and around the Aegean Sea. Huge areas of the world have not been mentioned, so that it is time to look briefly at what was happening in Western Europe, most of Africa, America and Australia.

EUROPE: CELTS

In Europe, outside the Mediterranean zone, the climate was generally too cool, and the population too sparse for what we call civilization to develop at an early date. Nevertheless, there was plenty of fertile land and as people from the Aegean area moved northwards, farming settlements were set up in Bulgaria, Yugoslavia, southern Hungary, Rumania and along the east coast of Italy as early as 5000 BC. During the next 2000 years, farming spread into Western Europe, into France, the Netherlands and along the coasts of Spain and Portugal. In Britain, Denmark and southern Sweden, the hunting peoples learned to grow grain and keep livestock. Copper was being worked from about 3500 BC in Spain, Italy and in Balkan countries north of Greece, while from 2000 BC, bronze was being produced in many places. Increasingly, Europe's coasts and rivers were explored by more advanced peoples from the Near East in search of copper, amber and tin.

By 1800 BC, Indo-European peoples had settled most of Western Europe where, from Spain and Brittany to Scandinavia and Britain, they erected huge *megalithic* (large stone) monuments as tombs, temples and sacred objects. In Britain, the Beaker Folk, so-called from the shape of their drinking vessels, raised the most striking of these Megalithic sites at Stonehenge in southern England. The hewing, transport and erection of the great stones must have called for the organization and feeding of huge numbers of workers on a scale not so different, perhaps, from that of ancient Egypt.

From 700-600 BC, iron-working peoples of Central Europe were certainly in touch with the Mediterranean civilizations, so that some of the arts and skills of Egypt and Greece began to influence the lives of the farmer-warriors of Britain, France and Germany.

These were the Celts, a vigorous warlike people who had occupied a large part of Europe north of the Alps and, pressed by other barbaric peoples from the east, had moved into Western France, Northern Italy, Spain and the British Isles. On their way eastward, some had settled a region in Turkey called Galatia.

Known also as Gauls, the Celts lived in tribes ruled by chiefs and priest-leaders called Druids. Constantly at war with one another, they usually settled in or around hilltop strongholds. They loved fighting, jewellery, horses, wine and feasting and, while they may have learned much about the arts of pottery and bronze-working from their contacts with Greece and Rome, their art was their own. They decorated bowls, vases, shields, helmets, horse-harness and chariot fittings with coloured enamel and created marvellous shapes, curves and geometric designs. Some of the finest examples of Celtic art have been found at a settlement in Switzerland called La Tène.

The Celts or Gauls who entered Britain brought with them ox-drawn ploughs and, later (from about 500 BC), the knowledge of how to smelt iron-ore and make weapons and tools of iron.

Britain got its name from Brythons, Celtic tribesmen who were close kin to the Gauls in France and the Belgae, a powerful tribe who occupied much of what is now southern England. These and others, like the Iceni who seized East Anglia, the Brigantes and Parisii of the north and the Cantii of Kent,

This magnificent example of La Tène metalwork dates from the first century BC and was found at Gundestrup in Jutland, Denmark. Round the silver cauldron are figures of gods and goddesses, some holding human beings and others holding fabulous creatures.

Statue of Narwa, Kushite administrator
at Thebes during reign of Amenartis,
sister of Kushite Pharaoh Shabaku,
716-695 BC.

were the people who came to be known as Ancient Britons. It was they who
fought Julius Caesar's expeditionary force, then lived for some 400 years
under Roman rule and were later driven into the hills and forests of the west
by Anglo-Saxon invaders.

Celtic language and poetry still survive in Wales, Ireland (Irish), Scotland
(Gaelic) and Brittany (Breton).

AFRICA: KUSHITES

Africa presents us with a fascinating puzzle. It seems certain that the first
man to use stone tools did so in East Africa, but there the story ends, for he
made next to no progress in that area nor, it seems, anywhere else in the
continent, except Egypt. Great changes of climate may have made life very
difficult and may have wiped out entire populations. We know, for example,
that the Sahara Desert was formerly a fertile area of grasslands and forests.
Egypt had little influence upon the rest of the continent. The Libyans learned
something from her about agriculture and warfare and, much later, south of
Nubia in northern Sudan, the kingdom of Kush emerged. By 730 BC, the
Kushites had defeated the Egyptians and established a dynasty of five Kushite
pharaohs. However, they were no match for the Assyrians, so they left
Egypt (660 BC) in order to extend their kingdom southwards into Sudan.
With their capital at Meroe, they built up an iron-using civilization that
lasted for several centuries.

Olmec figure from Mexico: basalt figure called 'The Wrestler'.

AMERICA: OLMECS

The first inhabitants of North America were Old Stone Age people who got there from eastern Siberia by crossing a thin strip of land which joined the two continents. It is by no means certain when these migrations began, but the oldest traces of man which have been discovered point to a date around 10 000 BC. Gradually, over a great many years, these people worked their way southwards, hunting small animals and later making spears that enabled them to kill mammoths and bison. They gathered wild plant foods and eventually learned to cultivate maize, the corn that was to become their main foodstuff.

By 2000 BC, maize was being grown in most parts of Central America and was beginning to reach Peru in South America. In Mexico, people were living in villages, growing crops and making little pottery figures, usually of females, but we know practically nothing else of their lives, religion and arts.

Then, quite suddenly, in about 1000 BC, arose the first civilization of America, that of the Olmecs, a people who lived on the eastern coast of Mexico. Here they built massive stone temples in the jungle and worshipped a jaguar-god, for whom, it seems, they carved figures and masks in jade and great heads with sinister expressions. Olmec jaguar-worship, with the building of earth and stone pyramids, spread through Mexico and to the

58

Chavin peoples of Peru; the gods of the later Aztecs were descended from those of the Olmecs, this mysterious people whose culture sprang up in a swampy jungle and disappeared in about 400 BC. Five centuries were to pass before their descendants built the great city of Teotihuacan in Mexico and the Maya people erected the first of their remarkable temples.

AUSTRALIA: ABORIGINES

The aboriginal inhabitants of Australia probably came down the chain of islands between the Malaysian Peninsula and Australia by way of Java and Borneo. It is believed that they were there about 20 000 years ago, at much the same time as the Magdalenian artists were painting marvellous pictures in caves in south-western France. Having made the crossing, the Australian aborigines followed a nomadic Stone Age way of life, hunting game, gathering food in the form of grubs, small creatures and edible vegetation and adapting with great skill to a harsh environment. It seems unlikely that they came into touch with any other type of culture until the Europeans arrived at the end of the 18th century.

'Four running women' — a joyous example of aboriginal art discovered in a rock-shelter in Arnhem Land, Northern Territory.

59

12 Rome
1000 BC – AD 476

Thousands of years ago, stone-using tribes lived in Italy and then, during the second millenium BC (2000-1000 BC), Indo-European invaders came from the north, making their way through the passes of the Alps and across the wide valley of the River Po. These Italic tribes, which included the Samnites, Latins and Umbrians, used copper and bronze and, from about 1000 BC, became skilful iron-workers.

Another people called the Etruscans arrived at about this time, probably by sea from Turkey, bringing with them a written language and considerable skill as potters, jewellers and bronze workers. They settled just north of the River Tiber, building walled towns on hills rising out of the coastal plain. Further south in Sicily, Greek colonists came to live in city-states which they built as trading centres along the coasts.

According to legend, Rome, one of the small cities of the Latins, was founded besides the Tiber in 753 BC. Well-sited for trade and defence, the city attracted settlers and became strong enough for the Romans to lead a revolt of the Latins against their Etruscan overlords. After much fighting, they succeeded in capturing Veii, the Etruscan capital (396 BC), and wiping out almost every trace of this artistic people, though they learned many things from them, including the Phoenician alphabet and how to use arches in building.

In 390 BC, not long after this victory, Rome was captured and burnt to the ground by the Gauls, Celtic warriors who had occupied the Po valley. However, they failed to take the Capitol, a fortified hill on which stood the temple of Jupiter, and were eventually driven away.

The aggressive energetic Romans next embarked upon a series of wars in which they defeated neighbouring Latin tribes and the Samnites, before turning their attention to the rich civilized Greek cities in the south. The Greeks sent for help to Pyrrhus, king of Epirus, on the Greek mainland. He brought over a powerful army and won several victories, but the Romans refused to accept defeat and, by constantly raising fresh armies to renew the struggle, forced Pyrrhus to quit. The Greek cities surrendered and, by 272 BC, Rome was mistress of Italy.

While the Romans were extending their power, they were also learning how to govern themselves. For the first two centuries or so of the city's existence, they were ruled by kings, but the seventh and last of them, Tarquin the Proud, proved so tyrannical that they drove him out and, in 509 BC, Rome became a republic.

The state was governed by two magistrates called consuls, appointed for one year and assisted by various lesser officials and a council of elders called the Senate. All were *patricians*, members of the ruling class of wealthy nobles and, for a long time, the rest of the people - farmers, craftsmen and other workers, known as *plebeians* or the *plebs* - had next to no say in the government. However, after bitter struggles, they won the right to elect two officers, called the *tribunes*, whose duty was to check injustice and look after the interests of the common people.

By degrees, the plebs also secured the right to be elected to any office, even that of consul, and to sit with the patricians in the Senate.

In those early days of the Republic, a citizen of Rome lived a simple hard-working life. He tilled his parcel of land outside the city or, if he was rich, directed his servants and slaves to do the work. His home consisted of a number of rooms grouped round an open courtyard, the *atrium*, which generally had a shallow pool in the middle and, against one of its walls, a shrine on which offerings were made to the household gods who protected the inmates and kept away bad luck.

The master conducted daily worship at home and also saw to it that his children were brought up to honour the national gods. These closely resembled the Greek deities, with Jupiter and his wife, Juno, ruling a large family of gods and goddesses. They included Mars, the god of war, Neptune, the sea-god, Mercury, the messenger, Venus, the goddess of love, Ceres, the Earth-mother, Minerva, goddess of wisdom, Diana, goddess of hunting and many others.

Reverence for the gods, obedience to elders and the law, duty to Rome and readiness to serve her and fight in her armies, were the virtues which a citizen taught to his sons. At least, this was the ideal, and in later years, Romans liked to look back to their city's early years as a golden age, when men were loyal, honest and brave.

Unlike the Athenians, the Romans were not generally artistic or inventive. They did not think deeply about human behaviour or ideal government; nor did they care particularly for trade or theatre or athletic exercise. They were practical people, energetic, ambitious, warlike and greedy; above all, they were good organisers with a flair for ruling other people and extending their empire.

Carthage, founded by the Phoenicians, stood on a headland of North Africa and, by the 3rd century BC, it had become the foremost merchant city in the western Mediterranean. Carthaginian colonies were scattered along the coasts of Africa, Spain, southern France, Sardinia and Sicily, and

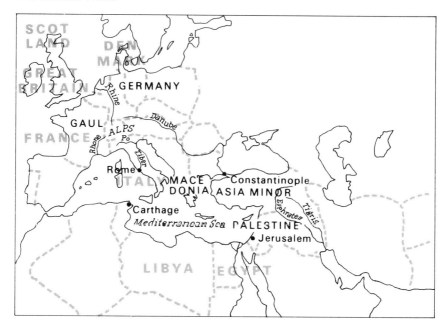

their seamen controlled the carrier-trade in iron, silver, tin, gold, corn, wine, olive oil and cloth. When Rome won control of Italy, the Carthaginians realised that a rival had arisen who could threaten their position as a trading power and it was not long before a quarrel over a city in Sicily led to war.

The Carthaginian or Punic Wars began in 264 BC and lasted, off and on, for more than a century. The first contest which took place in Sicily and on the sea, ended in victory for the Romans who, with their usual tenacity, built a fleet of war-galleys and eventually defeated an enemy who had started with infinitely more knowledge of naval warfare.

Although defeated, the Carthaginians were not broken. They had suffered severe losses but were still strong enough to resume the war in 218 BC, when their brilliant young general, Hannibal, assembled a large army in Spain, including cavalry and forty elephants, and marched them into southern France, across the Rhône and through the snow-bound passes of the Alps into the plain of northern Italy.

The Romans, scarcely able to believe that their enemy had performed this superhuman feat, hastily despatched two armies, but Hannibal easily beat them and then won an overwhelming victory at Lake Trasimene. He marched on south, hoping to raise the Italian tribes against Rome, but they held off and he found himself dogged by Quintus Fabius Maximus, a Roman general who, at the head of a new army, followed the Carthaginians everywhere, but refused to be drawn into battle.

In 216 BC, when they abandoned these cautious tactics, the Romans met the worst defeat in their history. Hannibal totally destroyed their army at Cannae, where 80 000 men were said to have been killed.

Great commander as he was, Hannibal still could not deal the knock-out blow. He lacked the siege engines and numbers of troops to capture Rome; reinforcements failed to arrive from Carthage because the Romans now had command of the sea, and he had enemies at home who did not wish him to triumph. Nevertheless, he continued the fight in Italy for another twelve years and only returned to Africa when Carthage was threatened by a Roman army. In 202 BC, he was completely defeated by Publius Cornelius Scipio at the battle of Zama and Carthage had to accept a humiliating peace.

It had been a desperate struggle and, in Rome, there were those who still feared Carthage might rise again. Their leader in the Senate, Cato, used to end every speech with the words 'Delenda est Carthago' ('Carthage must be destroyed') and, in 150 BC, an excuse was found to start the Third Punic War. For four years, the city of Carthage held out against a besieging army, the people suffering terrible hardship from famine, until, in 146 BC, the survivors surrendered. All were killed or sold into slavery, every building was destroyed and the ground itself was ploughed up, so that no trace of Carthage remained.

During these wars and for several years afterwards, the Roman armies continued to bring more lands under Roman rule. By 133 BC, they included Spain, Libya, Macedon, Greece and much of Asia Minor; among later additions were Crete, Syria, Palestine, Gaul and Egypt.

Territories outside Italy were divided into provinces, each ruled by a governor, called a pro-consul, who commanded the army, dispensed justice, built towns and collected the money and produce which had to be sent to Rome as tribute. This vast increase in territory brought enormous wealth and power to the Roman State. It also brought many problems. The rich became extremely rich, for there were ample opportunities for governors, officials and tax-gatherers to amass money in the provinces while, in Rome, as trade increased, merchants, bankers and money lenders were able to make fortunes.

In Italy, much land had been laid waste during the Punic Wars and family farms disappeared, as men were called up for the army or as farming became unprofitable when corn came in from the provinces. Rich men were able to buy up farms and turn them into big estates worked by slaves who, being numerous and cheap, were so harshly treated that many fled to join the robber-bands that terrorised the countryside. From time to time, slave revolts occurred, the most famous one being led by a gladiator called Spartacus who defeated three Roman armies before being killed in 71 BC. Loss of the farmlands drove many men to Rome but, owing to the huge number of slaves, jobs were scarce and wages low, so the poor existed as best they could, crowded into high blocks of slum tenements, thrown up in the damp low-lying parts of the city.

To deal with this situation, the Roman government provided corn as a free dole for the poor and, to keep them amused, built public baths and put on chariot races, wild beast shows and contests between gladiators who were specially trained to fight and die in the arena.

Many of the poor managed to exist as 'clients' or hangers-on of rich men, who gave them money and gifts in return for their votes at elections and for services which might include supporting a patron on public occasions and 'dealing with' the clients of rival politicians. Amid these evils, there were still magistrates and governors who tried to carry out their duties honestly and to observe the old Roman virtues but, in general, the Senate and the police officers - the *aediles* - were powerless to maintain order or to cure the hatred between rich and poor. Attempts at reform were made by the Gracchi, two brothers, Tiberius Gracchus (163-133 BC) and Gaius Gracchus (153-121 BC), who, as tribunes, wanted to break up some of the big estates and give land to the poor, but their enemies stirred up riots and both were murdered.

When Rome was threatened by Celtic tribes - the Teutons and Cimbri - who invaded southern Gaul from Germany, a general named Marius became head of the State. He was elected consul in 107 BC and re-elected for five years in succession, contrary to the rule which decreed that a consul should serve for one year only. However, this gave Marius time to build up an army of paid troops and, with Sulla, a young patrician, to defeat Rome's enemies.

The Senate found itself confronted by a successful general backed by an army loyal to him rather than to the State and a bloodthirsty struggle ensued between Marius, supported by the common people, and Sulla, the Senate's champion. After Marius' death, Sulla, who had led a successful campaign in Asia Minor, returned to Rome as a dictator, took away the rights of the Assembly and the tribunes, and restored the power of the Senate by massacring thousands of members of the popular party.

By these drastic measures, Sulla restored order for a time but it did not last after he died in 78 BC. The Senate proved incapable of ruling firmly, corruption was rife and no leader seemed able to command public support until there emerged the man who came to be called 'the Greatest of the Romans' - Gaius Julius Caesar.

Caesar, born into a patrician family, won over the common people by spending vast sums of money (most of it supplied by rich supporters) on free food and entertainment. In 59 BC, he was elected consul and, at the end of his year of office, with the help of his friend and son-in-law, a distinguished general named Pompey, he became governor of Gaul.

The Pont du Gard near Nîmes in Southern France, one of the finest Roman aqueducts outside Italy. Built in the time of Augustus, it consists of three tiers of arches, the lowest being of six arches, the second of eleven arches and the third of thirty-five smaller arches carrying the water channel.

This gave him what he wanted most, the chance to win glory at the head of an army for, although he had already shown himself immensely gifted as a politician, orator, scholar, poet and writer, he had only limited experience as a military commander. In a series of campaigns which lasted from 58-51 BC and included two expeditions to Britain, he defeated the warlike Gauls and added a rich province to the Roman State. Moreover, through his leadership and courage in battle, he won the devotion of his battle-hardened soldiers.

The Senate, sensing danger, ordered Caesar to disband his army and return to Rome, where Pompey had joined his enemies. After some hesitation, Caesar led his troops across the River Rubicon and occupied the capital.

Later, he conducted another series of brilliant campaigns in Spain, Greece, Egypt, Syria and Asia Minor, defeating Pompey and all the forces of the Senate.

Pompey was killed in Egypt and, in 46 BC, Caesar returned to Rome, the undisputed master of the Roman world and, in the short time left to him, he introduced a programme of reforms that would have benefited all classes of the populace, especially the poor. Towards his enemies, he showed mercy, but a party of them, hating his reforms and fearing that he intended to make himself king, stabbed him to death in the Senate House in March 44 BC.

There followed a civil war that lasted for 13 years and, at its end, Caesar's great-nephew, Octavian, emerged victorious, when his admiral Agrippa defeated the fleets of Mark Antony (Octavian's rival for supreme power) and Cleopatra, Queen of Egypt, seventh and last of the Ptolemy rulers, at the battle of Actium (31 BC), off the west coast of Greece.

Octavian, who became known as Caesar Augustus, is generally regarded as the first Roman Emperor, though he never took that title himself. A man of infinite ability and wisdom, he ruled an empire with a population of a 100 million for 44 years, giving it peace, prosperity and an administration so efficient that, in spite of the follies and wickedness of many of his successors, it continued to work for 200 years. It is he, rather than his great-uncle, who deserves the title, 'the Greatest of the Romans'.

Dividing the Empire into forty-three provinces, he concentrated on giving them just government, rather than conquering new territories. To defend the frontiers, he created a standing army of 25 legions (a formation of from 3000 to 6000 soldiers) in which the soldiers served for 20 years, while, at home, he formed an Imperial bodyguard (the Praetorian Guard), a police force, a fire service and an efficient Civil Service. He decreed that a census should be held so that taxes could be raised justly, and he introduced a great programme to build new roads and provide water-supplies, to suppress pirates and robbers, and to create an imperial postal service linking the provinces to Rome. Among other achievements, he had Carthage rebuilt, so that it grew into the largest city in the west after Rome.

Augustus encouraged writers and artists, and, during the Augustan Age, Virgil, Horace, Livy and Ovid were writing their poems, satires and histories. He was also a great builder, who boasted, 'I found Rome built of brick and am leaving it built of marble.'

Augustus was succeeded by his stepson Tiberius (AD 14-37), an able ruler but a suspicious evil man. He was followed by Caligula, cruel and insane, Claudius, the scholarly cripple, during whose reign Britain was added to the Empire, and Nero, a vicious buffoon, who committed suicide in AD 68, the last Emperor of Caesar's family.

In the reign of Augustus, in about 4 BC, there was born in Palestine, a Jewish carpenter's son, named Jesus. When he was grown to manhood, he began preaching a new kind of religious faith based on love, which soon won a great many followers, especially as he performed a number of miracles. He claimed to be the Christ or Messiah, the long-promised earthly King who would free the Jews from subjection and restore their kingdom.

But the priests and elders of the Jewish faith looked on his teachings as a threat to their authority and they saw to it that he was brought to trial for blasphemy in Jerusalem, before Pontius Pilate, the Roman governor. Against his better judgement, but to avoid trouble, Pilate allowed Jesus to be crucified with two criminals. According to his followers, Jesus rose from the

The Colosseum in Rome, the vast amphitheatre begun by Vespasian and finished by Domitian in AD 82, which seated upwards of 50 000 spectators beneath a huge awning protecting them from the sun. Lifts from underground passages brought gladiators and wild animals up to the arena in which they fought and died.

dead and ascended into Heaven, for he was none other than the Son of God.

This belief spread rapidly, especially among the poor, to whom the new religion called Christianity gave comfort and hope. Thanks chiefly to Paul, the first missionary, it soon reached cities along the Mediterranean coasts and then Rome itself, where Paul and Peter, one of Jesus's original disciples, were imprisoned and put to death during the reign of Nero.

The Romans worshipped many gods, but the Christians declared that there was only one true god and would not recognise the divinity of the Emperor. Moreover, they liked to meet together privately for prayer and they disapproved of slavery and condemned the cruelty of the Games. To the Roman authorities, therefore, Christianity was a danger to the State and must be crushed out of existence.

For more than two centuries the Christians were persecuted, especially during the reigns of Nero (AD 54-68), Decius (AD 249-51), and Diocletian (AD 284-305) when thousands were put to death. Some of the emperors were less severe, and Christianity continued to spread, for its teachings about a just and merciful God and the life after death appealed to people of all classes throughout the Empire.

The Arch of Caracalla at Djemila, Algeria, where Roman streets are still used by present-day villagers.

From AD 69, for about a century, life within the borders of the Empire was generally peaceful and prosperous. In the provinces, the people were encouraged to live in neat orderly towns, graced by handsome temples, theatres, arenas and public baths; a marvellous road system linked town to town and province to Rome, and along the roads flowed the merchandise, produce and ideas of a remarkable civilization in which conquered people were proud to become Roman citizens. This was the period of the Five Good Emperors - Vespasian (AD 69-79), a great general, Nerva (AD 96-8), Trajan (AD 98-117), a Spaniard who pushed the boundaries of Rome north of the Danube and eastwards to the Tigris, Hadrian (AD 117-38) who travelled ceaselessly in order to bring stable government to the provinces, and Marcus Aurelius (AD 161-80), a soldier, a scholar and a man of piety and goodness.

But, from the accession of the worthless Commodus in AD 180, the Empire began to decline. It was to last for more than another two hundred years and there were to be emperors like Septimus Severus (AD 193-211), Diocletian (AD 284-305) and Constantine (AD 306-37) who managed to bring back some kind of order, but the decay which had set in could not be cured.

Power had passed to the legions which made and unmade emperors as they pleased. At times, rival emperors fought for supremacy; between AD 211-84, twenty emperors were murdered and, in one year, no fewer than six were elected and overthrown. Without strong government, trade, justice and the people's morale declined; corruption increased and, in spite of the vast wealth in private hands and heavy taxation of the provinces, there was not enough money to pay the salaries of public officials, to support the unemployed and to meet the gigantic cost of the Imperial Court. There were other causes of weakness, such as the run-down condition of farming and a declining population in Italy, partly due to pestilence brought by the army from the East. But infinitely more serious was the remorseless pressure of barbarians all along the Roman frontiers.

From the forests and the steppes of Siberia, nomadic hordes of Mongols, Turks, Avars and Huns were on the move and, as they pressed towards the west, the German or Teutonic tribes of northern Europe found themselves being uprooted. Franks, Burgundians, Alemanni, Lombards, Goths and Vandals moved west and south, crossing the Rhine and the Danube, so that they pushed into Gaul, Spain, Africa and Italy itself. Many of them settled peacefully inside the Empire and served in the Roman legions; others, notably the Goths, Vandals and Alemanni, kept up continuous attacks along the frontier of the Roman Empire and, as fast as one group was driven back, another pressed in elsewhere.

Diocletian (AD 284-305) realised that the task of ruling the Empire and commanding its armies in the field was too great for one man, so he divided it between two rulers, one, his friend Maximilian, to live in Italy and he himself to rule the eastern part of the Empire from Nicaea in Asia Minor.

Constantine (AD 306-37), called 'the Great', reversed this plan by defeating his rivals to become sole Emperor. Yet he introduced more drastic changes when he transferred the capital from Rome to a new city called Constantinople which he built on the site of old Byzantium at the entrance to the Black Sea. He also accepted Christianity and decreed that the Christians must no longer be persecuted.

After his death, the Empire was again divided and, as the barbarian attacks fell increasingly on the west, there was less and less contact between the two emperors. In AD 401, the Goths, under their leader, Alaric, invaded Italy where they were defeated by a great general, Stilicho, himself a Vandal in the service of Rome. But he was murdered and, in AD 410, Alaric captured the city of Rome itself. Not long after this, the Goths were persuaded by the western emperor, to drive the Vandals out of Gaul and to settle there themselves, causing the Vandals to move on to Spain and North Africa, where they seized Carthage. Meanwhile, the Picts from Scotland and the Angles and Saxons from Denmark and Germany had invaded Roman Britain and destroyed the civilization they found there.

In AD 451, Attila led the ferocious Huns into Gaul but they were defeated at Châlons by the Goths who joined forces with the Roman army. Four years later, Vandals from Carthage sailed up the Tiber and fell upon Rome, plundering its treasures and carrying away 30 000 citizens into slavery.

After this disaster, the power of Rome as an empire came swiftly to an end. The provinces were overrun and, by A.D. 476, the German chief, Odoacer, deposed the last Emperor, Romulus Augustulus. But Roman civilization was not totally destroyed. Many of the barbarians became Christians, learned the Latin language and adopted Roman law and customs. Moreover, in Constantinople, Roman culture, mixed with Greek and Asian influences, was to survive for another thousand years.

PART TWO

The Medieval World

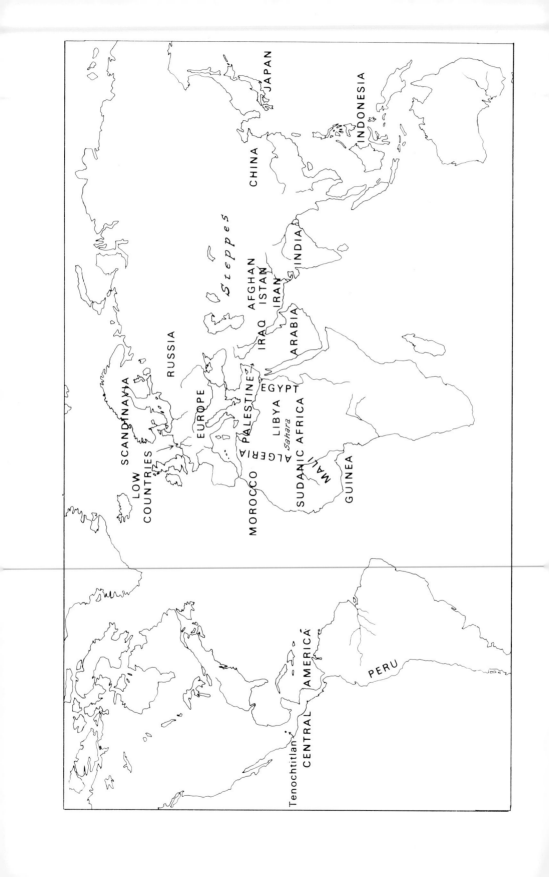

INTRODUCTION

If we could look down, as though from another planet, at the world during the thousand years or so up to 1600, we should probably be struck, first, by the fact that most of it was thinly populated and uncivilized. Great stretches of practically uninhabited forest, plain, desert and mountain separated the civilized areas - China, India, Byzantium, the Islamic countries, Europe, Central America and Peru (there was none in Australasia) - from one another, so each tended to be individual and different in some respects from the rest.

Traders and Buddhist monks certainly travelled between India and China; Crusaders came into contact with the Arab world and a few brave travellers, like Marco Polo, journeyed to the end of the earth. But these contacts were few. Most people never moved more than a few miles from the place where they were born, nor knew that the Chinese, say, or the English, even existed.

Yet, although communication was so difficult and knowledge of other peoples so scanty, we can see some similarities between the civilizations. All of them depended upon agriculture; all of them had a large peasant class whose labour supported the nobles, priests and warriors; all of them relied for power upon the muscles of men and animals, and some also used wind and running water; in all of them, religion was a dominant, sometimes *the* dominant force in people's lives.

Looking down, we would also notice that, from time to time, some of the most desolate areas in the world produced eruptions which had violent effects upon the civilized regions. These were the great invasions by nomadic tribes - Huns, Avars, Turks and Mongols - who poured out from the steppes of central Asia to fall upon the settled lands of China, India, the Middle East and eastern Europe and to terrorise their peoples for nine centuries.

Bedouin tribesmen of Arabia burst out from their desert homeland in the 7th century to conquer lands to the east and west, converting those who submitted, so that the Islamic faith spread along the North African coast into Spain, down into Sudanic Africa, across the Middle East into central Asia, India and Indonesia.

The third wave of invaders were the Norsemen or Vikings from Scandinavia who plundered and settled the islands and coastal fringes of western Europe, and also settled themselves in Italy, Russia and Byzantium.

The conquerors all came from lands so harsh that those who survived childhood grew into hardy, tireless fighters, but, in addition to their stamina and ferocity, each group possessed an advantage over the peoples whom they attacked. With the Vikings, it was the longship; with the Huns and Turks, their skill as archer-horsemen; with the Mongols, their disciplined cavalry and, with the Arabs, their ardent faith that death in battle against unbelievers would be rewarded by life in Paradise. Moreover, the Arabs, Mongols and Vikings inspired such terror that their enemies were usually beaten before they got into battle.

Religion had a profound effect upon the lives of everyone and, in all the civilizations, except, perhaps, in China, priests played major roles as teachers, leaders and statesmen. Buddhism, oldest of the three world religions and the first to spread beyond the society in which it was born, made its chief impact upon China and Japan, while Islam, with its remarkable power to appeal to different peoples, spread far beyond the Arab world to India, central Asia, China, the Sudan and Mali. The Christian Church, divided at an early date into the Eastern Orthodox and Roman Catholic Churches, was to be divided again by the Protestant rebellion. Its worldliness and the misdeeds of some of its clergy and supporters must not tempt us to forget that Christianity itself, with its power to inspire men and women to the highest ideals, was the chief civilizing influence in Europe. By the 16th century, it had been carried to America by the Spaniards and Portuguese, but had not yet become a world religion.

Still surveying this span of a thousand years, we would notice that, in spite of widespread plagues and disasters in the 14th century, the world's population was steadily growing, though it was still small by modern standards. In 1500, the whole of Europe contained about 100 million inhabitants, as against some 450 million today, while China may have had 150 million compared with more than 1000 million today.

Since the chief occupation everywhere was cultivating the land, most people lived in villages, but, as trade and manufacture expanded, towns increased in size and numbers. But they were still small. A 16th-century European town of average size contained about 5000 persons, a city like Norwich, 20000, Florence, 90000, while London at the time of Queen Elizabeth's death in 1603, was bigger than Paris with 200000 inhabitants, though smaller than Tenochtitlan when Cortes and the conquistadors set foot in Mexico.

Most people were smaller and less well fed than we are, and they died younger, a great many of them in infancy and women in childbirth. Comparatively few persons survived their forties; Henry VIII of England, at 50, spoke of being in his 'old age' and, in reaching 70, Philip II of Spain was almost unique among kings, though the indomitable Eleanor of Aquitaine was still journeying about Europe at the age of 80. Women tended to die before their husbands, doubtless because of the dangers of child-bearing and the drudgery of their lives. In law, education and social life, women almost everywhere were treated as men's inferiors, an attitude supported by the Christian Church. The lives of Muslim women were even more restricted.

Throughout this period, we see the emergence of states, most of them

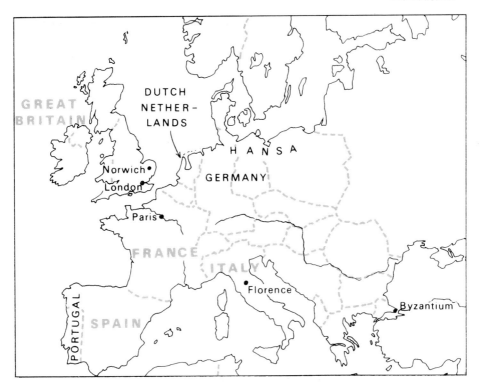

kingdoms, in which an individual, almost always a noble, rises above the rest through his prowess in war, assumes the crown and founds a dynasty. Kingship, sanctified though it might be by religious awe and ceremony, depended upon the monarch's character; if he were weak or stupid, his mighty subjects - feudal lords and princes, whether in Japan, India or France - would overthrow him and fight among themselves for power until one of their number triumphed. Sometimes, usually in China, the peasants rose against their oppressors and overthrew the ruling class.

From the 14th century, many kings were able to advance their power, because, with increased wealth, they could hire armies strong enough to subdue rebellious lords and, with cannons, to destroy their castles. Moreover, in some countries, but not yet in Italy, Germany or India, the ruler could appeal to the patriotism of his people, as men began to think of themselves as, say, Englishmen or Frenchmen, different from foreigners - and, usually, superior to them!

The tradition of the king taking counsel from the great men of his realm was an old one and, from assemblies like the Witan, Diet and States-General, there developed the idea of a parliament, called together as a rule to raise taxation. Cities, holding much of a country's wealth, therefore came to choose representatives to sit alongside lords and archbishops. Where monarchy was weak, some of the cities of Italy, the Low Countries, the Rhineland and the Hansa (an alliance of north Germany), came to be practically independent states, governed, not by nobles, but by an upper class of successful citizens

From about 1500, a dramatic change takes place in world history, as, with the discovery of America and of a sea-route to India and the East, Europeans from countries bordering on the Atlantic, viz. Spain and Portugal, followed by the Dutch Netherlands, England and France, begin their domination of the globe, which puts an end to the separateness of civilizations.

To a very considerable degree, their penetration and settlement of distant lands, their astonishing conquests and seizure of the lion's share of the world's trade were due to their development of weapons and ships that were markedly superior to all others of their time. To these advantages could be added the Europeans' adaptability, enterprise, pugnacity and greed. For better or worse, the world was to become theirs for the next four-and-a-half centuries.

1 Byzantium
330 – 1070

The Eastern or Byzantine Empire came into existence when the Roman Emperor, Constantine the Great, founded Constantinople in AD 330 on the site of an ancient Greek city called Byzantium.

After Constantine's death, the Roman Empire was divided into two parts, the West ruled from Rome and the East from Constantinople, but, whereas Rome was soon to be overwhelmed by barbarians, Constantinople managed to survive for another thousand years. The city itself was almost impregnable, since it was surrounded by water on three sides and defended on the fourth by a massive three-fold system of walls and towers. By military strength, treaties and bribery, the emperors held their enemies at bay until, in 527, there came to the throne a man whose greatest ambition was to win back the lost lands in the west.

A mosaic of the 6th century in the Church of San Vitale, Ravenna, Italy, showing the Emperor Justinian with his retinue making an offering of gold.

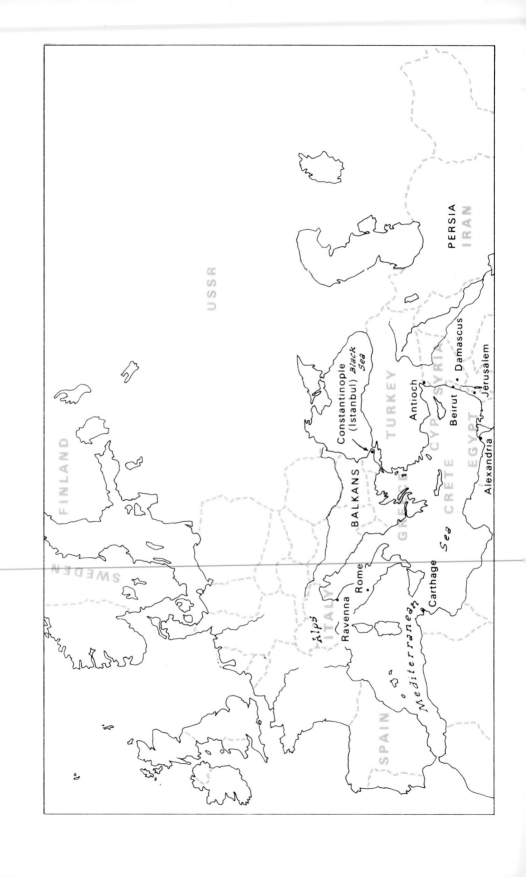

To a large extent, Justinian succeeded His finest general, Belisarius, defeated the Persians and then crossed to North Africa with a first-class army which captured Carthage from the Vandals. Next, he invaded Italy (537) to attack the Ostrogoths and recover Rome; imperial armies also reconquered southern Spain from the Visigoths and, at sea, Byzantine fleets held the mastery of the entire Mediterranean.

It was said that Justinian worked so hard that he never slept and also that he never made a decision without consulting his wife, the intelligent and beautiful Theodora, a former actress and daughter of a circus animal-trainer. At all events, this remarkable man ruled the expanded empire with masterly skill and embarked upon a vast programme of public works, filling Constantinople with marvellous palaces, libraries and baths. The magnificent Church of the Holy Wisdom, at St Sophia, with its ceiling overlaid with pure gold, took 10 000 men five years to build; another splendid building was the Church of San Vitale in Ravenna. Justinian also founded or rebuilt many towns and cities throughout the empire, in which Damascus, Antioch, Beirut and Alexandria became renowned centres of learning and trade.

Nowadays, Justinian is best remembered for his Code of Laws. Over the centuries, the Romans had made and changed so many laws that they baffled even the most learned judges, so the Emperor ordered a team of experts to examine hundreds of books and reduce what was best into a four-part Body of Civil Law which has influenced the legal systems of many countries to the present day.

Justinian's laws were mostly written in Latin and he himself was the last Eastern Emperor to speak Latin, but, by the end of the reign, he was using Greek, the language of most Byzantines, who, more and more, came to think of themselves as Greeks rather than Romans. In religion, Justinian never succeeded in uniting the eastern and western Churches. There had long been differences between the two communities and the Byzantines refused to accept the supremacy of a Roman Pope, so that, in later years, the Eastern Orthodox Church became quite separate from Rome.

In order to pay for so many wars and splendid projects, Justinian had to inflict heavy taxes on his subjects and, after his death, most of the territories which he had recovered were lost. His successors tried vainly to ward off Persian attacks in the east, while a Germanic people called Lombards crossed the Alps to occupy northern Italy and the Slavs and Avars, warlike tribesmen from the steppes, pressed into the Balkan Peninsula of south-eastern Europe.

Recovery began in 610, when the Emperor Heraclius came to the throne. A brilliant general, he won back many of the lost territories, recaptured Jerusalem and drove the Persians back to their own country. But, within a few years, Persia and much of the Byzantine Empire was overwhelmed by new enemies, the invincible Arabs or Saracens, who, inspired by their faith in Allah and his Prophet Mahomet, swept in from the Arabian desert to conquer Persia, Syria, Egypt and the rest of North Africa.

Constantinople itself did not fall. Thanks to its superb fortifications, its defenders repulsed every attack for a quarter of a century and, in 678, defeated an enemy fleet so heavily that the Arabs gave up naval warfare. The Byzantines' victory was mainly due to their use of 'Greek fire', a mysterious substance made up of naphtha by some secret process, which was fired from tubes or thrown in jars at the Arab ships with deadly effect, since it could not be extinguished by water.

In the next century, another outstanding emperor, Leo III ('Leo the Isaurian', 716-41) twice repulsed formidable Arab attacks on Constantinople and won back a great deal of imperial territory, but Italy had to be given up and henceforward the empire consisted mainly of Greece and Asia Minor (modern Turkey), an empire that was now Greek in spirit and achievement.

Throughout the ceaseless struggle against Arabs, Bulgars and Russians, Byzantium survived through the strength and professionalism of its armies and navies, and through the Emperors' use of their immense wealth to reward allies and bribe foes. Byzantines became renowned for their guile, their polished manners, double-dealing and cruelty. The Empress Irene, for instance, had her own son blinded in order to usurp his throne; she died in 803, having failed to come to terms with Charlemagne, founder of the Holy Roman Empire. By that time, Byzantines regarded all Westerners (whom they called 'Franks') as uncouth barbarians, while they, for their part, considered the 'Greeks' to be devious tricksters, and this mutual dislike was to have tragic consequences during the period of the Crusades.

The Isaurian emperors were followed by the Macedonian dynasty, founded by Basil I in 867, which lasted until near to the end of the 11th century. It was a time of vigorous rule, when the Byzantines generally held their own with their enemies and reduced the danger from the Bulgars by persuading them to become Christians. Indeed, Basil II adopted a frightful form of 'persuasion', when, after a great victory, he blinded 15 000 Bulgar prisoners and sent them home to their countrymen!

A new foe appeared in the 9th century when bands of Viking warriors from Finland and Sweden sailed down the Russian rivers to the Black Sea and launched furious attacks upon the great city which they called 'Micklegard'. Once again, Constantinople held firm, but the Emperor thought it wise to grant trading rights to the Norsemen and to take some of the warriors into his service as members of the Varangian Guard, a renowned fighting force which served the Imperial cause for over 450 years.

In the 10th century, under such emperors as Nicephorus II and John Tzimisces (969-76), Byzantium's armies drove the Arabs out of Asia Minor,

Crete and Cyprus, besides recovering Syria, which had been in Arab hands for three centuries. But, just when the Eastern Empire seemed to have reached a new peak of power and stability, its frontiers were overrun by tribesmen from the east called Seljuk Turks who speedily occupied great areas of imperial territory and, from about 1070, threatened Constantinople itself.

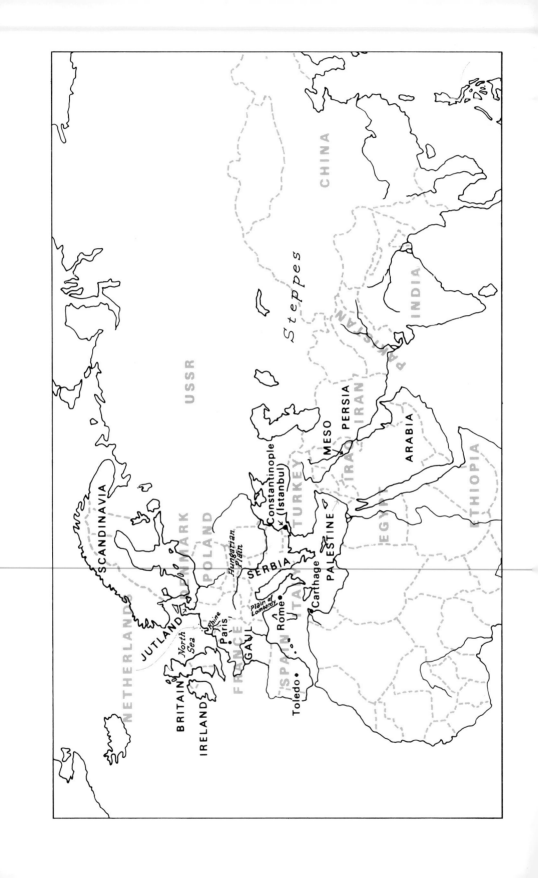

2 Christianity Spreads
450 – 1385

Halfway through the 5th century, the Roman Empire, already tottering, was assailed by hordes of Huns, fiercest of all the Asiatic nomads. Some had pushed south into India, others moved west, to the dismay of the Germanic tribes dwelling in lands alongside the Empire's borders.

The Hunnish leader, Attila, known from his ferocity as 'the Scourge of God', invaded Gaul, where the Roman nobleman, Aetius, at the head of an army composed largely of Goths, Franks and Burgundians, met him in battle not far from Paris. It was a bloody indecisive struggle, but, for once, Attila was halted and he retreated eastwards across the Rhine, and then turned south into Italy.

The Christian bishop of Rome, Pope Leo, went to meet Attila and asked him to spare the city. For some reason, he agreed to do so and led his warriors back to the Hungarian plain, where he died in 453. At his death, the German tribes revolted against the Huns, broke up the once victorious horde and drove the survivors back to the steppe-lands from which they had come.

This was the end of the Hunnish threat - but also the end of the Western Empire. Aetius was murdered and there was no authority strong enough to hold together the barbarian peoples who had settled inside Rome's boundaries and served in her armies. The last Roman emperor was deposed in 476 by a German chieftain named Odoacer and in Western Europe there followed a long period of confusion and disorder, which is sometimes called 'the Dark Ages'.

In Italy, Odoacer was soon overthrown and killed by the Ostrogoths (i.e. eastern Goths from the Black Sea area), led by Theodoric, who restored order and prosperity for a short time. As we have read, Belisarius captured Rome, but Byzantine rule did not last long, for a Germanic tribe, the Lombards, invaded the peninsula and settled down on the northern plain, now called Lombardy.

Visigoths (western Goths) and Burgundians (Germanic tribesmen) seized parts of Gaul, but an energetic people called Franks moved in from across the Rhine. Their leader, Clovis (481-511), drove out the Visigoths and founded a kingdom which came to be known later as France; at this time it included modern Belgium and the Netherlands.

Meanwhile, the Vandals, a fierce Germanic people, made their way to North Africa where they captured Carthage, and the Visigoths took possession of Spain. They accepted Christianity and, making Toledo their capital, created a society which cared for art, learning and culture.

Thus, although the West was no longer Roman, it did not fall entirely into barbarism. The peoples who threw off Roman rule had lived for too long on the borders of the empire or within its boundaries, not to be affected by Roman ways. Many of them greatly admired Roman customs and dress; they developed languages based on Greek and Latin (though not in Britain and Scandinavia) and they gradually adopted Christianity, which had become the official religion of the Roman Empire a century before its collapse.

At the head of the Western Church stood the Bishop of Rome. St Peter the Apostle had died there and the guardianship of his bones gave the bishop a special place among other bishops. Moreover, Rome for centuries had been looked upon as the capital of the world, so he seemed justified in taking the name of Pope or Father. When Pope Leo persuaded Attila to lead the Huns out of Italy, he was also seen to have taken the place of the Emperor, a ruler who spoke in the name of St Peter.

But not everyone accepted the Pope's authority. The Patriarch (or bishop) of the Eastern Church in Constantinople certainly did not, nor did the Christians in Egypt, known as Copts, who belonged to the Coptic Church; nor did the Nestorian Christians of Mesopotamia and Persia. The Copts and Nestorians had somewhat different beliefs from other Christians and were regarded as heretics by Rome and Constantinople. The Franks accepted Christianity in 497, but, as yet, like the Goths in Spain, they paid little heed to the Pope.

Christianity had reached Britain during the Roman occupation and had been carried to Ireland by St Patrick early in the 5th century. However, in southern and eastern Britain, Christianity and almost every trace of Roman civilization were wiped out by the Anglo-Saxon tribesmen who crossed the North Sea from the plains and marshlands of Jutland, Germany and Denmark to settle in a land more fertile than their own.

The Britons fought long and hard against the invaders, but they were steadily driven back into Wales, Cornwall and Strathclyde, where, in hilly country, they managed to hold out and preserve Celtic traditions. In Wales, they clung to the Christian faith and some crossed over to the western tip of France which is still called Brittany and where the Breton language is akin to Welsh.

Scotland and Ireland, neither of which was conquered by the Romans, were also inhabited by Celtic peoples - the Irish and the Scots in Ireland and the heathen Picts in Scotland. The Scots crossed over, subdued the Picts and gave their own name to the country they occupied and into which they

Den steward vergele so vunnd dar qval yue den muuste alssver
vor dem schiff das er den hiell vff gib als ober

St. Brendan and the
Whale from a 15th cen-
tury manuscript. The
Irish saint, said to have
been born in Tralee in
Kerry in AD 484, was
the legendary hero of a
voyage across the Atlantic
to the 'Promised Land of
the Saints' and of count-
less adventures, such as
landing on a whale in
mistake for an island.
Variations of the legend
are found in many lan-
guages; geographers and
navigators, including
Columbus, believed in the
existence of St. Brendan's
Island and several expeditions set out in search of
it, until in 1759 its
appearance was explained
as a mirage.

In die liifft wolte tragen vrd viel der wider herunder
als ob er in abgrund wolte vallen dem selben schiff was
das vff dem schmidt gewachsen goltz vnd ertz do wardt su als

brought Christianity, for St Ninian (*c.* 360-432) converted the Southern Picts,
while St Columba, in about 560, founded a monastery on the island of Iona,
from which the Christian religion was carried to the rest of Scotland.

From Rome, Pope Gregory the Great sent St Augustine to Britain (596) to
convert the Anglo-Saxons, but his mission had only limited success and it
was Celtic missionaries from Iona who carried Christianity into the
kingdoms of Northumbria, East Anglia and Mercia. In 644, the English
Church accepted the Pope's authority and became part of the religious
organisation of Western Europe.

Missionaries from Britain, notably Willibrod (658-739) and St Boniface
(675-754), went abroad to what is now the Netherlands to convert the
Frisians, but the heathen Saxons in Germany held out until Charlemagne
made them accept Christianity (864) at the point of the sword. The Slav
peoples of eastern Europe, Bulgars, Serbs and Russians, were won over to the
Eastern Orthodox Church of Constantinople, but Poland (*c.*965) and
Hungary (*c.*1000) became obedient to Rome. The Scandinavians were

A wall painting of c. 900, possibly depicting the celebration of Palm Sunday, from a Nestorian temple in Sinkiang, a remote province of western China.

converted in the 11th century and the last heathen peoples in Europe, the Prussians and the Lithuanians, in c. 1285 and c. 1385.

From Egypt, as early as 350, the Coptic Church sent missionaries to convert Abyssinia (Ethiopia) and, somewhat later, the Nubian kingdoms in the southern part of the Nile Valley. Between the 7th and 11th centuries, the Nestorian Church carried Christianity from Persia to India, east into China and south into Arabia, so that, although Christianity did not take lasting root in Asia, a few Christian communities survived for centuries.

The spread of Christianity (and learning) was chiefly brought about by monasteries. The first monks followed the example of St Anthony, who, in the 3rd century, retired to a hermit's existence in the Egyptian desert. The idea of living a solitary life devoted to prayer spread to Syria, Italy and Gaul, while, in the Celtic Church, a monastery consisted of a group of separate huts or cells, each with a single occupant.

However, a different kind of monastery developed in Italy, where, at Monte Cassino, St Benedict (*c*. 480-547) introduced a set of Rules for monks living together in a community, whereby each day was divided into set periods for worship, prayer and work. Benedictine monasteries quickly appeared throughout Western Europe and it was from them that missionaries set out to convert the heathen.

As new kingdoms emerged, the peoples of the West were linked together by the Christian religion, the Latin language and the Pope's authority. But in the Byzantine Empire, an Emperor still ruled, whose supremacy was accepted by the Patriarch, while in Syria, Palestine, North Africa and (later) Spain, the advance of Islam overwhelmed almost every trace of the Christian religion.

St. Benedict, by Hans Memling, the 15th century Flemish painter.

3 The Empire of Islam
570 – 1174

In about 570, a boy named Mahomet (also known as Mohammed and Muhammad) was born in Arabia at Mecca, a market town on the Red Sea. Arabia, a harsh desert land, crossed by caravan trade routes from eastern Asia to Syria and Egypt, was inhabited by Semitic tribesmen who worshipped pagan idols, but were acquainted with the religious beliefs of Jews, Christians and Persians (whose national religion was based on the teachings of the prophet Zoroaster).

Mahomet grew up to become a merchant, but, as the result of a dream in which the angel Gabriel spoke to him (the same Gabriel who had visited Mary, mother of Jesus), he became convinced that he was chosen to be the Prophet of God, whom he called Allah.

Like Jesus, Mahomet began to preach and win disciples. His message that Allah, the God of Abraham and the Jews, was the true and only God, angered the elders of Mecca, since they made a good income out of pilgrims to a sacred relic called the Kaabah Stone. In 622, Mahomet had to flee for his life to the oasis town of Medina, where he won a great many converts to his new religion called 'Islam', meaning 'submission', since they had to submit themselves utterly to Allah. These believers, known as Muslims or Moslems, marched on Mecca, but they met with little opposition, for the Arabs had become ready to accept Allah and, by the time Mahomet died in 632, the whole of Arabia had been converted.

The Prophet was followed as leader by Abu Bakr, who took the title of Caliph (which means 'successor') and raised an army to carry the faith into neighbouring lands, where the unbelievers ('infidels'), were given the chance to accept 'there is no God but Allah and Mahomet is his Prophet'. The alternative was death or heavy taxation, though Jews and Christians were treated more leniently, since they were 'People of the Book', who believed, like the Muslims, that the Old Testament was the word of God. Islam's holy book, the Koran, containing Mahomet's teachings and rules for living a good life, was the first piece of Arabic literature committed to writing and the forerunner of thousands of books of poems, stories and learning.

Abu Bakr and the two caliphs who succeeded him waged holy wars so successfully that Persia, much of the Byzantine Empire, Syria, Palestine, Egypt and Libya were overrun by the Arab warriors. Each Islamic state was

Every Muslim tries to make the pilgrimage to Mecca at least once in his lifetime. Here, from a manuscript of the Baghdad School, is a party of medieval pilgrims on their way to Mahomet's birthplace.

governed by a local ruler owing allegiance to the Caliph. By this time, he lived in Damascus, because the first dynasty or *caliphate*, the Omayyads, had moved there from Medina in 658.

Abd al Malik, one of the greatest of the Omayyad caliphs, introduced a standard coinage into the Islamic empire, improved communications and made Arabic the official language. He also built the Dome of the Rock in Jerusalem, a most famous mosque that was erected on the spot where,

according to tradition, Abraham led Isaac to the sacrifice and where Mahomet ascended to heaven.

However, in Persia, the converts to the new faith resented being ruled from Damascus and, led by Abu al Abbas, a descendant of Mahomet, they raised a revolt and, in a bloody struggle, all but wiped out the Omayyads and established the Abbassid dynasty which ruled the Islamic empire from 750 until about 1100. For their capital, they founded a new and splendid city at Baghdad, on the banks of the Tigris in Mesopotamia.

In a second wave of conquests, the Muslims pressed eastwards into Afghanistan, India and even to the borders of China. In the West, they carried the faith and the sword all along the length of North Africa into Morocco and Spain and, for a time, across the Pyrenees into France. Here, in 732, they were defeated by the leader of the Franks, Charles Martel, and forced to withdraw, but, known as Moors, they stayed on in southern Spain for the next 500 years. An Omayyad prince who had escaped death during the struggle with the Abbassids, set up an independent caliphate, with its capital at Cordova, a beautiful city of mosques, palaces, workshops, public baths and libraries said to house over 400 000 books and manuscripts. Meanwhile, from Morocco, Islamic armies carried Mahomet's teachings across the Sahara and south along ancient trade routes into Ghana, Mali and Nigeria.

The Arab conquerors who, not long since, had been nomadic robbers, were truly remarkable people, for they quickly absorbed the culture and learning of occupied lands in which they built splendid cities at Damascus,

Cairo, Baghdad, Bokhara, Samarkand and Cordova, filling them with mosques, palaces, schools, universities, workshops, public baths, hospitals and libraries.

For centuries, the whole Islamic empire, a vast area stretching from the borders of China to Spain, was linked by a common religion, a common language and a common coinage. It was crossed by trade and pilgrim routes, along which merchants and scholars carried the ideas and learning of one land to another. Thus, the knowledge of ancient Greece and Egypt, of Persia, India and Rome, was translated into Arabic, so that in science, medicine, mathematics, geography and astronomy, the Arabs were far, far ahead of Christian Europe.

In Baghdad, in the Golden Age of the Abbassids, when the great collection of stories, the *Arabian Nights* was being gathered, the Caliph Haroun al Rashid (786-809) presided over a Court renowned for its wit and learning, where poets, story-tellers and musicians entertained a ruler who founded schools to spread the knowledge of the Ancient World.

But the unity of Islam did not last. After the independent caliphate had been set up in Spain, Morocco created its own dynasty and, in the 10th century, the Fatimids in Egypt were defying the Abbassid Caliph of Baghdad. Thenceforward the story of Islam is one of separate dynasties, quarrels and intrigues, though Islamic religion and culture continued to expand and to appeal to non-Arab peoples.

From the Asiatic steppes, the warlike Seljuk Turks (Seljuk was the name of a great chieftain) moved into the Middle East, captured Baghdad and, in 1071, defeated the Byzantine army at the battle of Manzikert. Converted to Islam, they had no patience with the former Arab tolerance towards Christians whom they persecuted with such zeal that Pope Urban II called upon the princes of Western Europe to launch the First Crusade. The Seljuks fought the Crusaders valiantly and their leaders, called Sultans, who ruled in the name of the Abbassid caliph, set up strong governments for a time, until, in the 12th century, one of their governors, Saladin, made himself Sultan of Egypt and founded the Ayyubid dynasty that ruled from Egypt to Mesopotamia.

One of the puzzles of history is the frequent eruption of conquering tribesmen from the steppe-lands of Asia. How did that area of desert and grassland, with its bitter winters and burning summers, support the warrior-hordes who, time after time, swept like torrents across the settled lands? The probable answer is that it never could support them for long. It seems likely that there were periods of milder weather and abundant rainfall which produced more grass than usual and therefore more flocks, herds and horses. Fewer children died in infancy and, in these circumstances, along with the custom of one man taking several wives, the population exploded.

Portrait of Saladin (1138-93) painted when he was in his early forties. Sultan of Egypt and Syria, Saladin was a good general, a chivalrous foe and a patron of learning and the arts.

The nomads' traditional skills as horsemen and fighters provided a supreme chieftain or *Khan* with a ready-made army of tireless warriors and, in Saladin's time, just such a leader arose in Genghis Khan. Having united the tribes of Mongolia, the mighty conqueror invaded China and then turned west to overwhelm the Muslim states up to the borders of eastern Europe. Genghis died in 1227, but his successors stormed on through Russia into Poland and Hungary. In 1258, they captured and destroyed Baghdad itself, city of the Caliphs and the most splendid centre of Islamic culture. Their advance was halted when they were at last defeated at the battle of Ain Jalut (1260), near Nazareth, by the army of the Mamelukes, a new ruling group of Egypt and Syria.

During their campaigns, these ferocious conquerors were themselves conquered by the Islamic religion and absorbed by the peoples whose lands they occupied. The vast empire created by the Mongolian horse-archers soon broke up into a number of Muslim khanates, whose territories stretched from Russia to the borders of India and China. As we shall see later, the next upsurge of Muslim power would establish the Ottoman Turks at Istanbul (Constantinople) and a Mongol Emperor at Delhi.

4 Charlemagne
768 – 887

In the year 768, there came to the throne of Frankland, (a kingdom that consisted of most of modern France and Western Germany), a grandson of Charles Martel, 'the Hammer', who had defeated the Muslims at Tours. The young monarch, also named Charles, was destined to become known as Charlemagne, Charles the Great.

By the standards of his age, he deserved the title. A giant of a man, he defeated the Saxon tribes who raided his eastern borders and forced them by brutal means to accept Christianity, vanquished the Lombards in northern Italy, invaded Spain to attack the Moors, wiped out the dreaded Avars of Hungary (Mongolian tribesmen who had terrorised eastern Europe) and added parts of Germany and Italy to his empire.

But Charlemagne was much more than a conqueror. A Christian, with a sharp inquisitive brain and a genuine love of learning, he realised that Europe's greatest need was education, for apart from the clergy, hardly anyone, even the nobles, could read and write. Compared with the Islamic world, Western Europe was uncivilized.

Gold reliquary (receptacle for relics) in the form of a bust of Charlemagne in the Treasury at Aachen. It contains fragments of his skull and was ordered by the Emperor Frederick Barbarossa in the 12th century.

With the help of an English monk named Alcuin, Charlemagne founded schools, built churches and abbeys and made the Palace School at his new capital, Aachen (Aix-la-Chapelle) one of the greatest centres of medieval learning. He divided the empire into 'counties', each with a Count, who was compelled to rule justly, since he was subject to visits by 'missi', royal inspectors who continuously toured the kingdom to make certain that Charlemagne's commands were obeyed.

In the year 800, Charlemagne re-visited Rome, where he had earlier rescued Pope Leo III from his enemies and restored him to the papal throne. On Christmas Day, in St Peter's Church, the Pope picked up a golden crown from the altar and crowned his protector Emperor of what became known as the Holy Roman Empire, a vast tract of Europe which, in one form or another, was to survive for a thousand years.

Thus, to the indignation of the Byzantine Emperor (who still claimed to be ruler of all the old Roman Empire), the West now had its own Emperor and a dream of a united Europe. It was never much more than a dream, even though it persisted for centuries, for the genial old tyrant died and after his son, Louis the Pious, had failed to keep order, his successors divided the empire into three parts.

Charles the Bald took the western part, Lothair took the central part, a narrow strip, running from Lotharingia in the north right down to Rome, while Louis the German acquired the eastern lands which Charlemagne had conquered. The Kingdom of Lothair was soon absorbed by the other two and from them emerged the Kingdoms of France, Germany and Italy. A descendant of Charlemagne, Charles the Fat, was crowned Emperor of all these, but he proved to be hopelessly feeble and his deposition in 887 was followed by a period of misrule and anarchy.

During the centuries of turmoil that followed the break-up of the Roman Empire, a system emerged in Western Europe known as the feudal system.

Victorious chiefs had usually rewarded their followers with gifts of land and, from about the 6th century, Frankish kings insisted that every lord, in return for his estates, should take an oath of loyalty or allegiance, swearing to fight for the king and to bring with him a company of armed men. A great noble, holding large territories, would grant estates on similar terms to some of his principal knights, who, in their turn, made grants to lesser men. On every estate, the peasants or serfs, along with their wives, children, huts, implements and domestic animals, belonged to their lord; they had to obey him, pay various dues and work his land; in return, they received protection and the right to cultivate a certain amount of land in order to feed themselves and their families. Thus, every man had a lord, a richer, more powerful man, to whom he owed service and loyalty, so that medieval society was like a pyramid, with the mass of the peasants at the base and the king at the top.

The danger was that great lords, relying on the allegiance of their own people, could defy the king's authority or even overthrow him. Only the most powerful and determined kings could keep the lords under some sort of control and often the best way to do so was to go to war with a neighbouring country.

5 Vikings attack Britain
787 – 1042

Towards the end of his reign, Charlemagne tried, with little success, to repel sea-raiders who attacked the north-eastern coasts of his empire. They were the Norsemen or Vikings from Scandinavia, who, for the next 200 years, were to fill the peoples of Europe with dread.

Until about the middle of the 8th century, the Germanic barbarians living in Norway, Denmark and Sweden had existed as best they could by farming the narrow valleys and plains of their homelands. They had played no part in the overthrow of the Roman Empire, but now they suddenly burst out from their fiords to plunder and kill with remorseless fury.

Perhaps it was a sharp increase in population leading to a shortage of land that drove younger sons to take to piracy, but they could not have made such a spectacular success of robbery and, eventually, of settlement overseas, if they had not invented the longship.

These magnificent vessels, each about 24 metres long and carrying 80 warriors, were sturdy enough to withstand Atlantic storms and manoeuvrable enough to traverse the rivers of Europe so that their crews could go ashore where they pleased to plunder lands which possessed few defences, no national armies and no warships of their own.

The Vikings from Norway favoured the Outer Route, sailing out into the Atlantic and southwards to attack the coasts of Scotland. Then, with the Isle of Man as their base, they fell upon Ireland, where the monasteries were filled with priceless treasures. Some of the Norsemen ventured to the Faroes and as far as Iceland; Erik the Red founded a colony in Greenland in 982 and his son, Leif, actually reached the mainland of America, nearly five hundred years before Columbus.

The Danes took the Inner Route across the North Sea to Britain and down the coast of the Low Countries to pillage the rich farmlands of France. At first, they went home each autumn with loot from the abbeys which stood conveniently near the coasts and from sacked towns like London, Rochester, Nantes, Bordeaux and Paris. Other Vikings plundered Lisbon and Cadiz or sailed past Gibraltar into the Mediterranean to attack the Italian cities of Pisa and Lucca.

The Swedish warriors went by the Overland Route down the rivers of Russia and captured the flourishing city of Kiev in the Ukraine. In 865, they

organised a fleet to sail onward down the Dneiper and across the Black Sea to besiege Constantinople itself. Only a great storm saved the fabulous city from destruction.

But the treasure of Europe was not inexhaustible. Sometimes, the Vikings would agree to forego plunder in return for regular tribute - the 'Danegeld' - which the Anglo-Saxons and the Franks were forced to pay, but, increasingly, the robbers decided to settle in the lands which they had

Stone slab with a carved picture of a Viking longship, its sail set and the steersman at the steering-oar. AD 700, Gotland, Sweden.

harried, and they soon showed themselves to be skilful farmers, craftsmen, and shrewd traders who readily took to town life.

ALFRED THE GREAT

In 787, when the first Viking raiders went ashore in Dorset, England was a prosperous country. The Anglo-Saxons had long since adopted Christianity and merged their small kingdoms into three main ones, Northumbria, stretching up to Scotland, Mercia in the centre and Wessex in the south. With its long undefended coastline, its navigable rivers and undulating plains, the country was specially vulnerable to attack by bands of sea-pirates. Isolated raids were soon followed by organised attacks in which fleets of longships took part and whole companies of warriors spent the summer plundering the countryside.

By 855, 'the heathen host' stayed on through the winter; Northumbria, East Anglia and Mercia were overrun, before the Viking army moved in force against Wessex, whose kings had been putting up a stout resistance for years. In 871, Alfred of Wessex fought no less than nine battles, until even the Danes had had enough. They made peace and withdrew into Mercia. Six years later, in a surprise attack, Alfred was heavily defeated and, his army broken and the kingdom apparently lost, he fled into the marshes of Athelney in Somerset. But the men of Wessex rallied and, in 878, Alfred won a great victory at Ethandune, near Bridgwater, laid siege to the Danish stronghold and forced their leader Guthrum to sue for peace.

98

By the Peace of Wedmore, it was agreed that Guthrum should turn Christian and the Danes should withdraw to the eastern part of the country, known as the Danelaw, but Wessex and half of Mercia were to remain free.

At long last, the Vikings had been contained. Alfred had saved Wessex and Christianity in England, and, for the last twenty years of his life, he devoted himself to restoring his ravaged kingdom. To guard against further attacks, he reorganised the Saxon army, had 'burghs' (fortified towns) constructed and warships built in order to meet the enemy at sea. He rebuilt London and several other towns, sent abroad for monks to replace those who had been slaughtered, founded schools and, to encourage learning, himself translated and wrote books.

Like Charlemagne, but more humane, Alfred was the most remarkable man of his time - one of the few rulers in history who truly deserved to be called 'the Great'.

CANUTE

Alfred founded a line of splendidly successful kings, for his son, Edward the Elder, conquered the Danelaw and persuaded the Danes to accept his rule. Alfred's grandson, Athelstan (925-40), known as the first King of all the English, added southern Scotland to the kingdom, while the third great ruler, Edgar (959-75), aided by St Dunstan, Archbishop of Canterbury, gave England a golden age of peace and good government.

This happy situation did not last long. In the following reign, fresh waves of Vikings began raiding England anew, whereupon the king, Ethelred, called the Redeless, meaning 'ill-advised', paid them Danegeld to go away. Naturally they came back for more and Ethelred, in desperation, ordered the massacre of all Danes living in England. Among the slain was the sister of Sweyn Forkbeard, King of Denmark, who arrived with an army to take terrible revenge.

Ethelred fled abroad and, by 1017, Sweyn's son, Canute, had become king of both Denmark and England. All Alfred's work seemed to be undone when England and southern Scotland became part of a Scandinavian sea-empire, for Canute had also conquered Norway. Fortunately, he turned out to be an able ruler, who adopted Christianity and kept peace and order in his realms.

Canute's two sons died in quick succession and, in 1042, the English Witan (a council of bishops and nobles) offered the crown to Ethelred's son, Edward, a pious weakling, known as 'the Confessor', who allowed the kingdom to be run by a powerful earl, Godwin of Wessex, and, later, by Godwin's son, Harold.

Viking weapons from a collection in Oslo.

6 Normans and Magyars
911 – 1087

While the Vikings were raiding Britain's coasts and seizing its farmlands, others were inflicting such damage to France that in 911, the French king, Charles the Simple, made a treaty with Rollo the Norse leader, whereby Rollo and his followers were given a sizeable tract of land which henceforth became known as Normandy.

These Vikings, now called Normans, had to receive baptism and to do homage to the French king as their nominal overlord; it was tacitly agreed that they could go on raiding Brittany. With their usual adaptability, the Normans quickly settled into their new land, adopted its language and became good farmers, ardent Christians and builders of churches. Their inborn love of fighting found an outlet in making war on the Bretons and in quarrelling among themselves, so that they not only became expert cavalrymen but, to defend their estates, they invented a fortification known as a *castle*, which at this time usually consisted of a wooden tower on an earth mound or *motte*.

Meanwhile, Central Europe was suffering attack by hordes of ferocious nomads called Magyars or Hungarians who had moved westwards from the grasslands of southern Russia and settled on the Hungarian plain along the middle reaches of the Danube. From this gathering ground, they launched attacks upon more settled and civilized lands, burning, looting and carrying off women and children as captives. Between 896 and 955, they made raids into Bavaria, France, Saxony, Lotharingia and Burgundy; some of them penetrated as far as Italy and Spain.

In face of this menace, the German nobles elected Duke Henry of Saxony ('Henry the Fowler') to be their king and he made a truce with the Magyars, paying them tribute to gain time in which to train an army to fight on horseback like the nomads. In 955, Henry's son, Otto, finished the job. At Lechfeld, near Augsburg, he won a victory so complete that the Magyars who survived the slaughter, fled back to the Hungarian plain, never to return to the west. In about the year 1000, their king, St Stephen, persuaded them to become Christians and their days as nomadic raiders were ended.

After the battle, Otto's troops proclaimed him Emperor and, as Otto I, he put an end to civil war in Germany, revived the eastern part of the Holy Roman Empire as a German possession with large territories in Italy, and made himself protector of the Pope and the Latin Church. During his reign, which lasted until 973, he exercised a kind of protectorate over France, received tribute from Poland, Bohemia (W. Czechoslovakia) and Denmark, made war on the Slavs (tribesmen, who, from the Carpathians in Central Europe, became the forbears of Russians, Bulgars, Serbs, Croats, Poles and Czechs), and deposed one Pope in order to replace him by his own nominee. He can be said to have been the founder of Germany.

A battle between Hungarians and Mongols (here called Turks) on a bridge over the Danube. The Hungarians are on the left and the Mongols attacking them have been depicted with knightly helmets and a Crescent symbol on their banner. (From a decorated manuscript with the date 1244 in the text.)

THE NORMAN CONQUEST OF ENGLAND

When Edward the Confessor died in January 1066, the Witan passed over the rightful heir, Edgar the Atheling (prince), and chose Harold, the son of Earl Godwin of Wessex, to be king. This was their right and they did so because Edgar was only a boy, whereas Harold had been effectively ruling the country for some time, was popular (at least in the south) and had proved himself as a warrior in a campaign against the Welsh.

But there were two other men claiming the throne. One was Harold Hardrada, King of Norway, who coveted the land which had formerly belonged to Canute, and the other was William, the illegitimate son of the Duke of Normandy by a tanner's daughter, who from boyhood had had to fight hard to secure his father's lands and to ward off attacks by the King of France. William based his claim on the fact that he was related to Edward the Confessor, who, he said, had promised him the Crown. Moreover, Harold, when a prisoner-guest in Normandy, had sworn an oath to support his claim.

Unfortunately for Harold, his two enemies attacked at the same time, for there is little doubt that he would have overcome them separately. All through the summer of 1066, he waited in southern England with a fine

103

A scene from the Bayeux Tapestry showing part of the Norman fleet crossing the Channel with men and horses on board. The ship on the right is William's, for at the mast-head is the Cross-banner sent to him by the Pope. The Latin words are part of an inscription saying, HERE DUKE WILLIAM IN HIS GREAT FLEET CROSSED THE SEA AND CAME TO PEVENSEY.

army, while his fleet patrolled the Channel to deal with William's invasion force, but contrary winds prevented the Normans sailing. In September, news came that Harold Hardrada had landed a Viking army on the York-shire coast and was advancing inland; at this, King Harold marched north and, in a great battle at Stamford Bridge, practically wiped out the Norse invaders.

While his battered army was resting after its victory, Harold learned that Duke William had landed unopposed in Sussex, where he had erected a fort and was laying waste the countryside. The Saxon king immediately set off, marching so fast that many of his weary troops could not keep up with him; nor would he heed his brother's advice to wait for reinforcements to come in from distant shires. Angrily, he declared that he had beaten one invader and would drive the Norman Duke into the sea.

One 14 October 1066, they met on Senlac Hill, near Hastings, where, in a desperate battle, fortune swayed to and fro all through the day, but, by nightfall, Harold lay dead, surrounded by the bodies of his household troops, the hus-carls, who had fought dauntlessly to the end.

By this single victory, a kingdom far bigger and infinitely richer than Normandy, fell into William's grasp and he had no intention of letting go. With speed and sagacity, he imposed a Norman aristocracy upon the leaderless Saxons, rewarding his followers with estates, building motte-and-bailey castles at strategic points, crushing revolts with ruthless severity and retaining vast quantities of land and wealth for himself and the Church.

William the Conqueror did not introduce the feudal system into England, for there was already a complex system whereby every man owed duty to his lord. What he did was to make the holding of land and the obligations of tenants much clearer and stricter, with the King himself as the sole land-*owner*. By scattering their estates about the kingdom, he prevented his nobles from becoming over-mighty in any one area and, by retaining real power in his own hands, this iron man established the strongest monarchy in Europe.

To his sons and their descendants, William bequeathed a stable, well-organised kingdom, increasingly filled with splendid churches and rich monasteries. In literature and at Court, the language was French, but, gradually, English prevailed, and the conquerors and the conquered became one people, an energetic, aggressive people destined to play a major role in European and world history.

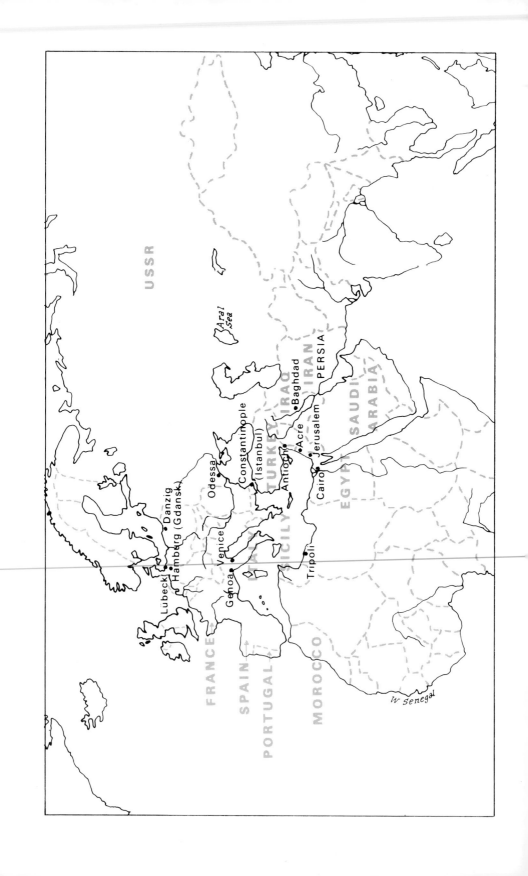

7　The Crusades
1061 – 1291

The Norman Conquest of England can be regarded as the greatest accomplishment of the Norse sea-rovers whose daring carried them to Iceland, Greenland, America, France, Russia and Constantinople. They also founded a kingdom in the Mediterranean world.

A few years before Duke William invaded Sussex, the sons of the Norman knight, Tancred de Hauteville, landed with a small force on the Muslim-held island of Sicily and, with the Pope's blessing, set about the Saracens with such vigour that they soon conquered the island. Roger Guiscard became King of Sicily, adding to his possessions the greater part of southern Italy, which his brother Robert had already seized. Thus emerged a remarkable Norman kingdom, fertile, rich through its trade with eastern lands, cultured and tolerant, because its motley population included Frenchmen, Italians, Greeks, Christians, Jews and Muslims. It was to play an important role, as a half-way house, during the Crusades.

After their early conquests, the Islamic warriors from Arabia had settled down to live tolerantly with their Christian subjects and neighbours in Palestine and Syria, but, suddenly, the peace was disrupted by the arrival of a ferocious people called Seljuk Turks. Some 300 years earlier, they had migrated from the Steppes to the east of the Aral Sea and had been converted to Islam; then they overran Persia and, in 1055, captured Baghdad. Thence, they poured into Asia Minor, defeated the Eastern Emperor and occupied Syria and Palestine, where they fell upon the Christian inhabitants, slaughtering them or selling them into slavery. The pilgrims' route from the West to Jerusalem was closed.

In the fighting, the Eastern Emperor lost so many of his finest troops that he wrote from Constantinople to the Pope, asking him to send some companies of Frankish knights, since they were known to be the best cavalrymen in the world. Pope Urban II did more. He preached to the Franks so eloquently that they agreed to put aside their own quarrels in order to rescue Jerusalem from the infidels or 'unbelievers' - each side regarded the other as 'unbelievers'!

Letters were sent to kings and princes all over Europe, while wandering preachers like Peter the Hermit aroused such enthusiasm among the common people that a host of peasants set off for the Holy Land, without

A cavalry clash between Crusaders, armed with Norman swords and shields bearing the Cross, and Saracens equipped with their curved swords and round shields, one with the Islamic crescent. Below: in camp, off-duty, Crusaders pass the time playing a board game which may be draughts. (from a 14th century manuscript, *L'Histoire de Guillaume de Tyre*)

weapons, stores or money. Most of them perished on the way, or were massacred with contemptuous ease by the Turks.

However, formidable armies from France, Normandy, Germany and Italy, journeyed to Constantinople, whence they fought their way down through Syria and into Palestine. In 1099, in spite of heat, drought, difficult country and incessant attacks by the Turks, they captured Jerusalem, where their joy at rescuing the Holy Places did not prevent them slaughtering the Muslim population.

Violent, greedy and often treacherous to one another, the Crusaders had nevertheless achieved a triumph of courage and faith. Some returned home but others stayed on to fight the Turks, build castles and carve themselves estates which they ruled as feudal lords. Within twenty years, they founded four Crusader kingdoms, known collectively as *Outremer*, (which meant 'overseas') of which the principal one was the Kingdom of Jerusalem. Its king, Baldwin I, claimed overlordship of the others: the County of Tripoli, the Principality of Antioch and the County of Edessa.

For almost 200 years, in the face of every kind of difficulty, Outremer somehow survived. New Crusades were launched (there were at least seven in all), with fresh armies setting out from Western Europe, led by the greatest monarchs and warriors of their time, but even Richard the Lionheart failed to capture Jerusalem after it had been re-taken by Saladin in 1187.

Italian merchant-cities, especially Venice and Genoa, grew rich on Crusader traffic and trade; one Crusade, the Fourth, was diverted by the Venetians from its original objective, Egypt, to Constantinople (1204), where knights wearing the Cross of Christ savagely looted the city which had been the bastion of Christianity for centuries. Two Crusades did make for Egypt in the hope of entering Palestine from that direction, but they failed to capture Cairo. The Children's Crusade of 1212 was a pathetic tragedy, but the Holy Roman Emperor Frederick II of Hohenstaufen, a man so gifted that he was nick-named *Stupor Mundi*, 'the Wonder of the World', actually regained Jerusalem by cunning, and crowned himself King. The city was soon lost; the great Crusader castles surrendered one after another and, when Acre fell in 1291, crusading came to an end.

A few hundred mounted knights, supported by hired foot-soldiers, and the two great Military Orders of the Hospitallers and Templars, had tried to hold a narrow strip of territory in an alien land. When the Muslims put aside their own quarrels and united their forces, they were bound to sweep the Westerners into the sea.

But there were some gains. The Crusades attracted many of the most violent and aggressive lords, so their absence was a boon to the homelands they left for ever, while those who served in a campaign lasting a year or two and then went home, had come into contact with people and ideas far more civilized than in the crude society of Western Europe. Manners were more gracious, knowledge of medicine, science and mathematics more advanced. New cloths - silks, damasks, cottons and muslins - found their way into the West, along with strange fruits and spices, fine jewellery and glassware. The Crusaders also brought back with them what was less of a gain - new knowledge of castle-building, siege-engines and military tactics.

The reconquest of the Holy Land was not the only goal of the Crusaders, for there were heathens to be fought in other places, notably in Eastern Europe and Spain. The shores of the Baltic Sea and the vast plain lying east of Saxony were inhabited by tribes speaking a Slavonic tongue and worshipping heathen gods. Urged on by their bishops, companies of German fighting men, calling themselves the Knights of the Sword and the Knights of the Teutonic Order, campaigned for generations against these tribesmen, until the pagans had perished or accepted Christianity.

There was, of course, more to be won than the souls of men. The lands of the Slavs were rich and well-worth having, once forests had been cleared, marshes drained and towns built. Along the Baltic coast, little fishing villages were to become thriving ports, such as Hamburg, Lübeck and Danzig, whose merchants controlled most of the sea-trade of northern Europe. The task of converting the heathen and colonising the northern plain was one of Germany's greatest achievements in the Middle Ages.

In the 8th century, Muslims from North Africa had overrun Spain and Portugal, where they created a civilization of cities and universities that far outshone the uncouth societies of Western Europe. But, in northern Spain, the small Christian kingdoms of Leon, Castile, Aragon and Navarre survived and, when the Emirate of Cordova broke up in 1031 into rival petty states, a counter-attack began to be launched.

Strongest of the Christian states was Castile, whose armies, aided by Crusader knights from France, Germany and Italy, drove south so successfully that, in 1085, King Alfonso VI captured Toledo. This led to the invasion of the peninsula by the fanatical Almoravids from Morocco, who defeated Alfonso and checked the Christian advance. Less tolerant than the previous Arab rulers, they drove many Christians and Jews to take shelter in the Christian kingdoms.

The struggle went on and when Pope Innocent III persuaded Aragon, Castile and Navarre to unite their forces in 1212, the Christians won a great victory at Las Novas de Tolosa. Further victories forced the Moors to retreat until, by 1248, they occupied only the mountainous land of Granada and here they stayed until most of them were driven out of Spain in 1492.

As a result of the reconquest, Castile and Aragon emerged as the leading powers in Spain, while Portugal, formerly a mere county round Oporto, became a separate kingdom.

8 T'ang, Sung, the Mongols and Ming 220-1644

The Han Dynasty, with its vast empire and contacts with the Roman world, broke up in about 220 and was followed by the period known as China's 'Dark Ages' or the Six Dynasties, which lasted until 580.

It was a time of turmoil and civil war, of upstart generals and short-lived emperors, of invasion by Turkish and Mongolian peoples pressing in from the Steppes. Yet writers, scholars and poets managed to survive; histories were written, libraries founded and statues carved in styles that showed traces of Greek and Indian influence.

Buddhism, brought in by missionaries and pilgrims from India, now took root in China, for its teachings appealed to the people, so that many Chinese

Figure of a horseman of the Six Dynasties period, AD 265-589. Chinese artists and sculptors seem to have been fascinated by horses, which were not native to China but came from the Mongolian steppes. Nevertheless, the Chinese improved horse harness and invented stirrups in the 4th century.

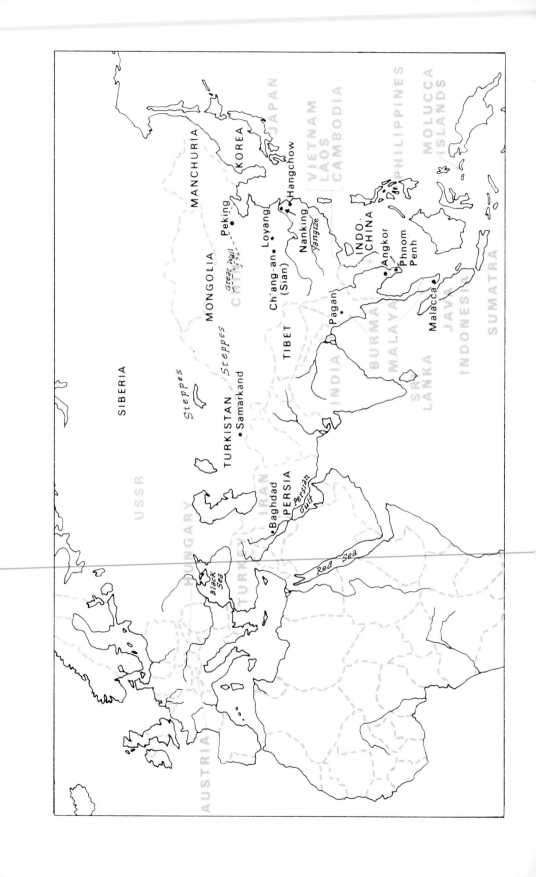

monks made the long journey to India to find out more about Buddha and his teachings.

Revival of China's unity began during the short-lived Sui Dynasty (580-618), whose two emperors successfully fended off the Turks, made war on the Koreans and compelled no fewer than five million peasants to construct a magnificent waterway, the Grand Canal, from Loyang to the Yangtze River.

In 618, just four years before the *Hegira*, when Mahomet fled to Medina, a young man named T'ai Tsung founded the brilliant T'ang Dynasty, which lasted for three centuries. He and his successors extended Chinese power over Korea, Manchuria, Mongolia, Turkistan and Tibet, so that they ruled an area even larger than the Han empire. They made contacts with the outer world, as goods and ideas flowed along the Silk Road from India, Persia and the lands of western Asia to Ch'ang-an (or Sian), the Chinese capital, which, by now, was the greatest city in the world.

The T'ang emperors kept the same form of government as the Ch'in and the Han, appointing the governors and officials, retaining the civil service examinations and encouraging the teachings of Confucius, rather than those of Buddha.

They built palaces, founded schools and libraries and attracted scholars and painters and poets to their court. In the reign of the Emperor, Ming Huang, two of China's most famous poets, Li Po and Tu Fu, created lovely pictures of everyday life and Wu Tao-tzu, regarded by many people as the greatest of all Chinese artists, painted his reputed masterpieces. Pottery became ever more beautiful and the emperor liked to converse with Hsuan Tsang, a Buddhist monk, who wrote a detailed geographical survey of his travels to India.

Perhaps the greatest event in the T'ang period was the invention of printing, which began with wooden blocks used to print designs on textiles. The Japanese, visiting the Chinese court, seem to have taken the lead in cutting Buddhist charms and holy signs on wooden blocks, and this led to the fashioning of movable type. The earliest printed book is said to be a Buddhist scripture, produced in 868 and found in a cave in 1907.

As with all empires, decay set in; the people, oppressed by heavy taxes, broke into rebellion. Asiatic nomads, especially the Khitans, attacked across the frontiers and, in 907, the last T'ang emperor was deposed. The empire fell apart, as one province after another set up as independent states or were occupied by the barbarians. After a period of turmoil, known as the Five Dynasties, a man of exceptional ability, Chao Kuang-yui, founded the Sung Dynasty in 960.

As emperor, Chao had to accept the loss of a great part of northern China to the Khitans, but he restored order in the rest of the country and ruled with tolerance and moderation. After his death, the Chinese had to retreat

Detail from a miniature from the court of Akbar the Great, showing Genghis Khan (top right) praying to the sky-god on the Kipehak Steppe, southern Russia. These plains were the farthest west that the great conqueror ever penetrated, but he sent mounted warriors like those seen here (bottom right) to ravage Bulgaria and neighbouring lands of eastern Europe.

114

further south, where the city of Hangchow became the new capital of Southern Sung. For a time, the emperors went on trying to expel the Khitans from their northern lands but, finding this impossible, the third emperor accepted the situation and agreed to pay the invaders an annual subsidy. As a result, China gained a century of peace and the Khitans settled down, only to be overcome in their turn by another nomadic tribe, the Kin or Chin, the 'golden people' who, by the first half of the 12th century, made themselves masters of the north and founded their capital at a place now called Peking.

Meanwhile, Southern Sung created what is generally regarded as one of the golden ages of Chinese civilization, when, thanks to the emperor's peaceful policies, literature and the arts flourished, printing was much improved by the introduction of movable type; astronomy, medicine and botany were studied and new inventions included the art of making porcelain, gunpowder and, possibly, the abacus or counting-frame.

At this time, the Chinese took to ship-building and sailing on the eastern seas to Java, Sumatra and even perhaps to Egypt and Sicily. They invented a compass and increased their trade with Japan, India and the countries of south-east Asia.

THE MONGOLS

The Sung Dynasty, which is remembered as a time of peace and beauty, was to fall in 1279, when, for the first time in her history, the whole of China was conquered by non-Chinese. In the vast plains of Siberia, a land of grass and stony deserts, the Mongols lived nomadic lives, wintering on the southern steppes and grazing their great herds of horses and cattle on the summer pastures in the north. Temujin, son of a chief or khan of these warrior-horsemen, managed to defeat and then unite all the tribes, so that they hailed him as the Great Khan, and allowed themselves to be transformed into a disciplined army.

In 1207, Genghis Khan led his cavalry squadrons into China, where they poured across the Great Wall to devastate the northern half of the country and sack Peking, the Chin capital. Leaving able generals to continue the conquest, Genghis himself turned west to sweep across Afghanistan and Persia to the shores of the Black Sea. Even the Turks could not withstand the hordes of tireless horse-archers and when the city of Samarkand was taken, its 30 000 Turkish defenders were slaughtered in a single night.

The great conqueror died in 1227, leaving his empire to his three sons, who invaded Russia and penetrated far into Austria and Hungary. Another horde destroyed Baghdad, the city of the caliphs and just when it seemed as though Western Europe would be overwhelmed by the invincible Mongols, the warriors withdrew of their own accord into their distant plains, leaving behind them a legend of unequalled savagery.

Mongol horsemen dash onwards, ignoring Chinese forces standing on the defensive. It was the Mongols' ferocious zest for conquest, their mobility and acquired skills in siege craft that made them invincible.

Three Mongol kingdoms emerged the Lordship of the West, amounting to modern Russia; the Lordship of the Levant, which included Asia Minor and Persia; and the Lordship of Turkestan in central Asia. While the rulers of these territories engaged in ceaseless wars with one another, one of Genghis Khan's grandsons, Kublai Khan, set himself up in Peking as Emperor. Brought up in China, educated by Chinese sages and taught the religion of Buddha, Kublai was more cultured than his barbaric forbears. Energetic, intelligent and possessing the Mongol genius for war, he overcame the valiant resistance of the last Sung emperor and, by 1260, brought the whole of China under the rule of the Mongol or Yuan Dynasty.

Kublai Khan could not rest there. He was, after all, the grandson of Genghis Khan, and he added Korea to his possessions, sent an army to punish the Japanese for raiding his coasts, invaded Burma and exacted tribute from Indo-China, Tibet, Malaya and Java. These expeditions marked the limit of Mongol power, which began to decline after Kublai Khan's death in 1294, because the throne passed to his grandson, a child, and, in the absence of a strong emperor, the Chinese rose against their Mongol overlords.

A number of major rebellions took place and one of the leaders, Chu Yuan-chang, overcame his rivals and established the Ming Dynasty (meaning 'Glorious') at Nanking in 1368. The Mongols put up a prolonged resistance but, by 1388, they were finally defeated and driven back to their grasslands. Their rule had been catastrophic, for agriculture and industry had declined and whole areas had gone out of cultivation, so the first task of the Ming rulers was to restore productivity, encourage trade, repair the ruined irrigation systems and move vast numbers of people to re-populate the devastated areas of the north.

The Emperor, exercising more authority than in Sung times, was assisted by a new ruling class called 'the gentry' and a standing army commanded by officers drawn from military families. With firm government and internal peace, China recovered its prosperity, as farm production rose and new crops were grown, such as cotton and sorghum, a grain suitable for dry regions; later on, in the 16th and 17th centuries, European traders introduced maize, potatoes, peanuts and tobacco.

The capital was moved north to Peking again, where the Emperor Yung Lo (1403-24) built in magnificent style a new Imperial City inside the main walled city, with yet another inner city, the Forbidden City, where the royal family lived.

To improve communications, the Grand Canal was repaired, so that goods and foodstuffs could be transported from the Yangtze valley to Peking without the risk of storms and pirates along the sea-coast. Industry prospered, especially the making of cotton cloth, silk and porcelain, and merchant groups were set up to control the immense volume of goods which had to be distributed throughout the country and collected together for export. Yung Lo sent a fleet of warships to Cambodia, Malaya, Thailand and Ceylon (Sri Lanka) to trade and demand tribute. Expeditions also reached the Persian Gulf, the Red Sea and the coast of East Africa, but the Chinese were not seamen at heart and, after Yung Lo's death, the voyages ceased.

The Ming Dynasty which lasted for 300 years, had to adopt an aggressive policy in its early years, when the Mongols were driven back and campaigns were launched to reduce Korea and Annam (Vietnam) to vassal states, but, after an invasion of Mongolia in 1449 resulted in the emperor's capture, the Ming abandoned the idea of further expansion. In fact, China became less and less interested in the outer world and more in favour of isolation, though in the 16th century, it had to withstand fresh attacks in the north from the Mongols and along its coasts by Japanese pirates. A great effort had to be made to save Korea after it was invaded by the Japanese general, Hideyoshi, in 1592.

Under these strains the Ming wilted. The emperors gave up trying to rule and power fell into the hands of the eunuchs, men originally appointed to take charge of the women's apartments of the imperial palace, but who had become court favourites, notorious for their greed and cruelty. Taxes were high and, in face of oppression by soldiers and secret police, the people in several regions of China took up arms. In 1644, one of the rebel leaders, Li Tzu-ch'eng, captured Peking, where the last Ming emperor committed suicide, but his hopes of founding a new dynasty were dashed by the invasion by the Manchus of Manchuria, a state lying to the north-east. Their leader, Nurhachi, crossed the Great Wall and set up the Manchu or Ch'ing Dynasty, which ruled China until 1911.

14th century blue-and-white Ming vase with scenes from a historical romance. The Ming Dynasty (1368-1644), established after the Mongols were expelled, is celebrated for its fine porcelain with coloured glazes, its literature and memorable architecture, including the Imperial Palace at Peking.

A 10th century Javanese bronze statue of Manjusri, who personifies the god of wisdom and Buddhist enlightenment.

SOUTH-EAST ASIA

The countries of South-East Asia - principally Burma, Thailand (Siam), Laos, Cambodia, Vietnam, Malaya, Sumatra, Java, Borneo, the Philippines and the Moluccas or Spice Islands - are one of the oldest inhabited areas in the world, whose roots go far back into prehistory. One of the earliest discoveries of man's origins was made in Java, where 'Java Man', like 'Peking Man' and 'Heidelberg Man', lived and hunted perhaps half a million years ago.

Many cave sites and Stone Age remains have been found in this region, as well as the widespread Bronze Age culture which produced beautifully-made Dong-Son bronze drums. Iron may have been used first in Thailand, as early as 500 BC, and it seems clear that South-East Asia had a number of flourishing societies before the arrival of Indian and Chinese influences from about the 2nd century AD.

Tonking (North Vietnam) was annexed at an early date by its powerful neighbour, China, but Burma, Thailand, Cambodia, Java and Sumatra became strongly linked to India, through trade and religion. Hindu and Buddhist temples were built throughout the region, and those at Pagan (Hindu) in Burma and at Angkor (Buddhist) in Cambodia are exceptionally magnificent. There were also many links with China and, from about the 7th century, the Srivijayan empire of Sumatra controlled the sea-trade passing through the Straits of Malacca.

From the late 13th century, the temple states declined and were replaced by new states, such as Ava in upper Burma and Mons, with its capital at Pegu in lower Burma; the strongest Thai kingdom was called Ayutthaya, while Phnom Penh replaced Angkor as the chief city of Cambodia. Mongol invaders penetrated Burma and, from China, the Mongol Emperor, Kublai Khan, demanded tribute from Champa (South Vietnam), Thailand and Burma, which seems to have been paid, but its expeditionary force to Java came back empty-handed.

119

Meanwhile, the empire of Srivijaya was replaced by that of Malacca, which became a sultanate, as Muslim traders brought with them the religion of Islam, which spread to northern Sumatra and Java, the Spice Islands and Mindinao in the Philippines. However, Buddhism kept its hold on Burma and Thailand.

The first Europeans to arrive in this region were Portuguese, who reached Malacca in 1509 and, two years later, captured the Sultan's capital and built a great fortress there. From this base, they pushed on to the Spice Islands (Moluccas) where they built a fort at Amboyna and ousted the Muslims from the lucrative trade. The navigator, Magellan, reached the Philippines in 1521, and the Spaniards, who later named the islands after King Philip II, introduced Christianity and developed a regular sea-route from Mexico to Manila, taking silver there in order to return with Chinese silk. By 1598, the Dutch had arrived in Java and, a few years later, made Batavia (modern Jakarta) the headquarters of their huge trading organisation, the Dutch East India Company.

9 The Founding of Japan
c. 100 – 1636

China, by its size, vast population and wonderful civilization, had a tremendous influence upon all its neighbours, and upon none more so than Japan.

Japan consists of several mountainous islands, separated from Korea by straits 150 kilometres wide, while there are over 800 kilometres of open sea between Japan and the Chinese mainland. This isolation made the Japanese self-conscious, unaccustomed to foreigners and convinced of their own superiority to all other peoples.

The first inhabitants of the islands were ancestors of the modern Ainus of northern Japan, a people with a Stone Age culture who, in about the 1st century of the Christian era, were pushed eastward and northward by Mongoloid invaders from Korea. Related to the steppe-dwellers of Siberia, they were fighting-men on horseback, carrying long swords, bronze mirrors and semi-precious stones, curiously curved in the shape of a large comma.

The religion of the early Japanese was a simple nature worship, called Shinto, based on a feeling of awe in the presence of anything remarkable in nature - a waterfall, mountain peak, a large stone or even an insect.

The invaders were organised into scores of clans, each ruled by a high priest or priestess, and one of these clans, the Yamato, became strong enough to win overlordship of all central and western Japan and even over parts of southern Korea. From the priest-chiefs of the Yamato clan stemmed the Japanese imperial family and the Japanese state - a loose association of clans under one supreme clan.

Understandably, Chinese culture had a strong influence and, from the 4th century onwards, the Japanese were using a form of writing derived from Chinese script. A great many Chinese and Koreans settled in Japan, bringing with them the Buddhist religion, though this never fully displaced the cult of Shinto. Among those converted to the new faith was Crown Prince Shotoku, who sent a large embassy to China in 607, which brought back a great deal of Chinese learning.

Fascinated by Chinese culture, the Yamato court decided to turn Japan into a replica of China, with a similar centralised government and civil service. Since the capital of T'ang China was the great city of Ch'ang-an, the Japanese started in 710 to build a similar city at Nara in the Yamato plain.

Wide thoroughfares were laid out, flanked by splendid palaces, and Buddhist temples, but, in 794, this city was replaced by a new one at Kyoto, a grandiose capital whose remains can still be visited today.

The greatest period of learning from China lasted from the 6th to early 9th century when, with the decay of T'ang and the rising self-confidence of the Japanese, a spirit of independence arrived. Embassies were no longer sent to China; the Japanese developed their own writing, their own literature and styles of painting, sculpture and architecture. Centralised government gave way to the rule of estates by powerful nobles and landlords. From the middle of the 9th century, one of the court families, the Fujiwara, won complete mastery over all the others and even over the Emperor himself, for he was made to marry a Fujiwara daughter and to abdicate when their son was old enough to take his place as puppet of his mother and her father.

In later centuries, strong emperors sometimes asserted themselves, but the Fujiwara family managed to retain their virtual monopoly of high court positions until the early 19th century.

During the 10th and 11th centuries, life at court was gracious and cultivated; noble families lived in houses consisting of a central pavilion linked to lesser ones by corridors or bridges; the whole would be set in a formal garden. Partitions and screens were painted with exquisite landscapes; court poets wrote love poems and verses describing the seasons, the country-side and its flowers; writers produced diaries, memoirs and novels about this brilliant artificial society. 'The Tale of Genji', written by the Lady Murasaki in about 1000, is perhaps the world's earliest novel.

But, away from the court, life was quite different. In the provinces, the dominant figure was the armed knight on horseback, who, like the feudal lords in Europe, held complete power over the lives of his peasants and, with the aid of other mounted fighting men, defended his estates against his enemies.

Clan warfare which went on continuously without interference from the capital, came to be centred on the rivalry between two great families, the Taira and the Minamoto. The Taira triumphed for a time, but, in a bitter war that ended in 1185, the Minamoto wiped out their rivals, leaving Yorimoto, their leader, in complete command. Deciding to allow the Emperor and the Fujiwara to carry on the pretence of governing, he moved away to Kamakura (near to modern Tokyo) and took for himself the title of *Shogun*, meaning 'Generalissimo', since he commanded the only strong fighting force in Japan.

The country's first military dictatorship was now established, for, by controlling the knights who ruled the estates, the Shogun was able to control Japan and all classes of society. Nevertheless, the Emperor's prestige and religious duties allowed him to appear to be the Head of State during the

Carved wooden figure of a
seated priest: late Kamakura
period (13th-14th century).

next 600 years of feudalism, when the real power was held by warrior-aristocrats.

The Minamoto family was overthrown soon after the death of Yorimoto, but the Kamakura system was carried on by the Hojo family, whose head, calling himself the 'Regent', controlled a puppet Shogun who controlled the puppet Emperor!

This dictatorship was put to the test in 1281, when the Emperor of China, Kublai Khan, despatched a huge fleet, with cavalry and soldiers totalling 150 000 men, to subdue Japan and add it to the Mongol empire. Against this host stood only a small number of knights, accustomed to single combat, but, when the landing was made at Hakata Bay, they manned the defensive wall they had constructed and were fighting with desperate valour when a typhoon descended on the fleet and destroyed the entire invasion force.

After this heroic episode, the Kamakura system broke up, because as the number of knights increased and they became poorer, the ties of loyalty to one another and to the Hojo grew weak. In an uprising in 1333, the Hojo family was wiped out and, after vain attempts to restore the Emperor or to put a Shogun back in power, the country came to be divided into a large number of more or less independent domains, each owned by a feudal lord, or *Daimyo*, who built himself a castle and, backed by his attendant knights and an army of peasants trained as foot-soldiers, ruled his little kingdom as an absolute monarch.

123

Nijo Castle, Kyoto (the ancient capital founded in 794). For centuries, it was the home of a usually powerless Emperor and his court until, in 1868, Meiji moved the capital to Edo and renamed that city Tokyo.

During the next two-and-a-half centuries of turmoil and civil war, the Japanese continued to make great strides forward in trade and the arts. At Kyoto, the powerless Court became a centre for artists and writers; the great Buddhist monasteries attracted men of learning and culture, especially *Zen* monks from China (Zen was a Buddhist sect devoted to meditation) who painted landscapes and picture scrolls portraying everyday life and famous events like the defeat of the Mongols. They also introduced the arts of landscape gardening, flower arrangement and the tea ceremony, an elaborate and graceful way of serving tea. This period produced the Nō drama, in which religious dance was combined with poetry chanted by actors and the chorus.

Trade came to be organised by guilds of merchants who dominated the growing commercial city of Osaka and imported goods from China, India and South-East Asia, such as silks, books, porcelains and copper cash, for the Japanese relied on China for their coinage. In return, they exported raw materials, such as sulphur, timber, mother-of-pearl, gold and pearls and also some manufactured articles, notably folding fans, painted screens and curved swords whose workmanship rivalled the famous blades of Damascus and Toledo.

By the 14th and 15th centuries, the Japanese had taken to the sea so successfully that they outsailed the Koreans and took charge of practically all the commerce of the China Sea. Then they ventured further afield and set up Japanese trading and sea-faring communities in the principal ports of South-East Asia. Nearer home, some of the mariners turned to piracy until, in the time of the Ming Dynasty, Japanese pirates became a scourge, as they ravaged the coasts and sacked Chinese cities.

Meanwhile, in Japan itself, the more powerful Daimyo tended to overcome their weaker neighbours, until, in 1568, a Daimyo named Oda Nobunaga seized Kyoto itself and then captured Osaka to make himself master of central Japan. He was followed by his general, Hideyoshi, who, from his military base, the great castle of Osaka, crushed all resistance and imposed peace and unity on the whole country.

Possibly to occupy his armies or to satisfy his own ambition, Hideyoshi then decided to conquer China, which he meant to attack via the peninsula of Korea. His invasion of 1592 made good headway, but the Koreans, with Chinese aid, put up such a stiff resistance that, when Hideyoshi died in 1598, the Japanese abandoned their first attempt at overseas conquest.

This fiasco brought the Tokugawa family to power as the country's military and political rulers, a family so numerous and resourceful that they kept the country in their grip until the middle of the 19th century. To maintain Japanese unity and to prevent the spread of foreign ideas, they forbade travel abroad and put a stop to ship-building and to most of the overseas trade which had been growing so successfully. Thus, from about 1636, Japan became isolated from the rest of the world, a tranquil society kept in order by the Tokugawa secret police, but one which dropped behind Europe in scientific and industrial achievements until its awakening in 1868.

Tokugawa Ieyasu, a former vassal of Hideyoshi and founder of the Tokugawa Dynasty, which ruled Japan for over 250 years (1603-1868). During this long period of peaceful isolation, art, literature and a realistic form of drama called *Kabuki* flourished, and scholars began to compile a 240-volume history of Japan.

10 The Medieval Papacy
c. 850 – 1417

During the 9th century, the reputation of the Western Church sank to a low level. The Pope had little influence, even in Italy, and, in other countries, the great bishops, lordly rulers of towns, villages and huge estates, mostly owed their appointments to the king or to some powerful family. As vassals, they paid feudal dues to their overlord and recouped themselves at the expense of lesser clergy, who, in turn, extorted all they could from the common people.

Furthermore, as Benedictine monasteries grew slack, the monks tended to forget their vows and their Founder's ideals of a life dedicated to prayer, chastity and poverty. However, the year 910 brought the foundation of a new monastery at a place called Cluny in eastern France. There, the monks adopted a strict, pious way of life which was so much admired that, by the next century, their example and the building of many more Cluniac 'houses' (there were 36 in England alone) led to widespread reform of the Church.

But, as the Pope regained his prestige and authority, he was bound to come into conflict with monarchs who claimed control over *all* their subjects - clergy and laymen alike. William the Conqueror, for instance, took care to make his invasion of England respectable by obtaining the Pope's blessing and a banner, but, once he had won the kingdom, he made it clear that he was going to be master of the English Church and he quietly refused to accept that the Pope was his overlord.

The next Pope, Gregory VII, a most determined character, announced that he alone had the right to appoint a bishop and to invest him with the staff, ring and robes of office. In Germany, the Holy Roman Emperor, Henry IV, took up the challenge and appointed a bishop of his own choice, only to be promptly excommunicated. To his dismay, he found himself abandoned by his own nobles, who readily seized the opportunity to rebel. This was the Pope's most powerful weapon. Subjects of an excommunicated prince were no longer bound by their oaths of allegiance and therefore might raise a rebellion; the clergy would preach against him; his son-and-heir's right to the succession would be disputed and neighbouring kings would be urged to launch a crusade and invade his realm. Henry IV had no choice but to submit, and for three days in January 1077, the Emperor had to stand barefoot in the snow outside the castle at Canossa in Italy, waiting to beg the Pope's forgiveness.

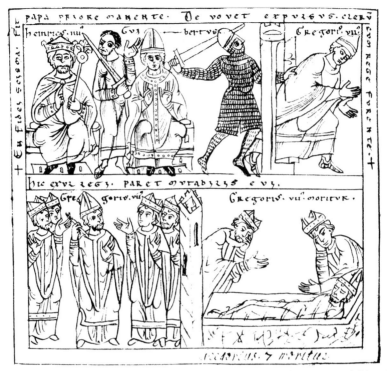

Revenge for Canossa: the Emperor Henry IV returns to Rome with an army and drives Pope Gregory VII out of the Holy City. He goes to southern Italy and dies there in exile.

The humiliation at Canossa provided spectacular proof of the Pope's authority, though it did not put an end to the argument. Indeed, Henry IV returned to the attack, captured Rome and drove Gregory into exile, where he died; but Henry never fully restored order in Germany and the struggle between Emperor and Pope went on for generations.

The Emperor Frederick Barbarossa (1152-90) also invaded Italy and deposed Pope Alexander III; Frederick's son, Henry VI, through warfare and marrying Constance of Sicily, greatly enlarged the Emperor's possessions in Italy (which alarmed the Popes) and his son, Frederick II of Hohenstaufen, 'Stupor Mundi', that strange monarch who toured his domain with a harem, a menagerie and a bodyguard of Muslim warriors, quarrelled so bitterly with one Pope after another that he spent most of his reign under excommunication and at war with the papal armies and allies.

Innocent III, Pope from 1198 to 1216, and guardian of Frederick II as a child, not only claimed power over all the princes, but did much to prove that his claim was true. He made Philip Augustus of France put aside Agnes of Merau and take back his lawful wife; he compelled Ladislaus of Poland and

Emperor versus Pope: the Pope triumphs. After Frederick Barbarossa deposed Alexander III, he returned to Germany for six years. His next expedition to Italy was a disaster; defeated in battle and wounded, Frederick had to recognise Alexander as the rightful pope and then lie full length before him and kiss his feet.

the kings of Aragon and Leon to do his bidding; he deposed the Emperor Otto IV, and organised crusades, including the Fourth Crusade which brought Constantinople under the rule of Rome for 57 years. During his pontificate, Sicily, England, Ireland, Aragon and Portugal all became papal *fiefs* (i.e. territories held by permission of an overlord) and, by excommunication, he forced King John of England to accept his nominee, Stephen Langton, as Archbishop of Canterbury; later, he declared Magna Carta null and void and excommunicated the barons who had devised it. His commands were obeyed from Norway and Lapland to Bulgaria and Constantinople, and no Pope, before or since, has held such universal power.

The life's aim of Frederick II, 'Stupor Mundi', was to make Sicily and Italy into a united kingdom within the Holy Roman Empire. This policy presented a serious threat to the Church, because the Papal States in the middle of Italy would have been engulfed. This was the real reason why the popes excommunicated Frederick and aided the cities of Lombardy in the north against him. It also explains why Pope Innocent IV devoted his career

129

During this period of strife, Christianity still prevailed: here, in Giotto's fresco at Assisi, Pope Innocent III gives St. Francis his approval of the Rule of the Franciscan Order of friars, whose work among the poor made them the best-loved of all the religious orders.

to defeating Frederick and wiping out his descendants.

Innocent IV gave the Sicilian kingdom of Sicily and southern Italy to Charles of Anjou, brother of Louis IX ('St Louis') of France, a king so pious that it was almost impossible to think of him opposing the Holy Father. The title of Holy Roman Emperor went, after an interval when there was no emperor, to an Austrian, called Rudolf of Hapsburg.

But, to pay for the Papal wars, the Church had to impose heavy taxes, especially in France and England, and this aroused angry resentment, so that, when Pope Boniface VIII announced his supreme authority in 1302, it was the French king, Philip IV, 'the Fair', who sent troops to arrest him, causing him such distress that he died. Philip then had a Frenchman elected Pope as Clement V and in 1308 the Papal See was removed from Rome to Avignon, which was then on the border of southern France.

For almost 70 years (1308-77), French Popes resided at Avignon where the luxury and corruption of the papal court became an open scandal. Clement V packed the college of Cardinals with Frenchmen, high positions in the Church were bought and sold, relatives of the Popes obtained rich offices and papal taxes were increased everywhere to pay for the court's extravagances.

During this period, Italy and Rome itself were in a ferment, as rival parties, the Ghibellines and the Guelfs, fought each other in every part of northern and central Italy. The Ghibellines had originally been supporters of the Emperor, while the Guelfs sided with the Pope, but, after the destruction of the Hohenstaufens, the names were taken over by local parties, the Ghibellines being the champions of the ruling aristocrats and the Guelfs of the merchant class.

However, in spite of the disorders, the Pope returned to Rome in 1377, but the joy of the Italians was short-lived, for there followed an even more disgraceful state of affairs – that division of the Western Church into two camps which is known as the Great Schism (1378-1417).

The real cause of the split had nothing to do with religion; it was political, for the Italians wanted the Papacy, with its power and riches, for Italy, while the French meant to go on dominating the Papacy, as they had done at Avignon. Each side therefore elected its own Pope – Urban VI, an Italian, and Clement VII, the French candidate – and the rest of Christendom took sides, with Italy, England, Hungary and the Holy Roman Empire (Germany and Austria) supporting Urban VI, while France, Scotland, Savoy, Castile and Aragon declared for Clement VII.

In time, each party elected a successor and the battle lasted for forty years, until a Council of the Church met at Pisa in 1409 to settle the scandalous situation. The Cardinals put aside both Popes and elected the Cardinal of Milan as Alexander V, which only added to the confusion, for there were now three Popes! Finally, in 1417, the Council of Constance got rid of all three and ended the Great Schism by electing an Italian, Martin V, to St Peter's throne.

Throughout Europe, the Church's reputation had been seriously damaged, but the opportunity to make a fresh start was ignored, for Martin V and his successor had no intention of allowing the Council to bring in reforms. Meanwhile, two movements of protest arose in widely separated countries. In England, a priest named John Wycliffe attracted widespread support for his biting attacks upon the Church, its wealth, corruption and ceaseless demands for money. He denied the authority of bishops and of the Pope himself and went on to query the Church's teaching about the eucharist or Holy Communion, when Christians partake of wine and bread, as at the Lord's Supper. Wycliffe himself escaped punishment for his views but, after his death in 1384, his followers known as Lollards, who went about the country preaching, were subjected to persecution and a number were burnt alive as heretics.

Wycliffe's writings found many admirers in far-off Bohemia (part of Czechoslovakia today) where John Huss was burnt at the stake for his violent attacks on the Church, but his preaching aroused such feeling that the Hussites took up arms and, in bitter fighting, defied five crusades which the Pope sent against them. Peace was signed with Rome in 1416, but the Hussites and the Lollards had set the stage for the Protestant Reformation in the next century.

131

11 France and Henry Plantagenet 987 – 1216

During the 10th and 11th centuries, when Otto I of Germany and his successors as Holy Roman Emperor were the leading monarchs of Europe, the land of France was of little importance. Charlemagne's western kingdom had dwindled to a collection of duchies, counties and states, whose rulers, barely able to control the ambitions of their own nobles, were engaged in a perpetual struggle with their neighbours.

In 987, Hugh Capet was elected to the throne of France. His lands, grouped around the cities of Paris and Orleans, were not extensive and he was neither rich nor powerful. However, he had the support of the Church and his claim to be the overlord of practically every French duke and count was grudgingly acknowledged, because it suited the great lords to accept the king's supremacy, since it confirmed their own power over their vassals.

For the next three-and-a-half centuries Capetian kings followed one another in unbroken male succession and, as each king had his son crowned during his own lifetime, election to kingship came to be forgotten and the principle of the crown passing from father to son was established.

At first, the Capetian kingdom was small. In the south-west, far from Paris, lay the duchy of Gascony and the county of Toulouse; to the north of them, the great duchy of Aquitaine was ruled by its dukes as a separate state; Brittany kept its ancient independence and Normandy had become so strong in the 11th century that Duke William could defy the French king and defeat him in battle. There was also Anjou, whose energetic counts increased their territory so successfully that Henry I of England (the Conqueror's third son) betrothed his widowed daughter, Matilda, to Count Geoffrey, nick-named 'Plantagenet'.

In this situation, French kings had to walk warily, but Philip I (1060-1108) managed to make some small gains during the wars in Normandy between the Conqueror's sons. Louis VI (1108-37) continued this policy and seemed to have achieved a master-stroke when he married his young son (afterwards Louis VII) to Eleanor of Aquitaine, who, at 15, had inherited all the lands and riches of that duchy.

In England, Henry I's death was followed by civil war, because the barons broke their oath to accept Matilda and transferred allegiance to her cousin

Stephen. For nearly 20 years, they enjoyed themselves mightily, building illegal castles and fighting among themselves or for one or other of the rival claimants. Meanwhile, Matilda's husband, Geoffrey, seized Normandy.

On Stephen's death in 1154, the English crown passed to Matilda's son, Henry Plantagenet, who became Henry II of England and, at a stroke, the most powerful monarch in Europe, for this dynamic young man had already married Eleanor of Aquitaine after her divorce from Louis VII. Therefore, with her vast domains, Geoffrey of Anjou's lands, Normandy and England, he found himself ruler of a kingdom that stretched from Scotland to the Pyrenees - and later he extended it by conquering Ireland in a lightning campaign in 1171.

133

The murder of Thomas à Becket in Canterbury Cathedral, 1170, by four knights who had left Henry II's court in Normandy and crossed to England after the King had upbraided his nobles for not dealing with the defiant Archbishop.

Possessed of inexhaustible energy - men said he never sat down, except to eat, and then briefly - Henry toured his realm incessantly, in order to settle disputes and administer justice, to bring disobedient barons to heel and to compel them to destroy illegal castles. His grandfather, Henry I, had founded the Exchequer and a system of control over money matters that gave the English king more power over his subjects than was enjoyed by any other European sovereign and Henry II introduced trial by jury and travelling judges. Royal justice came to be prized and looked upon as a right.

Yet, for all his talents as a man and a ruler, Henry experienced the bitterness of failure. For years, his wife, Eleanor of Aquitaine, was his beloved partner, ruling much of his continental possessions for him, sharing his duties and seeing to the upbringing of their large family, but these two headstrong passionate people quarrelled so furiously that she left him to live in her own domain and to encourage their sons to rebel against their father, so that, when she was captured, he kept her a prisoner for 15 years.

In his desire for order and justice, Henry came into conflict with the Church - and lost the battle. When his friend, the Chancellor, Thomas

Effigy of Henry II at Fontevrault Abbey in Normandy, where Queen Eleanor's effigy lies next to him.

à Becket, was made Archbishop of Canterbury, Henry believed that he would be master of Church affairs in England and able to put an end to the scandal of Church courts which enabled many a rogue to escape justice. But Becket flatly refused to do his bidding and, after an explosive quarrel, four of Henry's knights hacked the Archbishop to death in Canterbury Cathedral.

Henry died in 1189 and was succeeded by his son, Richard I, who, as Richard Coeur de Lion, won fame as a Crusader, but he failed to re-capture

Coronation procession of Richard I, Coeur de Lion, from a French chronicle of the 15th century, which accounts for the unlikely costumes. Richard is shown walking beneath a canopy with the two archbishops; his treasure chest and his crown are carried in front of him.

135

Jerusalem from the Saracens and, through the cost of his military campaigns and the ransom demanded by the Holy Roman Emperor Henry VI after his capture on the way home, he laid a heavy burden of taxation upon the English people.

Richard was followed by his brother John, whose reputation is perhaps blacker than he deserved. More able and a better ruler than Richard, he was, however, faithless, prone to spells of idleness and, far worse in the eyes of his barons, apt to lose wars, for Philip Augustus of France overran many of the English possessions on the continent, including Normandy.

In 1215, the English barons forced John to set his seal to a document called the Magna Carta, whereby he promised to settle their grievances and rule according to the 'customs of the realm'. The barons had no thought for anyone except themselves and the King had no intention of keeping his promise; indeed, he was absolved by the same Pope who had formerly excommumicated him! A civil war broke out, in which John was doing well, until he died suddenly whilst on campaign and was succeeded by his infant son Henry III.

The importance of Magna Carta was not what it really said, but what people thought it said. They became convinced that Englishmen could not be taxed without their consent nor imprisoned without trial, that the king must rule according to the law and not trample on the rights of freemen. As time went by, it became the rallying-cry of the oppressed, a banner to be raised against tyranny.

12 The Celtic Peoples of Britain 432 – 1485

IRELAND

The Romans never attempted to conquer the Gaelic Celts who had settled in Ireland from about the 6th century BC, and, although the Gaels (the Irish) came into contact with Roman civilization through peaceful trade, they felt no sense of shock or calamity when the Empire collapsed.

The people were ruled by petty kings who, in theory, gave allegiance to a 'High King', but, in the absence of a common enemy from abroad, there was no unity, only a constant state of feuding between rival chiefs and their followers.

In the 5th century, St Patrick, who as a boy had been captured in South Wales by Irish pirates, converted the Irish to the Christian religion and, although he could not cure their love of fighting, his mission led to a marvellous flowering of art and literature at a time when most of Western Europe had fallen into the Dark Ages.

The Irish built churches and monasteries, which they filled with jewelled, richly-enamelled crosses and vessels; they wrote poetry and heroic legends, produced exquisitely illuminated manuscripts like the *Book of Kells*, and sent scholars and missionaries to continental countries.

Towards the end of the 8th century, Viking sea-pirates began raiding the coasts and plundering the monasteries at will until, when the booty was almost gone, they founded settlements at Dublin, Waterford, Wexford, Cork and Limerick, from which they traded with the continent.

Eventually, in Brian Boru, the Irish found a leader who made himself High King of all Ireland and won a great victory over the Vikings at Clontarf in 1014. Alas, Brian was killed in the moment of triumph, so that the unity which he had forged fell apart and Ireland relapsed into petty strife.

A century after the Norman Conquest, Henry II of England obtained the Pope's permission to invade Ireland in order to bring it more closely into contact with Rome and to put its Church in order. First, he sent over Strongbow, Earl of Pembroke, who, with a well-armed force of Anglo-Norman knights, captured Dublin; he married the daughter of an Irish king, Dermot MacMurrough, and, on Dermot's death, made himself King of

This 8th century example of Irish-Celtic metalwork was found at Athlone in County Westmeath. Known as the Athlone Plaque, it was the bronze ornament for a book cover.

Leinster. In 1171, when Henry appeared in person to assert his authority as Ireland's overlord, the Irish chiefs accepted him without much demur, probably feeling that, as soon as he went back to England, they could carry on as before.

But they found that the Anglo-Norman barons and knights carried on as they pleased, seizing land and spreading piecemeal across the country. In and around Dublin, in an area called 'the Pale', Henry II's system of government was put into effect, with a Justiciar, representing the overlord, a parliament, counties, sheriffs and law-courts, as in England, but, beyond the Pale, the Anglo-Norman adventurers defied the royal authority, ruling their little domains as they pleased, marrying Irish wives and adopting Irish ways.

Yet there was no real fusion between the two peoples, for the Anglo-Normans or the English, as they became, were devoted to the feudal system, with its primo-geniture (whereby estates passed to the eldest sons) and allegiance of freemen to their lord and his heirs. The Irish would have none of that; they attached themselves to a lord of their choice and the contract ended with his death.

As years passed, whenever the English were engaged in continental or civil wars, the Irish broke into rebellion, and it became clear to the English authorities in Dublin that, far from completing the conquest of a subject race, their best hope was to hang on to what they possessed. The trouble seemed to be that the great Anglo-Irish families outside the Pale had become too involved with the Irish. Therefore, by the Statutes of Kilkenny, passed in 1366, the English were forbidden to intermarry with the Irish or to adopt Irish customs under penalty of torture or losing their titles. Although such laws were almost impossible to enforce, they kept alive the idea of two separate races.

WALES

The Angles and Saxons who overran most of Britain made little or no attempt to conquer the Celts who lived in the west, in the country they called Cymru, that is Wales. In this mountainous land, a number of small kingdoms emerged - Gwynedd, Powys, Dyfed, Gwent and several others whose rulers, calling themselves princes, constantly fought one another, until, sometimes, one more able or warlike than the others, would rule almost the whole of Wales. Rhodri the Great (844–78) and Hywel the Good (d.950) were two who united the Welsh for a time.

The Welsh did not have to wait long after the Battle of Hastings before their country was invaded by the Normans. William the Conqueror gave border lands to some of his most able barons, who soon began to push westward, advancing along the valleys and plains, especially in the south, and

building castles to secure their gains. The Welsh, who were good archers and nimble guerrilla fighters, put up a fierce resistance, but, for the most part, they could only hold on to the hilly, less fertile areas of their homeland.

However, like the Irish, they could be relied upon to strike back whenever their enemies relaxed their guard or became involved in civil war. Then the Welsh would raid across the border, burn a few villages, drive off the cattle, take some prisoners and return speedily to the hills where they could easily defy the English, for they were adept at setting ambushes and avoiding pitched battles.

In the 13th century, a Prince of North Wales, Llewelyn the Great (d. 1240), who married a daughter of King John of England, fought continuously against his father-in-law and the Marcher lords who defended the Welsh Marches or border country. Although forced eventually to acknowledge the English king as his overlord, Llewelyn extended his lands and, at one time, captured Shrewsbury.

His grandson, Llewelyn the Last, came to be known as Prince of Wales, when almost all the Welsh chiefs swore an oath of loyalty to him as their leader. He made many gains during the troubled reign of Henry III of England but, after Henry's son Edward I came to the throne, the tables were turned, for, Edward, a dour painstaking general, invaded Wales (1282) with a well-equipped army and, using a fleet to prevent corn from Anglesey reaching the mainland, trapped Llewelyn and his followers in the mountains of Snowdonia. To avoid starvation, Llewelyn broke out and was making south to raise the men of Brecon, when he was killed near the castle of Builth. His death put an end - or almost an end - to the long struggle, for, by building a chain of great castles to overawe resistance, and towns to encourage peaceful trade, Edward brought the whole country under English rule.

There was one more major rebellion. In 1400, during the reign of Henry IV of England, a descendant of Welsh princes, Owen Glendower (or Owain Glyndwr) led a revolt with such success that, at the height of his power, he called a Welsh Parliament, made alliances with France and Scotland, corresponded with the Pope and made plans to build universities.

But, although Owen captured several of the great castles and received help from a French army which landed on the coast of Pembrokeshire, he was opposed by a brilliant young general, the future Henry V, who wore down Welsh resistance, until Owen's forces melted away and he himself died an outlaw. Some seventy years later, in 1485, the grandson of a Welsh gentleman named Owen Tudor became Henry VII of England.

SCOTLAND

The Romans named the northernmost part of Britain Caledonia. Like Ireland it was inhabited largely by Gaelic Celts who had settled there several centuries earlier. These barbaric tribesmen, whom the Romans called *Picti*, meaning 'painted men', because they daubed themselves with war paint, proved so troublesome that two emperors, Hadrian and Antoninus Pius, built walled fortifications right across the country to keep the tribes in check. Nevertheless, there was a good deal of trade and contact between Caledonia and the more pacific region to the south.

After the Romans left, the Picts moved south to harry northern Britain, but Angles established themselves in Lothian between the Forth and the Tweed, and they also founded the kingdoms of Bernicia and Deira, which were united into the kingdom of Northumbria. Meanwhile, as the Britons were pushed back to the west, some of them, the Welsh, crossed the deserted wall and occupied Strathclyde in south-western Scotland.

In the 6th century, Celts called Scots crossed from Ireland to settle the kingdom of Dalriata, a region nowadays known as Argyll. Like the Welsh in Strathclyde, they were Christians and they fought bitterly against the heathen Picts, until an Irish monk, St Columba, who had founded a monastery on the island of Iona in 563, travelled to the stronghold of the Pictish king and converted him and his people to the Christian faith.

For a time, in the 7th century, Northumbria gained the overlordship of all the northern kingdoms, including Pictavia, but the Picts struck back, with victories over the Northumbrians and the kings of Dalriata, so that it seemed as if the Picts and Scots would be united under a Pictish king. However, from about 795, when they sacked Iona, the Vikings fell upon Scotland, plundering the Celtic monasteries, burning, slaying and seizing land.

The Picts strove hard to beat back the invaders but, weakened by continuous fighting, they were overcome by an uprising of the Scots of Dalriata, whose king, Kenneth Macalpine, defeated the Vikings and made himself ruler of all the mainland north of the Forth-Clyde, which henceforward began to be called Scotland. Its capital, where all the Scottish kings were crowned, was Scone in Perthshire.

For the next century, Macalpine's successors continued to fight the Vikings; several kings died in battle and then there appeared on the scene a new enemy in the shape of the English, for Alfred the Great's vigorous descendants overcame the Vikings (or Danes) in northern England and began to press hard upon Scotland. In 937, Athelstan, King of the English, won a shattering victory over a great host of Scots, Vikings and Welsh, as a result of which the Scottish king had to do homage as Athelstan's vassal.

Malcolm II, who became king of Scotland in 1005, also had to accept the English king (Canute), as his overlord, but he still managed to add Lothian and Strathclyde to his kingdom, so that its boundaries advanced to the Cheviots and the Tweed, much what they are today.

The reign of Malcolm Canmore (Malcolm III 1058-93) is an important one in Scottish history, for he married Margaret (St Margaret), sister of Edgar the Atheling, great-nephew of Edward the Confessor and the rightful heir to the English throne; she was a cultured woman whose influence had a civilizing effect on the northern court. Having paid homage to William the Conqueror, Malcolm asserted Scotland's independence in the next reign, but was killed at Alnwick fighting the English.

But, although there was enmity, there were also close ties with England and long periods of peace. Scottish kings and nobles married English wives and, through their lands, became English barons, doing homage to English kings. David I (1124–53), who was educated in England, introduced Norman customs, manners and the Norman feudal system into the country, built abbeys, reformed the law and gave charters to towns.

David's grandson, William the Lion, sided with Henry II's sons against their father, but, when he invaded England in 1174, he was defeated and captured, whereupon Henry shipped his prisoner overseas to Normandy and refused to release him until William had done homage for all his possessions. For 15 years Scotland was a vassal country of England until, in 1189, Richard I, eager to go on Crusade, sold back all that his father had won.

The next two reigns, those of Alexander II and Alexander III, were mainly peaceful and prosperous, and when King Hakon of Norway attacked the west coast in 1263, the Scots defeated the invaders at the battle of Largs. This victory enabled Alexander III to add the Hebrides, a Norwegian possession, to Scotland, but, in 1286, Alexander was killed in a riding accident, leaving as sole heir to the throne, his three-year-old grand-daughter, Margaret, the 'Maid of Norway,' the only child of his daughter who had married King Eric of Norway.

The situation in Scotland was being closely watched by Edward I of England, who, having made himself master of Wales, saw the opportunity to bring Scotland, and therefore the whole island of Britain, under his control. He secured the consent of the Pope and the Scottish nobles to marry the Maid of Norway to his son, Edward of Carnarvon, the first Prince of Wales, but the child died on her way to Scotland in 1290 and his scheme seemed to have come to naught.

However, when no fewer than eleven Scottish nobles put forward claims to the throne and civil war seemed certain, the Scots turned for advice to Edward I, known to be a wise and honourable dispenser of justice. As arbitrator, he stipulated that the successful candidate must accept himself, Edward, as overlord, and then decided in favour of John Balliol, on whom he put so much pressure that a rebellion soon broke out. Edward marched north in 1296 and, in a lightning campaign, overcame all opposition and made himself King of Scotland.

A little experience of the English as rulers so enraged the Scots that a band of patriots took up arms and, under a leader of genius named William Wallace, made such headway that Edward I had to march up from the south to Falkirk where, with his usual skill, he destroyed the rebel army. Wallace, betrayed by a fellow Scot, was executed with barbarous cruelty, but the spirit of resistance was by no means crushed.

A new leader arose in Robert Bruce, grandson of one of the earlier claimants to the throne. Bruce, who had served Edward I at court and in the field, had himself crowned at Scone and, although frequently defeated and at times a homeless fugitive, he managed to survive and then to make such ground that King Edward once again put himself at the head of an army that would finally crush this troublesome upstart. But, before he reached the Border, the old warrior died, leaving instructions that the campaign must be continued until Bruce was destroyed, instructions which his son, Edward II, completely ignored, for he speedily returned to London and the pleasures of life at Court.

Bruce took full advantage of his good fortune, so that, within five years, he had captured every castle in the country except Stirling. Its fall would mean that Scotland was finally lost to the English, so that even Edward II was forced to bestir himself.

The barons supported him and, in 1314, at the head of a great army drawn from all parts of the kingdom, Edward marched north to relieve Stirling and conquer Scotland. By superior generalship, on ground of his own choosing, Bruce routed the English army at Bannockburn and made himself master of the whole country. The victory was so complete that the Scots were able to raid deep into the northern counties of England, until, after many years of strife, the English recognised Scotland's independence and acknowledged Robert as the rightful King of Scotland. He died of leprosy in 1329, having realised his ambition, content on his deathbed to have lifted the sentence of excommunication laid on him by the Pope for murdering a rival in church more than 20 years previously.

13 England and France at War 1154-1477

After the Norman Conquest, one of the continuing themes in European history was the rivalry between England and France. Separated from each other by only a narrow stretch of water, with their ruling classes for many years closely related to one another, speaking the same language and with common interests, culture and religion, they nevertheless lived at enmity, each regarding the other with suspicion and malice.

Through inheritance and by marrying Eleanor of Aquitaine, Henry II of England ruled a great part of France, no less than Normandy, Anjou, Maine, Touraine, Gascony, Aquitaine and Poitou. In hope of weakening the English hold on these vast territories, the French king understandably supported Henry's rebellious sons against their father.

Louis' son, Philip Augustus (Philip II, 1180-1223) continued this policy, outwitting both Richard I and John of England, conquering Normandy and Poitou and making gains in the south, so that, by the end of his reign, he had tripled the size of France and made it into a strong, firmly-governed kingdom.

Louis VIII, who carried on his father's work, was followed by Louis IX, 'Saint Louis' (1226-70), one of the best-loved monarchs in history, a pious, noble-hearted man who, modelling his life on the ideal of Christian knight-hood, devoted himself to the good of his people and to fighting the Infidel.

His Crusades, however, were expensive failures, for, in an attempt to capture Cairo, he was taken prisoner and had to pay the Sultan of Egypt an enormous sum to ransom himself and many Christian captives. Years later, on the Eighth Crusade of 1270, he invaded Tunis but died before his army had made any headway.

Between these ventures, Saint Louis did much to promote peace in Europe, acting as arbitrator in disputes and even yielding some territory to Henry III of England in return for him doing homage for the remaining English lands. Louis also subdued the turbulent French nobles, ordered the building of roads and cathedrals and helped the university of Paris to develop into one of Europe's principal centres of learning.

Louis' successors were less wise and gifted. In Philip III's reign (1270-85), France lost the kingdom of Sicily, which had been given to Charles of Anjou

by the Pope, when, in an uprising known as the 'Sicilian Vespers' (church bells were ringing for Vespers), the people of Palermo massacred the French garrison and offered the crown to Peter of Aragon. Philip IV (1285–1314) who arrested Pope Boniface VIII and moved the papal court into exile at Avignon, quarrelled with Edward I of England and, to embarrass him, founded the French alliance with Scotland that was to last until 1560.

With Philip's death, the power of the monarch went into rapid decline, as the feudal nobles reasserted themselves and the Capetian line died out, so that the crown passed to the house of Valois. This enabled Edward III of England to claim the French throne on the grounds that, through his mother, he had a better right than Philip of Valois. So began the Hundred Years' War, that ill-named conflict which lasted off and on (mostly off) from 1337 to 1453. Its real causes lay in the English kings' determination to hang on to their last continental *fief* of Gascony, in their fear that French interference in Flanders would ruin England's woollen trade with that

146

prosperous region of the Low Countries, and in the English greed for plunder and ransoms.

At first, the English scored heavily, winning the sea-battle of Sluys (1340), a tremendous victory at Crécy (1346), and capturing the key port of Calais. Then the war was halted by the Black Death, a deadly pestilence carried in the bodies of fleas that lived on black rats. The epidemic probably originated in China, travelled to India and thence along the trade routes to the Middle East and Europe; Italian cities suffered terrible losses; in Florence, for instance, half the population died, and the plague moved on into France, Germany and Britain, wiping out perhaps a third of all the inhabitants, bringing trade - and war - to a standstill and filling people with such dread that, in parts of Germany, bands of demented men and women wandered about scourging themselves with whips.

The Black Death was the most malevolent outbreak of bubonic plague, but lesser outbreaks occurred again and again together with other epidemics, probably typhoid and influenza, which like famines, floods and droughts, were taken to be signs of God's anger against the wickedness of mankind. As a result of these disasters, the population of Europe, which had been rising steadily since about 1000, declined during the 14th century when much land went out of cultivation and villages, even towns, disappeared.

The peasants who survived the plague found themselves in many cases afflicted by fresh burdens, for with fewer men to work the land, overlords demanded a standstill in wages and a return to feudal duties in full. But, with the shortage of labour, workers naturally expected to be valued more highly and to be given better pay and more freedom.

In France, a peasant uprising called the *Jacquerie* occurred in the summer of 1358, when the murder of noblemen and their families was avenged by the slaughter of thousands of villagers and such merciless repression that the peasants were reduced to serfdom for centuries. English workers suffered less cruelly when, in protest against unjust taxes, some of them took up arms in 1381, captured some towns and marched to London.

The Peasants' Revolt soon subsided, for the insurgents, won over by 14-year-old Richard II's display of courage, went meekly home, only to find that his promises led to threats and executions. However, not all had been lost, for the lords had been too badly frightened to tighten the screws and, in England, the peasants gradually freed themselves from feudal duties.

When the war re-opened, the English, led by the Black Prince, won another shattering victory over an immense French army at Poitiers (1356), where the King of France, John II, and his son were captured and hundreds of the chief nobles killed. A peace treaty awarded Aquitaine and other territories to Edward III, who gave up his claim to the French Crown, but the treaty was no more than a truce, for the French, broken and practically

Edward III and the Black Prince enter the town of Caen in Normandy.

bankrupt, with their country devastated by the terrible English armies, refused to be conquered.

Under Charles V (1364-80), their fortunes improved, for the wily French king created a navy to dispute the seas and an army led by Bertrand du Guesclin, who avoided pitched battles and concentrated on harassing the English and capturing their castles. Du Guesclin used cannons so effectively that, in the campaign of 1369-75, he won back all the English overseas possessions, except Calais, Bayonne and Bordeaux.

There followed a disastrous period for both countries; in France, the feeble-minded Charles VI could not restrain the Dukes of Orleans and Burgundy in their violent struggle for power, while, in England, under the talented but foolish Richard II, there was widespread discontent, with religious dispute and, eventually, a revolt by a party of barons who deposed and probably murdered the King.

148

In 1415, Henry V, having revived the English claim to the French throne, landed an army in France, captured Harfleur, destroyed the French cavalry in the Battle of Agincourt and, with help from the Burgundians, conquered Normandy. By the Treaty of Troyes (1420), Henry received France itself, for he was to marry the daughter of the insane Charles VI, govern as regent and, after Charles' death, succeed to the throne. However, southern France declared for the Dauphin (Charles VI's son), and Henry V was about to start a new campaign when he died of camp fever, leaving to his infant son the kingdoms of England and France.

The boy's uncle, John of Bedford, pressed on with the war until Orleans was the last sizeable place in the hands of the listless Dauphin. If it fell, France must capitulate. Only a miracle could save her, and that miracle occurred when a peasant girl, Joan of Arc, took over the French army, saved Orleans, beat the English in battle and, within a year, saw the Dauphin crowned Charles VII in Rheims Cathedral. The rest was tragedy. Joan, captured by the traitorous Burgundians who sold her to the English, was tried for witchcraft and burned to death in Rouen market-place.

English and French cavalry in battle from *La Chronique du Temps du très chrétien roi Charles VII*. 15th century.

But she did not die in vain, for the French fought on so doggedly that the English grew weary of a war that brought no more victories; the Burgundians changed sides and, in 1453, the Hundred Years' War came to its end. The sole possession left to England was the town of Calais.

During the early stages of the war the ideal of chivalry took hold of the ruling classes of both sides; it implied that a true knight would behave honourably ('chivalrously') towards his opponents, especially if they were wounded or captured, and would treat women, children, the poor and the weak with compassion. Orders of knighthood came into existence, such as Edward III's Order of the Garter and the Duke of Burgundy's Order of the Golden Fleece, along with a whole literature of poems and romances. But, in practice, chivalry tended to be limited to the knightly class; the Black Prince, who treated the captured King of France with elaborate courtesy, could watch his troops massacre the common townsfolk of Limoges. Edward III and Henry V, both paragons of knighthood, behaved with horrifying cruelty to those who angered them and the conduct of the English soldiers was so inhuman that the Italian poet, Petrarch, travelling through northern France

A knight and his steed being armed for battle. An illustration from a French book of poems, c. 1415.

after the Battle of Poitiers, found the once-flourishing land reduced to a desert.

In the aftermath of the war, the English soon resumed fighting at home, where Henry VI's French wife, Margaret of Anjou, took up the cudgels on

151

behalf of her gentle husband and the Lancastrian party against the Yorkists, led by the Duke of York, a descendent of Edward III, who put in his claim to the throne.

The struggle between these parties, known as the Wars of the Roses, lasted from 1455 to 1485, with victory going first to one side and then to the other. Queen Margaret, fiercely triumphant for a time, met defeat; York's son came to the throne as Edward IV; poor mad Henry VI was murdered in the Tower and his son killed in battle. When Edward IV died, his brother Richard thrust aside his nephews and seized the crown, but Henry Tudor, last of the Lancastrians, returned from exile and on Bosworth Field defeated and killed the usurper Richard III. The victor was proclaimed Henry VII, the first of the five Tudor monarchs.

Fortunately for England, the Wars of the Roses did not bring devastation to the country, for no towns were sacked or even besieged and there was no massacre of civilians and not very much looting. The war, fought between nobles and their paid retainers, produced treachery, heavy battle casualties and murderous executions of captured nobles, but the ordinary citizens stayed aloof from the struggle, enabling trade and industry to flourish almost unimpaired. As for the barons, they had so much weakened themselves in wealth and numbers, that they could offer little opposition to Henry VII, when that cool-headed young man began to restore the royal authority.

France made a good recovery from the war, and Louis XI (1461-83) destroyed the mini-empire of Burgundy, which had arisen under Philip the Bold (1342-1404), uncle of the imbecile French King Charles VI. Through marriage and his own ability, Philip acquired Flanders and a string of territories along the French border; he ruled well, so that, under his son, John the Fearless, and his grandson, Philip the Good (1419-67), Burgundy became a rich and powerful 'middle kingdom' between France and Germany. Through changing sides, Philip the Good had much to do with the final defeat of the English, but there was no real trust between him and France, and his successor, Charles the Bold, proved no match for Louis XI, who formed a coalition against him and, after his death in battle (1477), annexed the duchy of Burgundy proper. However, he failed to seize Flanders, for Charles the Bold's daughter, Mary, had married Maximilian of Austria, a Hapsburg and son of the Holy Roman Emperor, who stoutly defended his wife's inheritance.

14 Life in Medieval Europe
1100 – 1350

Between about 1100 and 1350, conditions of everyday life were much the same throughout Western Europe, where frontiers were less definite than they are today and men thought of themselves as peasants, priests, burgesses or knights rather than as Frenchmen or Germans. To be sure, England was becoming more like a nation-state than any other country, partly perhaps because it was an island and partly because the English King's shire-courts gave the people better justice and a measure of independence from the power of the barons. But, in England, as elsewhere, it was feudalism that regulated most men's lives.

At the pinnacle of society, stood the king, the dispenser of justice, favour and, above all, land. Land was wealth; in theory, it all belonged to the king who granted estates called *fiefs* to his nobles, who, as *vassals*, promised to render 'aid and counsel'. Counsel meant supporting and advising the king; aid meant military service. In time, fiefs became hereditary possessions, passed from father to the eldest son, and a great vassal might do homage for his lands in France and England to both the French and English kings. He might therefore become just as rich and powerful as either of his overlords.

Castles abounded in medieval Europe; England had at least 400, France many more and Germany is said to have had 10 000. A castle was a lord's fortified home and the symbol of his position in society, as well as the stronghold which gave protection to his own vassals and to the peasants who worked his land. Until well into the 13th century, most castles were cold, draughty and uncomfortable, for there was usually only one great communal room in which practically all activities took place by day and where nearly everyone slept at night on straw pallets. The lord had his own *solar* which served as bedroom, reception room and council chamber and his successors often built themselves a range of larger, more comfortable rooms in the main courtyard, but the one thing in the swarming turbulent life of the castle which no-one had or expected to have was privacy.

Nobles belonged to one of two levels: the great barons who held huge estates and many castles and the lesser nobles, called knights in England, *chevaliers* in France, *hidalgos* in Spain and *ritter* in Germany, who received land from their feudal superior, lived in his household and served him with sword and lance. The knight's trade was fighting and he was bred to it from

Falconry, the highly specialised art of bringing down game-birds, which has its own rules, vocabulary and etiquette, was very much the sport of kings and nobles. The earliest and best treatise on falconry was written by the Emperor Frederick II, 'Stupor Mundi'.

boyhood; fighting gave meaning to his life, relief from the boring routine of peacetime life in the castle and the chance of riches from booty and ransoms.

Kings declared war and barons attacked their neighbours for gain, whereas peace often meant poverty. The landless sons of the lesser nobles had a vested interest in war and were forever ready to take sides in a quarrel or a civil war and to follow any leader to Ireland, southern Italy, Spain, the Baltic coast or the Holy Land, where they might win an estate or acquire a fortune.

The peasants who lived on the manors adjoining the castle were tied to the land, bound by law and custom to work for their lord all the days of their lives and unlikely to move away unless it was to follow the lord to war or, as in Germany, to the new lands which were being colonised in Prussia and along the Baltic coast.

The peasant or villein gave service for the land he held, two or three days' work every week on the lord's demesne, besides providing him with produce, eggs and eels, paying to have corn ground in the mill and, most hated of burdens, helping to build roads, bridges and castles. There were special dues to be paid, such as when the lord had to be ransomed or when his eldest son was knighted and, in France, there was a tax, called the *taille*, which the lord could demand whenever he wished.

There was a strong sense of community on the manor, where men had to share a plough and an ox-team, agree on the time for sowing their field-strips and when to cut the ripe grain. They shared the common land on which they pastured their animals and they all served the same lord, with whom they had in effect made a bargain that, in return for their labour, he would give them protection and justice in the manor court.

For the peasant, however harshly treated (his lot seems to have been hardest in Germany), was not a slave. He had his rights, hallowed by custom, which the lord was bound to respect and, where he was often absent, at court or at the wars, the peasant frequently had the chance to better himself. What is hard for us to understand is that men accepted that they were born different, destined by God to be nobles or villeins and never to be anything else. Class was fixed and even the blood of noble and commoner was supposed to be different.

War hit the peasants hard, when marauding armies ravaged the country-side and standing crops and villages went up in flames, but there were plenty of perils besides war. Above all else, the peasant dreaded a failed harvest and it happened all too frequently. During the 43 years' reign of Philip Augustus of France, for example, no fewer than 11 famine years were recorded, when countryfolk ate roots, acorns and bark and the children died of hunger.

There were epidemics too - plague, dysentery, smallpox, influenza, typhoid and other contagious fevers; leprosy was common and so were all kinds of skin diseases, including a torturing one called St Anthony's Fire. Polluted water, tainted meat, infected wounds and the penetrating damp of stone-walled rooms must have claimed many lives.

When he was ill, the peasant had no doctor to turn to, because physicians reserved their skills for the nobles, so he had to rely on the herbal remedies

Four months of the year, with occupations and signs of the zodiac from the Shepherd's Great Calendar, end 15th century.

March: a time for cleaning out ditches, ponds and moats, for pruning and for mending fences and enclosures round the little homestead.

May: the time when a young lord might ride out with a hawk on his wrist and his lady a-pillion. When young people might take a bath in company!

156

July: haymaking, when the tall grass is cut with the long scythe, raked, turned and put to dry in haycocks. The hay-crop is absolutely vital to lord and peasant, for it will be almost the sole feed for the animals kept through the winter.

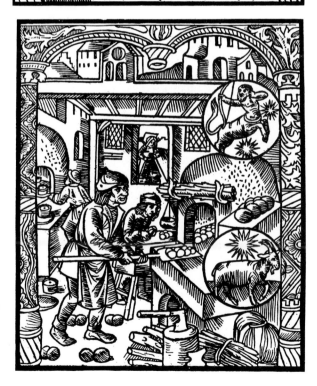

December: when field-work is normally at a standstill — though we can see through the window a woman using what looks like a breast-plough or a cultivator. Corn is threshed now, the wood-pile built high and the bakers kept busy making pies and loaves.

157

of the local wisewoman. The touch of a dead man's tooth was good for toothache; otherwise, the aching molar had to be pulled out by the blacksmith. Surgeons, though they ranked lower in society than physicians, were remarkably skilful, perhaps through constant practice, for they could set broken limbs and put them in plaster, carry out trepanning (boring into the skull) to relieve head wounds received in battle and tournament, operate for rupture, cancer and gall-stones, deliver babies by Caesarian section (cutting open the mother's abdomen) and even repair sliced noses with plastic surgery. For antiseptics, they cauterised wounds with old wine and the whites of eggs and, in place of anaesthetics, they made patients drowsy with strong drink or by holding to their nostrils sponges soaked in narcotics like opium and mandragora.

However, life was by no means all fear and misery. Those who survived these perils were extraordinarily tough and they had absolute faith in the power of God and His saints to protect them, for religion pervaded their lives and every activity from birth to death - ploughing, making a business deal, going on a journey, the harvest, a trial by ordeal or a marriage feast - called for the priest's blessing. A man was seldom out of sight of a church tower or the sound of its bell and it is estimated that in England there was a church for every 40 or 50 households in the land.

There were Church holy-days or holidays to enjoy, as well as the Christmas revels with mummers, jugglers and dancing. Men and boys played games with enormous zest - football, bowls, barley-break, curling, wrestling - and were often hurt in the process; tournaments and hunting belonged to the gentry, but everyone went poaching, for the excitement of the chase and the joy of getting fresh meat.

In good seasons, people ate well, even if the nobleman consumed too much meat and alcohol and the peasant's diet was limited and monotonous. The Englishman ate plenty of bread, cheese, curds, porridge and herrings; he drank ale and despised vegetables ('worts'), which he only ate when he had to, for he loved meat, all the more because it was none too plentiful, though there was frequently an old hen or a poached hare for the pot; a pig-killing called for a feast, but when a heifer or an ox had to be slaughtered, its carcase and hide were sold to a dealer, since a man needed money occasionally to buy salt and iron and to pay certain feudal dues.

Money, in fact, played a small part in everyday life, for wages and rents were seldom paid wholly in cash and even the great nobles were often short of actual money, so when it came to building a residence or getting fitted out for a campaign, they had to turn to the Jewish money-lenders or Italian bankers who did business all over Europe.

In France, the peasants lived mostly on bread, soups, fruit, vegetables and wine; in the north they drank cider. Italians ate coarse bread, onions, beans, turnips, garlic and pasta, while German peasants lived chiefly on dark rye bread, oatmeal porridge, boiled turnips, cabbage, sauerkraut and, occasionally, pork. German peasants dreaded becoming 'unfree', that is, becoming a serf, who was a chattel belonging to his lord and hardly better than a slave.

Unlike the lower classes, nobles ate white bread and a great deal of meat – beef, pork, mutton and venison, usually boiled rather than roasted, and all kinds of birds, from chickens, geese, swans, and peacocks to larks, curlews, snipe, herons and even vultures! At banquets, the cooks would serve fantastic dishes, such as a peacock with its tail spread, a pastry castle containing a roasted deer or a great pie filled with small live birds. A noble household spent a great deal of money on spices like pepper, cloves, ginger and cinnamon, and eastern luxuries such as sugar-loaves, almonds, figs, raisins and marzipan sweetmeats. The nobles drank wine, which was often mixed with spices or served hot (mulled) and their diet of meat and pastry, with very little fruit and virtually no vegetables, was probably less good for health and especially for the skin than the peasants' plain fare. However, they consumed a great deal of fish, on Fridays and especially during Lent when meat was forbidden; most castles and monasteries had their own fishponds and they were also supplied with vast numbers of eels by the manors, but people within reach of the coasts preferred sea fish, including porpoises, seals and whales; inland they had to make do with salted herrings and cod. Stockfish were fish split open and dried in the sun without salt; this made them so hard that they had to be hammered and soaked before cooking.

Between the nobles at the top of society and the peasants at the bottom stood a growing class of merchants, craftsmen and artisans, living in the towns and cities where they cherished their liberties and usually managed their affairs without much interference from king, bishop or lord.

Within its defensive walls, the town huddled round its market-square where stood the great church, the market-cross, the town-hall and the pillory. In the narrow, foul-smelling streets, craftsmen plied their trades in workshops on the ground floor of their own homes, which were mostly made of wood with thatched roofs, until stone or brick party walls and tiles came into use to reduce the danger from fire, which was so common that Rouen in France was burnt down no less than eight times in 25 years.

Land was scarce, so that if a man wanted to enlarge his house he built upwards by adding another storey, but, as a rule, the burgher's home consisted of two or three rooms above the shop, where, as in the castle, everyone lived in the main room and all the family slept in one bedroom. Servants and apprentices slept on the floor downstairs in the shop. Water had to be fetched from the public fountain and, contrary to popular belief, medieval people did take a bath now and again, usually in company! Some towns, especially in France and Germany, had a public bath-house, called a *stew*, where men and women bathed together and bath-ladies waited on the customers, washing heads, scrubbing backs and serving wine.

Owing to people's ignorance of municipal hygiene, townsfolk lived in perpetual danger from pestilence and, although the mayor constantly upbraided them for throwing their refuse into the streets, they seldom did more than dump it outside the town walls. Most houses had a privy, usually in the cellar, which was emptied on to the fields or into the river.

A great part of town life was organised by the guilds (or gilds), which were a sort of club to which the leading merchants belonged; each had its own rules, officers, meeting place and badge and in Florence, for example, the seven major guilds of bankers, lawyers, doctors, wool and silk merchants practically ran the city, fixing wages, prices and hours of work, organising defence and holding all the important municipal offices. In London, the various guilds of vintners, mercers, fishmongers, grocers, goldsmiths and so on were almost equally rich and powerful in their control of the city's business life. They also built and maintained churches, and founded schools and alms-houses. Craftsmen, excluded from the merchant guilds, formed their own craft guilds to fix prices, quality of goods, wages of journey-men and the training of apprentices. They helped members who were sick, looked after widows and orphans and sometimes supported a hospital or paid for boys to be educated.

In many cities, especially in Germany, a section was walled off for Jews, who were compelled to wear a yellow patch or the star of David on their garments, so that they were forever targets for abuse, and, from time to time, sickening violence. Anti-Semitic feelings, fanned by wandering preachers, blamed the Jews for any disaster, accident, famine or death of a child; savage persecutions took place right across Europe during the first two Crusades, when whole communities were put to death; Edward I of England was held in honour for expelling all the Jews from the kingdom; France did the same a few years later, Spain and Portugal followed suit. A great many Jews fled eastwards to Poland, Bohemia (W. Czechoslovakia) and Hungary; some went to Italy or made their way back into France and Spain as persecution died down. Always they survived through their courage and superior skills as doctors, lawyers, scholars and financiers.

From early times, the Church fostered education by training boys for the priesthood and monastic life. Cathedral or 'grammar' schools were founded in which such subjects as grammar, rhetoric and logic were taught, all in Latin, of course, as well as arithmetic, geometry, astrology and music. Secular schools i.e. schools unconnected with the Church, were opened in towns to provide education for the sons of the more prosperous burghers, but girls were usually taught their letters and domestic skills by their mothers Noble boys were taught by the household chaplain and girls were sometimes sent to school at a nunnery.

Universities came into existence in Europe early in the 13th century, though the idea of a university had already arisen in Spain, where, at Toledo, Arabs, Jews, and Spaniards shared their studies with Greeks, Frenchmen, Germans and Englishmen. The first university in Italy was at Salerno, followed by others at Bologna, Padua, Perugia, Siena and Florence, all of them dominated by the Church, though the Emperor Frederick II founded Naples University to train laymen to take the place of priests as his civil servants. Greatest of all universities was Paris, from which students went to England to found Oxford University; the universities of Vienna, Heidelberg and Cologne were started somewhat later.

Since all educated men spoke and wrote Latin, students could move easily from one place to another, taking degrees at, say Oxford and Paris and going on to Padua to study medicine. At entry, they were younger than modern undergraduates, going up at about 14 years of age to study for seven years for their degree. Most were sons of merchants and lawyers, though there were plenty of poor students, but not many from noble families, since it was beneath the dignity of a 'gentleman' to concern himself with book-learning. Rich or poor, students were notorious for their high-spirits and riotous behaviour and, not living in halls but in lodgings in the town, they were often so much at loggerheads with the townsfolk that a kind of running war went on for generations.

To sum up, life in medieval Europe was dangerous, brutal and short. It was an age of faith and superstition, a cruel age, in which there was little respect for human life or concern for suffering and injustice, an age dominated by men, in which the voice of a woman was hardly ever heard. But it was also an age of tremendous achievement in the building of glorious cathedrals and churches, in literature and art, especially that of book illustration; it contained the beginnings of our industrial society and made considerable advances in knowledge, government and the comforts of daily life.

15 Medieval Germany and Russia *c.* 550 – 1584

GERMANY

In 1273, some 20 years after Frederick II of Hohenstaufen had failed to realise his dream of uniting Germany and Italy into one empire, the German electors chose as Holy Roman Emperor, Rudolf I of Hapsburg (or Habsburg).

By this time, most of the Empire lay in Germany, which had become a patchwork of duchies, principalities, the kingdom of Bohemia-Moravia, more than 300 petty states and over 50 more or less independent cities. In theory, all were united under the rule of the Emperor and an imperial assembly, called the Diet; in practice, the dukes, counts, princes, margraves, arch-

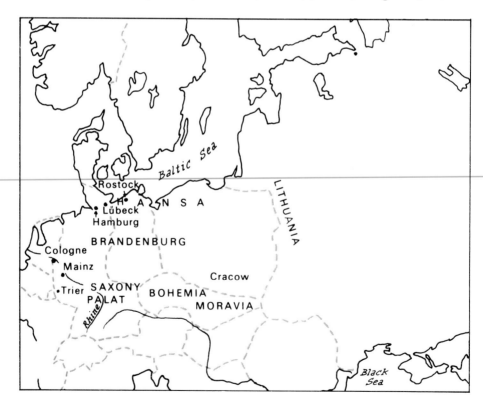

Portrait of the Emperor Maximilian I (1459-1519) by Albrecht Dürer. The coat of arms of the Hapsburgs can be seen on the left, encircled by the Order of the Golden Fleece. Maximilian of Austria, as he was before becoming Emperor, married Mary of Burgundy whose possessions included the Netherlands, and their son Philip's marriage to Joanna (daughter of Ferdinand and Isabella) led to the union of Austria and Spain. *Their* son was the Emperor Charles V.

bishops and minor nobles governed their domains as they pleased and only heeded the Emperor when it suited them to do so.

They choose Rudolf of Hapsburg because he was apparently too weak to impose law and order; however, Rudolf asserted himself so vigorously that he made a good deal of progress and through war and crafty bargaining, added the duchy of Austria to the family possessions. But he never ruled over Italy or Sicily. After his death, the imperial crown passed to the House of Luxembourg for more than a century, during which the privilege of electing the Emperor was secured by seven Electors only. By an agreement called the Golden Bull (1356), they were the Archbishops of Mainz, Cologne and Trier, the King of Bohemia, the Duke of Saxony, the Count Palatine of the Rhine and the Margrave of Brandenburg. This privilege not only made them sovereign rulers of their territories, but enabled them to sell the imperial title to the highest bidder.

In 1438, it went to Albert V of Austria, whose coronation began the Hapsburgs' long tenure of the imperial throne which lasted until Napoleon dissolved the Holy Roman Empire in 1806.

During Rudolf I's reign, three communities around Lake Lucerne formed a league to combat oppression by their German overlord; one community was called Schwyz, from which came the name Switzerland. This union developed into a confederation of Swiss cantons which in 1315 routed the imperial army and established the Swiss as the most formidable fighting men in Europe. The struggle for freedom went on for nearly two centuries, with

Peasants Dancing by Dürer, a marvellously vivid drawing in which the artist depicts the vigour, strength and almost frightening will to survive of those who toiled on the land.

the Swiss nearly always victorious, until, by the 'Perpetual Peace' of 1474, they won complete independence from the Hapsburgs.

In 14th-century Germany, while rival candidates fought and intrigued for the imperial crown, some of the northern sea-ports, notably Hamburg, Lubeck and Rostock, formed an alliance known as the Hanseatic League. Its members, eventually numbering about 150 coastal and inland towns, banded together for mutual protection and control of the 'Baltic Trade' between themselves and Western Europe. 'Factories' or trading centres were set up at Novgorod, Bergen, Bruges and London, where Hansa merchants enjoyed special privileges, such as paying lower customs rates than other aliens, because the products in which they dealt - cloth, naval timber, rope, furs, wools, corn, pickled herrings - were in great demand by countries which had not yet developed their own merchant shipping. In London, the German merchant or 'Easterling' was an important figure who gave his name in its shortened form of 'sterling' to England's standard coin.

So powerful was the League that the neighbouring countries of Denmark, Sweden and Norway obeyed its dictates, even so far as electing a king favourable to its policy. However, a decline set in during the 15th century, as the English and Dutch developed their own sea-going trade and, with other states, resented the League's monopoly of Russian products. In its hey-day, it had been a great commercial force, whose lasting work was the founding of towns in the eastern Baltic and opening up trade with Russia.

Between Germany and Russia lay Poland which, under the kings of the Piast dynasty in the 10th century, developed into a major Slav kingdom with its capital the city of Cracow. The Poles were converted to Christianity during the reign of Mieszko I (962-92), whose son, Boleslaw I (992-1025), called the 'Great', waged a successful war against the German Emperor and, to the east, pushed Poland's frontier almost to Kiev.

RUSSIA

Russia's history as a state begins in about the 6th century with the movement of East Slavs into forested country lying between the Black Sea and the Baltic, where they had to contend with Turkish nomads from Mongolia. To protect themselves, they built stockaded settlements at Kiev, Novgorod, and Smolensk, and when, in the 9th century, Scandinavian Vikings, called *Varangians*, came sailing along the great Russian rivers, the Slavs put up little resistance. They seem to have accepted the newcomers as their protectors and overlords.

In 865, a Viking or Varangian fleet sailed down the Dneiper to attack Constantinople, while, in the north, Vikings, under a leader named Rurik, established themselves at Novgorod. They soon dominated the whole area

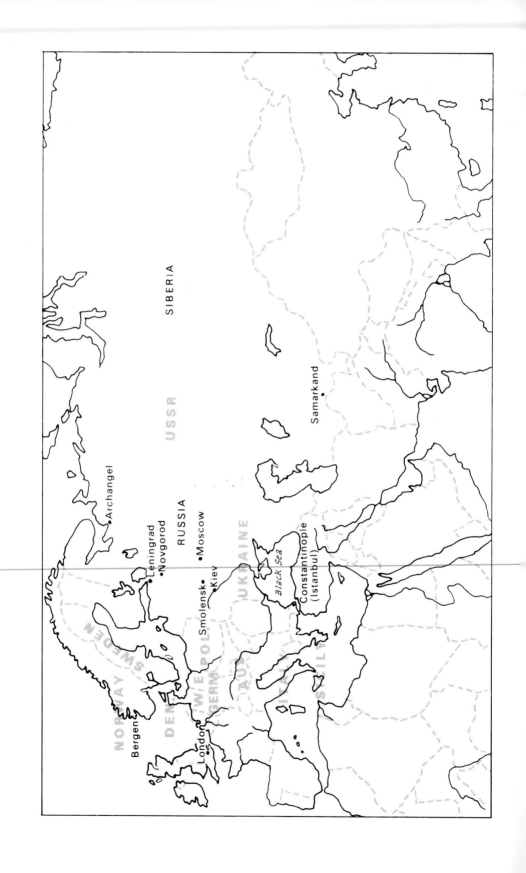

and, towards the end of the century, moved their headquarters to Kiev, which became the capital of Kievan Russia.

Having brought no women with them, the Vikings married local wives and, as they and their children merged with the Slavs, they looked more towards Constantinople than to Scandinavia and, in about 988, accepted Christianity. Kiev, growing rich from trade with the Byzantines, became famous for its magnificent churches.

As Kievan supremacy declined, the princedom of Moscow asserted itself and Novgorod grew into a great fur-trading centre and capital of an independent state, but, in 1237, the country was invaded from the east by the Golden Horde, an alliance of Mongolian tribes, among them the dreaded Tatars or Tartars.

Batu, grand-nephew of Genghis Khan and ruler of the Golden Horde, conquered all southern and central Russia, devastated Kiev in 1240 and moved on to attack Novgorod, now ruled by the Grand Duke Alexander Nevski. However, fearing that the spring thaw would trap his army, Batu withdrew to the Steppes.

Alexander Nevski, one of Russia's earliest heroes, earned the name of Nevski through a great victory on the banks of the River Neva (1240) over the Swedes who, intent on seizing part of Russia not occupied by the Tatars, had invaded the region where Leningrad now stands. After this victory, Alexander inflicted total defeat on the Knights of the Teutonic Order who had launched an invasion from Germany.

In spite of these triumphs, the Russians were hard-pressed to survive. Alexander's father, the Prince of Kiev, and Alexander himself had to journey to far-off Karakorum, hundreds of miles to the east in Mongolia, to do homage to the Great Khan and to beg humbly for mercy for their people.

From time to time, the Tatars renewed their raids and exacted heavy tribute from the Russians; then there emerged at Samarkand another descendant of Genghis Khan called Timurlain, or Timur the Lame, who raised a great fighting force, swept across Russia to Moscow, defeated the Ottoman Turks in Syria, invaded India, where he captured Delhi in 1398, and was about to attack China when he died in 1402.

Timur's empire soon fell to pieces, so that the Russians of the principality of Moscow, having beaten the Tatars in battle in 1380, were able to begin the long process of freeing themselves from their Mongol overlords. They had to pay tribute to them for another 100 years, but, in the 15th century, the Golden Horde broke up into a number of khanates, while Moscow, which had continued to grow in size and importance, took upon itself the task of bringing all Russian lands under one ruler.

Ivan III (1462–1505), Grand Prince of Moscow and the first to take the title of Tsar, trebled the size of his land by acquiring many provinces and

Ivan IV, called the Terrible, Tsar of Moscow and 'all Russia'. A monster of cruelty, who killed his own son, he was almost certainly insane towards the end of his life.

subduing the republic of Novgorod, which had for long been resisting the Swedes, the Germans and the powerful duchy of Lithuania, which at this time included much of modern Poland, Prussia and the Ukraine. Through his marriage to the niece of the last Eastern Emperor, Ivan brought Byzantine ways to the Russian court, which helped to make it unlike any in Western Europe.

His work was carried on by Ivan the Terrible (1533-84) who had to deal with a return of the Tatars. In 1571, they burnt Moscow yet again, but he drove them from Kazan and Astrakhan provinces and carried Muscovite power for the first time into Siberia. He made a commercial treaty with Queen Elizabeth of England, after Richard Chancellor had found a way to Archangel and overland to Moscow. A monster of cruelty, Ivan treated the *boyars* or nobles with appalling severity after they dared to murmur against his despotic rule; he directed the slaughter of 60 000 citizens in the streets of Novgorod and murdered his own eldest son. In his failings, he resembled Peter the Great, but, like him, he did a great deal for Russia.

16 Italy and the Renaissance
c. 950 – 1560

From about the middle of the 10th century, there arose in Italy, as in the Low Countries, a number of independent cities or 'communes', whose growth and importance rested upon trade.

Italy's geographical position made her the natural centre of commerce between Western Europe, the Byzantine Empire and the Muslim world, so that goods, such as spices, scents, ivory, olive oil, silk, timber, corn and salted fish, flowed into Italian sea-ports, whence they were carried at a fine profit to distant markets.

Venice was the first city to grow rich from this trade, because, as a Byzantine province (though, in fact, virtually an independent state), she was allowed to do business in Byzantine lands, where Venetian merchants had their own quarters in Constantinople and other cities, while Venetian fleets dominated the waters of the eastern Mediterranean. The First Crusade opened up lucrative trade with Syria and in transporting and supplying crusaders - trade that was soon shared by Pisa, and Genoa. Angered by the Byzantines' favours to these rivals, the Venetians took the leading part in diverting the Fourth Crusade to capture Constantinople in 1204. Governed by the Doge, or chief magistrate, and the Council of Ten, Venice became immensely rich and powerful, with considerable territories on the mainland, along the Adriatic coast and among the Greek islands. Its trading fleet, together with Genoese galleys, sailed every year to England and the Low Countries, laden with luxury goods for the ruling classes of Western Europe.

Meanwhile, the Italians began to develop their own industries, especially dyeing and finishing imported cloth and manufacturing fine woollens. Florence became the leading cloth-making city in Europe, while Lucca and Genoa were renowned for their silks. Industry and the carrying-trade

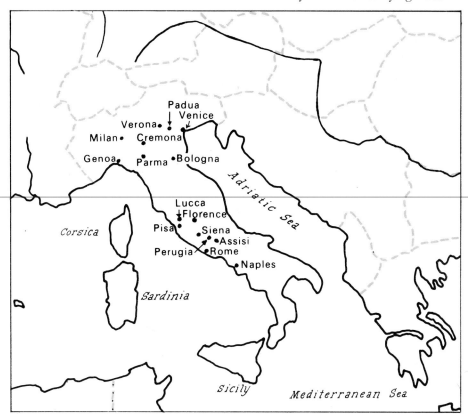

View of Florence c. 1495 with Brunelleschi's cupola of Santa Maria del Fiore in the centre. To the left can be seen the tower of the Palazzo Vecchio in the main square where Savonarola was burnt alive. The city was strongly defended by a great wall, with 70 towers, a deep moat and the River Arno for extra protection.

produced so much wealth that, from the 12th century, Italian businessmen became key figures in the principal cities of France, England and the Low Countries, where they opened banks, lent enormous sums to kings and nobles and acted as financial advisers to foreign governments. The gold florin of Florence and the Venetian ducat were great helps to international business because everyone could trust their value. However, even the astute Italians could suffer occasional disasters, as, in 1331, when Edward III of England failed to meet his debt of more than a million florins and bankrupted the Florentine firm of Bardi and Peruzzi.

Most cities, each with its area of surrounding countryside, came to be governed by oligarchies (small groups) of nobles and rich men, but, in some cases, the merchants, bankers and wool-dealers formed guilds which became strong enough to drive out the nobles and take over ruling the city. Disputes about trade and land led to almost incessant warfare, in which leagues were formed, with smaller cities allying themselves to larger ones for protection. Milan and Parma were sworn enemies; so, too, were Bologna and Cremona; Genoa dared to challenge Venice at sea, while, in Tuscany, Florence gained the upper hand over Pisa, Siena and Lucca. The 12th and 13th centuries brought a great deal of fighting and intrigue, when the Emperors Frederick Barbarossa and Frederick II ('Stupor Mundi') tried to bring the whole of Italy into the Holy Roman Empire and were resisted by the Popes and the Lombard League of northern cities, headed by Milan.

In these conditions, some cities came to be ruled by despots belonging to powerful families, like the Visconti and, later, the Sforzas of Milan, the Scaligers of Verona, the Carravesi of Padua and the Medici of Florence, who mostly took away the citizens' freedoms but provided them with security, magnificent buildings and schools of art and learning.

From about 1250, Italy's wealth and her long-established contacts with the Muslim world brought about that marvellous flowering of the arts known as the Renaissance - the 'rebirth' of the learning of Greece and Rome. Universities were founded in all the principal cities, where, although Latin was still the language of the Church and of scholars everywhere, books and poems began to be written in Italian by such masters as Dante (1265-1321), Petrarch (1304-74) and Boccaccio (1313-75), all Florentines. The cities came to be filled with beautiful churches, squares, palaces, paintings and sculptures, created by artists inspired by their observation of nature, their rediscovery of Roman models and their own experiments and new techniques. The greatest of these innumerable artists include Brunelleschi, the Florentine architect; Ghiberti and Donatello, both sculptors; Giotto, the

An anatomical dissection: a woodcut (by Jan Stephan van Calcar) for the title page of *De Humani Corporis Fabrica* (1543) by Andreas Vesalius, the greatest anatomist of his day and professor of surgery at Padua, Bologna and Basle. *Fabrica*, with its excellent descriptions and drawings, greatly advanced the practice of surgery, but Vesalius was condemned to death by the Inquisition for dissecting human bodies. Sent instead on a pilgrimage to Jerusalem, he died on the way home.

172

Journey of the Three Magi by Benozzo Gozzoli (*c.* 1459), in which members of the Medici family are seen as the Wise Men. The central figure in this section of the painting is Lorenzo the Magnificent, ruler of Florence for over 20 years, a ruthless politician and a patron of the arts.

master-painter of Florence, Padua, Naples and Assisi; Botticelli, Michelangelo, Leonardo da Vinci, Correggio of Parma and Titian, the Venetian painter - every one of them a genius.

At the time of the Renaissance, art was not separate from science and other branches of knowledge; Ghiberti said that a painter had to know grammar, arithmetic, geometry, philosophy, medicine, astrology, perspective, history, anatomy, 'theory' and drawing! Leonardo (1452-1519) moved on from painting to scientific experiments and discoveries; he dissected bodies to find out how muscles worked, investigated gases, designed weapons (including a kind of armoured tank), flying machines and a submarine and worked as an engineer designing canals and fortresses.

Of the principal cities, Milan became the most powerful for a time, under the rule of Galeazzo Visconti (1378-1402) and, after him, Francesco Sforza (1401-66) and Ludovico Sforza, called 'Il Moro', but Venice, which had maintained its supremacy over Genoa and the Turks for centuries, began to decline after the fall of Constantinople (1453), the development of the Cape route to India by the Portuguese and the dominance of Italy by foreigners.

Naples, Rome, Siena and Perugia all achieved great things, but it was to Florence, more than to all the rest, that we owe the glories of the Renaissance. The city, deriving its wealth mainly from cloth-making and banking, was for long governed by its leading merchants, from whom the Medici emerged as supreme rulers. Under Cosimo de Medici and his grandson, Lorenzo the Magnificent (d.1492), Florence reached its peak of splendour, but, within only a few years, it fell to the status of a duchy ruled by the Pope.

This eclipse of Florence and of Italy itself was brought about, first, by the French, for, in 1494, Charles VIII was invited in by Ludovico Sforza of Milan. He expelled the Medici from Florence and marched on to have himself crowned King of Naples. However, he was compelled to withdraw by the Holy League (the Emperor Maximilian - the Hapsburg prince who married Mary of Burgundy - Pope Alexander VI, Spain, Venice, Milan and England), formed to protect Italy, but his successor Louis XII (1498-1515) repeated the invasion, seized Milan and, in alliance with Ferdinand of Aragon, conquered Naples. The allies soon fell out, the French were defeated and Spain gained Naples, which, with Sicily, gave her control of southern Italy.

The French kept Milan for the time being and, in 1508, joined the Emperor, the Pope and Ferdinand in the League of Cambrai to attack Venice and share out her possessions on the mainland.

After much fighting and changing of partners, the new French king, Francis I, (1515-47) in alliance now with Venice, won the brilliant victory of Marignano (1515) over the others and recovered Milan, but he was soon engaged in a venomous struggle with his rival, the Emperor Charles V, grandson of Maximilian and through his mother, Joanna the Mad, possessor of Spain, Naples and America.

Charles' troops completely defeated the French at Pavia (1525) where Francis was taken prisoner and sent to Madrid. He recovered his freedom by promising to give up all his Italian claims, but speedily formed the Holy League with the Pope, Henry VIII of England and Venice. Once again, the Emperor triumphed, for his army of Spanish and German troops sacked Rome with horrible brutality and imprisoned the Pope. This dramatic success left Charles V master of Italy and, for the next 300 years, the country which for so long had led Europe in commerce and the arts of civilization ceased to have a history of its own.

But the upsurge of creative energy which originated in the Italian cities had by now spread northwards, helped by the invention of printing, which, in Europe, is generally ascribed to Johann Gutenberg (1389-1468) of Mainz, in Germany, and by the arrival in Western Europe of Byzantine scholars, who, after the fall of Constantinople, brought with them a great variety of ancient writings, including the New Testament in Greek, and learned works of science and astronomy.

All these books, old learning and new ideas were eagerly welcomed by

Portrait by Holbein the
Younger of Erasmus,
c. 1469-1536, the Dutch
humanist, whose teaching
and writings made him
the leading figure of the
New Learning in
northern Europe. He
travelled widely and made
visits to England to his
friend, Thomas More. He
was fully aware of abuses
in the Church, but
ridiculed the Lutherans as
likely to do more harm
than good.

William Shakespeare
(1564-1616): an engraving
on the title page of the
1623 edition (known as
the First Folio) of 36 of
his plays, which were
collected and edited after
his death by John
Heminge and Henry
Condell, two of his
former colleagues in the
Company called the
King's Men.

Self-portrait of Rembrandt (1606-69), the Dutch painter born at Leyden who spent practically all his working life in Amsterdam. A prolific artist, fascinated by the treatment of light and shade, he painted dramatic masterpieces such as *The Anatomical Lesson* and the *Night Watch,* hundreds of portraits, landscapes, religious paintings and tender studies of old people.

literate people. Men began to think for themselves and to ask questions, instead of merely accepting what the Church and medieval philosophers had taught them; their enquiries led to discoveries in science, medicine, mathematics and astronomy; they studied the world about them and human behaviour (some men of learning became known as humanists), and they dared to look critically at religion and the Church.

Most of the countries of Europe produced scholars, writers and men of achievement; in France, the most famous were the poet Ronsard and the writers Rabelais and Montaigne; in Spain, Cervantes wrote his immortal *Don Quixote*, while the leading English and Dutch humanists were Sir Thomas More, author of *Utopia*, Colet, Linacre and the learned Erasmus (1466-1536). Royal patrons like Humphrey, Duke of Gloucester, Henry VI and the talented young Henry VIII encouraged the arts and new learning in England which gave to the world the plays and poetry of William Shakespeare.

The marvellous schools of painting which suddenly emerged in the Low Countries and Germany produced Rembrandt, Van Eyck, the Breughels, Durer and Holbein, while Spanish painters included El Greco and Velasquez.

For its own reasons, the Christian Church had for long stifled scientific discovery, so that the Polish priest, Copernicus, needed courage to put forward the idea that the Earth was not the centre of the universe, but a planet of the sun. His work was carried on by Galileo, the Italian astronomer, who, with the aid of a home-made telescope, proved that the earth moves round the sun, though his discoveries were condemned by the Church and he was forced to deny what he knew to be the truth.

Portrait of Galileo (1564-1642), the Italian mathematician, inventor and astronomer, whose observations included the mountains and valleys on the Moon, the stars of the Milky Way, four satellites of Jupiter and sun-spots. His bold support of Copernicus' theory brought him into conflict with the Church, so that he was forced to deny his scientific creed and discoveries. However, he was able to retire to Florence and continue his researches until be became totally blind.

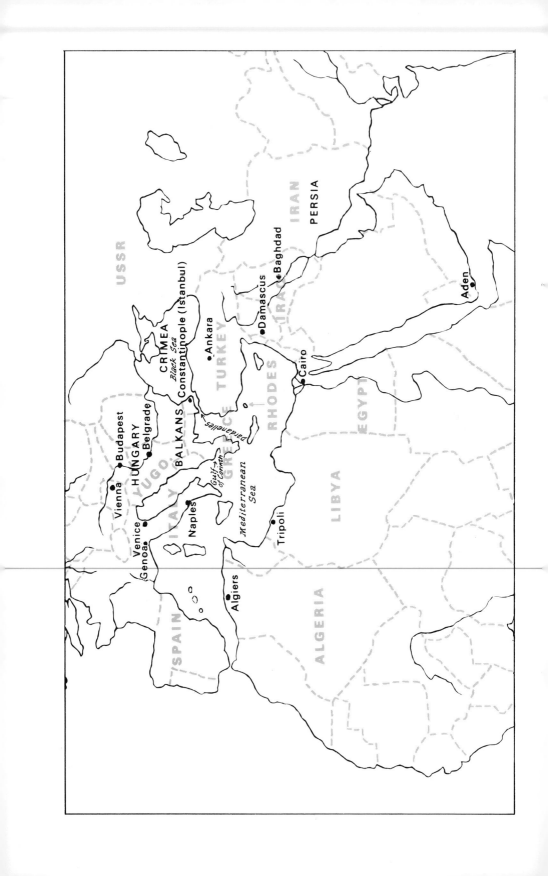

17 The Ottoman Empire
1300 – 1571

During the second half of the 13th century, a new dynasty of Turkish rulers - the house of Othman - arose in Asia Minor and became known as the Ottomans. Energetic and resourceful, they cleared out the last of the Crusaders from Syria (1291), crossed the Dardanelles into Greece and, by 1390, had made themselves masters of the Balkan Peninsula.

Their power was checked for a time by Timur the Lame, who completely defeated the Ottoman army at Ankara in 1402. But his empire was short-lived and the Ottoman Turks soon resumed their advance.

It became obvious that the Byzantine Empire and its capital, Constantinople, were doomed unless the Pope united the monarchs of Europe into a mighty alliance that would crush or, at least, repel the Muslim foe. But there was little chance of that, for the Eastern and Western Churches had long been bitterly hostile to one another and the Pope was not likely to proclaim a crusade to rescue Christians who refused to recognise his primacy.

Left to its fate, Constantinople, which had been the bulwark of Christianity for 11 centuries, fell to the prolonged assault of a vast army commanded by the Sultan Mehemet II, who bore the name of the prophet whom he served. Ironically, the last Byzantine emperor, who died sword in hand, was called Constantine, the name of the Roman emperor who founded the great city.

The capture of Constantinople in 1453 enabled the Turks to expand the Ottoman Empire and dominate the Near East; Mehemet attacked Hungary and, across the Black Sea, extended his authority over the Khanate of the Crimea.

Under Selim I (1512-20), the Ottomans defeated the Persians, whose power had been revived by the Safavid Dynasty; then, in a series of battles, they overcame the Mamelukes of Syria, the ruling class of that country and of Egypt, captured Damascus (1516) and marched into Egypt to take Cairo and put an end to the Mameluke Dynasty. Selim's successor, Suleiman the Magnificent (1520-66), advanced into Hungary, where he captured Belgrade, destroyed the Austro-Hungarian army at Mohacz (1526), took Budapest and laid siege to Vienna itself, but the city held out. Meanwhile, he beat the Venetians at sea and, by adding Rhodes, Algiers and Tripoli to his possessions, enabled his fleets to dominate the whole of the Mediterranean. Later, he completed the conquest of Persia, so that, by the time he died

The Siege of Vienna, 1529, from the Ottoman *Book of Skills* (published in Istanbul, 1588), in which the guns of Suleiman's army are trained on the Austrian capital. The Turks destroyed the suburbs, but the city was saved by heroic defence organised by Count Niclas van Salm.

campaigning in Hungary, the Ottoman Empire stretched from Algiers to Aden to Baghdad.

Deriving much of its wealth from Egypt, it was now the richest and most powerful of all the Muslim states, with its capital, Istanbul (as Constantinople was renamed), one of the most magnificent cities in the world, its army well-disciplined and its people efficiently governed.

Greatest of all the Sultans and known to his people as 'the Law Giver', Suleiman was a patron of the arts, a poet and a builder of wonderful mosques. His successor, Selim II, and the grand vizier, Sokolli, continued to expand the empire at a rate which alarmed Pope Pius V into forming a Holy Alliance to stem the Turkish advance. In 1571, Venice, Genoa, Spain and Naples furnished ships for a mammoth fleet of 300 vessels which, commanded by Don John of Austria, half-brother of Philip II of Spain, totally defeated the Ottoman navy at Lepanto in the Gulf of Corinth.

Although the Turks continued to threaten Eastern Europe for more than another century (they again attacked Vienna in 1683), their sea-power had taken a heavy blow from which they never fully recovered. In the second half of the 16th century, a long series of wars against the Hapsburg Empire and Persia drained their armies' strength and led to the empire's gradual decline.

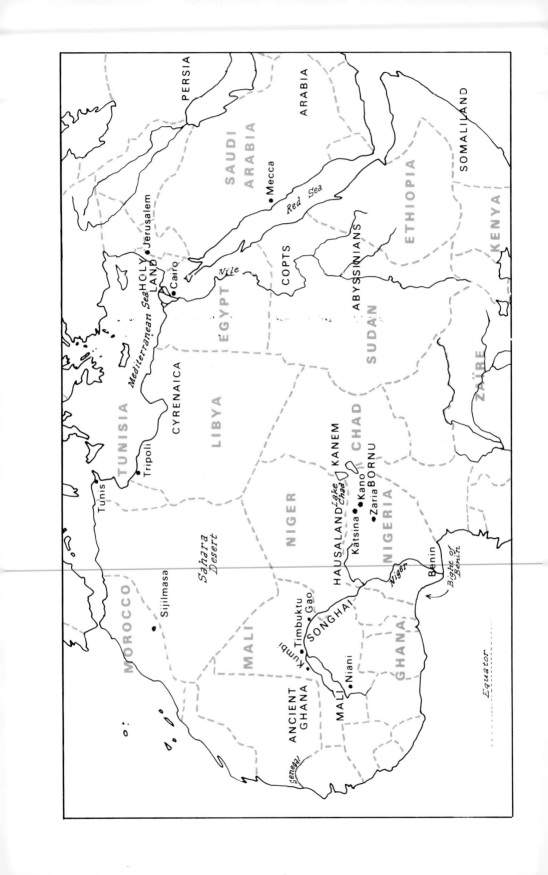

18 Medieval Africa
c. 640 – 1500

In the 7th century, Arabs, fired by the Islamic faith, conquered the whole of North Africa, easily defeating the Byzantine army in Egypt, overruning Cyrenaica and pressing on across the desert into the cultivated plains of Tunisia, where they built the city of Tunis and converted the Berber tribes to Islam.

Throughout this region, Christianity was eclipsed, except in Egypt and Sudan, where a minority known as Copts, established the Coptic church and clung to their religion for centuries. Everywhere else accepted the culture of Islam.

From North Africa, the teaching of the Prophet was carried south, across the Sahara Desert into the kingdoms of the 'Sudanic' region which stretches across sub-Saharan Africa from the Senegal river to the Red Sea. The principal kingdoms of this Sudanic area were ancient Ghana, Mali, Songhai, Hausaland and Kanem, lying north-east of Lake Chad. In these early kingdoms, semi-divine kings, ruling with the aid of a few high officials and district chiefs, held complete power over their people who lived by keeping domestic animals, chiefly cattle, and raising crops such as millet, wheat and beans. Trade seems to have been a royal monopoly.

At Sijilmasa, a great caravan centre in southern Morocco, traders would sell copper, cotton, swords and horses to Africans from further south in exchange for gold, ivory and slaves. The gold came from Ghana, a kingdom located in present-day Mali, some 800 kilometres north-west of today's Ghana; the Ghanaians did not mine gold themselves, but obtained it in exchange for salt from the more primitive people of the Wangara country, who jealously guarded the source of the precious metal. This trade had been going on since Roman times and, along its caravan routes, Arabs carried the faith of Islam into West Africa.

Near Sijilmasa, a holy man named Ibn Yasin preached a stricter, fiercer Islam to the Berber nomads, who, calling themselves Almoravids, swept out of the desert to conquer Morocco. Some went north into Spain to help defeat the Christians and, in the process, to seize the Caliph's power. The rest of the Almoravid horde marched south in about 1062 to attack Ghana, whose warriors put up such a strong resistance that it was 14 years before their capital, Kumbi, was taken and destroyed.

Decorated doorway of a clay-built house in Kano, Nigera, a city with centuries of importance as a caravan terminus for trans-Saharan trade. To this day, houses and walls are frequently re-surfaced in the traditional manner.

Ancient Ghana was so weakened by this struggle that the kingdom broke up into tribal units, but its place as the major power in the western Sudanic region was taken by the Mali empire, whose first great ruler, Sundiata (1230-55), expanded his territories and took control of the caravan termini and the gold trade.

Sundiata became converted to Islam and throughout the great period of Mali history, up to the end of the 14th century, his successors as *Mansa* (emperor) were all Muslims. The most famous of these was Mansa Musa (1312-37), who ruled a huge empire from his capital Niani, a great walled city, thronged with traders of many nationalities. Musa once went on a pilgrimage to Mecca, accompanied by an enormous caravan, with courtiers, warriors and 12 000 slaves clad in tunics of brocade and silk. In Cairo, he was said to have given away so much gold that its market-price did not recover for years. Musa brought back to Mali a number of Arab scholars and an architect to build mosques, palaces, schools and, at Timbuktu, a university which flourished for many years, until it was destroyed by invaders from Morocco in the 16th century.

Mali's wealth and good order began to decline in the late 15th century, when one of its vassal kings, Sonni Ali (1464-92), ruler of the Songhai people, asserted his independence and seized some of the Mali territories. Under his successors, the Songhai empire, whose capital Gao, on the bend of the Niger, lay some 1100 kilometres north-east of Niani, was even bigger than that of Mali. It lasted for about 100 years and then, after the defeat of its army by Moroccans in 1591, it broke up into small units.

East of Songhai were the Hausa City States, of which Zaria, Katsina and Kano became extremely prosperous as termini of trade routes across the central Sahara to Tunis and Tripoli. However, they never united to form a single Hausa state.

East again lay the Kanuri empire, founded by Kanem people from the east of Lake Chad, who moved to the south-west where the province of Bornu became a considerable power, exercising dominance over neighbouring peoples. The Kanuri kings, known as *mais*, kept in touch with the Muslim world, especially Egypt, from which they derived cultural ideas, laws and, from the 16th century, firearms.

South of the Islamic States lay the great tropical forest region of West Africa which is called Guinea (not the modern states called Guinea). We know little of its early history, because it was never reached by the Arab travellers who wrote about the Sudanic lands. It seems clear, however, that the peoples of Guinea had many contacts with ancient Ghana and Mali, and that they possessed remarkable skills in metal-working, pottery and sculpture. They lived in urban communities, from villages to large walled towns, from which they set forth daily to work in the fields, returning at night for safety to homes near the royal palace or the house of their chief.

One of the best known of these towns was Benin in Nigeria, which indeed was regarded by a Dutch traveller of 1602 as a city to compare with any major European city of the time. Capital of a rich and powerful kingdom, Benin has become famous for its marvellous bronze statues which were

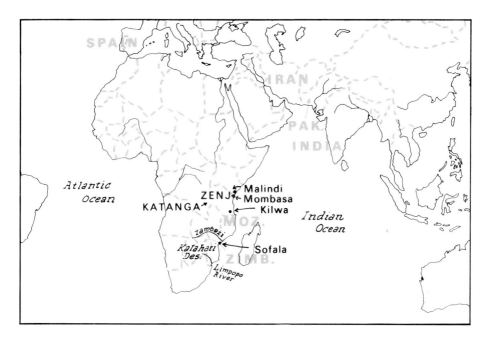

Bronze head of Queen Mother, Benin, where, at the time of the Europeans' arrival, bronze casting was a highly developed art. The Benin dynasty, one of the oldest in West Africa, maintained its royal traditions for over 500 years.

produced by generations of craftsmen to decorate the royal palace and shrines. From 1500, Benin and the neighbouring coastal states of Oyo and Akan came into increasing contact with Europeans, mainly Portuguese sailors who had explored the way round the great bend of West Africa into the Bight of Benin.

Just as West Africa and the Sudanic region were penetrated by Islam long before the arrival of Europeans, East Africa became well-known to Muslims from south Arabia and from the west coast of India. They called East Africa the Land of Zenj. From the 13th century, perhaps earlier, Arabs were living in stone-built towns such as Gedi, Malindi, Mombasa and Kilwa, all along the East African coast from Somaliland to Kenya and Tanzania. As the site for a settlement, they usually chose an island just off the coast, for this gave them security from attack by inland tribes, and, until the coming of the Europeans, there was no need for sea defences, since all the incoming ships were friendly trading dhows which sailed across the Indian Ocean laden with Islamic pottery, silk and cotton cloth, iron weapons, knives, tools and glass from Arabia and India. Using the north-east monsoon wind, the dhows reached the coast of Zenj between December and April and sailed back with cargoes of ivory, gold, tortoiseshell, rhino-horn, and slaves. Gold came from the land of the Karanga people (in modern Zimbabwe) and, like the ivory, was brought to the coast by Africans, for the Arabs did not penetrate far inland. They preferred to live in their island towns where they maintained African wives and became rich merchants. The children of these marriages became the Swahili people, whose language has a Bantu (African) structure and many Arabic words.

Kilwa, the principal town, was so prosperous that its Sultan minted his own copper coins, each bearing his name and a prayer to Allah. An Arab traveller, visiting the town in 1331, wrote, 'Kilwa is one of the most beautiful and well constructed towns in the world. The whole of it is elegantly built.' The Sultan also ruled Sofala, the main port for the gold trade of the Zambesi region, and levied duties on the sea-borne traffic along the coast. Malindi and Mombasa, for example, exported high quality iron ore to India to be manufactured into steel blades, and copper probably reached the coast from the Katanga kingdom.

Inland from Sofala, north of the Limpopo river in present-day Zimbabwe, some massive stone buildings were erected for a royal village or *zimbabwe*, between the 11th and 15th centuries by the Shona people whose ruler was known as Mwenemutapa or (Monomatapa). Great Zimbabwe is the only site in southern Africa where medieval stone buildings have been discovered.

In Africa, Christianity survived in the Coptic Church of Egypt and also in the mountainous country of Abyssinia (Ethiopia), whose emperor, courtiers and, after them, the people had been converted as early as the 4th century.

Churches and monasteries were built and there were close ties with the Coptic Church of Egypt, since both the Abyssinians and the Copts were regarded as heretics by the Roman Church.

The rise of Islam cut off the Abyssinians from most of the Christian world, but, for centuries, the Arabs never waged the *jihad* or holy war against them. Indeed, during the time of the Crusades, Abyssinian pilgrims went in their thousands to the Holy Land and Saladin himself gave them a church in Jerusalem.

As for the interior of Africa, we know little of its history before the 19th century, because the people there did not know how to write and the Arabs and the Portuguese who did understand writing rarely moved inland. We do know something of the movements of different types of Africans; originally there were three main races – Bushmen, short people, expert hunters, of whom a few still survive in the Kalahari Desert; Negroes, who entered Africa thousands of years ago but we do not know where from; they had round heads, flat noses and dark skins, and were farmers from an early date; Hamites who came from Asia during the Middle Stone Age; they had long heads, straight noses and brown skins, and were great cattle breeders.

From intermarriage of Negroes and Hamites, other groups emerged, of which the most numerous were the black Bantu people, whose great increase may have been due to the introduction into Africa (from about the beginning of the Christian era) of Asian food plants, mainly the banana and the yam. At all events, the Bantu spread over most of Africa south of the equator and, from about AD 1000, into East Africa where they were newcomers.

The slave trade, which went back to Roman times, expanded with the settlement of Muslim Arabs along the coast and the plentiful supply of incoming Bantu people who, captured in tribal wars, were sold to the Arabs and shipped to Arabia, India, Persia and even China.

Inland groups included Hamite tribes with little or no negroid blood, who moved down from Somaliland into part of Kenya. Another group, the Nilotes, came up the Nile from the Sudan, while Nilo-Hamites, who included the fierce Maasai, moved south to pasture their cattle on the grassy plains of Kenya and Tanzania.

This brief account of Africa's history from about the 7th century to the arrival of the Portuguese in the 15th century indicates that, while its rulers and peoples created their own empires, cities and ways of living, they were much influenced by their contacts with the Muslims. All of the north, from Egypt to Morocco, had become part of the Islamic world; trade and armed excursions took Islamic culture across the Sahara into the western Sudanic region and also along part of the coast of East Africa. A pocket of Christianity survived in Abyssinia, but the interior of the vast continent, indeed its shape and extent, remained unknown to the rest of the world.

19 India and the Muslim Invasions *c.* 500 – 1707

Towards the end of the 5th century, the ferocious White Huns from central Asia broke up the Gupta Empire and settled in the north, until they were defeated by a Hindu warrior-king named Harsha (d.647). From his capital city, Kanauj, on the upper reaches of the Ganges, Harsha extended his rule right across the country, though he was barred from the south by the warlike Chalukya people, who ruled the Deccan for about 500 years.

A famous Chinese traveller, Hsuan Tsang, lived for years at Kanauj, and left a vivid account of the civilized life at Harsha's court. But, after Harsha's death, India suffered a long period of unrest and confusion, during which many kings and dynasties struggled to survive or to master their neighbours.

By the 8th century, the Rashtrakuta kingdom dominated central India; Pala kings ruled Bengal and the Pratiharas held sway over a large area stretching east from the Punjab. In the south, the major powers were the Chalukyas and the Cholas. Arab invaders from Afghanistan made their way through the mountain passes into north-west India, where they conquered Sind in 712 and founded two small Muslim states. Their progress was checked by the Rajputs of Rajputana, who may have been descended from the White Huns and were now Hindu warriors belonging to clans which were perpetually at war with one another. In this warfare, the Rajputs cultivated a code of gallant behaviour rather like the chivalry of medieval Europe and they stopped their private fighting for a time in order to combine against the Muslim enemy.

In these troubled times, Indian civilization continued to flourish. Elaborately beautiful temples were built, statues carved, prose, poetry and philosophy written, while Buddhism spread far afield into Nepal and Tibet.

Over a long period, the border regions to the north-west came to be permanently occupied by Muslim settlers and it was from the Turkish kingdom of Ghazni, now Afghanistan, that Sultan Mahmud led a series of ferocious raids into India. At first, he came simply for plunder but, as Hindu resistance weakened, he was able to add the Punjab to his kingdom and, in 1021, to make the city of Lahore its capital.

This gave the Muslims a base from which they could drive deeper into the country and, 150 years later, another conqueror, Mohammed Ghuri, led

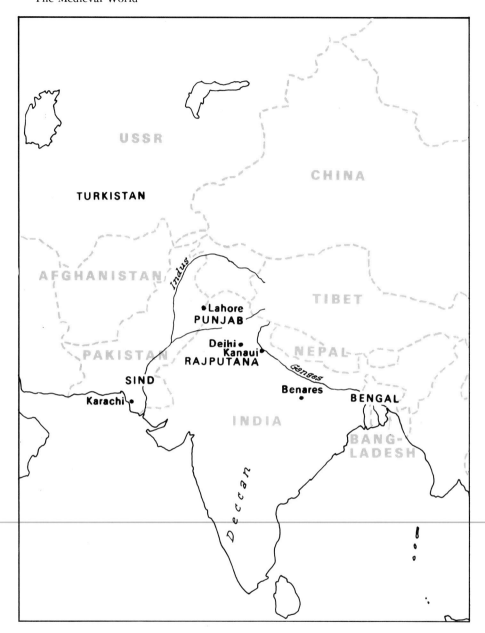

his warriors from Afghanistan across the Punjab and into Rajputana where he destroyed the Rajput army and pressed on down the Ganges plain to pillage the holy city of Benares. By 1206, he was the ruler of practically the whole of northern India, where his successor, Aibak, made the city of Delhi his capital and set up a dynasty known as the Delhi Sultanate, which ruled the north and much of the Deccan until the 16th century.

During this period, the Mongols under Genghis Khan rampaged across Asia and into Europe. Some made forays into India, but were beaten back, allowing Muslim scholars and artists from the devastated lands of central Asia and Persia to take refuge in Delhi and make it a centre of Islamic culture. However, the Mongols came back in 1398, when Timur the Lame captured Delhi with frightful slaughter and proclaimed himself Emperor of India.

Laden with fabulous booty, Timur soon departed, but the Delhi Sultanate, shaken by the invasion, broke up into separate quarrelsome states and the Hindu kings, notably the Rajputs, began to recover some of their old country.

In this weakened state, India was once again a prey to invaders and, this time, they came from what is now Russian Turkistan. Their leader, Babur, a descendant of Genghis Khan, defeated Sultan Ibrahim in a great battle near Delhi in 1526, overcame the Rajputs and founded the Mogul (or Mughal, a corruption of Mongol) Dynasty.

Babur, a more likeable man than most conquerors, was the first of a succession of emperors who gave India one of the most brilliant periods in its long history, an era whose golden age was the reign of Akbar the Great (1556-1605) who while still a young man conquered most of the sub-continent and then devoted the rest of his life to ruling this vast multi-national empire with wisdom and humanity.

Instead of trying to crush the Rajput chiefs, he won them over by making them his military allies, by marrying Rajput princesses and allowing the Hindus to practise their own religion. To help the peasants, he appointed officials to introduce fair taxation and study better ways of growing crops. He gave his subjects new laws, roads and schools, a police force and a reformed system of weights and measures, so they called him 'Guardian of Mankind'. At Court, Akbar encouraged both Hindu and Muslim artists and poets to express themselves in their own ways and he had temples and palaces built in a magnificent style that drew inspiration from Hindu and Islamic architecture.

Akbar's successors, though less gifted than he, were able men who expanded the empire into the extreme south and, under them, Persian manners, art and language came to have a lasting influence on Indian life. However, Akbar's great-grandson, Aurangzeb, a strict Muslim, introduced harsh anti-Hindu measures which aroused the hostility of the vast majority of his subjects. This factor, together with the constant drain on the north to pay for southern campaigns, and the rise of the warlike Mahrattas in central India, brought dire results, so that when Aurangzeb, last of the great Moguls, died in 1707, the empire was on the brink of ruin.

The reign of Akbar (1555-1605) was recorded by his minister Abul Fazl in the *Akharnama* (c. 1590), with its incomparable collection of miniatures. In the one reproduced here, Akbar is being entertained by Azim (or Adham?) Khan, his foster-brother and favourite, at Dipalpur, Punjab. It was this brother who was later accused of plotting against Akbar and flung to his death from a terrace of the palace at Agra.

20 The World Enlarged
c. 1290 – 1522

Although a few Vikings had set foot in North America in about AD 1000, the story of their brief visit had become lost and forgotten, and, until the 15th century, Europeans who thought about the matter at all, believed that the world was made up of three continents, Europe, Africa and Asia, grouped round the Mediterranean Sea.

Europe's contacts with the East had mainly been by land along the caravan routes which brought goods to the Black Sea and to Syrian ports, whence they were shipped to Western markets. Best known of the merchant travellers who braved the hardships of those immense journeys was Marco Polo, a Venetian, who, in the 13th century, travelled throughout China in the service of the Emperor Kublai Khan and came home after 23 years to write an account of a civilization of which Europeans knew practically nothing. The marvels he described filled his countrymen with incredulity, so they wrote him off as a champion liar - 'Millioni', 'Mr Millions', who made out that the Emperor's wealth and subjects were numbered in millions.

Nevertheless, it was clear that those distant lands produced immense riches. Crusades and pilgrimages had brought many Westerners into contact with the East; they had seen Constantinople and Damascus, had tasted new foods and brought back silks, carpets and jewellery and spices, which appealed immensely to the nobles and rich burgesses of rising towns. The Renaissance spirit of enquiry prompted men to read books and study old maps; desire for knowledge, an upsurge of enterprise - and greed - brought in the age of true world history.

But the way to the East was difficult and dangerous, for the empire of Islam barred the way and the few merchants who were allowed to pass through Muslim lands had to pay out so much in bribes and taxes that the goods they brought became almost impossibly expensive. Moreover, the volume of goods brought overland was small and the Italians, particularly the Venetians, held control of distribution throughout Europe.

A way had to be found by sea. The Chinese had made some considerable voyages in eastern seas; Arab dhows regularly crossed to and fro between India and East Africa, but not many European seamen had sailed south of Morocco or ventured far into northern seas or out into the Atlantic Ocean.

It was natural for the Portuguese to take a lead, for their sailors and

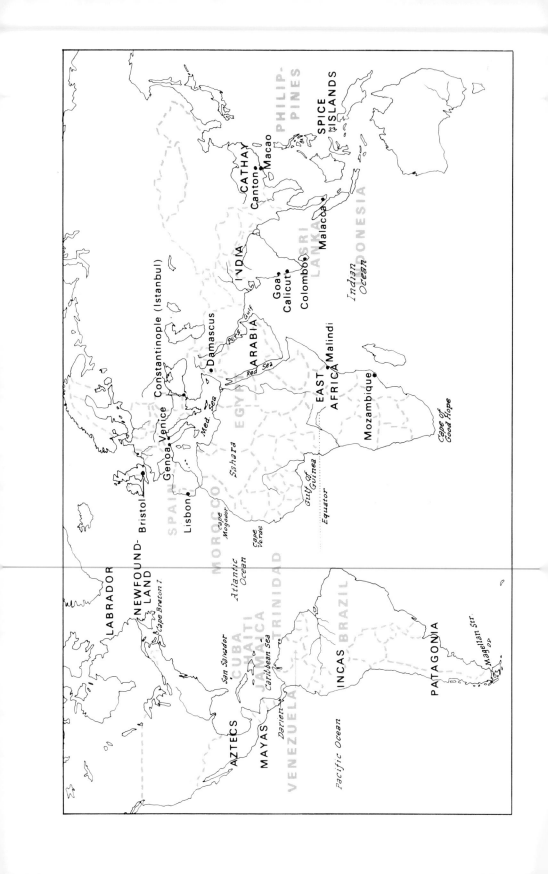

fishermen had been kept out of the Mediterranean by the Spanish and the Italians and had become used to coping with Atlantic storms. Henry the Navigator (1394–1460), son of King John of Portugal, began his life's work of encouraging exploration by collecting information and improving maps, ship-building, compasses and other navigational aids.

Prince Henry concentrated upon progress down the African coast, for he wanted Portugal to win a share in the trans-Saharan trade in gold and pepper that was in Muslim hands. Further, he hoped to find the legendary king, Prester John, who was supposed to rule a Christian kingdom somewhere in Africa, and who would help to overcome the infidels. There was also the possibility of finding a sea-route round Africa, though the ancients said that men would turn black and shrivel up before they could cross the boiling sea in the tropics.

Progress was slow but steady. By 1433, the Portuguese reached Cape Bojador; by 1444, Cape Verde Islands, where they planted a colony and, in the following year, the Senegal river. A fortress was built on the coast to protect the Guinea trade, the Equator was crossed without disaster, and, in 1486, Bartholomew Diaz rounded Africa's southernmost point. He would have sailed on but his nervous crew compelled him to return to Lisbon, where King John II told him that his 'Cape of Storms' must be re-named 'The Cape of Good Hope'.

These voyages and the epic ones which soon followed them were made possible by some important changes in ship design and navigational instruments. From about 1300, ships were built with a stern-post rudder in place of the steering-oar, and rigging gradually became more complex, as the single mast and sail were replaced by three masts, fitted with square and lateen (triangular) sails. Together with small sails, attached to a bowsprit projecting from the bow, these improvements made ships much more manoeuvrable and they could be built larger and stronger to withstand ocean conditions.

By the 15th century, navigators were well accustomed to using the mariner's compass and the astrolabe, an instrument used to find latitude by measuring the sun's or the Pole Star's height; they were also able to consult maps and charts prepared for them by navigational schools set up by rulers like Prince Henry and Charles V of Spain. Under the supervision of an official with a title such as 'Pilot-Major', voyages were carefully planned, sea-captains briefed and, after their return, cross-examined, so that the cartographers (map-makers) and hydrographers (surveyors of coastal waters, tides, currents etc,) could go to work.

While these maritime developments were helping the Portuguese to pursue their voyages, an important event occurred in Spain. In 1469, Ferdinand of Aragon married Isabella of Castile, a marriage which led to them being proclaimed joint sovereigns of Castile; ten years later, on his father's death, Ferdinand succeeded to the throne of Aragon and united the two realms into one kingdom. Spain's period of greatness had begun.

A vigorous ruler, Ferdinand curbed the nobles, introduced reforms and, less wisely, expelled the Moors and the Jews, from Spain. In a quarrel with Portugal, he obtained the Canary Islands, but had to agree not to interfere in the African trade. It was therefore essential for Spain to find her own route to the East.

This situation gave Christopher Columbus the chance to prove his theory that it was possible to reach the Spice Islands (now part of Indonesia) and China by sailing *westward* across the Atlantic. This Genoese navigator had spent some time in Lisbon, but, unable to persuade the Portuguese to back him, had moved to Spain where Ferdinand and Isabella provided him with three ships, crews and provisions to enable him to set sail in the summer of 1492. Two months later, he landed on the island of San Salvador, in the West Indies, which he believed to be off the coast of China. Although he found no sign of the cities and fabulous wealth of the Great Khan, he pushed on to Cuba and Haiti, which he named Hispaniola, New Spain. This must be Zipangu, Marco Polo's name for Japan, with the mainland of Cathay (China) somewhere to the west. Later voyages took Columbus to Jamaica, Trinidad, Venezuela and Panama, but he stuck to his original belief and died in 1506 without realising that he had discovered a vast continent lying between Europe and Asia.

By that time, the Portuguese had reached India, for on 21 May 1498, Vasco da Gama put in at the port of Calicut on the Malabar coast, where the local ruler, a Hindu, and his Muslim merchants were accustomed to trading with East Africa, Arabia, the Spice Islands and China. They did not look favourably upon the newcomers, but, after some difficulty, da Gama got away and returned safely to Lisbon with a cargo of pepper and cinnamon.

News of Columbus's discovery spurred the Portuguese to send out expeditions to overawe the ports of East Africa by cannon fire, to build forts at Malindi and Mozambique and to exact tribute from the unfortunate sultans with such greed that they ruined the coastal trade. Undaunted, they established themselves on the coast of India, defeated a fleet sent down the Red Sea by the Venetians and Egyptians and became masters of the Indian Ocean. Alfonso d'Albuquerque seized the town of Goa on the coast of India and made it the capital of the new Portuguese sea-empire in the east. He had a fort built at Colombo on the rich island of Ceylon (Sri Lanka), and, in 1511, pressed on to the East Indies, where he captured Malacca, capital of Malaya. This gave him the control of the route to the Spice Islands (the Moluccas) where he built more forts and settlements to take over from the Muslims the precious supplies of nutmegs, pepper and cloves which were carried away to Europe. By 1557, the Portuguese reached the coast of China where the Ming allowed them to build a fortified trading post at Macao, near Canton. Thus, with centres at Mozambique, Ormuz (an island in the Persian Gulf), Goa, Malacca, the Moluccas and Macao, most of the eastern spice trade fell into the hands of the Portuguese.

On the other side of the world, once Columbus had made his historic voyage, plenty of sailors and adventurers crossed the Atlantic in search of riches. In 1497, John Cabot, a Venetian navigator, sailed from the English port of Bristol to discover a route to Cathay; he reached Cape Breton Island, sailed along the coast of Labrador and discovered the fishing grounds of Newfoundland, but, since he did not bring home any gold or spices, his royal master, Henry VII, begrudged further expenditure and, for the time being, the English lost interest in voyages of discovery.

But others were more enterprising. In 1500, a Portuguese sea-captain named Pedro Cabral, possibly through sailing too far west on his way to India, reached the mainland of South America and claimed Brazil for Portugal. Next, Amerigo Vespucci, an Italian, in the service of Portugal, explored the coast of South America, which he realised was not part of Asia but, as he said in his writings, a New World, which came to be named America after him. No one knew how far it stretched, but it obviously lay between Europe and Asia, so, to reach Cathay and the Spice Islands by sailing west, men only had to find a strait through this inconvenient land-mass in order to break Portugal's control of the spice trade.

Meanwhile, by the Treaty of Tordesillas (1494), the Pope had given to Portugal the right to explore all lands east of a line drawn north and south 370 leagues west of Cape Verde, and to Spain all those west of it. Thus, Spain claimed sole right to the New World, apart from Brazil, some of which lies east of the line. Pope Alexander VI (Rodrigo Borgia), acting as an abitrator, made this share-out in order to prevent conflict between the two powers, but the up-and-coming maritime nations, the French, the English and the Dutch, were not going to accept a ruling by a Pope, least of all a Spanish Pope, to reserve the New World for Spain and Portugal.

Ignoring the great land-mass of North America, the Spaniards explored the Caribbean Sea, took possession of islands, built churches and began to convert the native people (whom they called 'Indians') to Christianity. Always, they longed for gold and a route to Asia and, in 1513, a soldier from Hispaniola, named Bilbao, led an expedition to the mainland, the Isthmus of Darien, from which he could see a new ocean, later to be called the Pacific Ocean. The mystery was solved. Asia must lie across this ocean and all that remained was to find the way to reach it.

That way was discovered by Ferdinand Magellan, a Portuguese captain who had already sailed by the eastern route to India and the Spice Islands. Dismissed for trading on his own account with the Muslims, he went to the

A fleet of canoes in the Philippines approaching two European ships with gifts and provisions, which do not seem to be well received by the men firing from a ship's pinnace. Magellan met with just such a reception when he reached the Philippines in 1521.

king of Spain who gladly provided him with the little fleet of five ships with which he set sail on 20 September 1519, searched all the way down the coast of South America for a strait, wintered in Patagonia, suppressed a mutiny and, in October 1520, found the straits which now bear his name. After 38 days of storms and hurricane-force winds, he brought his three surviving ships through these perilous waters into an ocean, which, by contrast, seemed so calm that he named it the Pacific Ocean.

Magellan had no idea that it was so vast. For 98 days, there was no sight of land, as the ships sailed north-west, borne along by the trade winds on a course that missed the South Sea Islands where the crews would have obtained food and water. In desperation, the men ate rats, mice and sawdust; they even chewed leather that had been soaked in sea-water, but many died of starvation and scurvy, before their captain brought them to one of the Philippine Islands. Here, in a skirmish with the islanders, Magellan and 40 of his men were killed. The survivors sailed on and, after more hardships, one vessel, the *Victoria*, with 18 men still alive, reached Spain three years after the expedition had set sail.

Magellan's was perhaps the greatest voyage in history; it proved that the world was round, it provided positive information about its size and the extent of oceans and continents, and it inspired countless mariners to set out on voyages of discovery. But when we speak of 'discovery', we ought really to add *by Europeans*, because the land and peoples which they 'discovered' had been there for a very long time! The Chinese and certain African peoples, for example, had developed their own civilizations with little or no help from outside; in America the Mayas, Incas and Aztecs had built their cities and vast temples without knowing that the Old World existed. What the Europeans did was to break into these more or less closed societies, to increase men's knowledge of one another and to stimulate world trade. These were great achievements but frequently they had disastrous consequences for so-called 'backward' peoples when they came into contact with the newcomers' religion, diseases, firearms and insatiable greed.

The Ambassadors, Holbein's striking portrait of two of the men who, like da Gama, Chancellor and Magellan, voyaged into the unknown to make treaties with outlandish rulers, to bring back knowledge and riches, or to perish in the attempt. Brave, self-confident, ruthless, they pose amid an odd assortment of navigational, astronomical and musical instruments. In the foreground is the distorted shape of a skull.

21 Europeans in America
c. 1519–1600

While Magellan was sailing across the world, Spanish soldiers - the *conquistadors* - moved in on to the mainland of America to conquer the Aztec and Inca empires, which collapsed with pitiful speed before the assaults of a handful of adventurers who possessed superior weapons and almost inhuman ruthlessness and greed.

As we saw in Part I (Chapter 11), America's first inhabitants came from Asia about 12 000 years ago, moved southwards, learnt to cultivate maize and, around 1000 BC, developed the civilization of the Olmecs, whose influence spread through Central America and Peru.

During the next 2000 years, three civilizations grew up in these regions: the Maya of Guatemala and Honduras, the Aztecs of Mexico and the Incas of Peru. The Mayas, who flourished from about AD 300 to 900, built cities, with massive temples and palaces of stone, ornamented with carvings and wall pictures; in the city of Tikal alone, two vast pyramid temples were surrounded by some 350 lesser temples and mansions. Their priests studied the stars, worked out a precise calendar and devised a system of arithmetic,

Mayan mask, sculptured in lava, a grotesque face with slit eyes, flat nose and open mouth like that of a child about to scream. This kind of face may have been the continuation of a very old tradition, for similar masks have been found all over Central America.

counting in twenties and making use of the figure nought, long before it was introduced into Europe from India by the Arabs.

In about 900, this remarkable civilization collapsed, perhaps because the peasants overthrew their priest-rulers, but a revival took place in the higher parts of Yucatan where new cities were built; however, from about 975, the Mayas came to be ruled by the Toltecs of Mexico, a warlike people who introduced their own gods and human sacrifice. Their principal cities were now Chichen Itza and Mayapan.

In the 13th century, the Toltecs and the Mayas were conquered by the Aztecs, a people who had only recently settled in the Valley of Mexico, where on the islands of a lake they built themselves a magnificent capital called Tenochtitlan, on whose site now stands Mexico City. From their lake-city, they exercised despotic rule over an empire of 38 provinces, with 450

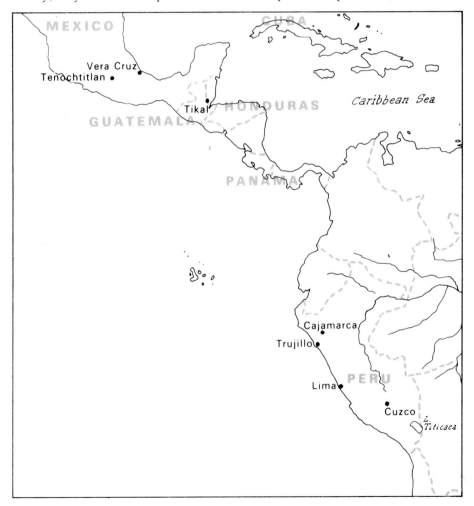

towns and some 15 million people who had to send them tribute and an unceasing supply of victims for sacrifice to the Aztec gods. This figure of 15 million was exceptionally large, for some 200 years later, England's population was only about 4½ million and that of France 8 to 10 million.

In the Andes mountains of South America, in what is now Peru, the Inca civilization grew out of earlier cultures, such as that of Chavin de Huantar, which between 1300 and 400 BC, produced stone temples to their cat-gods, and of the Paracas (400 BC–AD 400) who were expert weavers. A later Peruvian people, the Mochicas, built roads and viaducts to traverse the mountains as well as huge temples, like the Pyramid of the Sun at Trujillo, while, from about AD 1000, the Tiahuanaco people flourished in the plains south of Lake Titicaca, at 12 000 feet (3750 metres), the world's highest lake. By the 15th century, the Incas had organised most of the South American races into one empire which stretched from Ecuador to Chile and even included parts of Bolivia and Argentina. It was efficiently ruled by provincial governors appointed by the Inca emperor himself who, from his splendid capital at Cuzco, exercised a benevolent authority, so that the subject peoples did not hate their overlords in the way that the Mexican tribes hated the Aztecs.

The Incas built wonderful roads, with bridges and tunnels hewn out of the rocks; they piped water to irrigate the fields, organised a postal service with relays of swift runners, built factories for making cloth, pottery and jewellery and storehouses for emergency supplies of maize. They knew how to work gold and silver, but had no knowledge of iron, the arch or the wheel, no money and no written language.

In 1519, the Spanish governor of Cuba, fired by rumours of a city fabulously rich in gold, organised an expedition to the mainland. At its head was Hernando Cortes, the 34-year-old son of a poor nobleman who had come out to the New World in search of a fortune; brave, cruel and infinitely resourceful, he landed at a place he called Vera Cruz, burnt his ships to destroy any idea of retreat and advanced inland with no more than 400 men armed with guns and crossbows. He had, however, some cannons, 15 horses and a pack of fierce mastiff dogs, all of which were to fill the Aztecs and the subject Indian tribes with terror.

On the 200-mile march through jungles and mountains towards the Valley of Mexico, Cortes gained allies from the tribes who hated their Aztec oppressors. At length, the conquistadors reached Tenochtitlan, more magnificent than any city they had ever seen in Europe; to their surprise, they were welcomed by the Emperor Montezuma, who believed that Cortes was the god Quetzacoatl returning to claim his kingdom. He therefore greeted them with reverence and lodged them in one of his palaces. After touring the city and observing its wealth and the temples filled with reeking

Cortes meets Montezuma at Tenochtitlan. An illustration from an Indian account of the battles fought by the Tlaxacalans, allies of the Spaniards against the Aztecs.

skulls, Cortes suddenly kidnapped Montezuma and began to rule in his stead. At this, the Aztecs chose a new emperor and, in a bloody battle, drove the Spaniards out of the city, but Cortes was not to be beaten. From the surrounding countryside, he recruited a huge army of Indian warriors, with whose help he built a fleet of boats to cross the lake and destroy the beautiful city.

Cortes claimed Mexico for Spain and was rewarded by the Spanish King and Holy Roman Emperor Charles V with vast estates and the post of Governor, so that he ruled the country for several years, during which he explored the coastline and extended Spanish influence into Lower California.

When Bilbao sighted the Pacific Ocean, there was in his company a hardened adventurer named Francisco Pizarro, who stayed on in Panama to explore the country and work his way down the west coast of South America. On his journeys, he heard much about the wealth of the Incas, so, having obtained Charles V's permission to conquer the empire, he set out in 1530 with 180 men on what must have seemed an impossible adventure. But there was no limit to the tenacity of the conquistadors. So difficult was the country that it took them two years to penetrate to the city of Cajamarca in northern Peru, where they were well received by the Inca himself,

Atahualpa, whom Pizarro treacherously seized. In exchange for his release, the emperor offered the Spaniards a room filled with gold but, as soon as the treasure was amassed, Pizarro murdered Atahualpa and set out to capture the capital, Cuzco, and to slaughter the Inca nobles.

With its leadership destroyed, the empire collapsed and, like Mexico, became a province of Spain, ruled by a Spanish Viceroy, assisted by Spanish civil servants and Spanish priests. The new rulers – or the best of them – tried to establish an orderly society; they built many cities, including Lima, Peru's new capital, churches, hospitals and schools; priests and missionaries devoted their lives to educating the Indians and converting them to Christianity. But, in spite of these efforts, the real aim of the regime was to extract wealth, so that the native people were forced to mine the rich gold and silver deposits – work which was so uncongenial to them that they died in thousands or fled to the mountains. Within a few years of the conquests, the Indian population had been so reduced that the only way in which to find labour to work the silver mines, cattle ranches and sugar plantations was to import negro slaves from Africa.

In the Pope's division of the world, the Treaty of Tordesillas awarded Brazil to Portugal; Rio de Janeiro was colonised and, from the 1530's, emigrants went out to settle the coastal region, to found the city of Bahia as the capital and to establish sugar and tobacco plantations. The settlers' demand for labour brought a new importance to the Portuguese stations in West Africa, where slaves could be bought from African chiefs who enriched themselves by raiding neighbouring tribes. Angola, lying south of the River Congo, became the main supply base for slaves who were shipped from the port of Luanda to Brazil and thence, often, to the West Indies, where the Spanish settlers readily paid for slaves with silver.

This incessant demand for slaves arose from the fact that the growing of sugar and tobacco (and later of cotton) called for large numbers of workers in a climate that was too hot for Europeans to work out of doors; furthermore, the native peoples were not numerous and, if subjected to slavery, were inclined to disappear into the mountains and forests, or simply to sicken and die.

By 1600, it is estimated that upwards of a million Africans were landed in the New World, mostly by the Portuguese, but the slave trade was to become far bigger and more lucrative in the 17th and 18th centuries, when it was taken over by the Dutch, the French and, above all, the British, that is to say, by the leading maritime nations possessing the ships needed for that ghastly trade.

Portugal lost her independence in 1580, when Philip II of Spain made a successful bid for the crown. This meant that for the next 60 years, Spain held the lion's share of the world's silver and gold, spices and sugar, though, strangely enough, she gained little benefit from this astonishing good fortune.

In North America, in the great countries now called the United States and Canada, no civilizations developed like those of the Aztecs and the Incas, for the native inhabitants (later called Red Indians), although doubtless descended from the same people who had originally crossed the Bering Strait from Asia, never achieved similar levels of organised life in towns and cities. Under their chiefs, tribes, such as the Iroquois, Cheyenne, Pawnee, Blackfeet, Algonquin, Cherokee and the Huron, lived mainly by hunting, though they also grew maize in small fields round their villages. They knew how to make fire, pottery, canoes and transportable tent-houses, but had no domestic animals, except dogs, no wheeled vehicles and no knowledge of iron, though some knew how to work copper. Those in the south learned much from the Spaniards in Mexico and California; they stole horses and became skilful riders, and, in time, they acquired European weapons.

As yet, however, there was no clash with the white man, for after John Cabot's voyages, no-one took much interest in the lands lying to the north of the Caribbean. Jacques Cartier, the French navigator, certainly discovered the St Lawrence River in 1536, but there was no attempt yet at settlement. The Englishmen, Martin Frobisher and John Davis, tried to find the North-West Passage to China and Sir Humphrey Gilbert, the English navigator, perished on his way home from Newfoundland after a vain attempt to found a colony there. Two years later, in 1585, Sir Walter Raleigh sent out a party of colonists to Roanoke Island in the 'new land' of Virginia, but that project also failed and it was not until 1607 that the first European colony took permanent root in North America.

22 The Reformation and its Aftermath 1517 – 1600

The Catholic Church, with the Pope at its head, was for centuries the greatest civilizing influence throughout Western Europe. It founded schools and universities, inspired writers, philosophers, artists and musicians, taught men and women what to believe and, because it was the only Church in the West, gave them a sense of unity, no matter whether they were French or Italian or English.

Unfortunately, between about 1300 and 1500, the era of the Avignon Popes and the Great Schism, the Church's reputation sank lower than in the 9th century and, by this time, there were far more men of learning and idealism who realised its faults and dared to voice their opinions. The Renaissance, with its 'new learning', exchange of ideas and increase in medical and scientific knowledge, prompted them to question some of the teachings of the Church and the conduct of the clergy, including the Pope himself.

The monasteries had, generally, become rich land-owning institutions in which the monks lived comfortable lives and abbots, perforce, became worldly men of business; cardinals and bishops acted as statesmen and often lived in the magnificent style of princes, while many of the friars and parish priests were notorious for their greed and for keeping wives contrary to Church law. Nunneries, far less numerous than monasteries, were mostly small and rather poor; they existed chiefly as homes for well-to-do widows and spinsters and, while some occupied themselves with needlecraft and good works, there were frequent complaints of the nuns' love of finery and gossip.

What seemed particularly wrong was the practice called *simony*, whereby positions in the Church - say, a bishopric or a rich abbacy - were bought and sold; another evil was *nepotism*, the practice favoured by some high Churchmen of giving lucrative positions to nephews and other relatives, and it was wellknown that some of the Popes were elected as the result of bribery.

From time to time, men like Wycliffe, Erasmus, John Huss and Savonarola (d.1498), the friar of Florence, dared to protest against this widespread corruption, but the Church was so powerful that criticism could lead to

Woodcuts, the *Passional Christi und Antichristi,* from the studio of Lucas Cranach. In their zeal to attack the Catholic Church, Lutherans in Germany distributed many pictures such as these two which contrast the suffering of Christ with the Pope's life of ease and opulence. Some of the woodcuts were both violent and obscene.

charges of heresy, for which the penalty might be imprisonment or death. Both Huss and Savonarola were executed.

The man whose attacks on the Church led to the movement called the Reformation was a German monk named Martin Luther. On a visit to Rome, he was shocked by what he felt was the wickedness of the Papal court and, back in Germany, he became enraged by the sale of 'indulgences', pieces of paper which appeared to grant forgiveness of sins to anyone who paid a sum of money to one of the 'pardoners' who were touring Europe. The Pope had hit upon this means of raising funds to complete the rebuilding of St Peter's Cathedral in Rome and a Dominican friar called Tetzel was particularly successful in wheedling money out of the German peasants.

In 1517, when Tetzel arrived in his neighbourhood, Luther nailed to the church door at Wittenberg, a document attacking indulgences and other abuses in 95 'theses' or arguments. The effect was dramatic. In a short time, thanks to the new printing-presses, all Germany knew about the protest and could read the famous list of arguments. The Pope ordered Luther to withdraw his criticism and, when he refused to do so, issued a Bull, or papal order, excommunicating him. Luther and his supporters burned the Bull in Wittenberg market place, an act of defiance which brought about his condemnation as a heretic.

Luther's basic belief was that a man could achieve salvation only by faith in God and that he needed no priests or services of the Catholic Church to stand between him and God. At the Diet (assembly) of Worms in 1521,

Martin Luther
(1483-1546) by Lucas
Cranach, whose portrait
reveals the man's strength
of purpose, his peasant
origin, simplicity and rich
if sometimes coarse good
humour.

before the Holy Roman Emperor Charles V, the princes, dukes and bishops of Germany, he defended his beliefs with passionate sincerity, and, although the Emperor declared him an outlaw, he escaped punishment because Frederick of Saxony took him under his protection in the castle of Wartburg.

In any case, there was massive support for Luther in Germany. Many people felt that he was right in his attacks on the Church; the merchant class resented the drain of money to Rome and a number of German princes saw that breaking away from the Pope's authority meant breaking or at least weakening the Emperor's authority and therefore increasing their own independence. There was also the chance of acquiring the lands and wealth of the monasteries.

Charles V, a sincere Catholic, was much troubled by these events, for, with Spain to rule and at war with France, he wanted peace in Germany. His firmness won over some of the waverers, especially in the south, and a League of Catholic States was formed, including Austria, Bavaria and the Rhineland. Opposed to it was the League of Protestant States (they 'protested' against the Emperor's edict to put an end to Lutheran practices), mainly in the north, such as Saxony, Prussia, Brandenburg and Hesse.

Inspired by Luther's revolt, peasants in the Black Forest and central areas of Germany rebelled against their feudal overlords, but they looked in vain for support from Luther, himself the son of a miner. He even attacked their uprising in a pamphlet called 'Against the Murdering, Thieving Hordes of Peasants' and, after their defeat in the Peasants' War (1524-5), showed no compassion for their sufferings in the merciless punishment dealt out by the princes.

Luther, who lived until 1546, wrote many tracts, one of them a stinging reply to Henry VIII of England's defence of the Pope, but his greatest work was his masterly translation of the Bible into German. To a great part of the nation, he was a hero who had given them a new faith, but to many others, he was a heretic whose blasphemies only strengthened their loyalty to the old religion.

Germany remained divided and, after a war in which Charles V tried in vain to crush the independence of the states and to restore the unity of the Church, a kind of solution was agreed upon. By the peace of Augsburg (1555) each ruler was given the right to decide the religion of his subjects.

Meanwhile, another reform movement arose in Switzerland, where Ulrich Zwingli attacked the practices of the Catholic Church, though he and Luther did not entirely agree with one another. Zwingli, killed in a battle between Catholics and Protestants, was succeeded by John Calvin, a French lawyer, who, instead of bishops and priests, would have only ministers or elders chosen by their own congregations. Almost every kind of pleasure and light-hearted behaviour was regarded as sinful and at Geneva, which became the Protestant centre of Europe, Calvin set up a Church republic run by his own converts.

This strict gloomy faith (in which some men, 'the Elect', are chosen for salvation, while the rest of mankind are destined for eternal damnation)

JOHN KNOX

Engraved from Beza's Collection.

London Published 1 Jan.y 1798, by Robert Wilkinson N.º 58 Cornhill.

John Knox (1513-72), the Scottish reformer, whose Lutheran views caused him to be sent to the French galleys. Released, he eventually went to Geneva, where he met Calvin and became a permanent convert to Calvinist Protestantism. Back in Scotland, his fiery preaching won many converts and his unwavering hostility towards the young Mary Queen of Scots, together with her own mistakes, had much to do with her downfall.

211

Henry VIII with Henry VII by Holbein, who makes a telling contrast between the flamboyant prince of the Renaissance and his sober, much wiser, father.

spread into France, where the Protestants were known as Huguenots, into the Dutch Netherlands, parts of Germany and Scotland. From Geneva, John Knox returned to Edinburgh and, by his fiery preaching, converted most of the Lowland Scots to Calvinism, which in Scotland came to be called the Presbyterian religion. This conversion put an end to the old alliance between Scotland and France and led to the overthrow of the Catholic Mary Queen of Scots, widow of Francis II of France.

In England, the Reformation began by accident. Luther's teachings had made little impact and the Pope gave Henry VIII the title 'Defender of the

Faith' for his answer to Luther's 95 arguments. However, by 1527, Henry wanted a divorce from Catherine of Aragon, because she had borne him no sons and his eye had fallen upon Anne Boleyn. Unfortunately, the Pope, who would normally oblige an important monarch, was powerless to act, for he was virtually the prisoner of the Holy Roman Emperor Charles V, Catherine's nephew. Angered by delays that went on for years, Henry took the law into his own hands, had Cranmer, the Archbishop of Canterbury, declare his marriage void, married Anne and proclaimed himself Supreme Head of the Church of England.

The break with Rome was confirmed by Henry's seizure of the monasteries (1536-40), for, by selling off their vast lands to those who could afford to buy them, he won over to his side a large and influential class of the community.

But Henry was never a Protestant at heart and it was only after his death, in Edward VI's reign (1547-53), that the Reformation really made strides in England, owing to the return of converts from Geneva and the influence of sincere reformers like Protector Somerset, Cranmer, Hooper, Coverdale and Ridley. Queen Mary (1553-8), daughter of Catherine of Aragon, tried to put the clock back, for she married the Catholic champion, Philip II of Spain, and did her utmost to restore what she believed to be the true religion.

Her persecution of Protestants, mild though it was by continental standards, produced such a reaction that it was essential for her successor, Elizabeth (1558-1603), to find some kind of solution to a dispute that could tear the country apart. Her Settlement confirmed the separation from Rome and the Pope's authority; the monarch was made 'Governor' of the Church of England, services would be said in English and everyone had to attend church on Sundays. But there was to be no persecution and, as long as people did not openly challenge the official state religion, they could pray as they pleased. Elizabeth remarked that she had no wish to open 'windows into men's souls', and, in countless homes, Catholic services went on in private. The Elizabethan Settlement pleased neither side, but it worked and prevented the outbreak of religious war.

THE COUNTER-REFORMATION

To Roman Catholics, Protestantism was a terrible heresy. Anyone holding opinions different from the official teachings of the Church had always been considered to be a heretic and, from the late 12th century, the Inquisition was set up to deal with heretics. Inquisitors, i.e. investigators, who were usually Dominican friars, were sent out to question suspects and their powers to imprison, torture and execute the innocent and the guilty filled people with terror.

213

In Spain, Ferdinand and Isabella, with their chief Inquisitor, a monster of cruelty named Torquemada, used the Inquisition to get rid of the Moors and the Jews and to confiscate their property. However, as Protestantism took root in northern Europe, Catholics came to realise that it would not be defeated by terror; the Church must reform itself and elect Popes for their piety and powers of leadership, instead of for political reasons; their example would then encourage cardinals, bishops and priests to live and work as servants of God. Thus began the Counter-Reformation.

In 1534, a Spanish nobleman, Ignatius Loyola, who had been a soldier, formed the Society of Jesus to win back souls for the Catholic Church. Its members, known as Jesuits, had to be tough, brave and scholarly, for they took vows to give up their homes and to go out into the world to preach and convert the heathens and the heretics. Encouraged by Pope Paul III, they were brilliantly successful, winning back Poland and southern Germany to Catholicism and travelling all over the world as missionaries. Jesuits went to the New World to befriend and convert the Indians; they set up missionary stations in Africa, India, China and Japan and everywhere they went, they founded schools and colleges. These were often on the borders of Protestant countries, so they could educate boys to become priests and keep alive the Catholic faith.

The Holy Roman Emperor Charles V, who was greatly concerned by the state of the Church, urged the Pope to call a meeting to discuss ways of putting things right and from 1545-63, the Council of Trent (a place in Germany) met regularly to define Catholic beliefs and put an end to certain practices, such as indulgences.

These measures helped to purify the Church, but the Counter-Reformation was only partially successful. It failed to heal the split in the Christian Church, for, by 1600, half of Germany, Switzerland, the Dutch Netherlands, Sweden, Denmark, Norway, England, Scotland and Wales were Protestant countries. In most of them, there were still Catholics who practised their religion, often in secrecy and fear, as did the Huguenots in Catholic France. Protestantism never made much headway in Italy and Spain.

One thing was certain: there was no - or next to no - tolerance of one side for the other. People, like Queen Elizabeth, who had no strong religious feelings, were rare exceptions, for in an age which believed that the salvation of a man's eternal soul was more important than his life on earth, there was no room for mercy or an open mind.

23   Europe in the 16th Century

By his marriage to Mary of Burgundy in 1477, the Hapsburg prince, Maximilian (Holy Roman Emperor from 1493), acquired Burgundy and the Netherlands. He had to give up Burgundy to France, but the addition of the prosperous Netherlands to the Hapsburg territories in Austria and Germany made Maximilian the strongest monarch in Europe and involved him in almost continuous war with France and Venice.

Marriages proved to be more profitable than war. Maximilian's son Philip married the Infanta Joanna (daughter of Ferdinand and Isabella of Spain), so their son, who became the Holy Roman Emperor Charles V (1500-58), inherited Spain, its overseas empire, the Netherlands and the Holy Roman Empire. His brother Ferdinand's marriage to Anne of Bohemia and Hungary brought both these kingdoms to the Hapsburgs.

FRANCE

This situation provoked most of the wars, alliances, rebellions and religious persecutions of 16th-century Europe. France, encircled by the Hapsburg lands, was compelled to fight for survival and its king, Francis I (1515-47), young, unprincipled and brilliantly artistic, conducted a personal feud with his rival, the grave, conscientious Charles V. They fought mostly in Italy for possession of Milan because it blocked the route between Spain and Germany. Each monarch had his successes, but Francis, captured at Pavia in 1525 and later released, died without having made any headway against his rival. His son, Henry II, who married Catherine de Medici and recovered Calais from the English, followed his father's example in persecuting his Protestant (Huguenot) subjects, yet, in order to embarrass Charles V, sent an army in support of a *Protestant* rebellion in Germany!

Henry II, killed in a jousting accident, was briefly succeeded by his son Francis II (1559-60), husband of Mary Queen of Scots, and then by his second son, the 10-year-old Charles IX. By this time, the burning question in France was religion, in spite of the fact that the Huguenots were not very numerous, except in the west and in the little kingdom of Navarre on the edge of the Pyrenees. However, the Huguenots took Calvin's view that their

Titian's portrait of Charles V (1500-58), Holy Roman Emperor and King of Spain, whose dominions included the Americas, Spain, Naples, Sicily, Germany, and the Low Countries. He faced opposition from France under his arch-rival, Francis I, from Lutherism in Germany and from the Turks pressing hard on the Empire's eastern frontier. He fought long and hard to preserve the Catholic religion and the medieval ideal of the Empire; disappointed and worn out by the immensity of his task, he resigned the Empire in 1555 and retired to a monastery in Spain.

loyalty and obedience were to their Church, not to the state, a dangerous attitude to take in the 16th century, and, far more serious, a group of powerful nobles, led by Condé, Prince of Navarre, a member of the Bourbon family, and Admiral Coligny, supported the Huguenots in the hope of weakening the King's authority and increasing their own power. The extreme Catholics were led by the Duc de Guise and, later, by his son.

Catherine de Medici, ruling for her son, Charles IX, tried to restore peace by granting religious toleration, but, infuriated by her policy, the Guises fomented the Wars of Religion which lasted, on and off, from 1562-98.

In search of unity, Catherine arranged for her daughter to marry Henry of Navarre. The marriage took place on 18 August 1572, when thousands of Henry's fellow-Huguenots were gathered in Paris to celebrate the wedding. Queen Catherine, jealous of Coligny and now alarmed by the increase of Protestant power, authorised the murder of the Huguenot leaders. The opportunity was too good to miss by Catholic extremists and on 24 August, in the dark of night, some 8000 Huguenots were dragged from their beds and massacred. The slaughter continued for another month in the provinces.

The Massacre of St Bartholomew's Eve horrified Europe and left France isolated, but the struggle went on, until, in 1589, Henry III, the last of Catherine's sons to occupy the throne, was assassinated, leaving the way open for Henry of Navarre. As Henry IV, Navarre still had to fight the Catholic faction, but, finding that the majority of the nation would never accept a Protestant king, he decided to become a Catholic. 'Paris is worth a Mass!' he declared and, having at last entered the capital, this intelligent, likeable man devoted the rest of his life to restoring law and order.

In 1598, things were sufficiently calm for him to sign the Edict of Nantes, giving civil and religious toleration to the Huguenots, and with his chief minister, Sully, he continued to work for the country's good, until he was assassinated in 1610 by a religious fanatic. Considered by many people to be the greatest of all the kings of France, Henry IV strengthened the Crown's authority and founded the line of Bourbon kings who were to rule France for the next 200 years.

SPAIN

As we have seen, Spain's unification under Ferdinand and Isabella and the exploits of her mariners and conquistadors made her the richest country in Europe. In 1556, Charles V, worn out by the task of ruling his vast possessions, retired to a monastery and was succeeded as King of Spain by his son, Philip II. The Holy Roman Empire and the Hapsburg lands went to his brother, Ferdinand I, but Philip retained the Netherlands.

Philip was a strange man. Industrious, pious, so melancholy that he rarely smiled or took any pleasure, his unswerving aims in life were to make Spain supreme, to champion the Catholic Church and to wipe out heresy wherever it occurred. He rarely travelled to inspect his domains, to meet his subjects or to see how his orders were carried out, but remained all day and every day, year in and year out, in a room of the Escorial, the grim palace which he built not far from Madrid. He ruled by correspondence, sending out a ceaseless stream of instructions and advice to his officials in distant parts of the world, patiently sifting through the mass of reports and requests that came back to Spain and himself attending to every detail in every part of his empire.

Before his accession, Philip had married Queen Mary I of England, hoping thereby to improve Spain's hold on the Netherlands, but he failed to endear himself to his wife's subjects and, after a year, he deserted her in order to take over his inheritance.

Philip never shirked what he felt to be his duty. In Spain, he destroyed every trace of Protestantism and put heavy pressure on the Moors still living in Granada; he also intervened from time to time in the French Wars of

Religion and sent warships to join the fleet commanded by Don John of Austria when he defeated the Turks at Lepanto. He conquered Portugal in 1580 and, as well as concerning himself with the Spanish colonies in the New World, he had to find time to deal with the troublesome heretics of England and the Netherlands.

Yet, in spite of his infinite patience and industry, Philip left a shaky empire to his son by his third wife, Anne of Austria. Spain's wealth was largely an illusion, for her armies and navies were immensely costly; the Netherlands, instead of being an asset, became a drain on Spain's resources; English, Dutch and Huguenot pirates damaged her trade and, owing to inefficiency and dishonesty, only a fraction of the gold and silver from Peru ever reached the royal Treasury, so that Philip, apparently so rich, was, in fact, bankrupt. It was an age of inflation and the gold which did reach Spain was not invested in the industries and farming techniques which would have produced real wealth. Between the privileged aristocracy and the peasants there was no substantial middle class of manufacturers, merchants and properous farmers and thus, for these various reasons, Spain's greatness was short-lived and, from about 1600, a long period of decline lay ahead of her.

REVOLT OF THE NETHERLANDS

The 17 provinces of the Low Countries had long had their own ruling councils, called Estates, their rights and privileges, which Charles V had respected during the period when Calvinism took root in the northern part (now the Netherlands), while the southern provinces (now Belgium) remained Catholic.

In spite of the Netherlanders' prosperity and the importance to Spain of cities like Antwerp, one of the principal ports of Europe and the leading money markets, Bruges and Ghent, Philip felt it his duty to wipe out the Protestant heresy. Accordingly, during the rule of his half-sister, Margaret of Parma, he had Spanish troops sent into the country to enforce the work of the Inquisition, whereupon the Dutch, as the Netherlanders were generally called, broke into revolt, sacked churches and smashed images. Sterner measures were obviously needed, so Margaret was replaced by the grim Duke of Alva, who, at the head of an army of the toughest soldiers in Europe, imposed an iron rule, during which thousands of Protestants were executed and many more fled to England and Germany.

In their plight, the Dutch found a heroic leader in William of Nassau, Prince of Orange, affectionately known from his ability to keep quiet when it was wisest to do so, as William the Silent. He was, in fact, a German, who had inherited his title and been brought up at Charles V's court, where he became a Catholic and a favourite of the Emperor. However, the sufferings of his adopted people caused him to turn Protestant and, as an outlaw, to organise and lead the Dutch resistance.

He endured defeats, the deaths of three brothers, loss of his estates and fortune, but he never despaired and eventually the tide literally turned in his favour, for the Dutch, taking to the sea and calling themselves 'The Sea Beggars', played havoc with the Spanish shipping along the coast and, once, when the inland town of Leyden was about to be captured, came sailing to the rescue across the low-lying fields which William had ordered to be flooded. After this, Alva retired and, although the Duke of Parma took over command and the Spanish troops sacked Antwerp with such savage fury that the city never fully recovered, there was no way finally to subdue the Dutch.

Thus, in 1579, the seven northern provinces formed themselves into the United Provinces and, two years later, proclaimed themselves independent, with William the Silent as their president or *Stadtholder*. That fine man, who was called 'the wisest, gentlest and bravest man who ever led a nation' was assassinated in 1584, but his son, Maurice of Nassau, a brilliant soldier, carried on the struggle. Elizabeth of England sent help; English, Scottish and German volunteers fought alongside the Dutch and, although the southern provinces remained Spanish, Parma had to relax the pressure in order to prepare for the arrival of the Armada which was meant to put an end to the Anglo-Dutch partnership.

By 1609, the Spaniards had to agree to a 12 years' truce and, in 1648, the Dutch, by now grown rich, as well as powerful at sea, finally won their freedom; their country, the Republic of the United Provinces, soon came to be called Holland.

One of the truly remarkable features of this long struggle for national and religious survival was not so much that the Dutch grew rich whilst fighting a desperate war, but that in its latter stages, they created their golden age of painting. Rubens (1577-1640), Van Dyck, Franz Hals and Rembrandt were painting their masterly portraits and religious pictures while the fighting was still going on; Hobbema and Vermeer not long after independence had been won.

ENGLAND

The English, having been a scourge to France during the Hundred Years' War, withdrew from the continent after their defeat and, while the nobility devoted themselves to self-destruction during the Wars of the Roses, the bulk of the nation got on with the business of trade, manufacture, farming and fishing. Thus, when Henry VII came to the throne as the first of the Tudors, he acquired, not a ruined land, but a fairly prosperous kingdom, and, once he had overawed the nobles, he was able to amass a fortune, advance the power of the crown and arrange advantageous marriages for his children without getting embroiled in costly wars.

His son, Henry VIII (1509-47) a less wise but more colourful character, tried to cut a figure in Europe, first by joining the Pope, the Holy Roman Emperor and Ferdinand of Aragon (his father-in-law) in an attack on France and, later, by dangling England's support between the rivals, Francis I and Charles V. His military exploits were more expensive than glorious, and, ironically, the greatest victory of his reign was won during his absence in France, when, at Flodden (1513), the Earl of Surrey defeated the Scots with terrible slaughter. Among the slain was King James IV, whose heir, as so often in Scottish history, was a tiny child.

During these campaigns and intrigues, Thomas Wolsey practically ruled the kingdom, but the able upstart fell from grace when he failed to secure Henry's divorce; his successor, the odious Thomas Cromwell, organised the destruction of the monasteries, but, as the reign progressed, Henry took the reins of power into his own hands, ruling as a tyrant and striking down anyone who incurred his suspicion. No English king ever held such absolute power over his subjects, who, it must be said, mostly liked him for his flamboyant style and defiance of the Pope, but he left the kingdom far less secure than he had found it and, during the reigns of his successors, Edward VI and Mary I, England's fortunes sank still lower.

At her accession, in 1558, Elizabeth inherited a land whose Treasury was empty, its coinage debased, its people uneasy and divided by their religious beliefs. Her own right to the throne was doubtful; Henry II of France might well mount an invasion to put his son's wife, Mary Queen of Scots, in her place, while Philip of Spain could claim his dead wife's kingdom and, in the meantime, was offering to marry Elizabeth.

That she surmounted all these difficulties is the measure of her greatness. Luck, a wily adviser in William Cecil, and her own character and upbringing came to her rescue. She knew that Philip would never allow the French to dominate England and cut his sea-route to the Netherlands; moreover, as long as she kept him and the rest of the royal suitors on tenterhooks over her marriage, she could play for time, the time she needed to settle the religious question, to rebuild her father's navy and win her people's devotion. And so it happened. Henry II died and, within a year, his son, Francis II, also died, so that Mary, Queen of Scots went back to Scotland where John Knox had already broken the French alliance. He gave anything but a warm welcome to a Catholic queen and, within a few years, deposed from the throne through ill-fortune and her own folly, she fled to England where Elizabeth kept her a prisoner for 19 years.

Meanwhile, although Philip had his hands full with the multifarious business of his empire and the revolt in the Netherlands, he never gave up his intention to bring the English heretics and their double-dealing Queen to book. He sent Jesuits into the country to hearten the Catholic minority, agents to assist the plots surrounding Mary Queen of Scots and troops to help the Catholic rebels in Ireland, while, for her part, Elizabeth encouraged her sea-captains to rob the Spanish treasure-ships and sent 'underhand' help to the Dutch.

In 1586, Mary Queen of Scots was executed. At the end, she left her claim to the English throne, not to her son James, but to Philip himself, who, from his desk in the Escorial, planned the invasion with his usual attention to detail. A great fleet of warships and troop transports was assembled in Cadiz harbour, while, in the Netherlands, Parma put his men to work digging canals and building barges.

Drake's raid on Cadiz delayed matters, but, in 1588, the Armada, 130 strong, of which about 50 were men-of-war, set sail under the command of the Duke of Medina Sidonia, a mild man with no naval experience, whose master ordered him to make no attack on the English coast until he had joined forces with Parma.

On 19 July, the great fleet in crescent formation was sighted making slowly up-Channel and the English, commanded by Lord Howard of Effingham with Drake as vice-admiral, left their harbours to attack. Their 40 or so royal warships, faster, more manoeuvrable and lower in the water than the Spanish galleons, were supported by as many as 150 merchantmen and fishing-boats, but a part of the main fleet, under Lord Seymour, had been diverted to the Downs off the Kent coast to keep watch on Parma.

A running battle lasting nine days took place, in which the English damaged a good number of the enemy, but failed to break their formation, for the Spaniards' seamanship was of a high order and their gunnery unexpectedly good. On the 27th, Medina Sidonia brought the Armada safely to anchor off Calais; so far he had carried out his task to perfection and all that remained was to join Parma and invade England. But there was no sign of Parma and his army, for no precise rendezvous had been arranged; moreover (and this was the fatal flaw in Philip's plan) there was no friendly port along the coast with water deep enough to shelter the great warships.

Nevertheless, the situation was critical for the English commanders. Somehow they must break up the enemy fleet and, in the night of 28th, they decided to use fireships to achieve what their gunnery had failed to do. Eight merchantships were set ablaze and allowed to drift on tide and wind into the crowded anchorage. In the darkness, the Spaniards cut their cables and made out to sea as best they could, but dawn saw the fleet scattered along the coast, some already aground, some trying to reform but all without orders as the English squadrons sailed in to the attack. The crucial battle off Gravelines lasted all day, when the Spaniards suffered such damage that the invasion was now out of the question and Medina Sidonia's best hope was to save what remained of the fleet. With a south-west gale blowing up, all he could do was to sail north and return round the north of Scotland.

Howard kept up the pursuit until out of stores and ammunition, but the Spanish ships had greater danger to contend with, for Atlantic gales wrecked many of them on the rocky coasts and only 53 battered vessels got back to Spain, where Philip, displaying splendid dignity, refused to upbraid the hapless Medina Sidonia. 'I sent you out,' he said, 'to war with men and not with the elements'.

The Armada's defeat was not the end of the war, nor the end of Spain's navy. In fact, she recovered remarkably well and there were few successes for the English until 1598, when Howard, Raleigh and young Essex sacked the port of Cadiz to forestall another invasion attempt.

However, the legend of those summer days in 1588, when England stood to arms and the Queen went down from London to Tilbury to address her troops, while the sea-captains were tackling a mighty fleet - 'the greatest and strongest combination that ever was in Christendom' - provided a tremendous uplift in national pride and self-confidence. The English knew they had been saved by a miracle, but that surely proved that God was on their side and on the side of the Protestant cause.

Theirs was only a small country, with a population of perhaps 4 million, compared with France's 15 millions and Spain's 7 million. As mariners, they had nothing like the experience of the Spaniards and Portuguese, who had divided the world between themselves, so when the English did start making ocean voyages, they were regarded as trespassers and forbidden to trade. However, Willoughby and Chancellor, trying to find a north-east passage to Cathay (China), did reach the White Sea, north of Russia and Chancellor made his way to Moscow where he arranged a trading pact with Ivan the Terrible. Frobisher and John Davis explored the inhospitable seas of northern Canada, but, further south in the Caribbean and along the Spanish Main, Hawkins, Drake and other sea-dogs took to piracy, robbing the Spanish ships at sea and looting their settlements ashore. Like Magellan, Drake sailed round the world, amassing treasure and claiming California (New Albion) on the way, while, at home, Hawkins was patiently building up the navy that beat the Armada.

These exploits were only a part of the astonishing upsurge of enterprise and creative energy that occurred in Elizabeth's reign, when England suddenly produced so many men of action who wrote books and poems, built splendid houses and composed music. Raleigh was a courtier, soldier, writer, historian, explorer and would-be coloniser; Sir Philip Sydney, a hero-poet; Gilbert, an explorer and man of letters: Spenser, Ben Jonson, Surrey and Shakespeare wrote exquisite poetry, while composers like Dowland, Tallis

Elizabeth I (1533-1603) by or after G. Gower, one of the earliest English painters, probably in 1588, the year of the Armada, when, at 55, the Queen donned armour and rode down to Tilbury to address her troops, declaring that although she had 'but the body of a weak and feeble woman', she possessed 'the heart of a king'. By her courage and artful ability to keep both friends and enemies guessing, she saved England from disaster and created a legend to inspire her people. Yet, like her father (though for better reasons), she left problems in plenty for her successor.

and Byrd set poems to music. To compose verses, sing part-songs and madrigals, play an instrument and dance with solemn elegance or frenzied energy were necessary accomplishments for every educated person, while the newly-built theatres provided Londoners with marvellously varied entertainment. The plays of Dekker, Webster, Marlowe and Ben Jonson belong to their age, but Shakespeare was a genius who transcends time.

In less than 30 years, the Elizabethans produced more poetry, drama, essays, music and philosophy than in the two preceding centuries.

Elizabeth died in 1603. No British monarch, not even Victoria in her old age 300 years later, ever inspired such devotion, yet, against the glories of her reign and the rising prosperity of the middle classes, must be set the misery of the poor, widespread unemployment and vagrancy, rising prices and a shortage of land. In Ireland, there were rebellions and savage oppression and Parliament, abjectly obedient to Henry VIII, was beginning to voice its demand for a bigger say in the country's government.

The great Queen had never married, so the crown passed to her cousin's, Mary Queen of Scots' son, James VI of Scotland, first of the four Stuart kings, whose conduct and stupidity were to have disastrous consequences for the monarchy.

224

PART THREE

The European Dominance

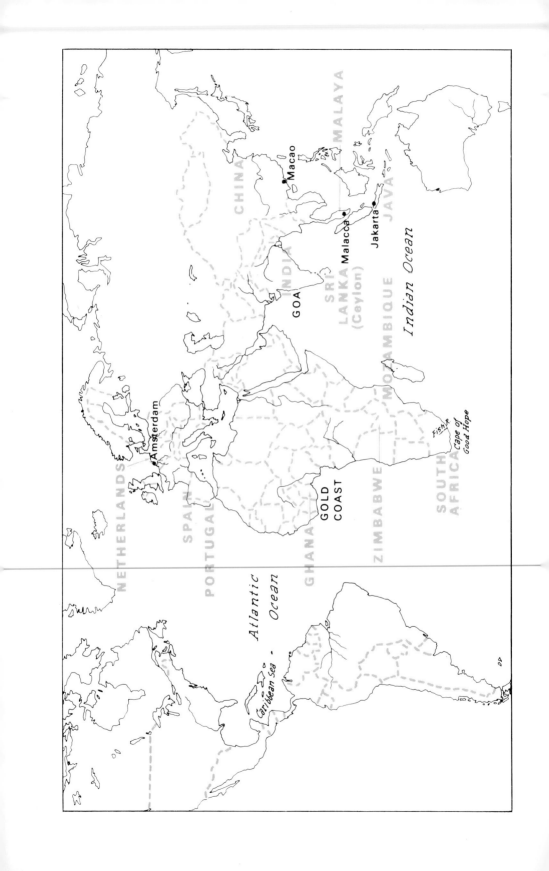

1 The Dutch Abroad
1602 – 50

During their struggle for freedom, the Dutch took to sea-faring with marked success. From attacks on Spanish shipping in home waters, they progressed to piracy in the Caribbean, where they harassed the galleons carrying silver to Spain.

Dutch merchants did business with the Portuguese, buying spices and silks brought to Lisbon from the East and re-selling them in European markets. However, when Philip II of Spain seized Portugal in 1580, this trade came to an end.

The Dutch were not deterred. Ignoring the Pope's division of the world into Spanish and Portuguese spheres, they made their own way to the East, rounding the Cape of Good Hope and sailing across the Indian Ocean to Ceylon (Sri Lanka) and Java, where they established Batavia (modern Jakarta) as their trading storehouse.

The Dutch East India Company, founded in 1602, soon broke the Portuguese control of eastern trade, for their ships were better armed, their trading goods superior and their officials sufficiently well-paid to give loyal service to the Company. After the Dutch captured Malacca, an important sea-port on the west coast of Malaya, in 1641, the Portuguese eastern empire dwindled to a few trading posts, such as Goa in India and Macao in China, leaving the lucrative trade in silks, spices, cotton, rice and sago almost wholly in Dutch hands.

The voyage from Amsterdam to Batavia took at least seven months and the Dutch found that they needed a landing place where they could obtain fresh water and stores. Consequently, a party of settlers, led by a surgeon named Jan van Riebeek, founded a victualling-station for the Company's ships at the Cape of Good Hope in 1652. After a hard struggle, they succeeded in raising cattle and vegetables to supply not only the Dutch vessels but ships belonging to other nations which called at the Cape.

At this time, South Africa was thinly populated by three main groups of people - the Bushmen, the Hottentots and the Bantu. The Bushmen, who had been forced southwards from central and eastern Africa by a more advanced culture, that of the Bantu, were hunters who lived in small groups of about a hundred. The Hottentots, who had similarly been pushed to the south by the Bantu, reached the Cape in about the 13th or 14th century and

Hottentots at Table Bay in the 18th century. Across the bay, on its south side, is Cape Town, South Africa's first city, with Table Mountain providing a magnificent backcloth.

developed a nomadic pastoral way of life depending on sheep and long-horned cattle. A remarkable increase in numbers of the Bantu in the Congo basin caused them to spread eastwards and southwards, and this movement compelled other peoples to migrate into parts of the continent that were practically uninhabited.

The Bantu used iron, grew millet and kept cows and goats; they moved slowly, but, by about AD 900, they had reached as far south as Mozambique and the first group, the Shona, had begun to establish itself on the borders of South Africa in Zimbabwe. The southernmost of the Bantu peoples, the Xhosa, arrived at the Fish River in South Africa in 1776.

As more settlers came out from the Netherlands, some of them chose to trek inland, moving their families and possessions by ox wagon to distant grasslands, where they lived isolated lives as cattle ranchers. Founded in this way, the Dutch Cape Colony came to be peopled by sturdy men and women calling themselves 'Boers' (from the Dutch word meaning a farmer), developing their own language into a form of Dutch now called 'Afrikaans', and employing black slaves, drawn from among the local Hottentots and brought from East Africa and Malaya.

228

The Boers, reared on the stern teachings of the Old Testament, regarded the black people as an inferior race fit only to be servants or, if troublesome, to be exterminated. Less docile than the Hottentots, the Bushmen raided the white men's farms, for, as hunters, they were naturally opposed to the settlers, but a more serious threat was that of the Bantu people whom the Boers called 'Kaffirs' ('unbelievers') and, from the mid-18th century, a number of merciless 'Kaffir Wars' took place, in which Europeans and Africans fought each other for land.

Not content with their control of eastern trade, the Dutch formed the Dutch West India Company in 1621 in order to take part in the Atlantic commerce. When Europeans found that sugar cane could be grown on the West Indian islands and that there were tremendous profits to be made from selling sugar in Europe, a great demand arose for slaves able to work in a hot climate. The obvious place to obtain them was West Africa where the Portuguese had been engaged in the slave trade for years, and the Dutch moved in with such determination that, by 1642, they had captured all the Portuguese forts along the Gold Coast.

For a time, they had things all their own way, carrying slaves and goods across the Atlantic to Spanish, English and French colonies. However, they were soon challenged by the French and English, who, from about 1650, realised that, with so much profit to be made, they too must have forts in West Africa. To a lesser extent, the Danes, Swedes and Germans also joined in the slave trade.

It worked this way: the European slave trader sailed to the West African coast with a cargo of guns, cloth, tools, knives, iron bars and alcohol, which he sold to the African chiefs in exchange for men and women who had been captured in tribal wars. He then sailed across the Atlantic to sell his human cargo at an enormous profit to plantation-owners in the New World. In addition, he usually carried a range of domestic goods that were eagerly bought by the settlers. With the money thus gained, he was able to buy sugar, silver and hides which he took back to Europe and sold at yet another profit. The 'triangular trade' as it was called, was so lucrative that an individual trader could enrich himself for life from the proceeds of two or three voyages.

2 Europeans Settle in North America 1536 – 1763

With the Spaniards firmly established in Central and South America, other Europeans (except the Portuguese in Brazil) had to content themselves with the cooler and apparently less wealthy lands to the north. Their object, at first, was not settlement but to find a way to the East.

In 1536, a French explorer, Jacques Cartier, discovered the Gulf of St Lawrence and sailed up the river as far as the site of Montreal. There he made friends with the local Indians who told him that he was in the land of Canada (the Huron-Iroquois word for a village) and that the kingdom of 'Saguenay', rich in precious stones, lay further to the west. Cartier never found the mythical kingdom and eventually came home to his native Brittany. However, some Breton fishermen went out to 'New France' and founded settlements on the shores of Newfoundland and in St Lawrence Bay.

In England, Sir Walter Raleigh, one of the most gifted men at Elizabeth's court, obtained permission to found a colony in the 'new land' to be named Virginia in honour of the Queen. The first expedition set sail in 1585, with a party of about 100 colonists who were put ashore on Roanoke Island lying off the coast of what is now North Carolina. From the start everything went wrong, for the Indians, friendly at first, could not supply foodstuffs indefinitely and the colonists had neither the skill nor the patience to grow corn and vegetables. They were therefore more than glad to be rescued in the following year by Francis Drake, himself returning from one of his Caribbean raids. Raleigh, still hopeful, raised the funds to send out a second expedition to Roanoke, but this, too, was a total failure, because it lacked the necessary stores to keep going until the colony got on its feet.

After these disasters, nearly 20 years passed before the next venture. Organised by the 'London Company in Virginia', a party of 105 colonists reached Chesapeake Bay in 1607 and built a settlement named Jamestown in honour of the new king, James I. Unfortunately, too many of the party were penniless gentlemen and ne'er-do-wells who had never handled an axe or a spade in their lives and the colony must have perished had it not been led by a man of resource and daring. His was Captain John Smith, an arrogant young soldier of fortune, who won the friendship of the Indians, traded with them for food and repulsed their attacks when they turned hostile.

The Virginia Company went bankrupt in 1624, but the colony was taken over by the Crown and began to prosper when a method was discovered of curing the Indian tobacco plant. In spite of James I's condemnation of the smoking habit, there was soon a brisk demand for tobacco in Europe, which presented a fine opportunity for younger sons of the English gentry to go out to Virginia to cultivate tobacco in big plantations worked by African slaves. In 1632, Lord Baltimore was granted no less than 7 million acres of land in Virginia, which he made into a new colony called Maryland after Charles I's wife, Henrietta Maria.

Carolina, lying south of Virginia, was founded in 1663 and, like its chief town, Charleston, was named after Charles II. Fifty years later, it was divided into two - North and South Carolina - for it had prospered from its principal

Earliest known illustration of a tobacco factory: from a history of the West Indies published in Paris 1667.

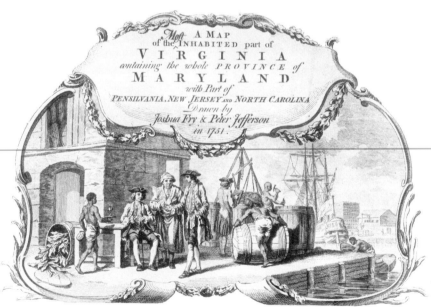

Sketch of a colonial tobacco wharf, from an 18th century map of Virginia.

An artist's impression of the Pilgrim Fathers landing, on 11 December 1620, at Plymouth Rock in Massachusetts Bay, where they built their first settlement.

crops, sugar and cotton, which, like tobacco, were grown on large plantations.

The last of the English colonies, Georgia, lying between South Carolina and Spanish Florida, owed its beginnings to General James Oglethorpe, a philanthropist, who obtained a charter from George II to found a colony for English debtors and persecuted European Protestants.

Meanwhile, a group of colonies, very different from Virginia and Carolina in spirit and climate, were struggling to their feet in the north. In 1620, an old ship called the *Mayflower*, left Plymouth in England for Virginia, carrying a party of 102 settlers, known to us now as the 'Pilgrim Fathers'. The leading group were Separatists, members of a strict Puritan sect, who had decided to seek a grant from the Virginia Company in order to found a colony in which they could live and worship in their own style. They first went ashore at Cape Cod and then built a settlement at a place they called New Plymouth, on the bleak coast of the colony that came to be named Massachusetts.

The local Indians proved to be friendly, but bitter weather and lack of food wiped out half the colony during the first winter. However, the survivors were saved by the arrival of stores, and, between 1628-40, Archbishop Laud's persecutions brought 20 000 Puritans from England. Most of them were well suited to the life of a pioneer - yeomen, craftsmen, sturdy farmer-

Penn's treaty with the Indians, 1683. As pacifists, the Quakers were opposed to fighting the Indians and Penn made a series of treaties with them for the purchase of land.

workers and small tradesmen, accustomed to hard work and imbued with an ardent, religious faith. The climate was harsh and the soil poor, but, by their own efforts and with help from merchant brethren at home, they founded a thriving colony, with Boston, its chief town and port.

Partly through religious differences, separate colonies came to be established - Connecticut and Rhode Island (1636), New Hampshire and Maine - to form a group known as New England, where Church elders presided over a kind of Bible Commonwealth of dour, earnest Protestants.

Between New England and Virginia, lay the New Netherlands, a central region, where the Dutch West India Company had bought Manhattan Island from the Indians and made it into a settlement called New Amsterdam. Its governor, Peter Stuyvesant, took strong measures against hostile Indians and did much to help the colony's expansion, but in 1664 he had to surrender to an English fleet sent out by James, Duke of York, brother of Charles II. Renamed New York, the settlement became the principal port of the Middle Colonies.

In 1680, Charles II repaid a royal debt by making a large grant of land in America to William Penn, a leader of the Quakers, another religious sect suffering a certain amount of persecution. Penn wanted to call his land 'Sylvania', which means 'woodland', but the King persuaded him to add his own name, so the new colony became Pennsylvania. Its capital was named Philadelphia, meaning 'brotherly love', and the good Quakers, practising what they preached, dealt honestly with the Indians who repaid them with friendship instead of hatred.

Thus, by the end of the 17th century, a long strip of English territory stretched down the Atlantic coast from New England to Spanish Florida. The people of these colonies looked to England to provide them with help and protection, but they already had their own elected Assemblies to run their affairs.

While these colonies were developing, the French were extending their influence over a vast area to the north and west. Samuel de Champlain, who first went out to Canada in 1603, explored part of the St Lawrence River, founded Quebec and helped his friends, the Algonkin and Huron warriors, to defeat the Iroquois. The New Englanders regarded these activities with hostility and, in 1629, they captured Quebec and had Champlain sent to England as a prisoner. He returned in 1633, when Canada was restored to the French, and carried on his work by encouraging younger men and Jesuit missionaries to get to know the Indians, their customs and languages.

Another remarkable Frenchman, René de la Salle, emigrated to Canada in about 1666 and spent several years exploring the country around and south of the Great Lakes. In 1681, at the head of a party of 50, La Salle travelled the length of the Mississippi down to the Gulf of Mexico to the spot where the city of New Orleans was to be built in later years. There he claimed the whole area watered by the great river and named it Louisiana in honour of Louis XIV.

Thanks mainly to de Champlain and La Salle, the French possessed enormous territory in North America. Much less numerous than the British and more closely supervised by their home government, they existed by farming alongside the St Lawrence River, fishing off Newfoundland and Nova Scotia, and trapping for furs in the endless forests. The tough Frenchmen got on well with the Indians, earning their respect for their skill as trappers and foresters and also because they traded fairly and had no desire to drive the Indians from their hunting-grounds.

At this time, there were probably between one and two million Indians living in the entire continent. Called 'Indians' because of Columbus's mistaken belief that he had found a new route to India, they were descendants of the aboriginal people who had crossed the Bering Strait more than 10 000 years earlier and had gradually spread inland and southwards.

Unlike the Maya, Inca and Aztec peoples, the North American Indians never rose above a primitive level of culture, because they were few in number considering the size of the continent, were weakly organised in numerous tribes and for the most part did not live in settled communities.

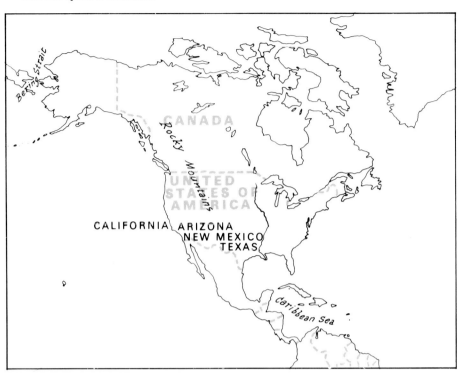

The tribes differed a good deal in appearance, language and occupation. The Eskimo-Indians of the Arctic area lived by fishing and hunting caribou, seal and walrus; the Indians of the north-west subsisted mainly on salmon and other fish; a number of small tribes like the Yorok and Pomo, skilled basket-makers, lived by hunting and food-gathering in California. To the south-west, in Arizona and New Mexico, the Pueblo Indians, named after the Spanish word *pueblo* for a village, grew maize, vegetables, melons and pumpkins in the river valleys, while in the same region the fierce Apaches and Navajo lived by hunting and pillage. Over the vast area between the Rockies and the Mississippi, the Plains Indians, whose tribes included the Blackfeet, Crow, Sioux, Cheyenne, Pawnee and Arapaho, depended for all their needs upon the buffalo (or bison), which provided them with food, clothing, tents, bone and horn implements and even a deity to worship. Lastly, the Woodlands Indians, of the Huron-Iroquois, Algonkin and Athabascan groups inhabited the eastern region from the Great Lakes down to Florida and Texas, living for the most part by hunting and primitive farming. The arrival of white settlers in such numbers that they soon outnumbered the entire Indian population caused tribes to move northwards into the forests, westward across the plains and down into the arid south-west. These migrations added pressure to the hunting-ranges, reduced the numbers of game animals and led to inter-tribal warfare.

Hostilities between the Europeans and North American Indians began in eastern Canada, where the first of the sealers and fishermen soon came into conflict with the local Eskimos. Southward, along the Atlantic coast and around the Great Lakes, there was already enmity between the Iroquois on the one side and the Hurons and Algonkin[1] on the other, when, in 1608, the French governor, Champlain, decided to help the Algonkin, thereby earning the undying hatred of the Iroquois. This had much to do with the eventual defeat of France in North America, for the powerful Iroquois tribes became allies of the English and fought alongside them for many years.

In New England, the most serious conflict was 'King Philip's War' of 1675-6, when the Wampanoag Indians, led by a chief called 'King Philip', wiped out a dozen settlements and bid fair to exterminate the colony. The settlers organised an army of militiamen who gradually got the upper hand and in the end virtually annihilated the tribe, though it was 1720 before they regained the western areas they had settled 50 years earlier.

In Virginia, the 1607 settlement at Jamestown came close to disaster from starvation and hostility of the local Indians under their chief, Powhatan. It was his daughter, Pocahontas, who is supposed to have saved the life of Captain John Smith, whose leadership brought the colony through its early perils. That friendship *was* possible between the 'pale faces' and the 'redskins' is shown by the fact that Pocahontas married an Englishman, became a celebrity in London and to this day is claimed as an ancestress by some of the 'first families' in Virginia.

The Ohio River runs west-south-west from Pennsylvania to join the Mississippi and in the 18th century its valley became an area of bitter dispute between the French and British, since it was the chief route to the west. To hold the Ohio Valley and link up Canada with Louisiana, the French built a line of forts which, according to the British colonists, infringed the territorial rights of Virginia. They realised of course that the French were barring their way to the interior and in the fighting which took place from time to time, a young officer named George Washington led his Virginian regiment with dash and reckless courage.

Thus, when the Seven Years' War broke out in Europe in 1756, there had already been years of unofficial fighting between the French and British in America and, as hostilities intensified, the position of the British colonists

Strictly speaking, Algonkin (Algonkian or Algonquin) is one of the 58 language stocks of American Indians; Algonkian tribes included the Blackfeet, Cheyenne, Chippewa, Cree, Delaware, Micmac, Ottawa and many others. Similarly, Iroquian was a linguistic stock whose tribes included the Iroquois, Hurons, Cherokee, Mohawks, Oneida, Six Nations, Wyandot, etc.

went from bad to worse. The local militiamen were undisciplined, the regulars were unused to fighting in backwoods and the English generals hopelessly incompetent, whereas the French, led by the brilliant Marquis de Montcalm, seemed certain of victory.

In England, William Pitt, who had taken charge of the war, saw what had to be done; he sent out new commanders, briefing them that the keys to the situation were the Ohio Valley and the French port of Louisburg, guarding the mouth of the St Lawrence River. Both must be taken. While the Royal Navy prevented French reinforcements reaching Canada, General Amherst secured the forts which had held the Ohio Valley and then went on to capture Louisburg. British warships could now sail up the St Lawrence River to Quebec.

The capital of French Canada, set high up on a cliff above the river, had already defied a strong attack and was apparently impregnable. However, Pitt chose 32-year-old James Wolfe, a nervy but dedicated protegé of Amherst, to command the operation and his army was brought safely up river by the Royal Navy to a point opposite the city where Montcalm commanded the French garrison. The siege lasted all through the summer of 1759 but, in spite of Wolfe's efforts, it seemed certain that the British would be forced to withdraw before winter set in.

In September, when Wolfe was ill and close to despair, a tiny path was discovered leading from a cove to the cliff-top and Wolfe, by getting his army up there at night and winning a decisive battle, in which both he and Montcalm were killed, assured himself of immortality.

In the following year, after Amherst had captured Montreal, the whole of Canada passed into British hands and when, in 1763, the Treaty of Paris ended this first world war, Britain was seen to have emerged with victory, prestige and a North American empire.

3 Monarchy Curbed
1603 – 88

When Elizabeth I died on 24 March 1603, the English crown passed as she had directed, to James VI of Scotland, the only son of her cousin, Mary Queen of Scots. The English people accepted him without demur as James I, for he was of Tudor descent and had been brought up as a Protestant; Parliament, which had begun to challenge the royal authority during Queen Elizabeth's reign, expected the newcomer to let it play a bigger part in governing the country.

James's success as ruler of Scotland was not repeated in England, where his animosity to the Puritans, his pro-Spanish foreign policy, and assertion of his Divine Right to rule without criticism from ordinary mortals made him exceedingly unpopular and drew various discontented groups together into a formidable opposition.

An event of James's reign whose dire consequences have lasted to the present day was the Plantation of Ulster (1608), by which the estates of Irish chiefs were confiscated after they fled abroad following their defeat at the battle of Kinsale at the end of Elizabeth's reign. Their lands in the six northern counties were 'planted' with Protestant settlers, mostly from Scotland and the London area (hence the name of Londonderry). Needless to say, this policy left the Irish with a burning sense of injustice.

James's son, Charles I, who succeeded him in 1625, was in some ways a more attractive character, but he was equally stubborn and quite untrustworthy. From wrangles over money, Charles and Parliament reached a stage of quarrelling about everything, so, from 1629, he followed his father's example of ruling without Parliament and raising income by taxes which the opposition regarded as illegal.

This was the basic cause of the English Civil War, for Charles's 'Eleven Years' Tyranny', as it was called, pointed all too clearly towards the continental type of absolute rule which Parliament was determined to oppose, even if it meant taking up arms against the lawful King. Furthermore, Charles had married a French Roman Catholic princess and there was a widespread (though mistaken) belief that he intended to reintroduce the power of Rome.

The Civil War which broke out in 1642, divided the country about equally. In every shire and town, even in families, some were for the King and some for Parliament. Most of the towns with their tradesmen and Puritans, took Parliament's side, while, in the country districts, people tended to stay loyal to the King. The gentry, High Churchmen and Roman Catholics were mostly Royalists, but there were still plenty of nobles and landowners among Parliament's supporters.

A grievous blow to the Royalist cause was the loss of the Navy, because it meant that Charles was unable to receive foreign aid, and he never held any of the major sea-ports, except Bristol. As regards money to finance the war, the King relied mainly on gifts from his supporters, whereas Parliament, with London and other centres of trade and wealth on its side, could raise loans and levy regular taxes.

If the King was to win the war, he had to do so quickly and all through 1643, when his forces were victorious everywhere, he seemed about to succeed. Yet somehow he was never able to deliver the knock-out blow. The real trouble was that the Royalists lacked a first-class general, a man of sufficient weight to persuade all the nobles and country gentlemen to put themselves and their followers under his command. Prince Rupert of the Rhine, the King's nephew, was too young and headstrong for the task; he could win engagements with the cavalry, but there was no body of disciplined infantry to finish off the enemy. Parliament, on the other hand,

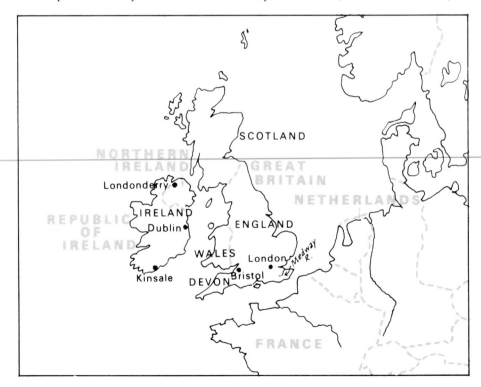

THE
CONFESSION 14
June 25 OF *1649*
Richard Brandon

The Hangman (upon his Death bed) concerning His behead-
ing his late Majesty, *C H A R L E S* the first, King of Great
Brittain; and his Protestation and Vow touching the same;
the manner how he was terrified in Conscience; the Appa-
ritions and Visions which apeared unto him; the great judg-
ment that befell him three dayes before he dy'd ; and the
manner how he was carryed to White-Chappell; Church-
yard on Thursday night last, the strange Actions that happened thereupon; With the merry conceits of the Crowne
Cook and his providing mourning Cords for the Buriall.

Printed in the year Year, of the Hang-mans down-fall, 1649.

Title page of a sensational 'confession', being the so-called death-bed repentance of the
Public Hangman who had beheaded Charles I only a few months before his own end. In
actual fact, there were *two* masked executioners on the platform; one of them, presumably
Brandon, brought down the axe; the other held up the King's head to the public. The other
two figures seen here would have been Juxon, former bishop of London, and Colonel
Hacker, commanding the guards.

found a born general in Oliver Cromwell, a country squire who raised his
own troop of God-fearing cavalry, got rid of the half-hearted commanders
and brought into existence the force of disciplined professional soldiers
known as the New Model Army. At Naseby in 1645, Cromwell destroyed
the Royalist infantry and effectively brought the war to an end. The King

Oliver Cromwell, a
drawing by Samuel
Cooper, when the Lord
Protector was about 50.

gave himself up to the Scots, thinking they would support a Stuart, but they handed him over to Parliament and retired across the Border.

Parliament had won the war and all that remained to be done was to disband the Army and get the King to promise to rule as they wanted him to. This was easier said than done. Charles's promises to friend or enemy were worthless and, after his intrigues with the Scots had led to a Second Civil War, which the Model Army won in a canter, Cromwell decided that 'the man of blood' must die. No-one could deflect Cromwell from carrying out what he believed to be God's Will and, therefore, contrary to the wishes of the greater part of the nation, Charles was publicly executed on 30 January 1649.

Having got rid of the King, Cromwell turned his attention to the Irish, who, driven by hunger and persecution, had massacred thousands of Protestants in a rebellion of 1641 and had later supported the Royalist cause. In 1649, Cromwell took the Model Army to Dublin and, in a few months, subdued Ireland with merciless severity. He then returned to deal with the Scots, who had invited Charles I's son to be a Presbyterian King and were about to invade England. With his usual efficiency (he never lost a battle), he defeated them and, in 1651, overwhelmed the Prince's army at Worcester, a final victory which he called 'God's Crowning Mercy'.

Thus, the Civil War, which had begun as a quarrel between King and Parliament, ended in the destruction of them both and, as usually happens in revolutions, in the emergence of a dictator, backed by the Army.

Not that Cromwell wanted to be a dictator; an M.P. himself, he had fought against the royal tyrant and his earnest wish was to see the country governed by God-fearing men – Puritans of course. Unfortunately, reaction had set in and, by this time, a free election would have returned a Royalist Parliament, so the only thing to do was for him to rule the country himself, as Lord Protector of the Commonwealth of Britain.

He ruled mildly at first, allowing a certain amount of religious toleration but, when his first Parliament, elected in accordance with a new constitution which gave great power to the Protector, dared to debate those powers, he sent the Members packing and began to rule more tyrannically than Charles I had ever done. Alarmed by plots and risings, he divided England and Wales into eleven districts, each under a Major-General, who maintained law and order and abolished every kind of 'frivolous amusement' and festivity, even including Christmas. The closing of ale-houses particularly infuriated the people, who loathed the Major-Generals and their régime, but, as long as Cromwell had the Army's support, there was no way in which they could overthrow him.

In foreign affairs, Cromwell was more successful, in that he revived England's name as a power to be respected. A quarrel over the carrying-trade at sea led to a naval war with the Dutch Netherlands, in which Robert Blake, a Parliamentarian general with next to no experience of the sea until he was fifty, proved to be one of Britain's finest admirals. Cromwell then made peace with the Dutch, formed friendly alliances with Sweden, Denmark and Portugal and, in the war between France and Spain, sided with France, in the mistaken belief that Spain was a greater danger to British interests than France.

Worn out in body and spirit, Cromwell died at Whitehall on 3 September 1658 when he was not yet sixty. Some historians have seen him as a great Englishman, tolerant, sincere, a military genius and the champion of liberty and the Protestant religion. To others, his fanatical conviction that he was an instrument of God turned him into a tyrant infinitely more ruthless than the monarch whom he destroyed.

At all events, his death revealed his failure to provide for the future. Neither his son Richard nor any of the generals could take his place and, from the welter of argument and disorder, one thing emerged with absolute clarity: that the overwhelming majority of the people wanted the kind of government they understood – a King on the throne and Parliament at Westminster. Amid an outburst of joy which the nation has seldom known before or since, Charles II rode into London on 29 May 1660.

The King's triumphant return and the end of the only republic in English history did not mean that the monarchy was just the same as it had been before the Civil War. Charles II had come back because Parliament said so and believed that he would uphold the Church of England. No-one suspected that the returned hero was in his heart a Catholic and an absolute monarch, for the cool, witty Charles had learned to keep his own counsel and he had no intention of suffering his father's fate or going back into exile.

During his reign the nation suffered a dire humiliation when the Dutch sailed up the Medway to destroy warships at anchor and there were two disasters afflicting the capital: the Great Plague and the Fire of London.

At this time, France was the richest, most powerful and most cultured country in Europe. Its monarch, Louis XIV, the all-powerful 'Sun King', was able to pursue his aggressive policies without any interference from a parliament and to set the style in personal grandeur for the lesser monarchs of Europe. Charles II, who admired all things French, made the secret Treaty of Dover with his cousin Louis, agreeing to join him in another war against the Dutch and to establish the Catholic religion in England when the time was ripe. In return, Charles was to receive a pension that would make him independent of Parliament. However, the Third Dutch War (1672-4) was inconclusive, so peace was made and Charles's niece, Mary, married the Dutch ruler, William of Orange.

Charles II's attempt to give freedom of worship to Catholics provoked such an outburst of anti-Catholic hatred that he had to lie low and weather the storm. Shrewdly biding his time until the uproar had died down, he suddenly overthrew his political enemies, dissolved Parliament and, with another grant from Louis XIV, ruled as he pleased for the remaining four years of his life, though he had seen enough to realise that it would be folly to try to restore Roman Catholicism.

His brother, the Duke of York, who succeeded him as James II in 1685, had no such scruples. An ardent Catholic (his first wife and both his daughters were Protestants), he soon had the country in a ferment through putting aside laws in order to favour Roman Catholics, enlarging the army and announcing that he could 'dispense' with any Act of Parliament. When the birth of his son provided a Catholic heir to the throne, a number of gentlemen sent a letter to the Netherlands, asking William of Orange, grandson of Charles I and son-in-law to James, to come over and save the English constitution and the Protestant religion.

William landed in Devon on 5 November 1688, with a small army, and moved cautiously inland. But there was no fighting in England. James was deserted by everybody - his soldiers, his best general, John Churchill, and even his younger daughter, Anne - so he fled the kingdom to seek help from Louis XIV, but, after a feeble attempt to regain his throne by raising the Irish, he accepted defeat at the Battle of the Boyne (1690) and retired to France to live out the rest of his life a pathetic pensioner of his French cousin.

The so-called 'Glorious Revolution' of 1688 was, in truth, an inglorious affair, marred by treachery and cowardice on both sides. However, the nation had got rid of the King without much trouble and, once he was gone, William of Orange and those who had invited him could make a deal.

Despite his ties with England, William had little interest in the country; he agreed to come only in order to get the support and money he needed to save the Dutch from his enemy Louis XIV. But, as an honourable man, he stuck to the bargain that gave him what he wanted. He and his wife, Mary (James II's elder daughter), agreed to become joint King and Queen and to accept the Bill of Rights by which the sovereign must be a Protestant, must not set laws aside, raise taxes or maintain an army without Parliament's consent. In other words, from now on, Great Britain, as England, Wales and Scotland began to be called, was to be governed by Parliament, not by the King. As Head of State, he still possessed a great deal of influence and prestige, but never again would the country be ruled by a despot.

The Civil War and the Glorious Revolution set Britain apart from the rest of Europe, in that its King became a 'constitutional monarch', who had to abide by the 'constitution', i.e. the laws and customs by which the country would be governed. This limitation of royal power was practically unique, for, in kingdoms like France, Spain, Sweden and Prussia, the King made all the major decisions concerning war, peace, finance and religion. The only country which resembled Britain was the Dutch Netherlands, a republic governed by an assembly called the States-General, which, in peril from Louis XIV's armies, had put its trust in the leadership of young William of Orange, great-grandson of William the Silent.

The events which brought Great Britain its constitutional monarchy were disastrous for Ireland. Cromwell's massacre of Catholics at Drogheda and Wexford, the Protestants' victory at the Battle of the Boyne, reduction of the bulk of the Catholic population to the level of serfs and the English government's determination to keep Ireland commercially poor and politically dependant created a legacy of bitterness which no-one managed to heal.

Medals and signatures of Stuart monarchs: James I, Charles I, Charles II, William and Mary.

4 The Thirty Years' War
1618 – 48

The German phase of the Reformation came to an end in 1555, when, at the Peace of Augsburg, Catholics and Lutherans agreed that each state should adopt the religion of its ruling prince. At best, this was no more than an uneasy truce, but at least it meant there was no more fighting for 60 years, until there broke out in 1618 a war so savage and protracted that, by its end, much of Germany had been reduced to a desert, its trade ruined and a third of its people dead.

This dreadful conflict was much more than a war of religion, for it was also a continuation of the struggle for power in Europe between the Bourbon kings of France and the Hapsburg rulers of Spain and the Holy Roman Empire. It became in fact a renewal of the earlier struggle involving the Valois and the Hapsburgs in the previous century.

A number of other issues brought more contestants into the ring. Sweden wanted part of northern Germany to secure her control of the Baltic and this was resented by the Danes; the princes and cities of Germany were afraid that the Catholic Emperor Ferdinand II intended to destroy their independence, so they fought, not for religion, but to keep the Emperor weak and Germany divided; Spain intended to crush the rebellious Netherlanders of the United Provinces who, for their part, regarded the war as a continuation of their struggle for freedom, while France came in to weaken the Emperor and get possession of Alsace. Worst of all, perhaps, were the warlords who fought for no cause at all, except pay and plunder. One of these, Ernst von Mansfeld, was so pitiless that the cry, 'God help those where Mansfeld comes!' went before him, as he led his cut-throat mercenaries to and fro across the land, burning, slaying and carrying typhus in their wake.

The war began in Bohemia (now part of Czechoslovakia), where the Protestants raised a rebellion against the Emperor, because they feared that he, a passionately devout Catholic, intended to wipe out their religion. This revolt led to the election to the throne of Bohemia of Frederick V[1], the young Calvinist ruler of the Palatinate on the Rhine, whose brief reign ended in disaster, with his defeat by the Imperial forces and the total subjugation of

---

[1] Husband of James I of England's daughter, Elizabeth, who became known by reason of their short reign, as 'the Winter Queen'. Their son was Prince Rupert of the Rhine; their descendant, King George I of Britain.

Bohemia. Frederick fled to the United Provinces of the Netherlands, where he endlessly busied himself trying to enlist help from other Protestant princes.

After his defeat, Frederick's own land, the Palatinate, passed into the Emperor's control, a valuable asset, because it stood on the land route from northern Italy to the Netherlands, along which Spain sent troops and gold to maintain her rule over the rebellious Dutch. This gain thoroughly alarmed France, since it meant that the Hapsburgs now held sway all along her land frontiers, from the Pyrenees, up the Rhine to the Netherlands. Furthermore, the Emperor's able general, Count Tilly, 'the monk in armour', inflicted a crushing defeat on the German Protestant army in 1623.

Cardinal Richelieu, the chief minister of Catholic France, therefore set himself to organise an alliance of *Protestant* powers - Sweden, Denmark and the United Provinces (he failed to persuade England to join) - to oppose the Hapsburg menace.

His plan misfired when Tilly and his co-general, the sinister, ruthless

Wallenstein, knocked Denmark out of the war and marched their victorious armies across Germany, capturing every fortress and town in their path. The Emperor seemed certain to triumph, when, at this point, Gustavus Adolphus, King of Sweden, took the field with the magnificent army which he had forged in the course of 20 years of war against the Danes, Poles and Russians.

Financed by Richelieu, Gustavus dramatically reversed the fortunes of war, defeating Tilly and sweeping through northern Germany to the Rhineland. At Lützen (1632), the Swedes must have destroyed Wallenstein, too, but for Gustavus being killed in the thick of the battle. With the loss of this commander of genius, the tide once more turned against the Protestants.

But, by this time, the war had ceased to be a religious conflict, for Richelieu had made up his mind to break the power of the Hapsburgs by putting French armies into the field in support of the German princes, the Swedes and the Dutch. Hence, for the next 14 years, Germany became a battlefield for the armies of half-a-dozen nations which reduced the country to a state of misery so terrible that, in places, the peasants were said to have taken to cannibalism. The Swedes, now led by Bernard, Duke of Weimar,

An incident of the Thirty Years' War painted by Velasquez: the Dutch commander of Breda surrenders the town to Spinola, the Genoese commander of the Spanish army. Spinola, moved by the courage of the Dutch during the six months' siege, embraces his enemy before the whole army.

were so heavily defeated at Nordlingen (1634) that Gustavus's Model Army ceased to exist and the German princes accepted the Peace of Prague, agreeing to quit the war.

The main action shifted to the Rhine Valley, where Richelieu's strategy was to cut the route from Italy and isolate the Spanish Netherlands (roughly the area of present-day Belgium). He took the Swedes into the French service and sent a force to attack the Spaniards and Milanese in Italy, but this great scheme was only partially successful, because Richelieu needed more troops than the 200 000 at his disposal.

From the Netherlands, the Spanish launched an invasion of France, but withdrew after Louis XIII and Richelieu inspired the Parisians to take up arms in defence of their country. In 1637, the Emperor died and was succeeded by his son, Ferdinand III, and, in the following year, with the French generally unsuccessful, there was talk of peace. Nothing came of it and the war dragged on. Innumerable sieges took place; one Spanish fleet was destroyed by the Dutch in the English Channel, another off the coast of Brazil; the Swedes recovered to beat the Austrians and the French occupied Barcelona.

A contemporary illustration celebrating the end of the Thirty Years' War, 1648. In the background are the cities of Vienna, Paris and Stockholm; in the foreground, weapons of war lie broken.

Richelieu died in 1642 and the king whom he served, Louis XIII, died soon afterwards, but one of his last acts was to give command of his northern army to a young man of 21, the duc d'Enghien, Prince de Condé, an appointment which decided the course of the war. At Rocroy (1643), Condé destroyed the Spanish army and, in the following year, partnered by another outstanding French general, Turenne, he annihilated the Bavarian army in three great battles around Freiburg.

The war ended in 1648, with the Peace of Westphalia, which awarded Alsace to France and part of Pomerania in northern Germany to Sweden, as well as recognising the independence of Switzerland and the United Provinces.

The attempt to restore Catholicism by the sword had failed and the Emperor's power was reduced to a shadow in Germany, though it remained real enough in Austria, Bohemia and Hungary. Spain, having lost Portugal, (which had raised a successful revolt in 1640), the United Provinces and her navy, could no longer play a leading role, and Germany, with all hope of unity gone, was to remain a weak federation of impoverished states for the next 150 years.

France had humbled the Hapsburgs and made herself the first military power in Europe, but, no sooner was the thanksgiving service over in Notre Dame Cathedral in Paris, than Cardinal Mazarin, Richelieu's successor, arrested his leading opponent, the spokesman for the Parliament of Paris, whereupon a civil war broke out, called the *Fronde*, which lasted for another 11 years.

5 Louis XIV, the Sun King
1643 – 1715

Louis XIII, dying in 1643, left the throne of France to his son, a 5-year-old child, whose mother, Anne of Austria, became Regent, ruling the country in company with her Italian minister Cardinal Mazarin. Hatred of this pair by the French nobles and the Paris mob led to the outbreak of rebellions known as the First and Second Fronde, during which the Court and young Louis XIV were driven from the capital and Mazarin fled the country.

However, the rebels were far from united and Condé, leader of the nobles, became so unpopular that Louis was able to re-enter Paris and Mazarin came back to restore the royal authority. As the real ruler of France, he lived on until 1661, when Louis XIV took the reins into his own hands.

Young Louis XIV makes his triumphal way through Paris in 1649, after the Fronde. The King, on horseback, is preceded by his Swiss guards. In the background are the Louvre of that epoch and the Pont Neuf.

251

Marble bust of Louis XIV by Bernini at Versailles. The Sun King possessed great energy and perseverance; he was intelligent and dignified and, under his despotic rule, France led the world in trade, military science, literature and art. Yet, by the end of his reign, the country was almost completely ruined.

The young king distrusted the nobles and loathed Paris, with its squalor and unruly citizens who had humiliated him as a child. He therefore decided to build a palace outside Paris, at Versailles, where Louis XIII had had a hunting lodge. There was to be a huge park, whose gardens, lawns and fountains were to supply the setting for the most magnificent residence in the world. Thousands of workmen toiled to clear and drain the land; hundreds of craftsmen were employed to decorate the vast state-rooms and salons that were filled with priceless furniture and lit at night by 10 000 candles burning in silver and crystal chandeliers.

To this grandiose palace, Louis summoned all the nobles of France, for he would have them reside at court, occupying themselves in a perpetual round of banquets, theatre-going, gambling and ridiculous ceremonies, such as attending the Royal Bedchamber to watch the King being dressed by highborn noblemen who vied with one another for the honour of holding a sleeve of the royal shirt! By keeping them engaged in these trival pursuits instead of plotting rebellions, Louis persuaded the nobles to believe that his Court was the centre of the world, which revolved about himself, the 'Sun King'.

In the early part of his reign, Louis was fortunate to be served by a number of able men of the middle-class who had been trained under Mazarin. Greatest of them was Jean Baptiste Colbert, the minister of finance for over 20 years, whose policy was to encourage industry and trade, improve the roads and waterways and create wealth for the glory of France and its dazzling monarch.

The royal income had to be increased to meet the cost of the King's
unbridled spending and this could only be done by means of taxation. Colbert
went to great pains to reduce dishonesty and improve the method of collection, but the evils of the French system were too deep for even the great
finance minister to cure, for the nobility and the rich clergy paid practically
no taxes and the middle-classes as little as they could get away with, so that
the cost of Louis' vast schemes fell almost wholly on the poorest citizens in
the land. Worse, the practice of tax farming, whereby a man bought the right
to collect taxes in a certain district, meant that barely half the money
squeezed from the poverty-stricken peasants ever reached the Treasury.

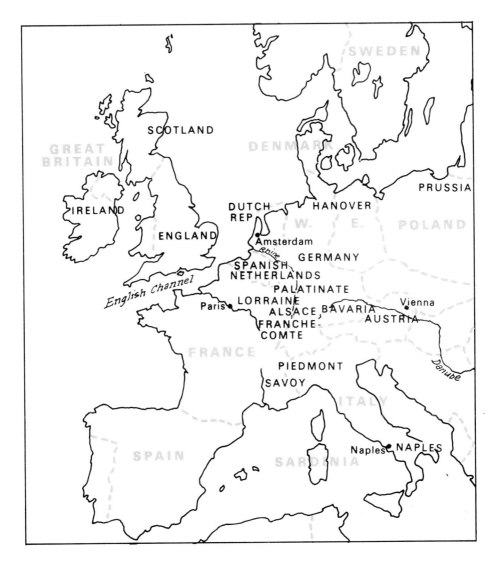

The splendour of Versailles was not likely to satisfy Louis for long; he had to find glory in war and on the death of Philip IV of Spain in 1667, he invaded the Spanish Netherlands, on the excuse that they belonged to his wife, the daughter of the late king. By now, he had the finest army[1] in Europe, with two excellent generals in Turenne and Condé (now restored to favour), and in Vauban, the greatest military engineer in history.

In the war of 1667, Turenne swiftly overran the Spanish Netherlands, capturing a string of towns and fortresses, and Louis also acquired Franche-Comté, a large province on his eastern border belonging to the Spanish Hapsburgs. These successes greatly alarmed the Dutch, since they knew that Louis' conquest of the Spanish Netherlands would be the prelude to an attack on their own country. They therefore brought a speedy end to their war with Charles II's England and formed a Triple Alliance with Sweden and England. This was enough to induce Louis to make peace and hand back Franche-Comté to Spain.

The vainglorious King could not forgive the setback to his military career by a people whom he detested as Protestant republicans, so he bought off Charles II of England with a huge bribe and, in 1672, launched his armies against the Dutch. By all the laws of warfare, the little republic should have been overwhelmed. But the Dutch fought with the stubborn courage they had formerly shown against the Spaniards; at sea, they held their own and, on land, they saved Amsterdam by flooding the countryside. They also overturned their republic and gave power to a dour misshapen young man named Prince William of Orange, who, like his great-grandfather, William the Silent, dedicated his life to saving the United Provinces from the invader.

After 6 years of war, a peace treaty was signed by which Louis recovered Franche-Comté and gained some important towns on his eastern border, though not a foot of Dutch soil. However, the frontiers of France were secure and the Sun King was the greatest monarch in Europe; at home, his power was absolute and France outshone the rest of the world in art, fashion and military science.

Just when he had the opportunity to improve his people's welfare and prosperity, Louis decided to make an all-out attack on the Huguenots, forcing them by cruel oppression to renounce the Protestant faith or flee the country. In 1685, he revoked Henry IV's Edict of Nantes, which had given them toleration, whereupon thousands of Huguenots, many of them traders and craftsmen, fled abroad, taking their skills in the lace, pottery and glass

---

[1] In size, the French army grew from about 50 000 in the 16th century to around 200 000 during the Thirty Years' War, to a quarter and even half a million men in Louis XIV's reign. It became a standing army, in which mercenaries were largely replaced by volunteers. A form of conscription was introduced in 1688.

Huguenot refugees landing at Dover in 1685. Louis' second marriage to Madame de Maintenon, who was herself governed by the Jesuits, is said to have been the reason why he revoked the Edict of Nantes. As many as a quarter of a million Protestants fled from France.

industries with them. The effect on French industry has been exaggerated, but every Protestant in Europe now looked on Louis as an ogre.

His next mistake was to invade and lay waste the small German state of the Palatinate belonging to the Holy Roman Emperor. He probably did this to distract the Austrians, since they were on the point of winning their age-long struggle with Turkey and he would prefer them to be engaged in a perpetual war on their eastern frontier rather than having them interfere with his own ambitions. He was therefore willing to give indirect help to the Turks, but the transfer of French forces to the Palatinate had a dramatic effect on Britain's history. It gave William of Orange time to slip across the Channel to oust the unpopular James II and to accept the English crown jointly with his wife Mary. Having suppresed the Jacobites (James's supporters) in Scotland and Ireland, William could turn to his life's task of defeating the Grand Monarch.

To oppose Louis, he organised an alliance of England, the Dutch Republic Sweden, Spain, Austria and Savoy, and, although, in the war of 1688-97, the French usually beat their enemies, the strain of fighting on several fronts and also at sea, proved so exhausting that Louis had to accept a peace which amounted to defeat. But the struggle was by no means over. Indeed, Louis XIV had still to fight the last and greatest of his wars - the War of the Spanish Succession. Spain, in decline, but still possessing a vast overseas

255

empire and most of Italy, had had for 35 years a sickly half-witted King named Charles II who had no children and was expected to die at any time. One of his sisters was married to Louis XIV and the other to the Emperor Leopold of Austria. Since both sisters had children, there were several claimants to the Spanish throne, but France was not going to let it go to Austria and the European powers were terrified by the thought of France becoming more powerful than all the rest of them put together. William III and Louis XIV, both anxious to find a middle-of-the-road solution, concocted a plan, by which France and Austria should share the Spanish possessions between them.

But no-one had consulted the Spanish people and, when the secret got out, they were furious that foreigners should decide to divide up their empire. Their dying King therefore made a will, leaving all his domains to his great-nephew, Philip of Anjou, Louis XIV's grandson.

Not surprisingly, Louis accepted the will and, as if to make quite sure that his opponents would take up arms, he seized some Dutch frontier fortresses and announced that only France would be allowed to trade with the Spanish dominions.

In the War of the Spanish Succession (1702-13), France, aided by Bavaria (whose Duke decided to support Louis XIV) and most of the Spanish nation, was opposed by Britain, Austria, the Dutch Netherlands, Prussia, Hanover, the Palatinate and Denmark. Their armies, on paper, outnumbered the forces which Louis XIV could put into the field, though it needed a commander of genius to get the best out of allies who were proudly independent, stubborn and suspicious of one another.

The English soldier, John Churchill, later Duke of Marlborough, was that man. Kept in the background by William III, who never trusted him, he took command of the main allied army on William's death in 1702 and, through his victories, brought Louis XIV's France to its knees. Hungry for fame and wealth, he possessed limitless patience with his difficult allies, matchless skill in detecting the enemy's weaknesses and such coolness in battle that he became a legend both to his own soldiers and the French.

His greatest victory occurred in 1704, when he dashed from the Dutch Republic across Germany and into Bavaria to join forces with Prince Eugene of Savoy, the brilliant Austrian commander who had already distinguished himself against the Turks. Marlborough and Eugene totally defeated the French and Bavarians at Blenheim, close to the River Danube, near Ulm, so that Vienna was saved and the French had to retire from Germany and go on to the defensive.

In a war of manoeuvres, sieges and counter-sieges, Marlborough reduced France to desperate straits. With her armies demoralised, the peasants starving and the Treasury empty, the country was facing total defeat, when the stubborn old King made one last appeal to his ragged soldiers. They responded so magnificiently that, with Marlborough removed from his command on charges of dishonesty, they halted the allied advance and the war petered out.

In the peace settlement of the Treaty of Utrecht (1713), France did much better than might have been expected. Her boundaries were left intact, for she kept Franche-Comté and Alsace-Lorraine. Louis XIV's grandson remained King of Spain as Philip V, which was what Louis had fought for, but he had to agree that Philip's branch of the Bourbon family would never inherit the French throne.

By reason of his bearing, achievements, wars and sheer longevity (his reign lasted for 72 years), Louis XIV played a major role in European history. His ambition cost his country dearly, yet France remained pre-eminent, for Louis created a legend which appealed to Frenchmen and nourished their love of *la gloire*. French literature and art, French military science, French fashions and manners still set standards for the rest of Europe.

Austria, disappointed that her Archduke had not gained the Spanish throne, received the Spanish Netherlands (now Belgium) as compensation, along with the Spanish possessions of Naples, Sardinia and Milan, so Austria became the dominant power in Italy.

Spain and Portugal retained their boundaries and their overseas possessions, but both had now fallen back to the second rank of powers and the Dutch, while keeping their cherished independence, had been so exhausted by the long struggle as to be permanently weakened. Dutch naval strength actually declined during the war, while England's navy grew stronger and stronger. The truly remarkable feature of the period was Great Britain's rise to the status of a great power. During Louis XIV's lifetime, the islanders endured civil war and a dictatorship; they executed one king and banished another and saw their Stuart monarchs supported by doles handed out by their rich cousin across the Channel; yet it was British gold, the British Navy and the genius of a British general which played the major part in bringing Louis down.

Foreigners regarded Britain with astonished admiration. Here was a country which not only accomplished a revolution with very little bloodshed, but had emerged from a long war richer and stronger than before. Her domestic position was greatly strengthened by the Union of England and Scotland in 1707 and her people enjoyed a good deal of religious freedom, a free press and parliamentary government, which, in an age of European despots, was little short of miraculous. No wonder that Voltaire, the great philosopher, who hated the tyranny in his native France, was delighted to visit a country where a man could write about what he pleased; or that another French visitor should declare: 'England is the freest country in the world. . . . And I call it free because the sovereign, whose person is controlled and limited, is unable to inflict any imaginable harm on anyone.'

William III died without children, so his sister-in-law, Anne, the second Protestant daughter of James II, became queen in 1702. Since none of her 17 children survived infancy, the crown was to pass by Act of Parliament to George, Elector of Hanover, a duchy in northern Germany, which had formerly been part of Brunswick territory. George was the grandson of Elizabeth, 'the Winter Queen', who, long ago, had married the Elector Palatine. But James II's son, who called himself James III since his father's death in 1701, had a much better claim.

One political party, the Whigs[1], supported George of Hanover because he was a Protestant, while the other party, the Tories[1] regarded James III as the rightful King, though they could not get over the fact that he was a Roman Catholic when they were staunch for the Church of England. So, while they hesitated, the Whigs stepped in and, on Queen Anne's death in 1714, proclaimed George of Hanover King George I.

The new King was a German, hardly able to speak English but fully aware that he owed the throne to the Whigs. He was therefore content that they should form the government and run the country, since he much preferred Hanover and went there as often as he could.

Thus, the Whigs entered into their long period of power, during which Robert Walpole, a rich Norfolk squire, became in fact, though not in name, the first 'Prime Minister', ruling Britain through his control of Parliament and of the Council or 'Cabinet'. For 20 years, from 1721-41, this cunning old cynic kept the country out of foreign entanglements, encouraged trade and 'let sleeping dogs lie', so that Britain built up the reserves of wealth that were to carry her through the wars that lay ahead.

[1] The Whigs received the name from the Whiggamores, Scottish Presbyterian rebels, while their rivals were dubbed Tories, after some Irish brigands.

6 The Northern Giants
1370 – 1795

Gustavus Adolphus, the founder of Sweden's brief era of military power, left his throne to his 6-year-old daughter Christina who grew into a brilliant young woman, a linguist, philosopher and art-collector who excelled in riding and sword-play. But the adult Christina shocked her people by turning Catholic and abdicating in favour of her cousin, Charles X.

Inheriting the military genius of Sweden's royal family, Charles attacked Poland and Denmark, which at this time ruled Norway and part of southern Sweden. He defeated them both but was denied total victory when the Dutch and the Austrians came to their assistance. His son, Charles XI (1660-97), another soldier-king, not only fought a series of wars to extend an empire which included Finland and the Baltic provinces of Ingria, Estonia and Livonia, but he also found time to curb the power of the Swedish nobles and to rebuild the country's finances.

Charles XII (1697-1718), who was known as 'the Wonder of Europe', came to the throne to face a coalition of enemies bent on destroying Sweden - Augustus of Saxony (the newly elected king of Poland), Frederick of

Charles XII (1682-1718), King of Sweden, succeeded his father whilst in his teens, which Denmark, Poland and Russia thought was a favourable time to crush Sweden. Charles defeated them all. A brilliant general, brave, clever and generous, he nevertheless exhausted his country's resources through his ambition and insatiable love of warfare.

Denmark and Peter of Russia. He won victories over the Danes and the Saxons, and went on to inflict a severe defeat on the Russians at Narva (1700), where Peter the Great's army was four times the size of his own. But the Great Northern War dragged on for years and, while Charles XII was campaigning in Poland and Saxony, Peter the Great found a general to occupy Sweden's Baltic provinces. Charles therefore marched into Russia, where, like other would-be conquerors, he met enemies far more deadly than the Tsar's soldiers.

Starvation and the Russian winter had already reduced his army by half, when, at Poltava (1709), it was practically annihilated. Charles himself escaped into Turkey, where he spent several adventurous years before returning to his native country. His death in a war against Norway, probably saved Sweden from total ruin. As it was, Russia, Poland, Denmark and Brandenburg divided the empire among themselves and the Swedish state, which for a century had played a role too big for its population and resources, retired to the back of the stage in favour of the new giants, Prussia and Russia.

At this point we must look briefly at the situation in eastern Europe during Sweden's period of greatness. Since the reign of Suleiman the Magnificent (1520-66), the Turks had been masters of south-eastern Europe, where they imposed a tyrannical rule over the Greeks, Bulgars, Serbs, Hungarians and Rumanians of that region.

It was fortunate for Europe that, during the Thirty Years' War, the Ottoman Empire was going through one of its periods of feeble inactivity, but, not long after the Treaty of Westphalia was signed, the Sultan appointed to the post of Grand Vizier an able and ruthless Albanian named Mohammed Kiuprili, who, with his successors also from the Kiuprili family, revived the Turkish fighting spirit.

The task of defending Christian Europe fell upon the Hapsburg Emperor, the Archduke of Austria, since his lands lay next to the Sultan's dominions, and, far from receiving help from his fellow-rulers in Western Europe, he found that most of them were well pleased to see the imperial armies desperately engaged along the eastern frontiers. His principal allies had to be the Venetians, who regarded the Turks as permanent enemies, and the Poles. Between 1370 and 1572, Poland had grown into a vast kingdom, which, thanks to union with Lithuania, stretched from the Baltic coast to the Black Sea. Under kings of the Jagellon dynasty, Poland made great advances in culture and prosperity, partly owing to the arrival of many Jews taking refuge from persecution in Western Europe, but when the last Jagellon king died in 1572, the Polish nobles, disliking strong government, decided that henceforward they would elect the monarch in order to make sure that he would have no power to overrule the Polish Diet - an assembly of quarrelsome nobles.

In 1587, they chose as king, Sigismund, a prince of the Swedish Vasa family, who, by adopting the Catholic religion, aroused the enmity of Protestant Sweden. During the almost continuous wars of the 17th century, Poland suffered a deluge of invasions by Swedes, Muscovites, Brandenburgers and Transylvanians, as well as a major Cossack uprising in the south. Among Poland's losses was the Duchy of Prussia which went to the Elector of Brandenburg.

One glorious episode relieved the gloom. John Sobieski, a Polish nobleman who had been elected King, led the Poles to victory after victory over the Turks and then, in 1683, saved Vienna itself, by destroying the Turkish army which had advanced through Hungary to lay siege to the city. After this triumph, the Austrians pushed the Turks back across the Danube and forced them to cede Hungary and Transylvania to Austria and the Ukraine to Poland. Turkish power was not destroyed, but, after the relief of Vienna, it went on to the defensive, as its European territories were whittled away by the armies of Austria and Russia.

Although the great-hearted Sobieski brought military fame to Poland, he could not check his country's decline, which continued through the reign of the next king, Augustus of Saxony, when the Swedes devastated the land. Even Charles XII's defeat at Poltava brought no relief, for the real victor was Peter the Great of Russia. From then on, Poland became a satellite state and her history a catalogue of disasters and betrayals right up until 1945.

Sobieski (1624-96), the general whose victories over the Turks caused him to be elected King of Poland in 1674 as John III.

Peter the Great (1672-
1725), the founder of
modern Russia.

In 1689, Peter Romanov was made joint Tsar of All-the-Russias with his idiot half-brother. As a child, Peter narrowly escaped death in a palace revolution and fled with his mother to a remote township where, without any schooling or discipline, he grew into a savage-tempered young giant, whose greatest pleasure was to play crazy war-games with the local boys.

For a time, the young Tsar continued his hooligan ways, but, at 24, he suddenly decided to rule and to make Russia as strong as the countries he had heard about in the West. His vast country, stretching endlessly eastwards, consisted of many states and peoples who only vaguely recognised the Tsar of Moscow's authority. Contact with the outside world had been almost solely with Constantinople, which accounted for the fact that the Russians belonged to the Byzantine or Eastern Orthodox Church.

It was a semi-barbaric society, without schools or universities; there were no handsome towns with law-courts and business centres, no sea-ports, except Archangel in the far north, which was frozen up for most of the year, and practically no knowledge of industry, trade or the civilized arts. The ruling class of nobles or *boyars* exercised despotic power over the serfs who toiled on their estates. Bearded and clad in flowing robes, the boyars wanted no change or interference in their lives, but they reckoned without the iron determination of a Tsar who was as savage as they, but infinitely more intelligent.

Peter knew that the great nations of the world possessed powerful armies and navies, so he decided to have them both. There was no problem in drafting 30 000 peasants a year into the army, to be taught drill and discipline, but a navy was a different matter; it would require seaports and the Turks held the Black Sea, while the Swedes ruled the Baltic coasts.

Realising that there was much that he did not know about ships, Peter decided to go to Western Europe and find out for himself. For five months he worked as a ship's carpenter in the dockyard of Amsterdam and then, at the invitation of William III, he crossed to England to continue his work in the Royal Dockyard at Deptford, on the Thames.

The Tsar went on to Prussia and Vienna, studying medicine, gunnery and military training, until he had to hurry back to Moscow on the news of a revolt by the Streltzy Guard, the crack royal regiment. By the time he arrived, the mutiny was over, but Peter ordered hundreds of the guards to be beheaded in the Red Square; many others were hanged and their bodies left in piles to show that the Streltzy was destroyed and the Tsar was absolute master of Russia.

He next dealt with the boyars, forcing them to discard their long robes and to shave off their beards; they were made to obey him, to pay taxes and have their sons trained to serve the state. He stripped priests and monks of their riches, dragooned thousands of peasants into the army or into labour battalions to build schools, libraries and academies of science. Putting

The long robes of Boyars being removed on the orders of Peter the Great, as part of his westernisation of Russia.

through these measures and various reforms (he introduced new industries, created a civil service and revised the calendar, the alphabet and the coinage), he forced Russia to accept western ideas and, although his cruelty and insane rages filled his subjects with terror, he could be generous to those who served him well.

In 1700, he was ready to join Denmark, Saxony and Poland in a war against Sweden, but, as we have read, Charles XII easily beat his raw troops at Narva in Livonia, adjoining the Baltic Sea. This defeat spurred Peter into re-training his armies so successfully that, while the Swedes were fighting their other enemies, he managed to occupy the Baltic provinces. Charles therefore invaded Russia but met with a disaster at Poltava (1709), from which Sweden never recovered.

By then, Peter had already begun to build a new capital where the River Neva flows into the Baltic. He dug the first turf himself and lived in a log hut in order to supervise the thousands of peasants, convicts and prisoners who were drafted there to build a city in a desolate swamp. Architects were brought from Holland, the use of stone anywhere else in Russia was forbidden, the nobles were ordered to erect mansions along the wide streets and 200 000 men died of exhaustion and fever, but, by 1718, St Petersburg[1] was completed, the finest city and one of the best ports in Europe. The Baltic ceased to be the 'Swedish Lake' and Russia had been given its window to the West.

By superhuman will, Peter the Great made Russia into a European power, a stupendous achievement, even if many of his reforms were ignored after his death. He did nothing to remove serfdom, to increase the people's happiness or to give them justice and culture, for what did a brute know of such things?

In north-east Germany, a poor little state, barely 100 miles long, with sandy soil and no coastline, natural resources or defensible frontiers grew almost overnight into a major European power.

The Electorate of Brandenburg, an outlying province of the Holy Roman Empire, came to be ruled from 1415 by the Hohenzollerns, a capable ruthless family from Nuremberg. The ruler was one of the seven Electors who chose the Emperor and, at the Reformation, Brandenburg became Protestant.

Prussia, lying some distance to the east, and separated from Brandenburg by the duchy of Pomerania and some Polish territory, had been conquered in

---

[1] Later re-named Petrograd and then Leningrad.

the 13th century by the Order of the Teutonic Knights who converted the heathen Slav population to Christianity and stayed on as rulers. The Duke of Prussia owed allegiance to the King of Poland. One of the Hohenzollerns was Grand Master of the Teutonic Knights and, on his death in 1618, Prussia became united to Brandenburg under a single Hohenzollern, though it remained a Polish fief.

During the Thirty Years' War, Catholic and Protestant armies reduced Brandenburg to such depths of poverty that the Elector George William fled in despair to Prussia, where he died in 1640. His son, Frederick William, the 'Great Elector', who ruled for the next 48 years, transformed the fortunes of Brandenburg/Prussia by a masterly combination of energy and cunning. Being on the winning side at the end of the war, he had a voice in the peace settlement and therefore obtained part of Pomerania which gave Brandenburg a piece of the Baltic coastline. When Louis XIV's persecution drove Huguenots abroad, he invited many of them to settle in Brandenburg to start industries and he also welcomed Jews, Catholics and Dutch peasants, who understood land drainage and the latest farming methods.

During the war between Sweden and Poland, he offered to support the Poles if they would give up their rights to Prussia. It thus became a permanent addition to Brandenburg (1660). The Great Elector's son coaxed the Holy Roman Emperor into letting him take the title of King and, since that title was not permitted within the Empire, he went to Konigsberg and crowned himself King Frederick I of Prussia. The name of Brandenburg dropped out of use and the new kingdom, with its capital in Berlin, was known henceforward as Prussia.

The second King of Prussia, Frederick William I, who reigned from 1713-40, was so eccentric as to be scarcely sane. At a time when every monarch tried to copy the elegance of Louis XIV's Versailles, this ferocious brute lived like a miser, begrudging every penny that was spent on anything, except the upkeep of the army. By creating this powerful army (he actually used it only twice), by his frugality and hold over his obedient hard-working subjects, Frederick William made Prussia the leading state in Germany. Despising culture and learning, his fury fell upon his son, the Crown Prince Frederick, a delicate boy who loved music, poetry and literature, but was subjected to a régime of such brutality that he tried to escape to England. In 1740, when the old tyrant died, his son's friends thought that the poet-king, Frederick II ('the Great') would introduce a new era of benevolent rule. On the contrary, he soon proved himself a more ruthless, unscrupulous tyrant than his father.

The Emperor Charles VI had no son, but a daughter, the beautiful and gifted Maria Theresa, so he persuaded all the leading states of Europe, including Prussia, to agree to accept her as heiress to his hereditary thrones.

Maria Theresa (1717-80), Empress, ruler of the Holy Roman Empire, a woman of great spirit who fought long and hard against Frederick the Great, introduced many reforms into her territories and, with her able minister, Kaunitz, raised Austria to the status of a European power. Latterly, she governed in partnership with her son, Joseph; another of her ten children was Marie Antoinette.

Charles died in 1740[1] and Frederick II immediately seized Silesia, one of her richest provinces. This theft led to the War of the Austrian Succession, in which Prussia was joined by France, Spain and Bavaria, who were opposed by Austria, Holland, Savoy and Britain.

[1] Whereupon Maria Theresa became arch-duchess of Austria, Queen of Hungary and Bohemia. Her husband Francis, was elected Holy Roman Emperor in 1745.

During the war, a confused affair which lasted from 1740-48, the Jacobites made a last attempt in the 'Forty-five' to regain the British throne, but, in spite of Bonnie Prince Charlie's gallantry, the Stuart cause perished on the field of Culloden (1746) and, by the treaty that ended the war, Frederick kept Silesia for Prussia.

Maria Theresa was determined to win it back, this time in alliance with Austria's old enemy, France. They were joined by Sweden and Russia, now ruled by the Tsarina Elizabeth, but Prussia's sole ally was Great Britain.

From Britain's point of view, the Seven Years' War (1756-63) was primarily a struggle with France for overseas possessions and trade, and William Pitt the Elder, the first British statesman to envisage his country as an imperial power, supported Frederick with gold, rather than soldiers, because his policy was to use British forces to fight campaigns in Canada, the West Indies and India.

After some early disasters, Pitt's genius for organisation led to a string of victories. General Wolfe captured Quebec in Canada, Admiral Boscawen destroyed the French fleet off Cape Lagos, Admiral Hawke obliterated another in Quiberon Bay (southern Brittany), while, in India, Robert Clive's victory at Plessey brought the huge province of Bengal into the East India Company's control.

Meanwhile, in Europe, Frederick the Great was fighting a desperate war. Outnumbered by the armies of three great powers, he suffered defeats, extricated his shattered army and won victories against all odds through the dauntless spirit of his Prussian soldiers. Time and again, he scraped together another army and called on his men for one more effort, but his enemies closed in remorselessly, until, by 1762, the haggard little man was at his last gasp, his army broken, Prussia overrun and his ally, Britain, pulling out, now that its young king, George III, wanted an end to 'this bloody and expensive war'. Frederick's salvation was the death of Elizabeth of Russia, for her successor, Peter III, hero-worshipped the Prussian king and ordered his armies to withdraw. This enabled Frederick to come to terms with his other enemies, who were themselves near to exhaustion. By the Treaty of Paris in 1763, Prussia kept Silesia, but Frederick never forgave Britain for leaving him in the lurch.

'I have fought and struggled for twenty-three years', he said, forgetting perhaps that it was his own greed that had brought such suffering to his people. 'I intend to devote the rest of my days to my country's recovery'. Shabby, dedicated and demanding that everyone should work as hard as he did, he brought Prussia back to life, by giving special help to the worst-hit areas, building new villages, roads, canals, encouraging foreign settlers and starting banks, schools and new industries. In less than ten years, he had made Prussia strong enough to permit him to take part in another robbery.

Catherine II, the Great, (1729-96), the daughter of a German princeling, who ruled Russia as a 'benevolent despot' and greatly increased the dominions and power of her adopted country. Although extremely intelligent and the friend of Voltaire, she achieved little in the way of improving the lot of Russian people.

Catherine the Great (1729-96) was not a Russian, but a German princess who, at the age of 17, married Peter the Great's grandson, the insane young man who, as Tsar Peter III, saved Frederick in 1762. Catherine learned Russian, joined the Orthodox Church and contrived the murder of her husband in order to become sole ruler of Russia for 34 years.

She was not called 'the Great' because of her concern for the people's good but because she added new territories to the Russian empire. In wars against the Turks, her general Suvorov made gains extending to the Black Sea, the Crimea and the Caucasus; then she expanded westwards by carving up Poland in partnership with Frederick the Great and Maria Theresa of Austria. By the First Partition of 1772, Poland lost one third of its territory and became in effect a Russian province. Frederick's share enabled him to join Brandenburg/Prussia and East Prussia into one state, while Maria-Theresa, distressed by the robbery, gained Galicia: 'She wept', sneered Frederick, 'but took her share.'

In 1793, the Second Partition took place, when Russia invaded Poland and divided the spoils with Prussia. The Poles rose to arms under their hero, Kosciuszko, but, after a brave beginning, they were totally routed in 1795, when the last fragments of their country were seized by Russia, Prussia and Austria. As a separate state, Poland ceased to exist, but the Polish nation, its language, religion and culture, lived on defiantly.

7 The American Revolution 1760 – 87

George III was 23 when he succeeded to the British throne in 1760. Unlike the first two Hanoverians,[1] this pleasant conscientious young man felt himself to be an Englishman and he made up his mind to be an active king rather than a mere figurehead.

For a start, he pressed for an end to the Seven Years' War, which, to the angry disgust of Frederick the Great, was achieved in 1763, when the Treaty of Paris brought such gains and prestige to Britain. George managed to create a party of 'King's Friends' in Parliament, who, in return for places and pensions, supported his policies. Contrary to the opinion of his detractors, George was neither a tyrant nor, in the words of Tom Paine, 'the royal brute of England', but he was obstinate and lacked the ability to take a far-sighted view of the situation in America, a distant country which he had never visited.

By the Treaty of Paris, Britain's empire in North America had increased 20 times in size, for, behind the line of the 13 colonies running down the coast lay a vast territory stretching inland from the Appalachians to the Mississippi. To the more adventurous colonists, this presented an opportunity to push beyond the mountains into the plains and forests and, for those who did not want to be mere squatters, various colonists, soon to become famous, such as George Washington, Benjamin Franklin and Patrick Henry, began organising land companies to sell farms.

But, from England, George III issued a proclamation forbidding this expansion. The British government's view was that it would be best to avoid conflict with the French and the Indians, for there had just been an uprising called Pontiac's Conspiracy in which many settlers were massacred. No colony had voted to help British troops quell the rising and Britain was expected to keep a protective force of 10 000 men along the frontier without any contribution from the colonists.

By this time, they numbered about 3 millions, the majority of them of English stock, with a great many Scots, Irish, French, Dutch and Germans.

[1] George I (1714-27) and George II (1727-60). In 1714, on the death of Queen Anne, George, Elector of Hanover, was invited to become King of Great Britain in preference to James II's son, a Catholic.

Some had been fugitives from religious persecution, crime and debt, but there were many thousands of hard-working men and women who had been driven by poverty to brave the six-week voyage in order to find a better life in a new land. They were not likely to feel much loyalty towards the British crown or respect for the high and mighty gentlemen who came out as governors, judges and officials and looked down their noses at the colonists.

By law, the colonies were supposed to trade only with England, but, in practice, this rule was largely winked at and, during the recent war, colonists, especially in Massachusetts, had done extremely well from illegal trade with the West Indies and even with the French. They felt that the trade laws were restricting their country's development and that the cotton and tobacco industries, in particular, were unfairly controlled by London businessmen.

In short, there were grievances in plenty: as John Adams said, 'The revolution was in the minds and hearts of the people . . . before a drop of blood was shed at Lexington.'

To help pay for defence, the English introduced a Stamp Duty on all kinds of documents and newspapers. The amount was trifling and not a penny would go back to Britain, but the outcry was so furious that, on Pitt's advice, the Stamp Act was repealed. However, Charles Townshend, the Chancellor of the Exchequer, introduced customs duties on six articles, including tea, which revived public indignation to such a pitch that Lord North, the Prime Minister, took off all the taxes except the one on tea which amounted to threepence a pound.

But a threepenny tax, even for the benefit of the colonists themselves, was vile tyranny when it was imposed by a Parliament in which no American had a seat. 'No taxation without representation' became the popular cry, and, in Boston, Massachusetts, on 16 December 1773, a party of men dressed as Indians boarded three ships in the harbour and dumped the Company's tea into the water. In response to this act of defiance, Parliament closed the port of Boston and took away Massachusetts' right to self-government, but, more wisely, it also passed the Quebec Act, whereby all the territory north of the Ohio River was annexed to the province of Quebec and religious freedom was given to Britain's newly-acquired French Roman Catholic subjects.

King George and his ministers now succeeded in doing what the French and the Indians had never managed to do: they caused the colonists to unite, for, in September 1775, delegates from every colony, except Georgia, met at Philadelphia to express their grievances and form a 'Continental Association'.

Meanwhile, the new Governor of Massachusetts, General Gage, arrived from England, with troops who were quartered in Boston. The townspeople formed a committee of safety to organise resistance and a body of militia, called 'minutemen', because they were ready to turn out at a minute's notice. Learning that this committee had established an arms-store at Concord, Gage sent a detachment of troops to confiscate it. On 19 April 1775, the redcoats reached Lexington village near Concord, where they found themselves faced by a line of minutemen. Someone fired the first shot; 8 minutemen fell dead and the British went on to Concord to complete their mission. On the way back to Boston, they were harassed by sharpshooters, firing from the woods to such effect that about 270 soldiers were killed or wounded.

The Battle of Bunker Hill, 17 June 1775, from a painting by John Trumbull: Dr Warren, a leading 'rebel' lies dying on the wind-swept height as the British make a desperate surge to reach the top. In the picture, the mortally wounded British Major Pitcairn is being carried from the field.

The War of Independence or, as the Americans call it, the American Revolution, had begun. It was to last for 7 years and to end in humiliation for Britain and complete victory for the colonists. The numbers of troops involved in the war were small; Washington's army rarely amounted to more than 16 000 men and, in the bitter winter at Valley Forge, it shrank to 2400; Burgoyne's army at Saratoga Springs totalled 7-8000 British and German soldiers and, when Cornwallis surrendered at Yorktown, only 7000 men laid down their arms. In essence, a small number of regular soldiers trained to fight in European-style battles, took on the ultimately impossible task of trying to subdue a great number of half-trained men operating in a huge country which they knew infinitely better than their opponents.

After Lexington and an action at Boston, in which Gage lost 1000 men in capturing Bunker's Hill and showing that irregulars could take on professional soldiers, the Second Continental Congress met at Philadelphia to issue its Declaration of Independence and to appoint Colonel George Washington to command its army. Operations began with Congress ordering an attack on Canada, but the expedition led by Benedict Arnold was a complete failure, because, thanks to the Quebec Act, the French Canadians had no intention of joining the rebellious, mostly nonconformist, colonists to the south. Meanwhile, General Howe, who had succeeded Gage, sat tight at Boston, and Washington tried manfully to turn a motley collection of

Reading the Declaration of Independence on the first Fourth of July, 1776, as it may have taken place in any one of the thirteen colonies. Only one man waves his tricorn hat in excitement, the rest of the crowd listen gravely to what must have been momentous tidings.

civilians into a disciplined army. It was a daunting task, for the separate colonies, mean and jealous of one another, kept him short of munitions and stores, while the men themselves showed little aptitude for soldiering. Many refused to serve outside their own state; desertions were common, privates considered themselves as good as their officers and the officers quarrelled amongst themselves and, in some cases, went over to the enemy.

But Washington was equal to every call. Infinitely patient and tenacious, he hung on, slowly winning the army's respect for his skill and devotion, as he refused any pay for his services and sold land in order to feed and clothe his men.

Howe moved down to occupy New York, where he received an enthusiastic welcome, but when Washington retreated north, the British commander showed a strange reluctance to follow him. The explanation for this inactivity was that the British command thought the best plan was to sit still and wait for the colonists to collapse from their internal quarrels and lack of money and equipment. Decisive action would only lead to lasting bitterness, whereas, in fact, time was to prove America's best ally and, as Pitt said later, three years were spent 'in teaching the Americans how to fight.'

In 1777, King George and his advisers concocted a master plan to cut off Massachusetts from the rest of the colonies; General Burgoyne would march

In December 1776, Washington was retreating before the British advance across New Jersey when, on Christmas night, he suddenly turned about, recrossed the Delaware and defeated a corps of Hessian (hired German) troops at Trenton. This brilliant exploit was followed by another a few days later at Princeton.

The surrender of the British troops at Yorktow

from Canada down the Hudson Valley to be met by Howe advancing from New York. Unfortunately, the orders were never made clear and Howe went off on his own to beat Washington at Brandywine and capture Philadelphia. Meanwhile, Burgoyne's redcoats trudged on through wilderness country, attacked all the way by guerilla troops, until they came to Saratoga Springs, where, surrounded and outnumbered, they surrendered.

The effect was electrifying. This was the colonists' first real victory since fighting began; it wiped out Washington's defeat and, infinitely more important, it brought Britain's European enemies into the war. France had been watching the scene with interest and, in response to Benjamin Franklin's persuasive skill at Versailles, had been sending stores, money and a few privateers but, now, with the prospect of Britain engaged in a long struggle, she came in openly on the American side by despatching a fleet to the West Indies. Spain, seeing a chance to recover Gibraltar, joined France in 1779 and Holland, hoping to weaken England's maritime power, followed suit in 1780.

The whole character of the war changed. The British decided to concentrate mainly on a naval war, while trying to bring Washington to a decisive battle on land. Sir Henry Clinton, the new commander-in-chief, therefore turned his attention to making attacks along the American coast and launching a campaign in the south, where there were thousands of 'loyalist' supporters. Georgia came under British control and, in 1780, Charleston in South Carolina was captured with the surrender of almost as many men as at Saratoga.

9 October 1781. Painting by Van Blarenberghe.

However, when the combined French and Spanish fleets were joined by the Dutch, the balance of sea-power was tipped against Great Britain and things became even worse with the formation of the League of Armed Neutrality by Prussia, Sweden, Russia and Denmark to resist the British search of neutral ships for goods destined for America. This was the work of Frederick the Great in revenge for having been left in the lurch by George III. The Royal Navy could no longer keep up an effective blockade of French and Spanish ports or protect British merchantmen at sea, so that some 3000 ships were sunk, an enemy fleet cruised in the English Channel, Minorca and Gibraltar were besieged, West Indian islands lost and the Spaniards captured Florida[1] and the Bahamas. In India, the French threatened to destroy the East India Company.

In America, Clinton still hoped for victory, for Congress was practically bankrupt and Washington was trying desperately to keep his ragged army together. From Charleston, General Cornwallis advanced through North Carolina into Virginia, with the idea of joining forces with Clinton who would move from New York, so that together they could destroy Washington.

Loss of sea-power defeated this plan. A strong French force, led by the Marquis de Lafayette, was able to land and prevent Clinton leaving New York, so Cornwallis made for Yorktown on the coast to wait for reinforcements by sea. Washington realised that his chance had come; he

[1] Ceded to Britain in 1763 by the Treaty of Paris.

raced south and was joined by French troops so that, with an army totalling 16 000 men, he closed in on Yorktown and began battering away at the British defence lines. Meanwhile, the French admiral De Grasse arrived off the coast with 40 warships, too many for the British fleet to disperse. Hemmed in by land and sea, Cornwallis made desperate attempts to break out of the trap but he was forced to surrender on 19 October 1781. Yorktown was as decisive as Saratoga, because it convinced the British that they must end a war which many of them had not wanted and which they now realised they never could win.

Lord North resigned and King George accepted a government of men who had long proclaimed the justice of the colonists' claims, but, like the rest of the nation, they were in no mood to yield to France and Spain and, by an astonishing change of fortune, Britain soon extricated herself from what had seemed to be a desperate situation.

In the West Indies, Admiral Rodney destroyed the Franco-Spanish fleet; Gibraltar, which had held out for two years, was relieved by Admiral Lord Howe and, in India, the French plans came to nothing. Thus, when the peace was made by the Treaty of Paris (1783), Britain's losses were nothing like what might have been expected. The 13 colonies of course gained complete independence; France retained Louisiana and Canada stayed in the British Empire. Something had to be done for the colonists who had sided with Britain, for there had been savage fighting between 'Loyalists' and 'Patriots' and there were too many scores to be paid to leave the losing side to their fate, so thousands of Loyalists, mostly from southern states, were granted lands in Canada and many others found homes in England and the West Indies.

In America, the colonies had become states, but they were not yet united, for there were those who felt that there was no need for Congress or a strong central government, now that the war was won. They had fought for independence, and, having freed themselves from orders issued from London, they saw no point in taking orders from Philadelphia. It soon became clear, however, that the states needed an American government to protect their interests in economic and foreign affairs.

A sharp reminder of this need came from Massachusetts, where, in 1786, a Continental Army veteran named Daniel Shays led an uprising of debt-laden farmers who found ready support from people who were indignant about heavy taxation and the general set-back in trade. The insurrection, which had to be put down by the militia, reminded men of property that victory had left them with problems to solve.

So the gentlemen who assembled at Philadelphia in 1787 - landowners, planters, lawyers and businessmen - came together to devise a Constitution which would somehow create a strong government and yet respect the rights of states to manage their own affairs. Their leaders, headed by Alexander Hamilton, Benjamin Franklin and James Madison (Jefferson and John Adams were absent in Europe) worked out a brilliant compromise through their moderation and also through bringing George Washington to Philadelphia, the one man whom everyone would accept as President.

In a remarkably short time, less than a year, they set up a federal government, that is, one in which the states formed a union or federation and gave up some of their powers, such as those to levy taxes, raise an army, regulate trade, declare war and make treaties. But they kept control of such services as education, police, roads and hospitals.

Laws were to be made by Congress which, like the British Parliament, consisted of two Houses, an upper one, the Senate, with two members from each state, and a lower one, the House of Representatives, whose members were elected by popular vote according to the population of each state. The Head of the State and of policy-making was to be the President, elected by the states for a 4-year term. Representatives were to serve for 2 years and Senators for 6. The third branch of the Federal Government was the Judiciary, of which the Supreme Court could overrule laws even if they were passed by Congress.

On 30 April 1789, George Washington, 'the Father of his Country', became the first President of the United States; he served two terms of office, eight years, and was followed by John Adams, Thomas Jefferson and James Madison, all of them men of outstanding quality.

The young republic had got off to a good start. It was blessed with a number of great advantages, of which the first was that its leaders were not faced with the task of governing a huge backward peasant class, such as existed in most other countries, for this was a vigorous literate people, who understood the democratic system and were eager for every kind of advancement. The new Americans had ample territory, great natural resources (mainly agricultural at this stage), the legacy of European civilization and the important advantage of being so remote that they could work out their future without foreign interference.

17th century bronze
figure of Lakshmi, the
Hindu goddess of fortune,
mother of Kama, god of
love, and consort of
Vishnu. The festival of
Lakshmi is celebrated by
the writer caste in Bengal.
(Bronze from Polur Font,
near Arcot.)

280

8 India
1707 – 1901

Aurangzeb (1658-1707), sixth of the Mogul Emperors of India, extended the empire even further south than had Akbar, but, in his devotion to the Islamic faith, he persecuted non-Muslims so cruelly that he destroyed the harmony which Akbar had fostered and aroused such hatred that the Mogul power was brought to ruin.

The Mahrattas, warlike tribesmen whose homeland was the Western Ghats, a mountain range rising up to the Deccan plateau, took to raiding Mogul territory so persistently that Aurangzeb said of their defiant leader, Shivaji, 'My armies have been employed against him for nineteen years and nevertheless his state has always been increasing'. Shivaji's death put an end to any prospect of Mahrattan unity, but, from their hill strongholds, they continued to ravage Central India for more than a century.

Another people provoked by Aurangzeb's intolerance were the Sikhs, a community of warriors from the Punjab foothills of the Himalayas, where they had built the holy city of Amritsar on land given to them by Akbar. The murder of their Guru, or holyman, drove them into rebellion and, from a religious brotherhood, they became a formidable military power. Peasant revolts and the cost of continuous wars overstrained even Aurangzeb's resources and he died a fugitive, dreading the fate he had meted out to so many others.

A Mogul emperor continued to sit on the throne at Delhi, but he was an emperor in name only, for the hereditary *rajahs* and the Muslim governors of the provinces set themselves up as rulers of independent kingdoms. While the Mahrattas and the Sikhs kept up their raids and Afghan invaders came down from the north, wars broke out between a multitude of petty states and, with the collapse of strong government, bands of armed robbers called *thugs* and *dacoits* roamed the countryside. By the middle of the 18th century, India had fallen into such chaos that a handful of Europeans were able to establish themselves as the dominant power.

The Portuguese were the first Europeans to start trading in India and in Eastern seas, but they were soon supplanted by the aggressive, better-organised Dutch. On the last day of 1600, Elizabeth I, Akbar's contemporary, granted a charter to the East India Company, formed by a group of London merchants, whose aim was to finance trading voyages to the spice

islands beyond India. However, in 1623, officials of the more powerful
United East India Company of the Netherlands put to death 10 English
merchants at Amboyna in the Moluccas, a disaster which persuaded the
English Company to shift its activities to the Indian sub-continent.

There they had already been permitted to set up a 'factory' or trading-post
at the port of Surat within the Mogul empire and, by 1647, they had 27
small posts, among them Fort St George, which was to become Madras. In
1665, they acquired Bombay from the Portuguese, as part of the dowry of
Catherine of Braganza on her marriage to Charles II and, over in the east, in
Bengal, Aurangzeb allowed them to found a new settlement at a place which
came to be named Calcutta. For a long time, the English East India Company
concentrated on 'quiet trade', making its profits from local business,
commerce with China and the sale of Eastern goods like cotton cloth, coffee,
pepper, tea and indigo to European markets. To protect their merchandise

II. Dupleix .

Joseph Dupleix (1697-1763), the French Governor of Pondicherry, whose project to found a French empire in India was narrowly frustrated by Clive. After his recall to France, the French Company refused to reimburse him for the vast sums he had spent out of his private fortune and he died in poverty.

from robbers, they fortified their settlements and hired native soldiers (*sepoys*) to serve under English officers.

As yet, the Company had no ambitions beyond trade and seemed likely to play a lesser role than the French, whose Compagnie des Indes was directed and financed by the French government. Moreover, in Joseph Dupleix, the Governor-General at Pondicherry, they had a brilliant far-sighted administrator who was determined to expand French influence.

In 1746, the French captured Madras from the British and although, by the Treaty of Aix-la-Chapelle, it was handed back two years later, French prestige stood high from the success of their arms and through Dupleix's masterly skill in forming alliances and setting up puppet governments in Hyderabad and the Carnatic. By 1750, he seemed certain to triumph, for the British-supported claimant to the throne of the Carnatic was hotly besieged at Trichinopoly (Tiruchirapalli) and, when it fell, the British would be ousted from southern India.

At this point, there appeared on the scene a young man named Robert Clive, who, as an ill-paid junior clerk or 'writer', had been in Madras when it was captured, but escaped to join the Company's military service. Given a small force to make a diversionary attack on Arcot, he captured the town

Suraj-ud-Daulah (or Siraj or Suraja Dowlah), Nawab of Bengal, attacked the British merchants in Calcutta on the charge of fortifying the place without permission. His downfall was brought about by a conspiracy of Indian nobles supported by Clive. After the battle of Plassey (June 1757), he was captured and executed.

and held it for 50 days against a huge army. This spectacular feat changed the situation, for it saved Trichinopoly, restored British prestige and put their client Mohammed Ali on the throne as Nawab of the Carnatic. The French and their allies surrendered and poor Dupleix was recalled to France in disgrace.

Clive also went home for a time but, in 1756, he was back in India as Governor of Fort St David, 100 miles from Madras, when the action shifted to Bengal. There the young Nawab Suraj-ud-Daulah, offended by what he considered to be the British governor's impertinence, advanced on Calcutta with an army, whereupon the governor and senior officials fled down the river, leaving the garrison to its fate. It surrendered and 146 prisoners were locked up for the night in a small room of the fortress and, in the stifling heat of June, all but 23 were dead in the morning. Much was made of the so-called Black Hole of Calcutta, but it now seems likely that it occurred through someone's blunder, not as an act of deliberate cruelty.

War with France was known to be imminent (the Seven Years' War broke out in August 1756), and Clive, accompanied by Admiral Watson and 5 men-of-war, set out from Madras to re-take Calcutta. This he achieved in January 1757, and went on a little further to capture the French station at Chandernagore. Realising that Suraj-ud-Daulah was unpopular, he then made a secret deal with a noble named Mir Jafir that he would put him on the throne of Bengal. Financiers and some of Suraj's officers were in the plot and, in June, Clive marched from Chandernagore with 3000 men and 9 field-guns to confront the Nawab's army of 50 000 fighting men, supported by more than 50 cannons and some French artillery. The two armies met in the mango groves of Plassey, where, after a night of indecision, Clive decided to attack. The enemy's cannonade was ineffectual, Mir Jafir's contingent stayed aloof and Suraj, sensing treachery, fled from the field on a camel. Thus ended one of the decisive battles of world history, because it gave the British control of Bengal and all its riches.

Mir Jafir was installed on the throne as Nawab, in reality the puppet of the Company, and Clive, whose 'reward' amounted to £234 000 and an estate worth £30 000 a year, went home in triumph.

In the Carnatic, the French and the English were more evenly matched and the French general, Lally, captured Fort St David and laid close siege to Madras, but he was defeated at Wandewash (1760) by Sir Eyre Coote, who went on to capture Pondicherry itself. This was the end of French dominion in India; they were allowed to keep their trading-stations, but no garrisons, and in 1769 the Compagnie des Indes was abolished.

During Clive's absence in England, the British officials governed Bengal with scandalous rapacity, extorting bribes and ruining merchants through

Robert Clive (1725-74), 1st Baron Clive of Plassey (portrait by Dance), the brilliant soldier and administrator who, in less than 12 years' residence in India, ousted the French and brought the huge province of Bengal under British rule. His efforts to check corruption earned him the bitter enmity which Warren Hastings later had to face.

their wholesale corruption. Mir Jafir himself was deposed in favour of his son-in-law for a huge sum paid to the Bengal Council and then restored to his throne for another fortune!

It is important to realise that while this misgovernment was taking place in Bengal, vast areas of India knew nothing, so far, of the British and their French rivals. The Mahrattas, for instance, moved into the north to occupy the Punjab in 1758, which led to an alliance of Afghan tribes whose leader, Ahmad Shah, invaded the Punjab and crushingly defeated the Mahrattas at Panipat (1761), a battle in which hundreds of thousands of warriors took part. Ahmad Shah subsequently withdrew, leaving northern India in greater disorder than ever.

When Clive came back in 1765 as Governor of Bengal, he recognised that a trading Company had somehow saddled itself with the task of governing millions of people. Nobody had planned this. The chaotic state of the country since the collapse of Mogul rule, and the successful outcome of the struggle with the French had placed the British in control of a country where a small number of European troops with European artillery could be decisive. Clive suggested to Pitt that the British Government ought to take over these new responsibilities, but Pitt was unwell and out of office, so Clive introduced reforms which were heartily resented by those who knew that he had made his own fortune. He raised salaries, so that the Company's officials would have less reason to be dishonest and forbade them to take part in private trade or accept gifts. The Emperor Shah Alam, whose army had recently been defeated at Buxar by Major Hector Munro, granted the Company the provinces of Bengal, Behar and Orissa, with the *diwani* or right to collect taxes; in return, since he had been made homeless by the Afghans, Shah Alam was given a pension and a palace at Allahabad.

Clive left India for the last time in 1767, but the 'heavenborn general', as Pitt dubbed him, found no happiness in retirement and he killed himself in 1774 during one of the fits of depression to which he was subject. His work in India was continued by Warren Hastings, who had risen steadily in the Company's service until in 1772 he became Governor of Bengal and Governor-General of India in the following year. An energetic, if high-handed, administrator, he reformed the government, improved justice and used Company troops to support the Nawab of Oudh in suppressing the Rohilla Afghans on his northern frontier. Through checking the dishonesty of merchants and officials, Hastings made many enemies, in particular, one of his council, Philip Francis, who went home to agitate for the Governor-General's recall.

Hastings meanwhile had to deal with the situation which had arisen since France sided with the American colonies, for the main Indian powers — the Mahratta Confederacy, the Nizam of Hyderabad and Hyder Ali, ruler of

Mysore — formed a coalition supported by the French, whose fleet appeared in the Bay of Bengal. Acting with great resolution, Hastings seized all the French settlements, sent a military expedition to protect Bombay, made vigorous war on the Mahrattas and used all his diplomatic skills to weaken the coalition. When Hyder Ali overran the Carnatic, Hastings sent the renowned Sir Eyre Coote to save Madras and wage a long campaign against this formidable foe.

To pay for all these operations, Hastings raised money in various ways, through loans, taxes and threatening demands upon wealthy Indians. In Oudh, for instance, he extorted more than a million pounds from the *begum* or dowager-princess, but, unlike so many officials, he took nothing for himself and, on occasion, even contributed money from his own purse.

After his return to England, he had to face charges of 'high crimes and misdemeanours' brought against him by Francis and the Whigs. His trial dragged on for seven years and, at its end, the man who had saved the East India Company from extinction, was acquitted, though ruined financially.

By this time, the British Government had come to realise that it could not allow the East India Company to go on making wars and generally misgoverning huge provinces, so, in 1784, William Pitt the Younger put through Parliament his India Act, by which much of the Company's power was transferred to a Board of Control, whose 6 Privy Councillors would take responsibility for Indian affairs and would appoint the Governor-General. Business and administration would remain in the hands of the Company's Directors.

The British Government genuinely hoped that there would be no further acquisitions of territory and no taking on the role of an imperial power. Yet, within less than a century, British India covered nearly three-quarters of the sub-continent and the authority of the British Raj (rule) was acknowledged by the remainder. A number of outstanding Governors-General introduced reforms, especially of taxation, but were constantly drawn into wars and disputes which led to the take-over of yet more territory. Under Lord Cornwallis (1786-93), for example, another war with Mysore resulted in the defeat of Hyder Ali's son, Tipu Sultan, who ceded half his state to the British; in 1796, Ceylon (Sri Lanka) was conquered from the Dutch and, during the governorship of Lord Wellesley (1798-1805), the fourth Anglo-Mysore War led to annexations which extended British rule over nearly all southern India. Wellesley adopted a 'forward policy', partly out of fear of revolutionary France (Bonaparte's Egyptian expedition had been undertaken to secure the 'half-way house' to India) and partly out of his own ambition to make Britain the paramount power. He made 'Subsidiary Alliances' with princes who were supplied with troops and protection in return for territory and an undertaking to have no dealing with any other foreign power. One of

287

the Mahratta princes accepted such an alliance and when the others refused, they were defeated at Assaye (1803) by Wellesley's brother, Sir Arthur Wellesley, afterwards the Duke of Wellington.

Neither the Government nor the Director of the Company approved of this expansive policy and Lord Wellesley was recalled to England in 1805. His departure made little difference, for there were always disorders to be suppressed and territories to be taken over in the name of peace and progress. The marauding Pindari tribes were broken up and the Mahrattas finally defeated; Burmese aggression led to the acquisition of Assam (1826) and Lower Burma (1852), but intervention in Afghanistan, caused by fear of Russian influence, had a catastrophic outcome when 4500 troops and 12 000 camp followers were wiped out by Afghan tribesmen on their retreat from Kabul (1842). But the annexations continued - Sind, Oudh and, after two bloody wars with the Sikhs, the whole of the Punjab (1848), which was turned by the two Lawrence brothers into a model province, with good law-courts, low taxation and prosperity.

Lord Dalhousie (1848-56) revived an old Hindu custom - 'the doctrine of lapse' - whereby the dominions of a ruler who died without an heir could be taken over by the Paramount Power. Under this law, he annexed 7 small states in central India, so that no independent Indian state of any importance remained. Dalhousie also set about providing the 'blessings of civilization' - roads, canals, telegraph and postal services, new sea-ports and railways. English had already replaced Persian as the language of official business; many schools were opened and the universities of Calcutta, Madras and Bombay founded in 1857.

British rule was bringing peace, order and economic development; yet all was not well. Many of the changes had been too rapid for people who had followed their own ways of life for centuries; prohibition of *suttee* (whereby a Hindu widow threw herself on her dead husband's funeral pyre) and the arrival of Christian missionaries made many Indians fear for their religion. Muslims were hostile to education in English and the old ruling families were offended by the overbearing attitude of some of the British officials.

The Indian Mutiny of 1857 was sparked off by the issue of greased cartridges for the new Enfield rifles to the army of Bengal, in which sepoys heavily outnumbered the British soldiers. The grease was said to be made from the fat of cows, sacred to Hindus, and of pigs, loathsome to Muslims. In the atmosphere of resentment, this was enough to provoke mutiny and, at Meerut, the sepoys killed their officers and marched south to Delhi, where they restored the aged Mogul Emperor to his throne. But the mutiny lasted for only a few months and never spread much beyond the area around Delhi and the recently-annexed kingdom of Oudh. There were massacres, heroic actions and some terrible reprisals by the British troops, but the princes, the

Battery at Lucknow - the defenders on the look-out: during the Indian Mutiny (1857), the British Residency at Lucknow, capital of Oudh, was hotly besieged by the 'rebels' from 30 June until 25 September, when its tiny garrison was relieved by General Havelock. His force could only reinforce the garrison and the siege was renewed until 17 November when it was finally broken by Sir Colin Campbell.

Indian people as a whole and, most important, the warlike Sikhs, made no move.

Peace was restored, thanks largely to the good sense of the Governor-General, Lord Canning, who was nick-named 'Clemency Canning' for his refusal to listen to the clamour for savage punishment.

The Crown took over the government of India from the Company, and the Governor-General, who was later known as the Viceroy, became directly responsible to the Secretary of State for India. In a royal proclamation, Queen Victoria assured her Indian subjects that her greatest wish was to see them 'happy, contented and flourishing'; there would be no more territorial expansion, no interference with religious beliefs and worship but more opportunities for Indians to take posts in the government service.

But, in spite of fair words, things were never quite the same as before the Mutiny. Each side had lost confidence in the other; the British became a race apart, with their own exclusive clubs and pastimes and, while there were many who acquired an abiding love for India, the ruling class tended to adopt an air of superiority, convinced that Indians would never be capable of governing themselves and therefore it was their duty to hold the reins of power and to do their best to improve the condition of the vast population.

This attitude was naturally resented by the growing class of educated English-speaking Indians, especially as they found that they were debarred from higher posts in the government service. In 1885, when the first Indian National Congress met, its members voiced their grievances in demanding a greater share in the country's government and more rapid Indianization of the civil service. As nationalism took root and Muslims, fearing Hindu domination, began to organise their own conferences and defence associations, agitation grew sharper.

Thus, by the time of the death of Queen Victoria, Empress of India, Congress was demanding self-government, such as had been granted to the Dominions of Canada and Australia. Although vigorous reforms were put in hand, many difficulties stood in the way of the ruling power, the greatest being the irreconcilable enmity between Hindu and Muslim.

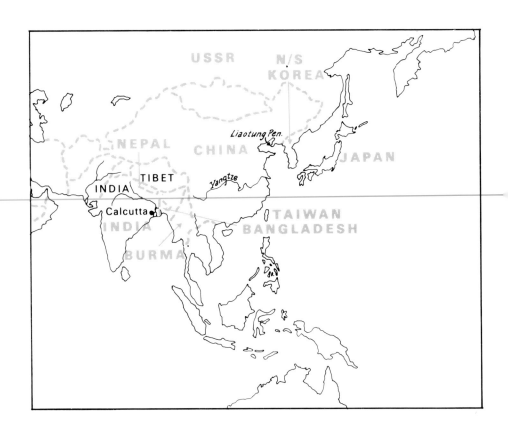

9 China of the Manchus
1644 – 1911

After the suicide of the last Ming emperor in 1644, the Manchus of Manchuria entered China and set up the Manchu or Ch'ing Dynasty, which lasted until 1911. The first of the two great Manchu emperors was K'ang Hsi (1661-1722), who did much to improve conditions in the vast country which was so often afflicted by rebellions, warlords and natural calamities like famines and floods. He continued to use the ancient form of government, whereby officials were chosen according to their performance in examinations on Chinese history, literature and the teachings of Confucius. In this way, a class of educated civil servants preserved China's culture for 2000 years through all the invasions and uprisings.

Tibet and Formosa were added to the empire in K'ang Hsi's reign, which covered the period when Louis XIV of France, Peter the Great of Russia, William III of England and Aurangzeb of India were ruling their countries. But the names would have meant nothing to the Chinese who regarded all foreigners as barbarians, considering their own country, which they called the 'Middle Kingdom', to be the centre of the world and all other countries to be their vassals. K'ang Hsi, however, did take an interest in European mathematics, science and music, and he enjoyed talking to Jesuit missionaries about the Christian religion, which he thought might be combined with the Chinese idea of Heaven and respect for the philosophy of Confucius. The Pope, however, did not agree.

K'ang Hsi's grandson, Ch'ien Lung (1736-96), was the other outstanding Manchu emperor. Like his grandfather, he expanded Chinese authority, adding Nepal, Burma and Annam (Vietnam) to the empire which reached its greatest extent during his reign. At Peking, he assembled a vast library, for which 15 000 scribes were employed in making copies of books and he encouraged the production of magnificent porcelains, as well as other works of art, such as jades, paintings, furniture, fans and wallpapers.

But, with the Chinese view of foreigners, it was difficult for Europeans to establish trade. A Ming emperor gave the Portuguese permission to set up a trading-post at Macao and the English East India Company had had a 'factory' since 1681 at nearby Canton, where, in Ch'ien's reign, a number of warehouses belonging to several other European nations stood in a row along the waterfront. Foreign merchants were not allowed to travel inland or to

Kuan-ti (God of War) in
famille verte porcelain of
the period 1662-1722.
Porcelain continued to be
an art form at which the
Chinese excelled.

trade direct with the Chinese; all business had to be done through a
government official and then only between the months of October and
March.

In hopes of improving this situation, the British sent out an embassy,
headed by Lord Macartney, whose 3 ships arrived at Tientsin, the port for
Peking, in 1793. Macartney, whose staff included scientists, artists and
musicians, brought with him a letter from King George III and 600 cases of
marvellous gifts. The visitors and their gifts were conveyed up the river to
the capital in barges, whose flags, unknown to the English who could not
read Chinese, bore the legend, *Ambassador bringing tribute from the
Country of England*. The Chinese, lining the river banks, did not think this
at all strange, for were not all the countries of the world subjects of China?

The Emperor Ch'ien Lung clearly took this view, for he accepted the gifts
and sent a reply to George III totally rejecting any idea of a trade agreement.
He consented to let the foreigners go on using Canton to obtain silk, tea and

porcelain, but these had to be paid for in silver, which was by no means to the Europeans' liking.

However, the British found something that the Chinese wanted even more than silver. This was opium, a drug produced principally in India, which turned those who smoked it into addicts, unable to work or take interest in

anything, except the dreams which the drug induces. The East India Company sold opium to British and American traders whose ships plied regularly between Calcutta and Canton, until Peking decided to put an end to a trade that was taking silver *out* of the country, so a commission went to Canton and destroyed 20 000 chests of opium, In the Opium War that ensued, British warships proved so superior to Chinese junks that they were able to bombard Canton and sail up the Yangtze to threaten Nanking.

The Chinese capitulated. By the Treaty of Nanking (1842), they agreed to open the ports of Canton, Amoy, Foochow, Ningpo and Shanghai to trade on equal terms, to give Britain Hong Kong as a naval base and to pay £21 million compensation for the opium destroyed.

A second clash occurred in 1858-60, after the Chinese had seized a British-registered ship, the *Arrow*, on a charge of piracy. This gave Britain's pugnacious Foreign Secretary, Lord Palmerston, the excuse to send an expedition which reached Peking and burnt the Emperor's Summer Palace to the ground. Again, the Chinese gave way, agreeing to open more ports, to allow diplomats in Peking and to pay another enormous indemnity.

Once Britain had forced open the doors of Ancient China, other powers demanded entry, so that France, Russia, Germany, the United States and Japan obtained ports from which to conduct their trade. In the 1880's, France annexed Annam, which became part of French Indo-China and Britain annexed Burma; the Chinese people suffered a worse humiliation in 1895 when their government was obliged to cede Korea, Formosa (Taiwan) and the Liaotung Peninsula to Japan.

There were many reasons for this pitiful decline from the days when Ch'ien Lung sent his contemptuous reply to George III; China had always been difficult to rule because its vast size and Ch'ien Lung had been followed by a number of feeble emperors. The choosing of officials by means of literary examinations had worked well for centuries, but, by this time, there had set in a resistance to change, just when new ideas and better means of production were needed to feed a population which had risen from 143 million in 1741 to 400 million in 1850. During this period, arable land increased by only 35 per cent, so, as more and more people tried to wring a living from their diminishing land-holdings, the peasants' lives became increasingly wretched.

Famines, rapacious landowners, heavy taxation and inflation induced many peasants to seek a way out of their misery by emigrating. Although this was illegal, agents were readily found to organise the traffic from village to neutral port, such as Portuguese Macao, whence millions of Chinese peasants were transported by ship to countries of South-East Asia, Australia and California (during their gold-rush years), the West Indies, Peru and any place where there was a demand for cheap 'coolie' labour.

Tzu-Hsi (1834-1908), Dowager Empress of China, who thought herself 'the cleverest woman who ever lived'. Yet, while her determination held the empire together for nearly 50 years, her refusal even to consider new ideas and social change brought China into civil war and foreign invasions, and brought about the end of the Manchu (or Ch'ing) dynasty.

In China itself, the peasants took up arms in one rebellion after another against a government which seemed powerless to improve their miserable existence. The greatest of these uprisings, the Taiping Rebellion, which lasted 14 years and cost over 20 million lives, was begun by a messianic figure, Hung Hsiu-ch'uan, whose version of Christianity appealed so strongly to the peasants of south China that they captured the city of Nanking, where they proclaimed the 'Heavenly Kingdom of Great Peace'. In the state which Hung founded, land was distributed equally and groups of 25 families formed the basic units of a society in which the popular vices of opium-smoking, drinking, polygamy, gambling, slave-owning and even foot-binding were forbidden.

From Nanking, the Taipings launched expeditions to conquer the rest of China, but, although the rebellion spread across 16 provinces, the movement came to be weakened by Hung's withdrawal from active leadership, the resultant struggle for supremacy among his subordinates and, in spite of its early success, the Taiping hostility to the teachings of Confucius. In the end, government armies, led by Confucian generals, suppressed the great rebellion. Nevertheless, it had a lasting influence, for it weakened the Manchu dynasty and helped to inspire later revolutionaries. More rebellions erupted; bandits infested the countryside and generals sent by Peking to restore order often set themselves up as independent warlords.

From 1861, for nearly 50 years, the ruler faced with this turmoil was a

Flight of Europeans from the Boxers - a cartoon in the Shanghai newspaper Tung-Kwang-Hu-Pao, 1900.

woman, a former concubine of the Emperor Hsien Feng. On his death, she seized power as the Dowager Empress Tz'u Hsi, ruling on behalf of her infant son and, when the boy died, this dynamic woman, vain, cruel and totally opposed to reform, contrived to put the 3-year-old nephew of the dead emperor on the throne so that she could continue to rule as regent.

Towards the end of Tz'u Hsi's reign, a secret society emerged which came to be known as the *Boxers*, from martial exercises similar to boxing which its members carried out. Believing that they themselves were immune to bullets, they proposed to cure China's troubles by expelling Westerners and destroying the Manchu government. Hence, in the Boxer Rebellion of 1900, they killed numbers of Christian missionaries, Chinese converts and foreigners; they then marched in force to Peking where they laid siege to the compound in which several foreign governments had their legations. After 55 days, a relief force made up of troops from 6 European powers, the U.S.A. and Japan fought its way in to raise the siege and take possession of China's capital.

Once again, the Manchu government had to accept humiliating terms, which only increased the people's hatred of foreigners and, in spite of some belated reforms from the old Empress, their determination to overthrow her

296

detested régime. For leadership, they looked to Sun Yat-sen, a doctor living in exile (a Christian, curiously enough), who organised uprisings which spread through the southern provinces where anti-Manchu feelings had always been strong. Tz'u Hsi died 3 years before the 1911 Revolution which ousted the last Emperor and proclaimed the Chinese Republic, with Sun Yat-sen as its first President.

Sun Yat-sen (1866-1925), the Chinese revolutionary leader, a doctor of medicine who lived abroad in Japan, America and Britain, organising at least ten unsuccessful uprisings from abroad until victorious in 1911.

10 Japan
1603 – 1919

Under the early rule of the Tokugawa *Shoguns*, who came to power in 1603 and ruled Japan as benevolent dictators for 265 years, Portuguese, Dutch and Spanish traders were welcomed and Jesuit missionaries made many converts to the Christian religion. But quarrels broke out when Franciscan and Dominican priests arrived and there was also ill-feeling between Spanish and Portuguese merchants, so the Shogun decided to expel them and to outlaw Christianity. By 1638, only a few Dutchmen were allowed to carry on a small amount of trade; all other dealings with foreigners, the learning of foreign languages and the building of ocean-going ships were forbidden.

In her isolation, Japan enjoyed peace and affluence and the Emperor remained a worshipped figurehead; the *daimyo* (feudal lords) were kept in check; their knights or warriors, the *samurai*, provided the class from which

Conference held 2 July 1863 on board the *Sémiramis* by French, British and Japanese officals, after the bombardment of a Japanese town (see page 300). Impressed by Western naval strength, the Japanese decided to study Western techniques of war.

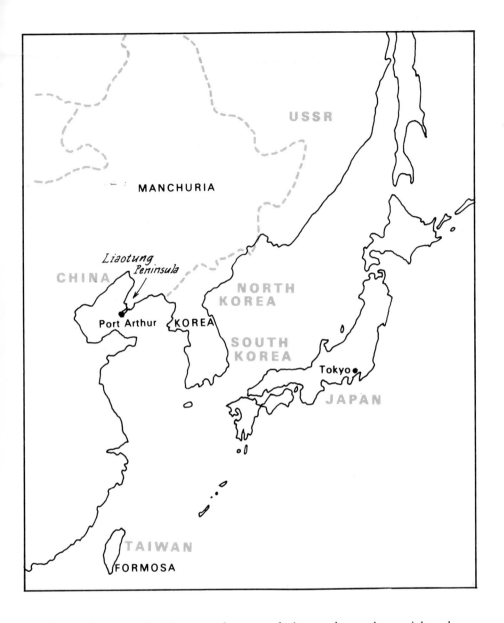

all government officials were drawn and, lower down the social scale, merchants, artisans and farmers lived prosperous, uneventful lives. By the end of the 18th century, the population of Edo (later called Tokyo) had risen to a million, but its existence was practically unknown to the Western world.

In 1853, 4 American warships arrived in Edo Bay and their commander, Commodore Perry, went ashore to present the U.S. government's request for the use of a Japanese port by American ships and proper protection for ship-wrecked sailors. The Shogun refused, but, when Perry returned in the following year with a stronger force, the Japanese, mindful of Britain's

victories in the Opium and *Arrow* wars in China, granted all that the Americans wanted. The British, the Russians and the Dutch were soon on the scene, making similar demands for trading concessions.

Not surprisingly, the arrival of foreigners and foreign goods had an upsetting effect upon a people who had lived so long in seclusion, and there was widespread indignation with the Tokugawa family for letting them in. Foreigners were attacked and their ships fired on, whereupon the combined fleets of the USA, France, Britain and the Netherlands bombarded a Japanese town. In 1868, an alliance between Court officials and some of the powerful daimyo resulted in the overthrow of the Tokugawa Shogun; the new government was headed by the Emperor Meiji, a boy of 15, whose reign lasted for 45 years, during which Japan was to advance from a backward oriental state to the position of a world power.

Japanese version of the battle in Tsushima Strait (27 May 1905) when the Russian Baltic fleet was practically annihilated by the Japanese fleet under Admiral Togo. Port Arthur, Russia's Manchurian base, had already fallen to the Japanese army.

Instead of trying to put the clock back, the young Emperor, guided by a number of able advisers, issued decree after decree to change totally the Japanese way of life. In his name, orders went out abolishing feudalism and the power of the daimyo, who were given pensions or official jobs; the samurai, forbidden to wear their traditional long swords, lost their privileged position; Western dress was introduced and a tremendous programme of school-building was undertaken to abolish illiteracy and to teach children educated skills and the importance of loyalty to the Emperor, the country and the family.

With the help of British, French, German and American advisers, westernisation went on at such an astounding pace that, within 30 years, the Japanese possessed railways, shipyards, mines, factories, iron and steel works, a powerful fleet and a modern army, with the banks and financial organisation to back their new-found might.

In 1889, a parliamentary system was founded, with an aristocratic Upper House, an elected House of Representatives, a Prime Minister and a Privy Council appointed by the Emperor. In practice, real power was in the hands of the army and navy chiefs, since they were not responsible to Parliament. It was they who decided to forestall Russia's imperialistic ambitions by sending an army to Korea, Formosa (Taiwan) and part of Manchuria. The next step to prevent Russia playing the dominant role in the decayed Chinese empire, was to demand the withdrawal of Russian troops which had moved into Manchuria during the Boxer Rebellion. When this was refused, the Japanese launched an attack in the Liaotung Peninsula, where they captured Port Arthur, the key naval base of this area, and amply demonstrated that the Tsarist forces were no match for Japan's westernized army.

Meanwhile, Russia had sent her Baltic fleet half-way round the world to the Far East, but the Japanese navy, commanded by Admiral Togo, fell upon it in the straits between Japan and Korea, and, in the battle of Tsushima, practically annihilated it.

In the peace treaty of 1905, arranged by the U.S. President Theodore Roosevelt, Russia acknowledged Japan's interests in Korea and transferred her lease of the Liaotung Peninsula and the railways she had built in southern Manchuria. Japan, the military ally of Great Britain since 1902, victor over Russia and China and now possessor of overseas domains, had suddenly become one of the major powers.

Relieved of competition in Korea, Japan quietly annexed that country in 1910 and there, as in Formosa, embarked on a programme of railway and factory-building with ruthless efficiency and little concern for the native inhabitants.

The First World War gave Japan the chance to make further gains for, as Britain's ally, she declared war on Germany in 1914, took over the German bases in China and seized German islands in the Pacific - the Carolines, Marshalls and Marianas, east of the Philippines - which she retained after the war. While the rest of the great powers were engaged in Europe, it was easy to put pressure on China, whose new republican government was presented with the notorious 'Twenty-One Demands' in 1915, which, in effect, ordered the Chinese to accept the Japanese as their advisers. The demands provoked such resentment that some were withdrawn and others watered down; nevertheless, Japan acquired many advantages, including a great increase in trade with the rich markets of Asia which had previously been dominated by European firms.

Thus, Japan went to the peace conference at Versailles in 1919 as one of the 'Big Five' to have her gains confirmed and to confer on naval disarmament as an equal with France, Britain and the USA.

11 Liberté! Egalité! Fraternité! 1789-94

The victory of the American colonists resounded across Europe; it inspired men who hated tyranny, especially Frenchmen whose government had helped to bring the young American republic into existence and whose soldiers had come home with glowing accounts of the land where ordinary people had won their fight for freedom.

The revolution which broke out in France only 8 years after the British surrender at Yorktown was not an isolated explosion. At about this time, there were serious uprisings in the Dutch Netherlands, Bohemia, the Austrian Netherlands and Sweden; America had the Shays Rebellion and, in England, hundreds were killed in the Gordon Riots of 1780. All these disturbances were essentially protests against authority, but none of them managed to bring down the government. How was it that an insurrection in Paris during the summer of 1789 became a revolution which no-one could quench?

For more than a century, France had been the leading country in Europe, outdistancing all the others in wealth, population, art, science and aristocratic splendour, yet, for all its magnificence, it was now on the verge of bankruptcy. This was still a feudal society, in which about a quarter-of-a-million aristocrats were supported by the toil of millions of illiterate half-starved peasants, while, between them, the *bourgeoisie* or middle-class, fumed with indignation at the privileges of the nobility and at their own lack of any say in how the country was governed.

The *Estates-General* or Parliament had not met since 1614, in spite of the fact that France had been almost continuously at war and had piled up enormous debts to pay for its armies and for the grandiose schemes of its royal autocrats. The help given to America had made the situation worse and, although minister after minister tried to relieve the country's financial plight, there was only one way in which it could have been done, which was to shift the burden of taxation from the poor to the wealthy classes. But not even an absolute monarch dared to overthrow the privileges of the nobles and the clergy.

There were other strains on the French people. The population had been rising faster than food-production, so labour was cheap and food was dear; a

303

series of bad harvests and outbreaks of cattle disease in the 1780's brought widespread distress and even famine in some areas.

To more and more Frenchmen, it became obvious that drastic changes were needed and, in their helplessness, they looked with a certain amount of hope towards Louis XVI, the young well-meaning monarch and his Finance Minister, Monsieur Necker, who was known to favour tax reform. But Louis was handicapped by his isolation from the people and by the behaviour of his wife, Marie Antoinette, the daughter of Maria-Theresa of Austria. In her frivolity, extravagance and, even in her beauty, the Queen came to stand for all that people hated in the privileged classes.

In 1789, the King agreed to summon the Estates-General, but, when the elected representatives gathered at Versailles, the Commons met such blank opposition from the other two 'estates' - the Nobles and Clergy - that they broke away to declare themselves the National Assembly and to swear never to go home until they had given France a new constitution.

Alas, they had no clear-cut programme and, as the weeks passed, with one high-flown speech after another, the situation in France became explosive. Food was scarcer than ever and riots broke out in several provincial towns, while, in Paris, a mob which had taken to the streets to protest at M. Necker's dismissal, broke into the army's arsenal and armed themselves with muskets.

On 14 July 1789, they captured the Bastille, a 14th-century fortress which was used as a prison for persons who had offended the King in some way, such as writing pamphlets to urge reform. There were, in fact, only 7 prisoners inside, but the fall of the Bastille was immensely important for two reasons: it had long been the symbol of royal oppression and its garrison offered no resistance to the mob. Louis XVI had concentrated 30 000 troops in and around Paris and, if they had made the slightest move to subdue the rioters, the Bastille would not have fallen. But, when the army stood aside and refused to fire on the citizens, the monarchy was doomed.

News of the Bastille spread like wildfire, law and order were overthrown, as the peasants took their revenge for centuries of oppression. In the country, they attacked the chateaux and destroyed ancient charters which recorded their feudal duties; in the towns, the bourgeoisie seized power from the royal officials and formed National Guard companies to defend themselves. In Paris, Lafayette, hero of the American war, took command of the Guard, but not of the mob, which marched to Versailles to bring Louis XVI and the royal family back to the city as prisoners.

As the Revolution grew more violent, power passed to the mob-leaders and to political societies like the Girondins, who still stood for liberty and fairly moderate policies, and the Jacobins, out-and-out republicans, who were led by Danton, Marat and Robespierre.

The capture of the Bastille by the Paris mob, the symbolic opening of the French Revolution.

J' somm' du Tier·Etat.

'Here's to the Third Estate!' A workman and a laundrymaid drink the health of the *Tiers Etat*, the Third Estate or the Commons, which included everybody who was neither an aristocrat nor a cleric.

In 1791, the King tried to escape, disguised as a valet, but he was recognised and arrested near the frontier, so that, thenceforward, he was treated as the enemy of the Revolution, all the more because his brother-in-law, Leopold II of Austria, and Frederick William of Prussia had decided to intervene. France declared war on both of them, but, as things went badly and a foreign army crossed on to French soil, the people's anger boiled over. An insurrection abolished the monarchy and, in an orgy of blood-letting, known as the September Massacres, hundreds of citizens, suspected of royalist sympathies, were executed by a newly-invented machine called the guillotine.

Showing equal fervour for the cause of freedom, the revolutionary armies drove the enemy back across the frontier and occupied the Austrian

Sketch by the artist David of Marie Antoinette on her way to the guillotine when, after vile treatment and viler accusations, she bears herself with courage and pathetic dignity.

Netherlands (Belgium), a success which inspired the government to announce that it would help any people to rise against their rulers. On 21 January 1793, Louis XVI, after his 'trial' in the name of Citizen Capet, went to the guillotine and, a few days later, France declared war on Great Britain.

In the war, Britain's main allies, Russia, Prussia and Austria, showed less interest in fighting France than in dividing up Poland among themselves and, within two years, that unfortunate country disappeared from the map. Pitt's policy - the old one of paying Britain's allies to do the fighting on the continent, while the Royal Navy kept command of the seas - therefore had scant success, whereas the French, fired with patriotic enthusiasm for their Revolution, carried all before them. They beat the Austrians in the Netherlands and took possession of the country; in the South of France, where a British fleet entered Toulon harbour to help the royalists, a young artillery officer, named Napoleon Bonaparte, deployed his guns so skilfully that the British were forced to withdraw.

While the French soldiers were saving the Revolution in the field, the politicians in Paris were engaged in a struggle for power from which the Jacobins emerged triumphant. Ignoring the Convention (successor to the National Assembly), they formed the Committee of Public Safety to run the government, liquidated the leading Girondins, executed Marie Antionette and instituted a Reign of Terror, when revolutionary tribunals throughout

Arrest of Robespierre (1758-94), leader of the Jacobins and, for a year, supreme ruler of France. His Reign of Terror led to his own downfall and reaction against the Revolution in which he believed so passionately.

France condemned thousands of persons to death, often on the flimsiest grounds.

At this time, when treachery and cruelty held sway, Robespierre, an accomplished young lawyer, became the real ruler of France for a year. The mob loved him for his apparent sincerity and total lack of interest in personal gain, so that his one remedy for opponents and suspects - the guillotine - was hailed with glee. In Paris, the number of executions went up to 80 a day. No-one was safe; not even Robespierre's own associates; he sent Danton, Hebert and Desmoulins to the scaffold; Marat was stabbed to death. But, at length, the tyrant overreached himself by proposing a law which threatened the life of every member of the Convention. A group of his enemies, led by Barras, suddenly arrested him and, on 28 July 1794, he was dragged to the scaffold to die without trial like so many of his victims.

With his death, the Terror came to an end and a group of Moderates in the Convention ordered an end to the Jacobin clubs, the release of thousands of prisoners, a new Constitution and an amnesty for royalists. They also decided to give executive power to a Committee of five, called the Directory, one of whom was to be the rascally but astute Barras who had arrested Robespierre.

With the Terror gone, it seemed just possible that *Liberté, Egalité* and *Fraternité* - those watchwords of the idealists -would be established. But the Parisians were in an ugly mood; the '*Reds*' had had their cherished Commune, the people's council, abolished; trade was bad; food was dear and, to the consternation of republicans, cries of 'Vive le Roi!' ('Long live the King!') began to be heard in the streets.

At this point, when the Convention was wondering what could be done, Barras remembered the young artillery officer who had distinguished himself at Toulon in 1793 and who was now in Paris looking for a military appointment. His name was Napoleon Bonaparte.

Portrait of Bonaparte (by Gérard) in 1803, when he was 34 years of age and First Consul. In the following year, he assumed the title of Emperor Napoleon I. He married (1) Josephine Beauharnais, a widow, and (2) the Archduchess Maria Louisa of Austria by whom he had a son, known as the King of Rome and Napoleon II.

12 Napoleon Bonaparte
1795 – 1821

On 4 October 1795, when royalists and extremists in Paris were about to take up arms, Paul Barras, commanding the Army of the Interior, sent for Bonaparte and asked him to serve under him.

'Where are the guns?' was Bonaparte's first question. They were 6 miles away, so he sent cavalry to bring them at top speed into the capital, where he placed them to fire directly down the streets along which the rebels would march towards the government headquarters, the Tuileries. When, with drums beating and muskets at the ready, they came into sight, he ordered his gunners to open fire and, with what he called 'a whiff of grapeshot', he put an end to the rebellion in half an hour.

As a reward for saving their skins, the Directory promoted Bonaparte at the age of 26 to the rank of full general and gave him command of the Army of Italy, which was already fighting the combined forces of Austria and Piedmont. By a series of brilliant victories, this astonishing young man crushed the enemy, fostered a spirit of revolution in the northern Italian states and created two republics under French protection - the Cisalpine Republic from the duchy of Milan and the Ligurian Republic round Genoa.

Having dictated peace terms to the Austrians and sent wagon-loads of looted treasures to France, Bonaparte returned to Paris like Caesar home from the wars and the Directory quailed at the arrival of the alarming hero they had created and looked round for some fresh employment for his menacing talents. Perhaps he would like the post of 'Commander of the Army against England'? Bonaparte declined. He would prefer, he said, to invade Egypt. The idea was quite attractive, since Egypt, nominally a province of Turkey, was weak and its conquest would supposedly enable France to strike at England's richest possession, India. Bonaparte himself wanted to make the expedition, not solely a military conquest, but a scientific and archaeological triumph.

The general who set out for Egypt in 1798, was not a Frenchman, but a Corsican of Italian descent whose father managed to get him sent to a military school in France, whence he entered the French army as an artillery officer. Bonaparte was 20 when the Revolution broke out and he had no doubts about continuing his army career, since at that time he had a keen sympathy for the oppressed and contempt for the privileged classes.

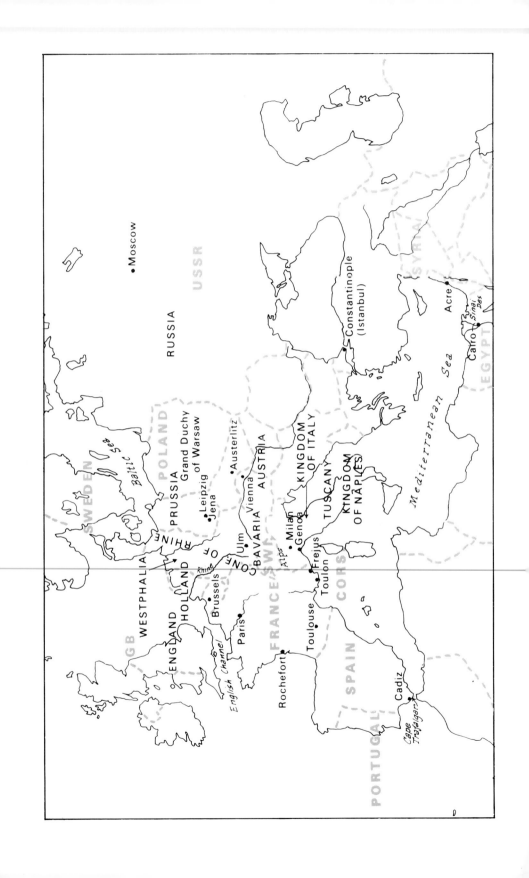

War and politics gave him chances to rise in the world and, as we have seen, he distinguished himself at Toulon, saved the Directory with his 'whiff of grapeshot' and became a general at 26, the adored 'Little Corporal' of his troops. No matter that his seniors resented his rapid promotion, no one could deny his brilliance on the battlefield nor the superhuman energy that enabled him to dominate everyone and every situation that confronted him.

His conquest of Egypt was a walk-over, for the gorgeously attired cavalry of the Mamelukes, the Egyptian ruling caste, were no match for French musketry and cannon-shot and Bonaparte entered Cairo in triumph. But 11 days later, Nelson, the English admiral who had been scouring the Mediterranean in search of him, destroyed the French fleet as it lay at anchor in Aboukir Bay, near the mouth of the Nile, and effectively cut off Bonaparte and his army from all contact with France.

Undismayed, Bonaparte advanced across the Sinai Desert into Syria in order to attack the Turkish army. Did he intend to capture Constantinople or to march across Iran to India? We do not know, because the garrison of the medieval fortress at Acre held out so stubbornly that the would-be conqueror was forced to retreat to Egypt.

Bad news awaited him. In his absence, the Austrians and Russians had invaded Switzerland (seized by revolutionary France in 1789), all his Italian gains were lost and the French government was in a state of collapse. Deciding to abandon his army, Bonaparte slipped away and, after an anxious voyage and a narrow escape from English ships, landed at Fréjus, just 15 months after he had set out from Toulon.

In Paris, hailed as the conqueror of Egypt, he was seen to be the one man who could save the country. Backed by the Army, he swiftly overthrew the government and, by the people's vote, became First Consul, with two other Consuls of no importance to assist him. He was now ruler of France and, while putting out peace feelers, he at once begun planning the swift victory which he needed to consolidate his power. Switzerland was again in French hands, so he crossed the Alps and came down into Lombardy, where, at Marengo, he would have been defeated, but for the Austrians' lack of fighting spirit. However, General Moreau won a more convincing victory at Hohenlinden, and the Allies accepted the Peace of Amiens and, by 1802, Russia, Austria and Britain had all accepted peace treaties.

Meanwhile, the First Consul was applying his extraordinary gifts to make France the orderly, just society which the revolutionary idealists had dreamed about. Working 16 hours a day to put right the chaos of 10 years, Napoleon, as he was now called, gave France an efficient system of local government; he ordered the building of schools, colleges, roads, canals and ports, and he encouraged trade and agriculture, so that France enjoyed a prosperity unknown for 130 years. Having set the country's finances in order, he turned next to its legal system and, presiding personally over the deliberations of a body of experts, reduced a mass of ancient customs and regional laws to a single code of some 2000 clauses, called the Code Napoléon, which gave all men equal justice and the right to trial by jury.

Extreme republicans had tried to root out religion, but Napoleon realised that the majority of Frenchmen wanted to practise the Catholic faith, so, in 1801, he made a peace or Concordat with the Pope so that the church bells rang again across the whole of France.

In these measures, Napoleon had the support of all Frenchmen, except the royalists and extreme revolutionaries. By the people's vote, he became First Consul in 1800, Consul for life in 1802 and Emperor in 1804, when, in Notre Dame Cathedral, Paris, in the presence of the Pope, he placed a gold laurel wreath on his own head and then set a crown on the head of his wife, Josephine.

But it was not enough for Napoleon to revive titles and Court ceremony and to settle down to the humdrum business of ruling a quiet and prosperous country. His restless temperament wanted glory - and where was it to be won except on the battlefield? So, in the war which had broken out again in 1803, he resolved to crush England first and then to bring the whole of Europe under his own control.

He assembled a great army on the cliffs opposite the Kent coast and ordered his naval commanders to break out of the harbours in which they were closely confined by the British Navy. It was two years before Admiral Villeneuve, commanding the French-Spanish fleet,[1] managed to escape from Toulon, but, instead of trying to win control of the Channel so that the invasion barges could make the crossing, he took refuge in Cadiz harbour, principally because he had no confidence in his fleet and wanted to save it from destruction. In furious disgust, Napoleon broke up the camps and marched away to Bavaria to deal with his enemies on land.

In October 1805, he crushed one Austrian army at Ulm; in December, he routed the main Austro-Russian armies at Austerlitz, a victory so complete that the Emperor Francis II accepted a humiliating peace, the Tsar withdrew his shattered forces into Poland and Pitt, his whole strategy in ruins, died of shock.

One piece of news alone relieved the Allies' gloom. Nelson enticed Villeneuve out of Cadiz and, on 21 October 1805, off Cape Trafalgar, destroyed the enemy fleet as a fighting unit to make England safe from invasion and to give her command of the seas for the best part of a century.

Napoleon's reaction was to decide to ruin the 'nation of shopkeepers' by closing the whole continent to British goods. The Baltic ports were still

[1] Spain had been a reluctant ally of France since 1796.

314

open, so he annihilated Prussia's army at Jena (1806) and moved on to defeat the Russians in the following year. The Tsar Alexander I, dazzled by Napoleon's personality, agreed to join the 'Continental System' that was to destroy Britain's commerce, but the British replied with their own 'Orders in Council', claiming the right to search neutral ships sailing to French-controlled ports. This policy made Britain extremely unpopular and led to an unnecessary but brief war in 1812 with the United States.

Napoleon was now at the summit of his fortunes. He abolished the Holy Roman Empire and parcelled the German states into the Confederation of the Rhine and the Kingdom of Westphalia under French 'protection'. The rest of Europe was to be ruled through his nominees, for he did not forget the members of his own family as long as they showed him proper respect. His brother Louis was made King of Holland; he gave Westphalia and an allowance of 5 million francs to his spendthrift brother, Jerome, and Naples to Joseph, before up-grading him to the throne of Spain. General Murat, who had married one of the Bonaparte sisters, received the Kingdom of Naples, another sister was made Grand Duchess of Tuscany and Josephine's son by an earlier marriage, Eugène, was put in charge of the enlarged Cisalpine Republic, now called the Kingdom of Italy, while Sweden was given to his friend, the French marshal, Bernadotte.

Napoleon ruled this empire well; he stationed French troops in all the vassal states, but his aim was to bring equality, justice and even self-government to the different countries, so he uprooted feudalism and introduced French ideas of progress and the Code Napoléon. Where he failed was in forgetting the national pride of peoples who had welcomed the French as liberators, but now found themselves ruled by a foreign despot who taxed them heavily, told them how to live their lives and ruined their trade by his ban of British goods.

Meanwhile, there was no doubt that his trade embargo was hurting Britain. Her trade with Europe fell to a trickle, though there was still one gap in the continental wall, as long as Portugal allowed British ships to use her ports. Napoleon therefore sent an army under Marshal Junot to occupy the country and he dealt with Spain, that reluctant ally, by forcing the King to abdicate in favour of his brother, Joseph Bonaparte.

Calling on Britain for support, the enraged Spaniards took up arms in a national revolt that was to tie down Napoleon's best generals and a quarter-of-a-million French troops for 6 years, for the Peninsular War was a classic example of how it is almost impossible to subdue a hostile population in a huge mountainous country, where 'a small army would be beaten and a large army would starve.'

Sir Arthur Wellesley, later the Duke of Wellington, who landed a British army in Portugal in 1808, had learned how to fight in a barren land during his campaigns against the Mahrattas in India, and, working closely with Spanish and Portuguese patriots, he kept the French at full stretch by advancing into Spain, then retreating back to Portugal, drawing the enemy into prepared defensive lines and, with the aid of his allies, advancing again to beat the hitherto invincible French in battle after battle. The ice-cool aristocrat wasn't afraid of them; he had studied their tactics and knew that they attacked in dense columns, so he trained his men to fight in line and hold their fire; the French made great use of their artillery, so he posted his men in trenches and behind ridges for protection and when the French cavalry appeared, his infantry formed squares and stood rock-firm against the fiercest charge. In 1813, Wellington drove the French back, step by step across Spain and over the frontier into France itself, where he finally beat Marshal Soult in Toulouse in April 1814. There, to his astonishment, he learnt that the Emperor Napoleon had abdicated.

While the Spanish war had been draining French resources and giving hope to the rest of Europe, Napoleon's friendship with the Tsar had turned sour and when Alexander re-opened trade relations with Britain, Napoleon decided it was time to put his rival down. In June 1812, he invaded Russia with an army of more than half-a-million men, one third of them French and the rest from so many of the occupied countries that it was called the 'Army of Twenty Nations'. He beat the stubborn Russians in one terrible battle without destroying their army, and, in September, entered Moscow where he awaited the Tsar's surrender. No-one came; the capital was deserted, the countryside stripped bare of supplies and, after a fire broke out, most of the city lay in ruins. A month elapsed before Napoleon realised his peril and ordered the retreat. It was 500 miles to the frontier and, as winter closed in on the endless columns, the dreaded Cossack cavalry attacked along the flanks. Snow, famine and the terrible cold did the rest.

The remnant of the Grand Army which crossed into the Grand Duchy of Warsaw in mid-December numbered fewer than 40 000 ragged survivors, and, by that time, their Emperor had left them, racing ahead by sleigh and carriage to raise fresh armies before Europe realised the extent of the disaster.

But the news had got out and Europe was up in arms to throw off the yoke. Prussia, Austria, Sweden and the German states declared war and, although Napoleon showed all his old brilliance in twice defeating them, his troops could not compare with those who had perished in the Russian snows.

At Leipzig, in October 1813, the allies beat the French and drove on towards Paris. Suddenly bereft of all support, Napoleon abdicated and went aboard an English frigate which carried him into exile on the island of Elba in the Mediterranean.

In less than a year he was back in France, where the people, already sick of

Napoleon leads his troops along a muddy road during the campaign of 1814, fought inside France itself, when Prussian, German, Austrian and other allied forces were driving towards Paris. Against odds, Napoleon never fought more brilliantly, but in vain, for Paris surrendered in March and he himself on 11 April 1814. This picture by Meissonier is one of many romanticised paintings which helped to create the Napoleonic Legend later in the century.

Louis XVIII's regime, greeted him with joy and the soldiers sent to arrest him fell into step behind their Emperor. Proclaiming his peaceful intentions to the world, he immediately raised an army of 130 000 troops with which he proposed to capture Brussels.

The Allied leaders, in conference in Vienna, broke up in dismay, but with pledges that they would raise enormous armies to destroy Napoleon once and for all time. For the moment, however, they could only muster a Prussian army under the resolute old campaigner Marshal Blücher and a mixed force of British, Dutch, Belgian and Hanoverian troops commanded by the Duke of Wellington.

Before these two armies could make contact, Napoleon attacked the Prussians, forcing Blücher to retreat, though the old general sent word to Wellington that he would join him as soon as possible. The Duke decided to fight a static defensive battle on carefully chosen ground, where he placed his numerically smaller army behind a long ridge south of Brussels near the village of Waterloo and awaited Napoleon's attack. It began at about noon on 18 June 1815, when the French infantry poured up the slope and were driven back by artillery-fire, musketry and the bayonet. The cavalry fared no better, but Napoleon kept up the pressure, mounting one assault after another on the Allied army, which hung on grimly with Wellington forever at hand to plug gaps and regroup his weary soldiers. As evening approached, dark masses of troops were seen approaching. They were Blücher's Prussians who had struggled all day across swampy ground to keep their commander's word to his ally.

In a last desperate throw, Napoleon ordered the Imperial Guard to attack but, in the face of superior firepower, they broke and fled and, with the vengeful Prussians smashing through the French right, the battle became a rout.

Not for the first time, Napoleon left his soldiers to fend for themselves and rode for his life to Paris, where a new provisional government told him to abdicate and leave the country. At the port of Rochefort, a British warship barred his escape to America, so he went aboard and, with astonishing cheek, wrote to the Prince Regent, asking for 'the hospitality of the British people!' There was no reply; he was taken instead to the remote island of St Helena in the south Atlantic, where he died in 1821, after spending his last years quarrelling with the governor and weaving his own version of his career.

Nineteen years later, his body was brought to France to be reburied in the Invalides amid an upsurge of hero-worship which launched the Napoleonic Legend. The tyrant who left his country defeated and weaker than when he positioned the guns at Toulon, became the Man of Destiny, the military genius, who spread the ideals of Liberty, Equality and Fraternity to the downtrodden peoples of Europe.

13   Ferment in Europe
1815 – 52

Napoleon's defeat did not destroy the impact of his extraordinary career; indeed, the Revolution's greatest influence outside France was to come in the years from 1815 to 1870. The Emperor's tyranny had awoken nationalism, a longing by people speaking the same language to throw off foreign rule; furthermore, the Revolution had spread liberalism and the idea of non-aristocrats having a say in government.

The representatives of the four victorious powers, Austria, Prussia, Russia and Britain, who met in Vienna in 1815, had small sympathy with these aspirations. They came together to prevent a renewal of French aggression and revolution, but, although they restored as much of the old régime as they could, they were less vengeful towards France than the Allies of 1919 were to be towards Germany.

France had her frontiers put back where they had been in 1790, and she also had to pay a war indemnity and accept occupation by allied troops for three years. Louis XVIII (the brother of Louis XVI, whose son had died) occupied the French throne more or less as a constitutional monarch; a Spanish Bourbon, Ferdinand VII, reigned from Madrid; another Bourbon was given the kingdom of Naples;[1] the Pope recovered the Papal States and Victor Emmanuel I received the Kingdom of Sardinia, which included Savoy on the borders of France and Piedmont in northern Italy.

Territories were re-arranged without any thought for feelings of nationalism. The Catholic Netherlands (now Belgium) were put under the rule of the Dutch Protestants; Austria was compensated for the loss of the Austrian Netherlands with virtually the whole of northern Italy, including Venice; Poland was re-divided, most of it going to Russia, and Prussia received gains right across northern Germany. The rest of Germany became a confederation of 39 states under the domination of Austria.

The leading figure at Vienna was Prince Metternich, an unbending aristocrat, whose policy was to preserve the Austrian Empire at all costs and therefore to prevent its German, Czech, Italian, Polish and Rumanian subjects even discussing ideas of freedom. Tsar Alexander, more idealistic,

---

[1] The kingdom of Naples was reunited with the kingdom of Sicily in 1815, to form once again the Kingdom of the Two Sicilies.

319

Prince von Metternich (1773-1859), the Austrian statesman who played the leading role in the settlement of Europe after Napoleon's downfall. For a generation, he was the arch-enemy of liberalism inside and outside Austria. In 1848, an uprising in Vienna forced him to take refuge in England; he later returned to Austria but took no further part in politics.

wanted a Holy Alliance of powers to promote Justice, Christian Charity and Peace, but, in practice, the rulers of Russia, Austria and Prussia were united in opposing liberalism and revolution wherever they might arise.

To her credit, Britain refused to join the enemies of liberty in Europe. Her Foreign Minister, Castlereagh, took the view that it was no part of the duty of the major powers to interfere in the internal affairs of other states and therefore Britain came to be regarded as the champion of liberty by peoples like the Greeks, Poles and Belgians who were chafing under foreign rule.

Revolts against the Vienna settlement broke out almost immediately, with the Austrians having to suppress risings in Piedmont and Naples, where Austrian troops upheld the rule of a despotic monarch. French soldiers went to the aid of the Spanish King against his own people and the Russians put down a Polish insurrection.

The Greeks were more fortunate in being able to take advantage of a rift between the two champions of repression, Austria and Russia. Metternich, well aware that a successful revolt of the Serbs, Greeks and other Balkan peoples against Turkish rule could lead to similar rebellions in the Austrian Empire, naturally upheld the Sultan's waning authority, but the Tsar, partly because of the close links between the Greek and Russian branches of the Orthodox Church, supported the Greeks when they rose to arms in 1821. And there were many others in Western Europe who felt a romantic kinship with the rebels, the most famous being the English poet, Lord Byron, who became the martyr-hero of the movement.

George Canning, Castlereagh's successor, did not intervene at first, because he felt that Turkey's defeat would make Russia all-powerful in the eastern Mediterranean, but, when the Sultan's Egyptian troops (sent by Mehemet Ali, an Albanian adventurer who had made himself master of Egypt) seemed bent on wiping the Greek nation out of existence, he joined with Russia and France in sending a fleet which completely destroyed the Turkish navy in Navarino Bay (1827). This victory made it impossible for the Sultan to overcome the Greeks and in the end he was compelled to recognise their independence (1830).

Louis XVIII came to his throne, it was said, 'in the baggage of the allied

armies', but this easy-going old gentleman had the sense to follow a middle-of-the-road course which enabled France to put her finances in order and take her place again as one of the great powers. His brother, Charles X, who succeeded him in 1824, was much less sagacious. A religious bigot, who believed that it was his duty to root out every trace of the Revolution and restore the *ancien régime*, he declared that he would rather 'chop wood than reign after the fashion of the King of England'. But when he dissolved the National Guard, abolished the Assembly and threatened the freedom of the press, the Parisian mob manned the barricades and, after three days of fierce fighting in July 1830, drove the King back into exile.

Lafayette, the veteran revolutionary, took charge of affairs to bring back, not a republic, but a constitutional monarch in the person of Louis Philippe, son of the Duke of Orleans, whose sympathy with the revolutionaries in 1789 had earned him the nickname, 'Philippe Egalité'. Publicly adopting the tricolor, Louis Philippe became the Citizen King, a benign figure in frock coat and top hat, who walked about the capital like any member of the *bourgeoisie* and gave his country 18 years of peace and advancing prosperity.

The July Revolution excited liberals everywhere and, in Germany, three rulers were forced to abdicate in favour of successors who promised to reform the constitutions, while, in Italy, the patriots were again crushed by

An incident during the aftermath of the Greek War of Independence: Greek insurgents resist government cavalry from a tower in Thebes, 1833. In the previous year, Greece had been saddled with Prince Otto of Bavaria as king and this led to unrest and revolts.

Liberty Leading the People by Delacroix was based on the July revolution of 1830. Barricades were thrown up in Paris and, after three bloody days of street-fighting, the restored Bourbon monarchy was overthrown.

Austrian troops. The Tsar Nicholas I, breathing fire and fury against all revolutionary doctrines, had to deal with another Polish rebellion and this helped the Belgians to break away from Dutch rule. Fighting took place in Brussels; Antwerp was bombarded by Dutch artillery, but the Tsar's preoccupation with the Polish revolt meant that there was no intervention by the eastern autocrat, so, with British and French support, the Belgians won the day. In 1839, the Treaty of London recognised Belgium as 'an independent and *perpetually neutral* state.'

The 1840's were years of hardship and distress throughout Europe, with a number of wet summers and ruined harvests. In Ireland, the failure of the potato crop of 1846 robbed most of the population of its staple diet and produced starvation; there were famines in France and Central Europe, along with a commercial slump that caused widespread unemployment. These circumstances gave a sharper edge than ever to radical agitation and, in 1848, the 'Year of Revolutions', governments in every major capital in Europe, except London and St Petersburg, seemed to be tottering. The storm broke in February in Paris, where the words *Socialism* and *Communism* had recently come into everyday use; Louis Philippe's government, pleasing enough to the wealthy middle-class, was now so unpopular with workers,

Emigrants arriving at Cork, 1851. After the Famine of 1846, when over a million died of starvation, the sole hope for Irish peasants was emigration and, as a direct result of their sufferings, a quarter of a million men, women and children crossed to Britain and a million left for America.

students and unemployed that a demonstration in favour of electoral reform suddenly became a rebellion. Within a couple of days, the Citizen King abdicated and retired to England; the Second Republic was proclaimed and a provisional government promised a new Assembly which would be elected by universal suffrage.

When the elections produced an overwhelming victory for the moderates, an enraged mob invaded the Hall of Assembly and overturned the government, at which the *bourgeoisie* called on the National Guard and regular troops to restore law and order. Four days of the bloodiest street-fighting ever seen in Europe resulted in victory for the Assembly, which then decreed a new republic to be ruled by a single chamber and a strong president.

In the plebiscite of December 1848, the presidential poll was headed by the 39-year-old nephew of Napoleon I - Louis-Napoleon Bonaparte - who had recently returned from exile in England. Nothing was known of his character or talents, but to all who wanted a 'strong man' to govern France, his name was enough to secure his election.

These events lit the fires of revolution throughout Italy and central Europe. In Vienna, a mob broke into Metternich's palace and the Chancellor, who had directed the affairs of half the continent for over 30 years, was forced to flee for his life. While the Austrian Emperor granted a liberal constitution (which he later revoked), Hungarians revolted in Budapest

324

against Austrian rule, Bohemian Czechs in Prague, and Italians in all their principal cities. With the Austrians fully engaged, the German states were free to have their own revolutions and to make their demands for elected assemblies, freedom of the press and an end to secret police. When the barricades went up in Berlin, Frederick William of Prussia made concessions and it looked for a time as if a united Germany was about to emerge. But after the Austrian armies had crushed the Italian and Hungarian revolts, it became clear that a union of German states would mean war between Prussia and Austria, whose Emperor now had the Tsar's backing. So Frederick William beat a retreat and German liberals had to abandon their hopes of unity.

For various reasons, the revolutions of 1848 all failed; the Austrian armies were too strong for the rebels and the rebels were all too often divided among themselves; violence and bloodshed frightened the middle-classes into accepting 'strong government' and, as in France, the crushing of the poor. However, the revolts had their effect on landowners, so that feudalism disappeared throughout central and most of eastern Europe, although, in Russia, a majority of the people remained serfs.

In the short term, changes took place in France which were by no means to the liberals' liking. The Second Republic had but a short life, for Louis Napoleon, taking skilful advantage of the parliamentary struggles between

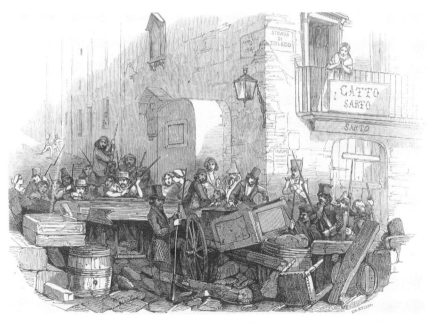

1848: street barricade in Naples, where Ferdinand II's troops suppressed a rebellion.

Conservatives and Radical Republicans, steadily increased his own powers, until, by the *Coup D'Etat* of 1851, he dissolved the Assembly and used the army to crush a popular rising in Paris and numerous risings in the provinces. The great majority of Frenchmen, weary of political struggles and alarmed by the violence, agreed by plebiscite to give Louis Napoleon the right to draw up a new constitution. He awarded himself what amounted to dictatorial powers and, in 1852, when the Second Empire came into existence, this clever, self-confident little man, who had dreamed since boyhood of achieving his 'destiny', was proclaimed Napoleon III, Emperor of the French.

Nicholas I (1796-1855), Emperor of Russia, who succeeded Alexander I in 1825. His reign saw a marked increase in state control of all aspects of Russian life, yet there was actual improvement in the lot of peasants and serfs. Main events abroad were successful wars against Persia and Turkey, the Polish revolt of 1830 and the Crimean War.

14 Independence for Latin America 1806 – 1911

The ties linking Spain with her American colonies were broken when Napoleon deposed Ferdinand VII and put his own brother Joseph on the Spanish throne. The colonists refused to recognise Joseph Bonaparte and several areas declared their independence during the Peninsular War, but a tricky situation arose after the restoration of Frederick VII in 1814. Those who had enjoyed freedom during his absence did not take kindly to his determination to re-impose rule from Spain and new republics sprang into existence with a speed unmatched until the ending of colonial rule in Africa in the 1960's.

Movements towards independence were afoot even before Napoleon seized control of Spain, because the *Creoles* (Spaniards born in America), who were the rich well-educated leaders of South American society, resented the home country's close rule and the patronising attitude of royal officials who denied them a proper share in the government.

The Creoles fought for independence from Spain, not for individual liberty for the rest of the people – the Indians, the Mestizos (mixed Spanish and Indian) and the Negroes, who together comprised some 80 per cent of the population and lived for the most part in servitude and misery. Hence, some of the governments set up after independence were just as repressive as any in Europe.

Three outstanding figures emerged as the founding fathers of Latin America: Francisco de Miranda, José de San Martin, and Simón Bolivar, the widely-travelled, deeply-read admirer of Napoleon who dedicated his life to liberating the Spanish colonies. Miranda, a Creole from Caracas who had served in the French revolutionary army, landed in Venezuela as early as 1806 with a small force, but had to return to exile in England, where he hoped to find support from the Duke of Wellington and others. This did not materialise, but he still made a second landing in 1811 and, with young Bolivar as his lieutenant, was making good progress, when an earthquake destroyed Caracas and demoralised his troops. The royal forces struck back and Bolivar and other officers, indignant at what they thought was Miranda's poor leadership, allowed him to fall into Spanish hands and he was sent across the Atlantic to Cadiz where he died in prison.

José de San Martín
(1778-1850), the South
American patriot, who
played a great part in
winning independence
for his native Argentina
and for Chile and Peru.

Bolivar fled to Jamaica and the cause of independence now rested principally with San Martin, a Creole born in what is now Argentina, where his father had been governor and where he became one of the leaders of an uprising against the Spanish authorities. Although Paraguay, situated immediately to the north-east, attained its independence in 1811 without much difficulty (the first of the Spanish-American colonies to do so), progress was so slow in Argentina that San Martin decided to move to Chile, because its people had already taken up arms. He led his 'Army of the Andes', a mere 5000-strong, over the mountain passes and down into Chile, where he joined forces with a rebel army led by Bernardo O'Higgins, the Chilean son of an Irish soldier, and together they overwhelmed the Spaniards in the Battle of Chacacuco (1817)[1]. In the following year, the rebels proclaimed Chile's independence. San Martin at once began to plan the liberation of Peru, Spain's most cherished possession, for which he received help from O'Higgins and Admiral Lord Cochrane, a British naval officer who organised a fleet to transport troops northward along the coast.

---

[1] This victory weakened Spanish rule in Argentina, though Spain did not recognise Argentine independence until 1842.

Simón Bolívar (1783-1830), the Liberator, who had far more success as a fighting general than as a peacetime ruler. His heroic achievements were never forgotten, but his dictatorial methods aroused opposition, so that Bolivia, Colombia and Venezuela all rejected him.

In 1820, San Martin landed his army on the Peruvian coast and won such popular support that the Spanish Viceroy abandoned Lima, enabling San Martin to enter the capital and proclaim the liberation of Peru (1821), with himself taking supreme authority and the title of Protector.

While these operations were going on, Bolivar was attacking the Spaniards in the north, where he occupied Bogota and liberated the province of New Granada, the old name for Colombia. Crossing the Andes eastward into Venezuela, he won the Battle of Carabobo, and, by adding the freed provinces of New Granada and Ecuador to Venezuela, founded a federation which he called Great Colombia. He was now ready to enter Peru from the north.

San Martin came to greet his comrade in arms – or was Bolivar his rival? They met at Guayaquil, Ecuador, in July 1822 and it seemed clear that they could not agree on a common plan, for San Martin wanted monarchies in the liberated states, whereas Bolivar had set his heart upon a federation of republics that would form a United States of South America. Rather than harm the cause for which they had both fought, San Martin resigned his authority in favour of Bolivar and left the country to die in poverty in France.

For the next two years, Bolivar and Sucre carried the war to the royalists, until, by the Battle of Ayachucho (1824), the Spaniards capitulated and agreed to withdraw all their remaining troops from Peru. This decisive victory marked the end of Spanish rule in South America and, to perpetuate the name of the great liberator, the people of south-eastern Peru founded a new republic called Bolivia.

Simon Bolivar had triumphed and, at only 42, his star seemed to be still rising, but, alas for his dream of a peaceful league of Spanish-speaking peoples, conspiracies and separatist movements soon showed that his compatriots did not share his enlightened aims. Discontent in Bolivia caused him to return to Colombia as president, but here, too, he was accused of dictatorial methods and, when Venezuela and Ecuador quarrelled, Great Colombia broke up into separate states and the great Liberator, pensioned off and removed from all authority, died a disillusioned man in 1830.

In freeing Spanish America from colonial rule, Bolivar was greatly helped by the friendly attitude of Britain and the United States of America. George Canning, the British Foreign Secretary from 1822, gave diplomatic recognition to the rebel governments and made it clear that the British Navy would be used to prevent any European expedition crossing the Atlantic to aid the royalists. In taking this line, he was of course protecting Britain's lucrative trade with South America, a point that was fully appreciated in Washington, where Americans eyed the British support for rebels with understandable suspicion. President Monroe and his Secretary of State, John

Quincey Adams, therefore felt it would be wise to define America's policy and, in December 1823, they issued the famous 'Monroe Doctrine' that any attempt by European powers to extend their influence in the Americas would be interpreted by the United States as an 'unfriendly act.'

In Portuguese Brazil, events took a different course from those in the Spanish colonies, because, when the French invaded Portugal in 1807, the royal family managed to escape to Rio de Janeiro, where King John VI established his court. After Napoleon's overthrow, he announced that, instead of going home, he would stay on in Rio and rule Portugal and Brazil as one kingdom. This arrangement pleased neither country and, in 1821, after an insurrection in Portugal, King John agreed to return to Lisbon, leaving the government of Brazil to his son, Dom Pedro. When Pedro realised that the home government intended to reduce Brazil to the status of a colony, he proclaimed its independence and, with popular support and naval help from Admiral Lord Cochrane (who had turned up in Brazilian waters), he overcame the Portuguese garrisons and, in December 1822, was crowned in Rio as the Emperor Pedro I.

Portugal accepted the situation, but the outcome was less than happy for Brazil, because Pedro turned out to be an autocrat and, after an unsuccessful war with Argentina[1], he was obliged to abdicate in 1831 in favour of his 5-year-old son, Pedro II. The boy's reign, which began officially in 1840, proved to be a long period of good government and great material progress. With internal peace and the arrival of immigrants of many nationalities, particularly Germans and Italians, production of coffee, sugar, tobacco and (after 1880) rubber increased by leaps and bounds; there was a spate of railway-building and the country was found to possess enormous mineral deposits.

However, in spite of these advances, there were some powerful opponents of the monarchy, including the big landowners (who were furious at the freeing of slaves) and Army chiefs annoyed by Pedro's peaceful policies. In 1889, an army of revolt forced the kindly old emperor to resign and Brazil became a republic, governed by a president whose dictatorial powers were backed by the military.

Mexico or New Spain, the fourth of Spain's great colonial possessions (the other three being New Granada, Peru and Buenos Aires), had been ruled by

---

[1] A war in which Brazil lost a province which became the independent state of Uruguay.

a Viceroy for 300 years since the death of the last Aztec emperor. The Viceroy's authority extended over Mexico itself, Texas, an area called New Mexico and California, but, during the French revolutionary period, a spirit of unrest flared into open revolt. The Creoles, jealous of the Spanish officials and angered by corruption, heavy taxation and restrictions on local commerce, led an uprising in 1811, when two priests, Hidalgo and Morelos, commanding forces consisting largely of Indians, attacked the royalists. They had some success, but the Creoles, realising that the Indians would demand the restoration of their confiscated lands, changed sides and the rebellion was crushed.

In 1821, when it looked as if a new liberal government in Spain would grant concessions to the Indians, the Creoles, joined by ecclesiastics and Spaniards, proclaimed Mexico's independence, with Augustin de Iturbide (who had taken a prominent part in suppressing the Indians) as the elected Emperor. He was soon overthrown and executed, whereupon a republic was proclaimed in 1824.

For the next 60 years, the history of Mexico was one of almost continuous warfare between rival generals who took sides as it suited them with various groups supporting the Church, the Army, a monarchy and the republic. The situation was made worse by the desperate poverty of the peasants and the concentration of wealth in a few hands. During these conflicts, Spain sent an expedition to try to reconquer Mexico (1829), the French bombarded the coast in retaliation for the looting of foreign shops (1838), and American settlers in Texas declared its independence and it was annexed by the United States. This led to the war of 1846-8, in which President Santa Anna was defeated by the American generals, Zachary Taylor and Winfield Scott, who captured Mexico City after severe fighting. By the peace treaty, the United States received Texas, California and the huge area called New Mexico, which included the present states of Utah, Nevada and Arizona.

Mexico suffered its next disaster at the hands of Napoleon III, who, on the pretext of restoring order and recovering the losses suffered by foreigners, sent a French army to overthrow the government and instal an Austrian archduke, Maximilian, as Emperor. Maximilian, who entered Mexico in 1864, announced a programme of reforms, excellent on paper, which could not be carried out, owing to the lack of a trained civil service and to the activities of republican guerillas. When the American Civil War ended in the following year, Maximilian was doomed, because the Americans could now concentrate on asserting the Monroe Doctrine of no foreign interference and Napoleon III, realising that his scheme had misfired, bowed to pressure and agreed to withdraw his forces. Abandoned by the man who had set him up, Maximilian was captured by the republicans, courtmartialled and shot on the 19 June 1867.

Left to its own concerns, Mexico suffered a further period of unrest, until it found in Porfirio Diaz a president-dictator who, between 1884 and 1911, put an end to political strife and enforced measures to foster the country's economic progress. To a large extent, he succeeded, but his policies benefited a small class of landowners and industrialists far more than the mass of people and he was overthrown by the Mexican Revolution of 1911, which once again reduced this luckless country to a state of confusion.

Pancho Villa at the head of his rebel troops in 1916. Villa, one of the most colourful characters of the Mexican Revolution, raised an army to support Francisco Madero, leader of the revolt against Diaz. After Madero's murder, Villa fought against the military bosses and actually captured Mexico City for a time. He was assassinated in 1923.

15 Ideas and Inventions
c. 1650 – 1919

Europe's domination of the rest of the globe from the 17th century onwards was partly due to the temporary decline of the great civilizations of Asia - India and China; the Chinese, it is true, were still a highly cultured people, but they had become inward-looking, unwilling to communicate with outsiders or to accept new ideas - and it was through the Europeans' readiness to put forward and to exploit new ideas that they came to make such a tremendous impact on the world.

From the time of the Renaissance, educated men had been discarding the age-old respect for authority, particularly the authority of the Church, in favour of reason and observation. Francis Bacon, sometime Lord Chancellor of England and a notable man of ideas, declared that 'the true . . . end of the sciences is that human life be enriched by new discoveries', a view that was developed by Descartes (1596-1650), the French philosopher and mathematician, who taught that the way to reach truth was to reject accepted opinions and to doubt everything. To do so often called for courage, as the founder of modern medicine, the English doctor, William Harvey, realised when he found himself well-nigh ruined by the fury which greeted his account of the circulation of the blood.

The age of Bacon, Harvey and Descartes was also the age of Kepler, the German astronomer, of Christian Huygens, the Dutch scientist and Galileo, the Italian inventor of the refracting telescope with which he proved the truth of the theory of the Polish genius, Copernicus, that the sun and not the earth is the centre of our universe. The scientific discoveries in the 17th century by these men and others, such as Boyle and Hooke in England and Leibniz in Germany, were carried forward in England by Isaac Newton (1642-1727), who discovered the Law of Gravitation and invented a new mathematical system called Differential Calculus.

Men with enquiring minds were encouraged when Charles II of England granted a charter to found the Royal Society, whose members met to discuss new ideas and investigate all kinds of phenomena. The French followed suit with their own Academy of Sciences founded in 1666.

The scientific revolution was now under way and, after Newton, the 18th century produced a number of remarkable men who, mostly without formal training, and usually having to devise their own apparatus, carried out their

Voltaire (1694-1778) holding forth to Frederick the Great in the palace near Berlin, during his 1750 visit to the monarch who had long been sending him his own poems to read. Frederick treated the French sage generously and Voltaire responded with gushing praise and hailed his host as the 'Philosopher King'. Later, in a bitter quarrel, each showed the unpleasant side of his character.

Statue of Edward Jenner (1749-1823), the originator of vaccination, whose investigation of the popular tradition that milkmaids who had had 'cow-pox' (a mild skin complaint) were immune from the dreaded small-pox led him to discover a way of saving the lives of countless children. Despite fierce opposition at first, Jenner eventually won world-wide acclaim and many awards and honours.

336

experiments and passed on their discoveries to the next generation of enthusiasts. Among them were Antoine Lavoisier (1743-94) the Frenchman who is often called the father of modern chemistry; Joseph Priestley, an English clergyman who discovered oxygen; Linnaeus, the Swedish botanist; Edward Jenner, whose treatment of smallpox in England made him one of the pioneers of preventive medicine; René Laënnec, a Frenchman, who invented the stethoscope; Alessandro Volta (1745-1827), the Italian physicist whose investigations into electricity were continued by Michael Faraday (1791-1867), assistant to Sir Humphry Davy, a leading scientist, whom he eventually succeeded as Professor of Chemistry at the Royal Institution, founded in London 1799. In his researches, Faraday carried out thousands of experiments and produced the first electric dynamo. In Britain, also, were Henry Cavendish, a rich recluse, who devoted his lonely life to science and John Dalton (1766-1844), a Quaker schoolmaster and chemist, who put forward his Atomic Theory long before anyone had heard of nuclear physics.

As well as the scientists - or 'natural philosophers', as they used to be called - there were other thinkers who concerned themselves with people's behaviour and the way they were governed. In Paris, a group of writers, influenced by Descartes and by the English philosopher, John Locke, produced a whole body of literary and philosophical works, of which the most famous was the 35-volume *Encyclopédie* (1751-72), which not only summarised all that was up-to-date in learning, but put forward the most advanced ideas of the time and dared to challenge the injustice of war, colonialism, the Slave Trade, taxation and the penal system.

This period came to be known as the Age of Reason; it was the time of the so-called 'enlightened despots', Louis XIV, Peter the Great and Catherine the Great, Joseph of Austria and Frederick the Great of Prussia, who believed that human progress should be guided and controlled by absolute rulers like themselves. It was also the time of intellectual rebels and apostles of freedom, like Tom Paine and Benjamin Franklin in the U.S.A.; Jonathan Swift, the Anglo-Irish satirist; the young Goethe in Germany; the French encyclopédistes and, above all, Voltaire and Rousseau.

Voltaire, born in Louis XIV's France in 1694, showed such contempt for accepted ideas and poked such devastating fun at the Church and the State that he changed people's ways of thinking and, by teaching three generations to hate oppression, became the hero-figure of the revolutionaries. Jean-Jacques Rousseau of Geneva, by contrast, was a visionary, who expressed in *The Social Contract* (1762) his belief that the remedy for society's ills was virtue, that in the ideal state everyone would work for the common good. His opening sentence, 'Man is born free but is everywhere in chains', fired the imaginations of countless idealists and was to be heard again in 1848 in the *Communist Manifesto* of Karl Marx and Friedrich Engels, who ended their pamphlet with these words, 'The ruling classes may well tremble at the thought of a communist revolution! The proletarians have nothing to lose in the struggle but their chains. They have a whole world to conquer - workers of the world, unite!'

Marx (1818-83) and Engels (1820-95) were both Germans and members of the International Communist Federation, one of many offshoots of the socialist movement which arose in France and England in the 1820's. The communists, mostly refugees and political outcasts living in various capitals (both Marx and Engels lived, worked and died in London), were fanatically republican and revolutionary. They advocated the violent overthrow of *capitalism*, the system whereby rich men owned factories and paid other men to work for them. Marx, who moved from Brussels to London in 1849, worked for years in the Reading Room of the British Museum on his book, *Das Kapital*, in which his theories were helped out by Engels' first-hand knowledge of English factories. In this book, which has had more influence on the world than any other in modern times, the authors predicted that the workers would rise against their capitalist employers and establish a classless society in which government and industry would be controlled by the workers. Neither man lived to see his theories come true, but revolutionaries in many countries continued to study *Das Kapital* and to plan the overthrow of governments.

A book which in its day aroused infinitely more anger and abuse than *Das Kapital* was the work of a gentle semi-invalid named Charles Darwin, who, as a young man, made a voyage to South America and the Pacific, as a naturalist on board a survey ship, H.M.S. Beagle. His observations convinced him that all living things (which he divided into groups and *species*) had developed over millions of years and those which survived did so through 'evolution', i.e. by changing and adapting themselves. When Darwin's book *The Origin of the Species*[1] came out in 1859 it was met by a storm of abuse and its author was denounced as 'the most dangerous man in England.', an atheist and enemy of religion and mortality, because his theory went against the Bible's account of the creation of the world in six days.

In putting forward ideas that outraged orthodox opinion, Darwin was as much a revolutionary as Karl Marx and it is difficult for us to imagine the horror with which people received the notion that man had evolved from amphibians and lower animals. But, like Newton, Darwin changed man's views of himself and the universe and when he died in 1882, he was buried in Westminster Abbey near to the tomb of Sir Isaac Newton.

---

[1] Its full title was *On the Origin of the Species by Means of Natural Selection or the Preservation of Favoured Races in the Struggle for Life*.

Until about the middle of the 18th century, most people in the world could well believe that life would go on much as it seemed always to have done, with the vast majority engaged in agriculture and almost the sole sources of power being wind, water and the muscles of men and animals.

In the next century and a half, the invention of machines, the discovery of new kinds of power and the concentration of large numbers of workers in factories produced changes so dramatic that they are rightly called the Industrial Revolution. It began in Britain, spread into some European countries and the United States, reached Japan towards the end of the 19th century and is still working its changes in many parts of the world.

Britain became the first industrialised nation for a number of reasons. Since William III's accession, the country had had a stable government and a Parliament filled for the most part with businessmen and landowners whose chief concern was their own and the country's prosperity. In short, the governing class, unlike the French nobility, was interested in commerce. Aristocrats, merchants, and the landed gentry were prepared to invest money in new factories, coal mines and iron works, confident that, in the Bank of England, the country had the soundest financial system in the world.

The changeover from cottage and small workshop industry to the factory system could not have taken place without the inventions of a number of remarkable Scots and Englishmen. As early as 1733, John Kay patented a Flying Shuttle that enabled a weaver to double his output; Kay's invention, originally intended for the woollen industry, was adapted by the cotton weavers of Lancashire and south-west Scotland. In their turn the spinners were provided with a better machine by James Hargreaves, whose Spinning Jenny (1754) did the work of 8 men; then came the Water Frame of Richard Arkwright, whose application of water-power to machines made large-scale production possible.

The early textile factories had to be built by the side of waterfalls and fast-running streams, but the change to steam power was soon to make it profitable to build factories in towns, where there was coal close at hand.

Men had known about the power of steam for centuries, but it was difficult to produce and harness. In 1698 Thomas Savery built a cumbersome steam-driven pump to pump water from coalmines, an invention which was improved by Thomas Newcomen, so that it came into use in many mines, in spite of its inefficiency and the huge amounts of coal that it consumed. The man who made it really work was James Watt, a Scottish instrument-maker, who corrected its faults by fitting a separate condenser (1769). By 1781, Watt had adapted his engine so that it would drive a wheel or a shaft and it was not long before steam-power was being used in factories to drive looms and all kinds of machinery.

The key to Britain's industrial lead lay in the rapid development of her coal and iron resources. At this time, she had more of either than any other country in Europe and her coal production rose from 6 million tons in 1770 to 16 million tons in 1816. For centuries, iron had to be smelted in forested areas where charcoal was produced but, in about 1708, Abraham Darby discovered that if coal was turned into coke, it would produced intense heat and therefore replace charcoal. The new process came into widespread use, especially where coal and iron were found close together and the country's output of pig-iron rose from 30 000 tons in 1760 to over a million tons in 1806.

An industrial country needs a good transport system to move raw materials and finished products, but, in the 18th century, Britain's communications could not compare with the fine roads and canals of France. To remedy this state of affairs, Turnpike Trusts were set up to improve roads by charging tolls, but more important was the work of two great engineers, Thomas Telford and John Macadam, who built a whole system of well-constructed main roads for the stage coaches, private carriages and wagons of the time.

But the new roads, however good, were not suitable for great loads of coal and iron, nor for Mr Wedgwood's pottery or the huge variety of goods turned out by Birmingham's workshops. These would go more smoothly and cheaply by water, and, when James Brindley completed his first canal in 1761, the price of coal in Manchester dropped by half. Brindley, an illiterate genius, was the greatest of the canal-men who, in the space of a few years, constructed a network of canals to link Britain's navigable rivers.

The first self-moving steam-engine was made by a young Frenchman, Nicolas Cugnot, who, in 1769, startled Parisians by dashing along in a one-seater steam-carriage at 9 miles an hour. When he overturned, the prudent citizens locked him up and abandoned the idea. In about 1784, James Watt's foreman, William Murdock, made a working model of a road locomotive, but Watt discouraged his experiments and it was Richard Trevithick who built the first high-pressure road locomotive (1801) and he also constructed the world's first railway locomotive to pull coal along a track at a mine in South Wales. Trevithick lost heart and it was left to George Stephenson to improve the primitive engines that hauled coal-trucks at a colliery in north-east England. His first great success came with the opening of the Stockton and Darlington line in 1825, the first public railway line in the world, but he is remembered chiefly for his work on the Liverpool and Manchester Railway and for winning the Rainhill Trials of 1829 with his famous locomotive, the 'Rocket'.

After this, there was no way of checking 'railway mania', as people tumbled over one another to subscribe money for building new lines, most of them planned and built by George Stephenson and his son, Robert, with

Coal-mining in Northumbria, north-east England, in about 1800, before the use of the Davy 'safety' lamp (invented 1816) and the introduction of underground railways and tubs. Hewn with pick and shovel, coal had to be hauled to the surface by ropes or carried on miners' backs up a series of ladders.

The 'Rocket', built by George Stephenson as his entry for the Rainhill Trials of 1829, which were held to find the best locomotive for the new Liverpool and Manchester Railway. Pulling a wagon-load of excited passengers up and down a stretch of line, the 'Rocket' reached a top speed of 29 mph to beat easily the three other entrants and win the prize of £500.

341

Isambard Kingdom Brunel the maestro of the Great Western Railway. By 1870, they had built a 13 000 mile network of railways, covering the length and breadth of Britain and revolutionising the transport of passengers, food, freight and mail.

A number of foreign observers had been present at the Rainhill Trials and, when railway construction in Britain was seen to be successful, the 'mania' spread to Belgium and France and across the continent to Russia. The United States, at once realising that railways would open up its vast territories, began to lay down tracks and, by 1840, was building its own locomotives. For the rest of the world, British workshops usually supplied the rolling-stock and British engineers supervised the construction of the lines.

Railways changed the world. They enabled manufacturers and farmers to transport goods and produce to distant markets, millions of people to travel unbelievable distances, generals to move armies and governments to control colonial possessions and to open up inaccessible lands. The first military railway made its appearance during the Crimean War (1854-6); railways were built for strategic reasons in India after the Mutiny of 1857; they played a major role in the American Civil War, which only briefly delayed the colossal task of building a line right across America, for, in 1869, the first through train completed its run from California to New York. By the 1870's, railways were being laid down in the United States at the rate of 10 000 miles a year.

South American railways were largely financed and built by Britain in order to bring wheat and meat to the ports for shipment to British markets. Similarly, in Australia, New Zealand and South Africa, railways supplied the means to open up remote territories, while, in Europe, railways carried millions of immigrants westward in their escape from poverty and persecution to lands of opportunity in the New World.

Alongside the railways ran the new electric telegraph, linking city to city and government to government at a speed even faster than the trains could travel. One advance led to another, so that before the 19th century was out, the first underground railway was opened in London (1863), the first overhead track in New York (1867), the first electric train in Berlin (1881) and the first diesel engine (1897), also in Germany. As a means of long-distance transport, railways had no rival for over a century, for, although there were cars and trucks on the roads before the First World War, the great expansion of road transport did not begin until the 1920's.

If steam-power could be applied to machines and vehicles, it ought to be able to drive a boat and, at the time when Trevithick and Stephenson were developing their locomotives, enthusiasts in France, Britain and the United States were trying to make steamboats work. Their experiments led to the successful construction of a steam-tug, the *Charlotte Dundas*, which, in 1802, towed barges on a Scottish canal. An American engineer, Robert Fulton, who had watched the little tugboat, went home and built the *Clermont*, America's first paddle-steamer, which began carrying passengers on the Hudson River in 1807, eighteen years before the opening of the Stockton-Darlington Railway. In 1819, a New York ship, the *Savannah*, crossed the Atlantic with steam-driven paddles assisting the sails; a year later, a cross-Channel steamship service was established and, in 1827, the Dutch *Curacao* made the first all-steam crossing of the Atlantic. After this, the story of steamships was one of progress in the face of ridicule by the die-hard supporters of wooden sailing-ships.

Brunel's *Great Britain* was the first iron screw-driven steamer to cross the Atlantic (1845) and, with the introduction of more efficient engines and the opening of the Suez Canal in 1869, the victory of steam over sail was assured.

Like the merchantmen, warships also had to change from sail to steam, from wood to iron and from iron to steel. Britain, whose policy was to ensure that the Royal Navy was more powerful than the combined fleets of all other powers, naturally kept a close watch on these developments and other innovations such as submarines, armour-plate and gun-turrets. In 1897, the Lords of the Admiralty were startled by the performance of the *Turbinia*, a small yacht fitted with a new type of engine called a steam-turbine, invented by Charles Parsons. Superior to any other type of marine engine, the steam-turbine was brought into use for warships and also for the great liners, which, until the development of long-distance aircraft, carried passengers and mail to every part of the world.

Britain's industrial lead was short-lived, because her example was speedily followed by countries like Belgium and France, which possessed coal deposits and plentiful labour. During the middle of the 19th century, German industry passed in a few years from cottage handicrafts to large-scale engineering works and steel, textile and chemical production, a transformation made possible by inventive skill, good financial arrangements and state encouragement of science and industrial research. State control and employment of foreign experts played a big part in building railways, mills and factories in Russia, which, it is sometimes forgotten, was one of the world's leading industrial nations by 1914.

No country's industry advanced so dramatically as that of the USA. In 1800, it was a group of states engaged principally in agriculture and cotton production; by 1870, it was a giant on its way to becoming the greatest industrial power in the world, whose growth was due to a capacity to invent every kind of machine, from Eli Whitney's cotton gin to Isaac Singer's sewing-machine, to enterprise, ruthlessness and huge capital investment.

Coal, the prime source of energy for machines and transport, soon had its competitors. Gas, a by-product of coal, was discovered by William Murdock, whose experiments led to the gas-lighting of houses, factories and streets. Gas-works, foul-smelling as they were, did a marvellous job in promoting greater safety, convenience and education, since the new lighting enabled people of all ages to read books after working hours in their homes and in 'evening institutes'.

Apart from the invention of gas-cookers, that was about the extent of the usefulness of gas. Electricity was an infinitely more important source of energy. Its existence was known in ancient times; it interested early scientists like Newton and Boyle and promoted experiments in many countries, but it was the British scientist, Michael Faraday who, in 1831, established that electricity could be generated. His discovery led to sending electric signals along wires and thence to the telegraph system.

These discoveries brought electricity into fairly limited use from about 1870, when it first began to replace steam for driving machinery. Electric lighting soon followed, when Swan, an Englishman, and Edison, the American genius, produced a successful filament lamp.

By 1900, small generators, domestic and street lighting, telephones, electric trams and underground trains had come into use; large-scale use of electricity in industry became possible when big power-stations were constructed, at first in the United States and Germany and, by the 1920's, in Britain. In most cases, the generators were driven by coal or oil, but another important source of power was moving water. Since 1886, the hydro-electric plant has been operating at Niagara Falls and this method of producing electricity by the action of water on a turbine was adopted in many countries, such as Switzerland, Norway, Australia and Egypt, where it was relatively simple to harness the power of water-falls and rivers.

Oil was known to some of the peoples of the Ancient World as a mysterious substance that seeped out of the ground in various places in the Middle East. It took the form of bitumen and 'naphtha' and was used to waterproof floors, caulk ships and make the deadly weapon known as 'Greek fire'. The substance had only limited use until, about the middle of the 19th century, shale oil began to be distilled in Scotland and James Young, a Glasgow chemist, discovered how to make paraffin, a fuel that is used in lamps, heaters, and cooking-stoves. A variety of this was produced in the U.S. as 'kerosene'. The first oil-well was drilled in 1859 at Titusville in the state of Pennsylvania, which was soon producing 10 million barrels of oil a year and this achievement led to the drilling of wells in Poland, Rumania and Russia and to the discovery of huge oil reserves in Venezuela and Texas.

In these early years of the industry, the most important products were lamp oil (kerosene/paraffin) and lubricating oil; the remaining products of distillation, especially petrol, were burned or thrown away. However, when enthusiasts, particularly in France and Germany, were trying to make a mechanical road vehicle less heavy than the 'steam carriages' of the 1820's, someone hit on the idea of using petrol as fuel for a light-weight internal combustion engine. Gottlieb Daimler, a German, produced a small petrol-engine in 1884 and, in the following year, Carl Benz built what is generally regarded as the first motor-car, a three-wheeled vehicle powered by a ¾ h.p. motor.

Four-wheeled cars began to be made, notably by Panhard and Levasseur in France, the world's leading manufacturer of automobiles in the 1890's. In Britain, the speed limit was raised to 14 miles an hour and, by 1900, many small firms were turning out cars one at a time, like coach-builders. Even the United States produced no more than 4000 vehicles a year.

However, in 1908, Henry Ford, a farmer's son from Michigan, USA, began mass-production of his Model-T car, which was cheaper and more reliable than its competitors. In 1909, he sold 10600 'tin-lizzies'; in 1914, nearly a quarter-of-a-million. The age of the motor-car had begun, with all that it was to mean for the industrialised countries of the world – vast automobile industries, fast travel without timetables, improved roads, immense riches for a few oil-producing countries, congested cities, declining railways and a death-rate accepted as inevitable.

From using a petrol-engine to propel a carriage along the ground, it was a short step – less than 20 years – to making the first aeroplane. Man had long been fascinated by the dream of flying – there were stories of the ancient Chinese lifting men into the air by means of kites, Leonardo's drawings of a flying-machine and various attempts to build weird airships and gliders. The first successful ascent by a human being was made in 1783 by a young Frenchman, De Rozier, who stayed up for 4½ minutes in a *Montgolfier* hot-air balloon. Hydrogen-filled balloons were used for military observation in Napoleon's time and, in the Franco-Prussian War of 1870, 65 balloons left Paris during the Siege, carrying passengers and mail. The next step was to make balloons long in shape and to power them with an engine, so they could be steered. The French pioneered this type and, in 1900, the German, Count Zeppelin, constructed the rigid-frame airship which was given his name.

Heavier-than-air machines developed from 19th-century model aircraft, and it was from the feats of a German gliding expert, Otto Lilienthal (killed in 1896), that the secrets of an aircraft's wing came to be understood. In America, two gliding enthusiasts, the brothers Wilbur and Orville Wright, built an aeroplane which made the first true powered flight at Kittyhawk, North Carolina, on 17 December 1903. It lasted for 12 seconds and was watched by 5 spectators. Several years passed before the Wright brothers' achievement attracted much interest, but, after a Brazilian, Santos-Dumont, made some flights around Paris and Louis Blériot flew across the English Channel in 1909, the public and some of the military began to realise that the aeroplane was going to be more than a plaything for daring young men.

The First World War brought tremendous advances in aircraft design and, when the war ended, thousands of trained pilots were ready to turn to civil flying. Passenger services between European capitals started in 1919, the year in which Alcock and Brown flew the Atlantic in a wartime bomber and the brothers Ross and Keith Smith flew from England to Australia. Through the 1920's and '30's, aviators like Cobham, Byrd, Lindbergh and Kingsford-Smith, made long-distance flights that pioneered the world's air-routes, though it was not until after the Second World War that a trans-Atlantic passenger service came into being.

Improvements in transport had much to do with the revolution in communications which took place in the 19th century. Postal services had existed since the time of Hammurabi and were set up by despotic rulers like Genghis Khan, the Han emperors and Louis XIV for their own use; private persons either employed messengers or bribed the official couriers to carry their letters. However, public services had been started in most European countries by the beginning of the 19th century; the coming of the railways then made it possible to organise a speedy and reliable system, which was made all the more efficient by adopting the use of postage stamps, introduced in Britain in 1839.

In addition to letters, the new post offices dealt with parcels and, as time went by, with money orders, savings bank deposits and telegrams. The idea of an electric telegraph had made some progress in Spain and Germany, when, in 1837, Samuel Morse, son of a Massachusetts parson, sent a message along a copper wire by means of a code which he had invented.

Within a few years, most of the eastern states of the USA were linked by telegraph lines; Britain and Germany followed suit with such success that, by mid-century, the new system was installed throughout Europe. A cable was laid across the Atlantic in 1865, and Europe was linked to India in the same year and to Australia in 1873.

The telephone derived from the telegraph and several inventors had been interested in the possibility of reproducing electrically the vibrations caused by a human voice before Alexander Graham Bell, a Scot who had moved to America, spoke that first telephonic sentence, 'Watson, come here, I want you', on 10 March 1876. By 1878, the world's first public telephone exchange was opened at New Haven, Connecticut, and the first automatic exchange (1892) also originated in America, where the new invention was developed so efficiently by private enterprise that there were nearly 9 million telephones in operation by 1912. In Europe, Germany, always leading the

Steam-cars were cheap to run, quiet and powerful. Here, in about 1898, on a Paris boulevard, Monsieur Serpollet prepares to demonstrate the virtues of his car. A Serpollet steam-car beat all the petrol cars in a race at Nice in 1902 and King Edward VII, a keen motorist, bought a Serpollet for his personal use.

way in electrical industries, took to the telephone more enthusiastically than France or Britain, where the telephone service became a state monopoly in charge of the Post Office.

Until about the middle of the 19th century, most newspapers adopted a sedate dignified style considered suitable for educated people. The spread of literacy, the invention of improved printing presses and the typewriter (the Remington No I appeared in 1876), removal of newspaper taxes and, in some countries, of censorship, led to the appearance of a new kind of popular newspaper. The Americans set the style with the *New York Herald* (founded in 1835), which specialised in vivid reporting, special enterprises, such as sending Stanley to Africa to search for Dr Livingstone, and large-scale advertising. After William Randolph Hearst made a fortune out of sensational journalism, Britain produced its own newspaper tycoons in the brothers Alfred and Harold Harmsworth (later Lords Northcliffe and Rothermere) whose *Daily Mail* (1896) and *Daily Mirror* (1903) became Europe's first mass-circulation 'dailies', although, for Sunday reading, the *News of the World* had had a large and avid readership since 1843.

347

The British public's appetite for newspaper reading - larger even than that in the USA - gave rise to a number of newspapers with circulations of more than a million copies a day. Although popular dailies were published in Europe - *France Soir* and *Le Figaro* in France, *Corriere della Sera* in Italy and the German *Frankfurter Zeitung* (1856) - they tended to have smaller circulations but probably greater political influence. Specialised journals and magazines found a ready sale in all the advanced countries of the world and played a role in education and entertainment similar to that of radio and television in the 20th century.

While these developments were taking place in industry and transport, changes were going on in farming that were so important that they are known as the Agrarian (or land) Revolution. In 1700, most of the world's people lived by working on the land; farming methods had hardly changed since the Middle Ages, but the increase in population meant that new methods of producing more food had to be found. Nowhere was this more true than in Britain, where, at the beginning of George III's reign, about half the land was still cultivated on the old open-fields system, whereby a mass of small freeholders and tenants produced on their scattered strips of land about enough food to feed their families in a good year and they were able to make ends meet by keeping a few animals on the common and working in their cottages at the loom and the spinning wheel.

This system was virtually brought to an end by the 3000-odd Enclosure Acts of George III's reign. Commissioners went round the country, measuring, surveying and listening to claims to the commons and pasture; when this protracted business was finished a number of compact farms emerged, practically all of them owned by better-off farmers and wealthy landlords, since the small man, having to face the costs of the enquiry and of hedging and fencing, was obliged to sell his strips for what he could get and become a farm labourer or take himself off to the towns to find work in one of the new factories.

It was harsh, but the only way to produce more food, because, once the land was divided into bigger units and farmed by men with capital, all kinds of improvements could be introduced. Land could be made more productive by manuring, marling (adding clay and lime to sandy soil) and drainage; a methodical rotation of crops was followed, with the growing of better grasses for hay and roots for winter feed, so that cattle need not be slaughtered every autumn and there would be fresh meat in the shops during winter. These practices, already common in the Netherlands, were made popular by enthusiasts like Lord 'Turnip' Townshend, Arthur Young and George III himself, who, as 'Farmer George', ran a model farm at Windsor. By careful

348

breeding, Thomas Coke of Norfolk and Robert Bakewell, a Leicestershire farmer, doubled the size of their sheep and cattle in a few years; Sir Humphry Davy suggested the use of artificial fertilisers; oil-cake was introduced as cattle feed, farming journals had a brisk sale and the Board of Agriculture was founded in 1793 to encourage the new 'scientific farming'.

Jethro Tull's seed-drill of 1701 was the fore-runner of agricultural machines, such as the horse-drawn hoe, an improved harrow with iron rollers, Andrew Meikle's threshing-machine of 1786, which was soon followed by a mechanical reaper, but, with labour still cheap and plentiful, there was no incentive to make much use of steam-power until towards the end of the 19th century. The reaping hook, scythe and even the flail remained in general use for many years, with the horse the all-purpose work animal except in parts of France and southern Europe, where oxen were commonly used.

American farmers, using steam-ploughs and McCormick harvesters, were able to extract enormous harvests from virgin soil and the high-quality wheat was carried by rail to the sea-ports to be shipped to Britain and sold at prices which brought ruin to the British farmer.

Switching to meat might have saved him, but the 1880's saw the introduction of refrigeration and the arrival of cargoes of frozen meat from Australasia and Argentina. With Britain's large industrial population, this dependence on imported food was an inevitable development for a crowded island which lived mainly by exporting manufactured goods.

The situation was different in other European countries, such as France, Germany, Italy and Russia, because they were less densely populated and possessed such large food-producing areas that they were virtually self-sufficient.

16 The Second British Empire 1788 – 1914

In the second half of the 19th century, Britain was the richest and probably the most envied and unpopular country in the world. As the first industrialised society, she became 'the workshop of the world', the supplier of every kind of manufactured article from locomotives, cotton shirts and printing presses to brass bedsteads and children's toys.

In addition to industrial know-how and some brilliant engineers and inventors, Britain possessed good supplies of coal and iron, a booming steel industry, thanks to the discovery of better methods of production by Bessemer and Gilchrist Thomas, plentiful labour (the population doubled in Queen Victoria's reign), a stable government and half the world's ocean-going ships.

To these advantages could be added an element of luck. Just when the United States was becoming a major threat at sea, the Americans became involved in their costly Civil War (1861-5), which enabled British ship-builders to forge ahead in the construction of steamships. Germany, another potential rival, was in the throes of her struggle for national unity; so was Italy, while France, after the glittering promise of Napoleon III's régime,

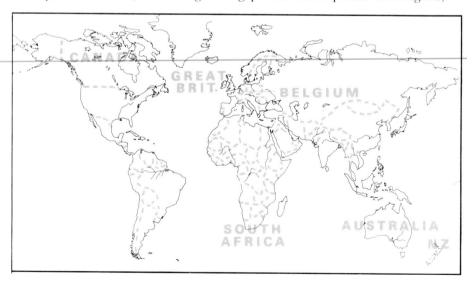

suffered defeat and national humiliation. Russia also had been defeated, (in the Crimean War), and, in any case, was of no importance in world commerce, while Japan was only starting to emerge from medieval seclusion. The industrial giants of the near future were still puny weaklings. Great Britain and Belgium were the only countries which had the majority of their people living in urban communities and, in 1870, Britain's volume of trade was more than that of Germany, France and Italy put together and was three or four times that of the United States.

Britain's prestige and influence on world affairs arose partly from her industrial lead and partly from her acquisition of a new empire, different from the one she had lost in North America. By 1815, she and Spain were the only countries which possessed large overseas territories, for the rest of the powers (apart from Russia in Asia and the Middle East) showed little interest in acquiring colonies. Spain was in the process of losing all hers, except Cuba, the Philippines and one or two islands; France conquered Algeria in 1830, but it was years before she obtained any more territories in Africa and Indo-China. Until about 1870, Germany, Italy and the United States were too concerned with their own internal affairs to bother about imposing their rule on other peoples.

CANADA

The country which set the pattern for Britain's management of her colonies was Canada, where, at the end of the American War of Independence, some 40 000 Loyalists left the new republic to settle in Canada, which meant that there were now more English than French, so, to prevent friction, Pitt put through the Canada Act of 1791 which created two separate provinces, Lower Canada or Quebec, with its mainly French population, and Upper Canada or Ontario, where many of the British had settled. Each had its own Assembly and was free to develop in its own way.

This arrangement worked well for some 40 years, but, by the 1830's, a good deal of animosity had developed between the British and the outnumbered French settlers; furthermore, both parties felt that there was too much government from London and not enough consideration for small farmers and recent immigrants. In 1837, these grievances led to the outbreak of two minor rebellions which alarmed the government into sending out Lord Durham to investigate the troubles. The Durham Report of 1839 recommended that Upper and Lower Canada should be reunited into one province and given what practically amounted to self-government. Even so, the plan did not remove the hostility between the two races and another solution had to be found during the American Civil War, when it seemed essential to safeguard Canadian independence. In 1867, an Act was passed to

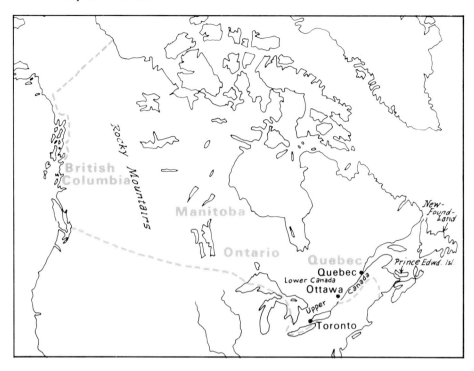

create the Dominion of Canada, which meant that, while the British monarch remained Head of State, Canada was otherwise completely independent.

Quebec, Ontario, the Maritime Provinces on the east and any others that would be formed out of the vast territories of the west became separate provinces, but each would send a representative to the Federal Government in the new capital of Ottawa. Things moved slowly at first, for Newfoundland refused to join and Prince Edward Island hung back; however, the new province of Manitoba joined the Confederation in 1870 and British Columbia in the far west agreed to come in in 1871 on the promise of a transcontinental railway, though the Canadian Pacific line was not completed until 1885.

Federation established a strong British dominion in North America, which steadily expanded as the young ambitious country carried out a vigorous policy of town-building and road and railway construction. The population increased, as a stream of immigrants, as many as 300 000 a year, began to occupy the vast western prairies. This situation alarmed the Indian and half-breed population, since they rightly feared that the advance of the newcomers would destroy the buffaloes on which they mainly depended for food and, in 1885, there occurred Riel's Rebellion, which lasted 3 months,

A Crowfoot Indian Chief
who remained loyal to the
government during Riel's
Rebellion. Louis Riel,
leader of the Metis or
French half-breeds,
organised the rebellion
against incoming settlers
to North-West Canada.
After the Metis and their
Indian allies surrendered,
Riel was executed at
Regina, Saskatchewan.

Pushing ahead with the Canadian Pacific Railway track, a project that represented nation-building in a vast land with only 4 million inhabitants.

until it was crushed by the Canadian army. Louis Riel, the leader of the uprising, was tried and executed.

After this unhappy occurrence, Canada enjoyed a period of great prosperity up to the outbreak of the First World War for, in addition to its riches in the wheatlands, timber and fishing industries, huge deposits of coal, nickel, gold, silver, cobalt and natural gas were discovered. Notwithstanding the influx of immigrants of many nationalities, the ties with Britain remained close and, in 1899, Canada at once sent troops to serve in the South African War.

The lesson which the British had learned from the loss of the American colonies had obviously sunk in, for the granting of self-government to Canada was to be followed in Australia, New Zealand and South Africa. Thus, instead of the Empire dissolving into separate states, it was to develop into a Commonwealth of Nations.

AUSTRALIA

The loss of the American colonies meant that Britain no longer had a convenient dumping-ground for law-breakers, until someone remembered Captain Cook's favourable report on a distant land in the southern hemisphere, which he had named New South Wales in 1770 and claimed for King George III.

After a minimum of preparation, a party of about 1000 convicts and guards sailed for Australia and landed at Sydney Cove in Port Jackson, New South Wales, in January 1788.

In a land whose soil and climate seemed to be totally hostile to Europeans, the settlement was saved from disaster largely by the zeal of Governor Captain Phillip, and, gradually, as more and more free settlers came out, as fertile lands were discovered and sheep were bred for wool, a thriving community was established on the edge of an unexplored continent.

The infant colony was confined to the coastal strip around Port Jackson (Sydney), until an exploring party crossed the Blue Mountains to reach the plains beyond. From there, pioneers pushed on to take possession of huge areas of grassland; one group moved north to found Brisbane (1825), the future capital of Queensland; others discovered the network of inland rivers and, in 1829-30, Charles Sturt travelled down the Murrumbidgee and the Darling rivers to the sea. Meanwhile, the Swan River Settlement (1829) around Perth met so many difficulties that a party of farmers moved east to what later became known as the state of Victoria. They were joined by another group from Tasmania (then called Van Diemen's Land), whose leader, John Batman, founded the settlement (1834) which became the city of Melbourne. South Australia owed its beginnings to Gibbon Wakefield, an

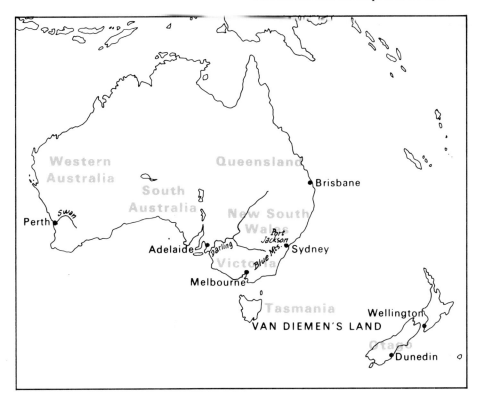

ardent believer in imperialism, who founded a society in London to promote yet another colony; its first shipload of settlers reached Kangaroo Island in 1836 and then moved to the mainland, where the official surveyor, Colonel Light, laid out the attractive city of Adelaide, named after William IV's queen.

The new country developed at a remarkable pace. Some men acquired vast holdings of land for sheep, while others, including ex-convicts, made fortunes out of commerce, liquor and money-lending. As a general rule, the farm-labourer from East Anglia, the Irishman from his poverty-stricken island and the Scot from his highland glen ate better, lived better and was a freer man than if he had stayed in the United Kingdom.

The failure of the Crown to provide land for immigrants led to 'squatting', i.e. the illegal occupation of land beyond the limits of settled areas, by resolute pioneers, who pushed on into the empty 'bush', where they built their homes and took possession of great tracts of territory.

But, when one speaks of the 'empty' bush, this is not quite accurate, for it was, in fact, the homeland of the Australian aborigines, who were too few and their way of life too simple to be able to put up the kind of resistance to

355

A group of Tasmanian aborigines in the 1860's. In 1847, the remnants of this dying race - 14 males, 22 females, 5 boys and 5 girls - were moved from Flinders Island in Bass Strait to the site of a former convict station at Oyster Cove near Hobart. Ten years later, only 5 men and 10 women were still alive.

(Above right) Sheep-shearing near Sydney in the 1860's.

(Below right) A miner's hut, Lithgow Valley, New South Wales. This is a Slab Hut, made with vertical 'slabs' of timber and roofed with bark. Photograph by the New South Wales Government Printing Office, 1900.

the white man which the American Indians did in the United States. The aborigines were driven from their hunting-grounds to make room for sheep and wheat; most of them perished (all were exterminated in Tasmania) and only a few survived in the most remote and arid parts of the continent. In all probability, nothing could have saved a primitive people from the onset of European civilization, European weapons, diseases and liquor, but, as in other parts of the world, it is a story which is almost wholly discreditable to Europeans.

356

Arrival of the Government gold cart at the Colonial Treasury, Sydney, on 21 August 1851, from a sketch by Marshal Claxton.

In 1851, gold was discovered in Victoria, an event which set off a 'gold-rush', a mad stampede that caused thousands to abandon their jobs and attracted 'diggers' from all over the world, so that Victoria's population leapt from 70 000 to 330 000. The fever soon spent itself, as the easily-won gold was exhausted, but the country was now more populous and the immigrants turned to farming, coal-, copper- and lead-mining and various mercantile occupations which in the long run produced more wealth than the gold.

By 1856, the four colonies, New South Wales, Tasmania, Victoria and South Australia were given self-government and Queensland joined them three years later. Western Australia, whose development had been slower, followed suit in 1890 and soon had its own dramatic gold-rush. But, so far, a small population scattered over vast distances, felt no need for federation, especially since there was a good deal of inter-state rivalry and 'cussedness', exemplified by the way in which neighbouring states built railways with different gauges! However, common sense slowly asserted itself and, after much argument, the Commonwealth of Australia came into being in 1901, with a central government consisting of a Governor-General, appointed by the British Crown, a Cabinet led by the Prime Minister and two Houses, the Senate and the House of Representatives, with members from each state.

358

Rev. Samuel Marsden landing at the Bay of Islands, where he first preached on Christmas Day, 1814. Marsden, chaplain to the convict settlement in New South Wales, went back to Australia for a time, leaving 3 missionaries - but it was 11 years before the first Maori was converted to Christianity!

NEW ZEALAND

Although Tasman, the Dutch navigator, sighted the two main islands which make up New Zealand in 1642 and Captain Cook explored their coasts in 1769-70, no-one took much interest in the country until Christian missionaries went there from New South Wales in the early years of the 19th century. They made some headway with the native inhabitants, a vigorous race called Maoris, who, they found, were already being corrupted by contact with European and American whalers, seal-hunters and escaped convicts, who were about the most violent and degraded ruffians on earth. In 1830, Samuel Marsden, the leading missionary, suggested to the Governor of New South Wales that he should send a British representative to New Zealand and take action to control the whaling settlements. However, neither the missionaries nor the British government supported Gibbon Wakefield in the plans which he was putting forward to turn New Zealand into a British colony.

Wakefield persisted. Enlisting aid from political, religious and business leaders, he succeeded in founding the New Zealand Company whose first party of settlers landed at Port Nicholson (now Wellington) in January 1840. Within days, William Hobson, a naval captain, arrived from Australia with

A Maori Chief in 1880. Most modern Maori tribes trace their descent from ancestors who came in a fleet of canoes in about 1350 from a place that was possibly the Pacific island of Tahiti. Certainly, they are Polynesians.

orders from the British government to annexe New Zealand, to deal fairly with the Maoris and prevent Europeans from defrauding them.

As Lieutenant-Governor, Hobson negotiated the Treaty of Waitangi with the Maori chiefs who yielded their sovereignty to the Queen and gave her the sole right of purchasing their lands. In return, she guaranteed the lands which they retained and gave them the rights and privileges of British subjects. Meanwhile, the Company had founded the town of Wellington and, as more settlers arrived, new towns were built all round the coast, often with the names of the settlers' place of origin, e.g. Dunedin, founded by the Free Church of Scotland and Christchurch, founded by the Canterbury Association.

Trouble soon arose because the Maoris held different views from the British on the ownership and sale of land; they also felt that their whole way of life was threatened by the Europeans. There were two Maori wars: the first one broke out in 1845 and was settled by the new Governor, Sir George Grey, an outstanding administrator who had made his name in South Australia.

This was the period of Lord Durham's celebrated Report on Canada and the British government decided to make similar provisions for New Zealand,

The Second Maori War:
an attack by British
troops on a Pah, a
stockade made of heavy
timbers.

which was divided into six provinces, each with its own elected council, which would send members to a Federal House of Representatives.

Grey did not approve of this 1852 plan, for he realised that the Maoris would never accept a form of government in which they had no voice. The Second Maori War, which broke out in 1860 and lasted until 1872, was a guerilla conflict in which the outnumbered Maoris fought with the courage of despair, for their cause was hopeless and, if they were to avoid extermination, salvation had to lie in partnership with the colonists. Grey, who returned for a second spell as Governor (1861-7), and George Selwyn, the first Bishop of New Zealand, did much to win the respect of the valiant Maoris, who in 1867 were given the right to elect 4 representatives to the House of Representatives. Slowly, they came back from the brink of extinction, to play a part in their country's development.

The colony prospered through its farmers' success in breeding a new type of sheep that yielded good wool and fine quality meat, and through the invention of refrigerated ships which carried huge quantities of New Zealand lamb to Britain. Discovery of gold in the western valleys of Otago in the '60's brought a gold-rush, with accompanying upsets and a dramatic increase in population.

The dominant figure of this period was Julius Vogel, a London Jew, who came to Otago via the Victorian goldfields, started the country's first daily newspaper, entered politics and, as Treasurer in the 1870 government, introduced his so-called 'grand go-ahead policy'. Thousands of immigrants were brought in; railways, roads and telegraph lines were built, and new industries, including woollen mills, foundries and paper mills, were started. Since these schemes depended largely on the government spending vast sums of borrowed money, they produced, not surprisingly, a financial crisis in 1894 and a good deal of distress.

Nevertheless, New Zealand gained essential public works and thousands more immigrants, Scandinavian and German, as well as British. By the beginning of the 20th century, the colonists were among the most prosperous people in the world and enthusiasts were hailing New Zealand as a sort of paradise of social reform. By that time, its government had introduced free compulsory education (1867), measures to settle industrial disputes and eliminate strikes, votes for women (1893), old-age pensions and state loans for farmers. This liberal programme was dear to the heart of the Premier, R.J. Seddon, who held office from 1892 until his death in 1906. A year later, New Zealand became a self-governing dominion; it had earlier refused to federate with the Australian colonies and was now a new nation standing on its own feet. The lawless haven for whalers and desperadoes had come a long way in 67 years.

SOUTH AFRICA

When Jan van Riebeek arrived at the Cape in 1652, he originally had no intention of starting a Dutch colony, merely of establishing a half-way port-of-call for ships sailing to the East. But the settlement grew and it was not long before Dutch farmers, known as Boers (strictly, Trekboers), began pushing inland across the veld towards the Orange River. Nor was it long before racial tension arose between Europeans and Africans.

The Dutch controlled the Cape until almost the end of the 18th century but, in 1795, Great Britain, at war with revolutionary France (which had overrun the Netherlands), seized this valuable outpost. It was handed back in 1803, only to be re-taken three years later and finally to have its occupation ratified by the peace settlement of 1815.

The years 1806-36 saw the transition of the Cape from a Dutch settlement into a British colony, partly through the arrival of the '1820 settlers', 5000 emigrants from England. This was also a period of continuous fighting (the so-called 'Kaffir' wars) between the whites and the Bantu peoples moving down from the north. Another conflict developed between white and white, Boer and Briton, for the two groups disliked one another and the Boers resented the presence of newcomers in a land where they felt

A view of Market Square and the Stadt Huis in Cape Town, 1832, a drawing by Sir Charles D'Oyly.

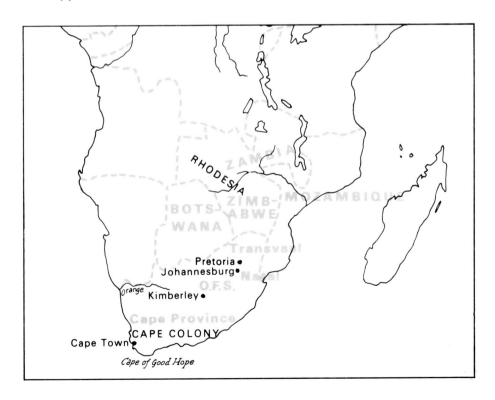

they had a prior right and they particularly objected to the arrival of British missionaries.

When Britain abolished slavery in her empire in 1833, the Boers, who owned a great many slaves, were so deeply offended that some 10 000 of them - the Voortrekkers - moved out of Cape Colony across the Orange River into Natal. But the Great Trek did not bring the hoped-for freedom, because the warlike Zulus of the area launched fierce attacks and the British decided to step in and annex Natal in order to protect Cape Colony. Once again, the Boers yoked their oxen and trekked northwards to found the states of Transvaal and the Orange Free State, and, once again, the scattered farmers found that they could not keep the Zulus in check. In 1877, the Transvaal was annexed by the British and this did not improve relations between the two races, especially as the Boers viewed with ill-concealed satisfaction the heavy weather which the British troops made of defeating Cetewayo, the renowned Zulu chief.

However, his defeat *did* make a case for the return of Transvaal and, when this was refused, the Boers took up arms and defeated a British force at Majuba Hill (1880). Gladstone, the British prime minister, true to his liberal principles, turned the other cheek and gave Transvaal back.

This situation was made all the more explosive by the emergence of Cecil Rhodes, a dynamic Englishman, who, having made a fortune out of a newly-discovered diamond-field at Kimberley (on the border of Cape Colony), used his wealth to form the British South Africa Company and recruit its own armed force. His aim was to bring all of South Africa under British rule and, in his way, stood the Boers, obstinately unaware of the 'blessings' which the superior Britons would bring to the black continent. Rhodes, now Prime Minister of Cape Colony, acquired Bechuanaland and then defeated the Matabele, whose land was declared a protectorate, renamed Rhodesia.

The Transvaal, now the only remaining obstacle, was suddenly convulsed by the discovery of gold in 1885. As in Australia and California, thousands of diggers poured into the country from all over the world, turning Johannesburg into a huge boom town and completely outnumbering the Boers. Their President, Paul Kruger - 'Oom Paul', the wily, resolute father of his people - made sure that the *Uitlanders* (foreigners) paid heavy taxes, but had no citizen rights, not even to vote.

A group of Uitlanders planned a rebellion, which Rhodes was to assist by getting his friend Dr Jameson to lead an invasion force of 500 volunteers. Due to muddle and misunderstanding, the uprising never took place and Jameson's Raid of 1895 was a resounding fiasco. The British government was universally condemned for an act of aggression against a small state; the German emperor sent congratulations to Kruger, Rhodes had to resign and the Boers were understandably jubilant.

In this mood and supplied with German arms, the Boers made ready to drive the British out of South Africa altogether. Jameson's Raid, Majuba Hill and Gladstone's well-known attitude had convinced them that they had little to fear, especially when Oom Paul could call on 60 000 well-mounted farmers to oppose a total force of only 14 000 British soldiers in the whole of South Africa. On the other hand, Kruger might have given a thought to the fact that Gladstone had gone and, in his place, Lord Salisbury headed an imperialistic government which had by this time acquired rights over large areas of Africa. Moreover, the British people, confident of their wealth and power, had woken up to the glory of possessing an empire. Aggressive patriotism ('jingoism'), had taken the place of meekness and liberal sentiments.

The South African War (also known as the Boer War), which broke out in October 1899, began with some startling reverses for the British, who were outnumbered, outgunned and out of their depth as regards knowledge of the country. However, the Boers made the mistake of besieging small garrison towns instead of sweeping through to Durban. In 1900, Lord Roberts and General Kitchener arrived with large reinforcements to relieve the beleaguered towns and defeat the main Boer army.

Three Boer generations in the war, 1900. Left to right: P. J. Lemmer 65, J. D. L. Botha 15, G. J. Pretorius 43, whose bearing shows their determination to oust the British.

A commando (military force) under General De Wet, crossing a drift or ford on the Orange River.

The last phase of the war, from November 1900 to May 1902, was a prolonged guerilla struggle in which the Boers, led by Botha, De Wet, Hertzog and Smuts, put up a most valiant resistance. Johannesburg and Pretoria fell, Kruger fled to Europe, but the 'commandos' and the farming populace would not give in, until Kitchener burnt the farms and put the civilians into concentration camps, so that they could no longer give aid to their fighting men.

These harsh measures brought the war to an end, and in the Treaty of Vereeniging, the British sought to pacify the situation by offering unvengeful terms. A grant was made to restore the farms and the two Boer republics became British colonies, with the promise of early self-government. This was granted in 1906 and, four years later, Transvaal and Orange Free State joined Cape Colony and Natal to form the Union of South Africa, the fourth self-governing Dominion of the British Empire.

17 America Grows
1803 – 1905

When George Washington took office as its first President, the United States made up only a small part of the continent of North America, for huge areas to the north, south and west belonged to Britain, Spain and France. Sparsely peopled by American Indian tribes, with a few Spanish forts and trading-posts, these territories were largely unknown to the Europeans of the Atlantic seaboard but, once the Ohio Valley had been settled, the West began to exert its fascination and to draw men towards the heart of the continent.

The first and greatest addition to American territory came in 1803, with the Louisiana Purchase. Roughly speaking, Louisiana was the area between the Mississippi and the Rockies that belonged in theory to France, which had ceded it to Spain in 1763 and claimed it back in 1800. This change caused Napoleon to think about reviving French colonies in America and deve-loping the port of New Orleans. The Americans were horrified and their President, Thomas Jefferson, sent representatives to France to let it be known that, if the French occupied New Orleans, the United States would make an alliance with Britain. In 1803, Napoleon therefore agreed to sell and, for the sum of 60 million francs (about 15 million dollars), the size of the United States was doubled.

Florida was bought from Spain in 1819 and the next big acquisition was at the expense of Mexico. American settlers in Texas staged a revolt and set up an independent state which was annexed by the United States in 1845. In the war that followed, Mexico was easily defeated and, by the peace of 1845, she had to surrender California, most of Arizona and territory that would one day become Utah and Nevada. By 1853, only 70 years since the Peace of Paris, the United States had grown from 13 colonies to 30 states, which stretched from coast to coast and the population had risen from nearly 4 million people to about 24 million.

Hardly had California been bought than gold was discovered at Sutter's Mill and, from 1849, thousands of diggers poured into the state to extract the precious metal in quantities that could only be compared to those which Spain obtained from Latin America in the 16th century. But wheat and cotton played an even more important role in shaping the United States' growth, for her river transport, canals and railways were built mainly to carry those products to the world's markets.

Wheat was the great frontier crop, for it grew prodigiously in the virgin soil, where, it was said, McCormick's harvester pushed the line of civilization 30 miles westward every year! American wheat was now in high demand in the industrial countries of Europe, especially Great Britain. So was cotton, which, thanks to Eli Whitney's *gin* (a machine which separated

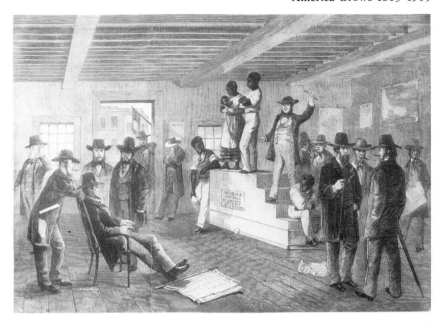

Slave auction in Virginia, 1861. Although rich Virginians had owned slaves for over 200 years, part of the state refused to join the Confederate cause and broke away to become West Virginia.

the raw cotton from the seeds), replaced tobacco as the prime crop of the South. Its exhausting effect on the soil caused southerners to move to Alabama, Mississippi and Louisiana and to continue to look for new land.

When Washington began his presidency, there were about 700 000 slaves in the Union, but the demand for cotton led to a big increase in the number of plantations and of slaves. By 1860, there were about 4 million slaves[1] providing the unskilled continuous labour required for cultivating and picking the crop. The whole economy of the South and the life-style of its rich aristocratic planters depended on slavery.

The opening of the West made men ask themselves whether the new territories were to be slave states or free. Texas already had slavery, but what about California, New Mexico, Kansas and Nebraska, which had not? Southerners felt that slavery was a right that should not be interfered with by outsiders, but, in the North, where a fierce abolitionist movement was gaining ground, most people were opposed to any extension of slavery.

As tension mounted, the Southerners came to look on the bustling industrialised North as an enemy, bent on destroying their prosperity and

---

[1] Importation of slaves was abolished in 1808, yet the slave population continued to rise through natural increase. Slaves were bred in Maryland and Virginia and taken to be sold in Alabama, Louisiana and other southern states.

Abraham Lincoln (1809-1865) in 1864. Throughout the agonies of a bitterly-fought civil war, Lincoln showed the highest qualities of statesmanship, steadfast courage and charity. Had he lived, the South would surely have been saved a great deal of suffering and humiliation, but, while he is rightly a national hero, it was he, the ardent democrat, who refused to allow Southerners freedom to leave the Union.

way of life. It was, they said, the right of each state to manage its own affairs and if this right was to be denied, then they would secede, i.e. leave the Union and found a separate nation.

To those who believed in federal government, the Constitution and the ideals of the Founding Fathers, this was a shocking view to take and no-one opposed it more hotly than the son of a restless western pioneer, Abraham Lincoln, who, despite his early lack of education in the backwoods, had become a lawyer and Congressman. In a series of public debates, Lincoln passionately upheld the Union, declaring, 'A house divided against itself cannot stand. I believe this government cannot endure permanently half-slave, half-free ... I do not expect the Union to be dissolved - I do not expect the house to fall - but I do expect it will cease to be divided'.

As the champion of the anti-slavery, pro-Union movement, Lincoln won the Presidential election of 1860, a sensational result which, at once, caused South Carolina to leave the Union. Another 6 states followed suit and met together to form the Southern Confederacy, with Jefferson Davis as President. They were joined a little later by 4 more states to make the number of 'secessionists' up to 11. Why did they do it? The probable answer is that the Southerners saw that the North was growing stronger and richer, so that they would soon be overpowered. It was now or never. As an independent nation, they could follow their own interests and probably acquire more land by annexing Cuba and Mexico.

The first step was to seize government properties, mints and forts in the South, but, at Fort Sumter, Charleston, the commander refused to submit. Confederate guns opened fire on 12 April 1861 and the Civil War began. It was to last four years, to cost over half-a-million lives and bring ruin to the South. With hindsight, one can see that the North, like Parliament in the English Civil War, was bound to win. It possessed far greater wealth, raw materials and industry; its population numbered 22 million against 9 million Southerners, of whom over one-third were negroes; it had 30 000 miles of railways, besides lake, river and canal routes, while the South had practically no industry or skilled workers and only two main railway lines.

Yet the South possessed a much stronger military tradition, for Southerners dominated the regular army and the cream of its officers resigned in order to serve the Confederacy. As a soldier, the Southerner proved hard to beat; led by such outstanding commanders as Robert E. Lee and 'Stonewall' Jackson, he reckoned he could 'lick any five Yankees' and, in the last stages of the war, when he was hungry, ragged and short of ammunition, he went on fighting to the bitter end. By contrast, the

Farewell to Fort Sumter, 3 February 1861. Wives and children wave goodbye to the soldiers quartered in that fort, as they steam past in the *Marion* on their way to New York.

Northern soldier was more difficult to train and discipline, and, in the early part of the war, he was led by generals who could not compare with Lee and Jackson. So it took the Union four long years to beat the Confederacy, years in which Lincoln met every set-back, difficulty and outburst of criticism with unshakeable resolve, until, as Commander-in-Chief, he found in Ulysses Grant, Sheridan, Thomas and Sherman, the generals he needed to win battles and wear the enemy down.

Much of the war was fought in the state of Virginia, where the Confederate generals, Joe Johnston, Lee and Jackson, mostly concentrated on holding the southern capital, Richmond. In a number of hard-fought battles, they repulsed or defeated their opponents, but the North, with its superiority in manpower and materials, was able to repair its losses and raise fresh armies. The Southerners stayed on the defensive for the most part and when they did advance into Kentucky and Tennessee, they were beaten by the hard-drinking brigadier-general, Ulysses Grant. He was no military genius, but he was tenacious, never made the same mistake twice and, of him, Lincoln said, 'I can't spare this man; he fights.'

When Lee pushed up into Maryland, he found so little support that he had to retire to Fredericksburg, where his ragged troops smashed the Union army's assault and won another victory at Chancellorsville, though the death of Stonewall Jackson was a mortal blow to their cause. Once again, Lee advanced north of Washington, whereupon Lincoln sent General Meade to intercept him and they met at Gettysburg on 1 July 1863. The battle in

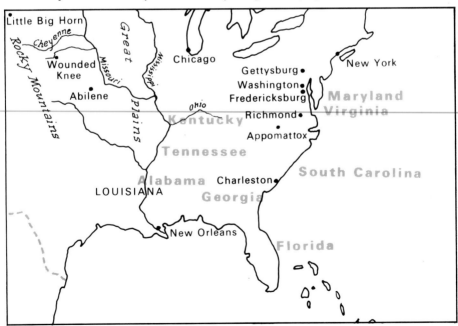

General McClellan, the Union commander, at Antietam, September 1862, a
savage battle from which Lee managed to
extricate his outnumbered army.
McClellan, a good but cautious general,
was dismissed for not annihilating the
enemy.

Confederate troops storming a Federal
stronghold during the early part of the
war.

which 40 000 men were killed, proved to be the turning point of the war, for
Lee lost a third of his splendid army, a loss he could never make good.
Defeated, though by no means broken, he returned southwards into Virginia
to keep up the struggle for two more years, but, from now on, it was
downhill all the way.

In 1864, Grant moved east to deal hammer-blow upon hammer-blow at
Lee. His losses were enormous, but he kept up the relentless pressure to
break the Confederate resistance and when Lee was forced to abandon
Richmond, the end had come. On 9 April 1865, he surrendered to Grant in
the village of Appomattox Courthouse.

Five days later, Abraham Lincoln was dead, assassinated by a southern
fanatic, who thus removed from the scene the one man to whom the ruined
South could look for moderation and justice. Throughout the long struggle,
Lincoln had never uttered one vindictive word against the Southerners and,
as the end drew near, had urged his followers to restore the Union 'with
malice towards none, with charity for all'. Now that he was dead, there was
no-one with the authority to restrain a vengeful Congress from imposing
'Reconstruction' on the defeated South, which meant dividing it into
districts ruled by major-generals who handed political power and financial

pickings to northern fortune-seekers, known as 'carpet-baggers', their Southern allies called 'scalawags' and to some of the freed negroes.

Although Lincoln had repeatedly said that his main aim was to save the Union and not to abolish or perpetuate slavery, he had proclaimed the freeing of all slaves in the rebel states in 1863 and, by an amendment to the Constitution, two years later, slavery was forbidden and they were given the right to vote. This meant that in all the ex-Confederate states, except Georgia, white voters were outnumbered by black. But it was not difficult for wily politicians to manipulate uneducated negroes who lacked leadership of their own race, and relied on the support of the occupying armies of the North. When these were removed in 1871, blacks soon disappeared from assemblies and public positions and whites regained control by means which included intimidation by secret societies, such as the Ku Klux Klan.

Even so, the Union had been saved, Lincoln's ideal of 'government of the people, by the people, for the people' seemed to be safe and the United States could resume its march towards becoming the richest nation on earth, even if it meant forgetting the blacks, the Indians and the poor whites.

Covered wagon going westward. This was the pioneers' mode of transport until the building of trans-continental railways after the Civil War. The great 'prairie schooners' on the Oregon Trail were invariably pulled by teams of oxen. Every-one, except the sick and the very young, walked alongside - all 2000 miles!

Geronimo, the famous Apache chief, one of the last to give up. In 1886, he surrendered to the U.S. army and was sent into exile in Florida. He was never allowed to return to his Apache homeland.
Copyright G. D. Hackett, NY

In the half-century that followed the Civil War, America's spectacular expansion took three main lines of development: movement across the prairies towards the Pacific, growth of big business and a surprising venture into imperialism. First came the brief era of the Wild West, when cowboys drove the cattle herds across the Kansas ranges to railheads like Abilene, Ellsworth and Dodge City, where the steers were slaughtered or transported alive to the abattoirs of Chicago. In 1871, Abilene alone handled 700 000 cattle, but, within a few years, thousands of European immigrants were challenging the cattlemen for a share of the Great Plains. The Homesteaders Act gave them each 160 acres of land to cultivate, so they planted corn and protected their crops behind fences of the newly-invented barbed wire.

Cattle and corn brought destruction to the buffalo herds and the Indian way of life. As land-hungry Americans pushed into the prairies, some of the tribes made treaties with the newcomers; others resisted fiercely, but all came to realise that the white man's word was worthless when land or gold were involved. In 1863, occurred the Sand Creek Massacre of Cheyenne Indians by the Colorado Militia; this led to open warfare and the general policy of herding the tribes into reservations. The Indians' reaction was to wipe out General Custer and his men in the famous action at Little Big Horn

(1876), but retaliation brought disaster to the Sioux and broke the resistance of tribes like the Blackfeet, the Comanches and the fierce Apaches. Geronimo, the last great Apache chief, surrendered to the American army in 1886 and the final act of violence was the slaughter of 300 Sioux at Wounded Knee in 1891.

While the cattlemen and the farmers were transforming the West, a generation of inventors, technologists and businessmen in the East were turning the United States into the world's leading industrial power. By the turn of the century, it stood first in production of wheat, cattle, cotton, petroleum, coal, gold and copper, in the output of iron, steel and manufactured goods and in mileage of railway, telegraph and telephone lines.

This remarkable expansion was due to a number of factors, apart from the country's immense natural resources; Americans seemed to be exceptionally enterprising, with an inborn optimism that was constantly fanned by stories of 'striking it rich'; a whole crop of inventions made their appearance, such as McCormick's harvester, Whitney's cotton gin, Edison's dynamo, Morse's telegraph, Bell's telephone and innumerable machines and methods that made mass-production possible. 'Big Business' played a dominant role when astute men got together to form giant corporations or 'trusts' to undercut rivals and buy up smaller firms. 'Captains of industry' emerged, like Cornelius Vanderbilt and J.P. Morgan, who made fortunes out of railways, John D. Rockefeller, the oil-magnate and Andrew Carnegie, the poor boy from Scotland, who built the steel industry. In this 'Gilded Age', as Mark Twain called it, the Duke family controlled tobacco; the Guggenheims, copper, and Philip Armour, meat-packing; by 1900, there were at least 300 millionaires in the USA.

Ruthlessly efficient business methods could flourish where there was a docile labour force and, between 1830 and 1910, more than 26 million immigrants entered the country, most of them poor and ill-educated; a quarter of them from eastern and southern Europe - Czechs, Serbs, Croats, Greeks, Italians, Poles and Russian Jews - who were ready to work long hours for low wages, to the angry dismay of native-born Americans and the rising trade unions. The immigrants settled chiefly in the big new industrial cities of the North-East and in the Pacific states, where they lived in appalling tenements. Yet America's dramatic expansion could not have taken place without them and, in return, America gave them what they had never had in their home countries - the hope of better times to come for themselves and, above all, for their children.

Exploitation of cheap labour was only one way of making money; there were price-fixing deals, violent suppression of trade unions, bribery of government officials and the formation of political 'lobbies' to press for favourable treatment of certain industries and for import duties on foreign

Russian immigrants landing in New York 1892. By then, the so-called 'old' immigration from Britain and western Europe had passed its peak and most of the newcomers were drawn from the impoverished countries of central and south-eastern Europe.

goods. Among those who tried to break the power of the giant trusts was Theodore ('Teddy') Roosevelt, President from 1901-9, a colourful character, who devoted his vast energies to attacking the trusts and introducing a 'square deal' for the workers.

As the economy forged ahead, Americans began to look beyond their own country for business opportunities, especially in South America, China and Hawaii. William Henry Seward, Secretary of State from 1861-9, was one of the first to see the need for bases to protect these interests and, in 1867, he obtained Midway Island, lying west of Hawaii. He also bought Alaska from Russia for over 7 million dollars, despite much opposition for paying that sum for a mass of ice!

When Cuba rebelled against Spanish rule in 1895, American sympathies and self-interest led to a war in which the United States defeated Spain in little more than 3 months. Cuba gained its independence, along with close commercial and political ties to America; Puerto Rico, the Philippines and the Pacific island of Guam were annexed and, after them, Hawaii (1898), with its magnificent anchorage of Pearl Harbor.

Thus, by the end of the century, the United States, somewhat to its own surprise, had acquired an overseas empire. 'Teddy' Roosevelt, an enthusiastic supporter of expansion, obtained permission to build the Panama Canal to enable the United States to dominate the Pacific and, in 1905, he played a leading part in arranging a peace settlement between Russia and Japan.

It was clear that George Washington's advice, in his Farewell Address of 1796, that America should have as little connection as possible with foreigners had been forgotten. The USA was now a world power.

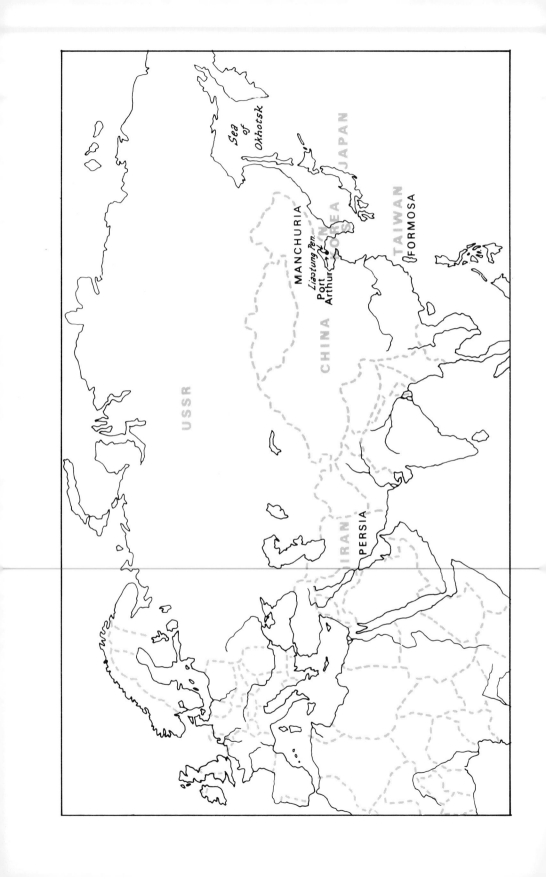

18 A New Europe
1823-1914

RUSSIA

One of the dominant themes of 19th-century European history was fear of Russia. Since Peter the Great's time, the Russian Empire had continued to expand until, by mid-century, it stretched from Finland and Poland to the Black Sea in the south and across Siberia to the Sea of Okhotsk in the far east. This expansion and Russia's enormous armies made the Powers apprehensive. Britain was fearful for India; there was general indignation at the Tsar's brutal treatment of the Poles and at his support of Austria in crushing the Hungarians in 1848. Moreover, it was abundantly clear that Russia intended to push down into the south-west, towards Turkey's possessions in the Balkans, in order to win control of the Black Sea and access to the Mediterranean.

Curiously enough, the country whose foreign policy made the other great Powers shiver, was a backward savage society at home. 88 per cent of the population were serfs, who owned nothing but were themselves owned by the nobles. Two-thirds of the land belonged to the Tsar and the Church, the rest was apportioned to the nobles who held it in trust, allowing the serfs to cultivate strips which just enabled them to feed their families in a good season. Provincial towns were primitive and mostly built of wood; there were few schools and universities, only a small number of teachers and writers, and hardly any prosperous merchants, shop-keepers and craftsmen.

Tsar Alexander I died in 1823 and was succeeded by Nicholas I, whose reign was variously described as an ice age, a plague zone and a prison, for he was an unyielding despot, intent upon controlling every aspect of national life by the rule of officials and secret police. Yet there was no revolution, only minor conspiracies and outbreaks of violence and crop-burning by serfs; in foreign policy, the Tsar continued to play a strong role and to look for an excuse to attack Turkey.

It came when a quarrel broke out between French Roman Catholic monks and Orthodox monks in Bethlehem, which was within the Turkish Empire. Declaring that he was the protector of all Orthodox Christians, the Tsar sent troops to occupy two Turkish provinces at the mouth of the Danube. The French Emperor, Napoleon III, was also looking for an excuse for war to

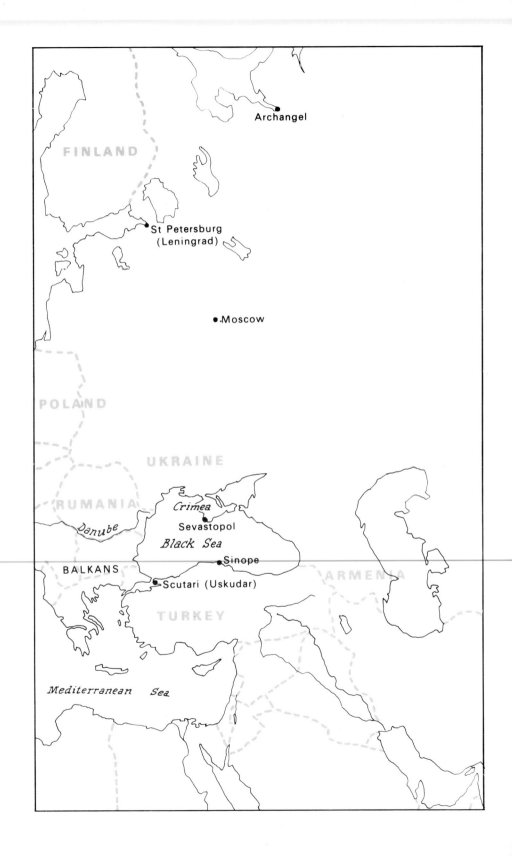

Archangel

FINLAND

St Petersburg
(Leningrad)

•.Moscow

POLAND

UKRAINE

RUMANIA

Crimea

Danube

Sevastopol

Black Sea

BALKANS

Sinope

Scutari (Uskudar)

ARMENIA

TURKEY

Mediterranean   Sea

Battle of Inkerman, November 1854, a bloody slogging match between infantry, in which the Russians lost 11 000 men and the Anglo-French armies 4000. The Russian failure to bring up their reserves resulted in the long siege of Sevastopol.

rally public opinion and to underline the fact that he was the great Bonaparte's nephew; he therefore sided with the Sultan and had no difficulty getting Britain to join in, since Palmerston and the general public were fiercely anti-Russia. When news came that Russian warships had wiped out the Turkish fleet in the Black Sea, off Sinope, France and Britain declared war in March 1854.

The Crimean War, one of the most useless and ill-conducted conflicts of all time, was confined to the area around the Black Sea port of Sevastopol, which was captured after a siege lasting a year and the loss of over 400 000 lives. The campaign was remarkable for the blunders of the military commanders, the bravery of the ill-equipped soldiers, the first war-time use of railways and 'iron-clad' warships and the emergence of a popular heroine in Florence Nightingale, an Englishwoman, who went out to run the British military hospital at Scutari and later made nursing a respectable profession for women.

The peace terms signed in Paris in 1856 proved to be as futile as the war itself. The Tsar agreed that no warships should use the Black Sea - and he repudiated this clause in 1871; the Sultan promised to treat the Balkan. Christians better - and failed to do so; the victors 'guaranteed' the Sultan's European possessions - and sponsored the formation of the new state of Rumania.

Tsar Alexandar II (1855-81), whose reign was marked by many reforms, as well as by social change based on railway development and industrialisation. His foreign policy was expansionist - towards the Balkans, against Turkey and into central Asia and the Far East.

However, one man was well-satisfied. He was Count Cavour, prime minister of Piedmont, part of the kingdom of Sardinia, who, by sending a few soldiers to serve in the war, obtained a seat at the peace conference and the chance to win support for his plans to create a Kingdom of Italy.

Meanwhile, in Russia, the new Tsar, Alexander II, had made up his mind to free the serfs, a momentous decision, which was of course opposed by the nobles, but he persisted and, in 1861, 40 million serfs became free peasants. Hailed as the 'Tsar Liberator', Alexander introduced more reforms in the hope of turning Russia into an efficient modern state; he relaxed censorship of newspapers and magazines, allowed students to discuss ideas that had been forbidden, introduced trial by jury, reduced the length of compulsory army service and set up local councils, with powers to build schools and hospitals.

Alas for his good intentions. As often happens when a government effects overdue changes, there was an immediate demand for more reforms.

The peasants were given land to farm, but they had to buy it from the landlords, who, they claimed, kept the best land for themselves. This meant they could barely grow enough food to exist and yet still had to find the annual payments, so that, in many cases, they were worse off than in the days of serfdom.

Removal of censorship and the spread of education led to the growth of revolutionary ideas, political clubs and terrorist organisations, some of them, like the *Nihilists* (Latin nihil means 'nothing'), pledged to destroy everything - government, family, marriage and life itself. In 1866, the Tsar narrowly escaped assassination. The shock convinced him that he had gone too far, so the clubs were closed down, censorship reimposed and severe measures taken to suppress all political activity, but, to no purpose, for on 13 March 1881, the 'Tsar Liberator' was killed by a bomb thrown by a Nihilist student.

The next Tsar, Alexander III (1881-94), put an end to all hope of reform, without being able to curb discontent and the growth of major political groups. His reign was notable for persecution of racial minorities - Finns, Poles, Ukrainians, Armenians and Jews - and for Russia's own Industrial Revolution. After emancipation, thousands of peasants had flocked into the towns, providing a cheap labour force, which encouraged European financiers to invest money in mines, oil-wells, steel-mills and factories. This brought a great increase in trade and industry, most of it state-owned, and a new class of industrial workers, whose hours, wages and living conditions were even worse than those in Western Europe half-a-century earlier.

By the turn of the century, opposition to the Tsarist government was becoming better organised. The more moderate elements wanted a representative parliament, free education and land reform, but the Social Democrats or S. D. Party, which was founded in 1898, based their beliefs on the ideas of Karl Marx and therefore stood for overthrowing the régime by revolution. In 1903, at a meeting held in exile in London, the party split into two groups: the *Bolsheviks* or majority and the *Mensheviks* or minority, which later became separate parties.

The Bolsheviks were led by Vladimir Ilyich Ulyanov, a professional agitator, who took the name of Lenin. In 1900, he fled abroad to avoid arrest and spent the next 17 years in exile, though he remained in close touch with revolutionary comrades who were organising socialist groups, called *soviets*, in the Russian factories.

Their chance to overthrow the government seemed to have arrived in 1905, after Russia had suffered a humiliating defeat by Japan. The policy of expanding the empire had gone on remorselessly in spite of all the domestic unrest and, since the Crimean War, a good deal of territory had been acquired at the expense of Turkey, Persia and China. In 1894, Japan's westernised forces compelled China to cede Korea, Formosa (Taiwan) and part of Manchuria called the Liaotung Peninsula. Russia stepped in and demanded this peninsula, which the Japanese, not being prepared for further action, had to give up. But they did not forget the insult to their pride and, in 1904, they suddenly attacked and sunk the Russian Far Eastern Fleet at Port Arthur and soundly defeated the Russian armies in Manchuria.

This disaster convinced the revolutionaries that their time had come and, at Christmas 1904, they declared a general strike. The 1905 Revolution began with a procession of workers in St Petersburg to present the Tsar with a list of their grievances, but, before they reached his palace, they were fired upon by soldiers and ridden down by the Cossack cavalry. This 'Bloody Sunday' gave rise to strikes, peasant uprisings and a mutiny of the Sevastopol fleet, which caused the Tsar Nicholas II to agree to the election of a Parliament or *Duma* and to grant such liberties as freedom of speech and the right to join political parties and trade unions.

If Nicholas had been sincere, he might have saved his throne, for there was still much support for moderate policies, but Nicholas, believing that he had been sent by God to rule the country and that reforms were mere 'senseless dreams', impeded the work of the Duma, ignored their decisions and dismissed those who offended him.

However, the situation calmed down, as industry continued to expand, wages improved and the Tsar's minister, Stolypin, introduced land reforms which produced a class of prosperous land-owning peasants, called *kulaks*. Revolutionary activity declined and might have died away altogether had not Russia mobilized her armies in 1914. Once again, an aggressive foreign policy led to war - a war that was to bring such chaos and misery that revolution became the only alternative to the Tsarist régime.

ITALY: THE RISORGIMENTO

When Count Cavour, the stout bespectacled Prime Minister of Piedmont took his seat at the Paris peace conference of 1856, Italy was not a nation, but a collection of small states ruled by foreigners, with the exception of the Papal States in the centre and Sardinia (comprising the island of Sardinia, Savoy and Piedmont), whose ruler, King Victor Emmanuel II, had given Cavour a free hand to modernise his mainland province. Cavour, rich, shrewd and extraordinarily gifted, speedily transformed Piedmont by building roads and railways, making Genoa into a major port and concluding trade agreements with Britain and France.

In the north of Italy, Lombardy and Venetia were ruled by Austria, while in a number of smaller states, like Tuscany, Modena and Parma, the aristocratic rulers were propped up by Austrian support. Down south, where Naples and Sicily, known as the Kingdom of the Two Sicilies, endured the tyrannical rule of a Bourbon King, Francis II, centuries of mismanagement had reduced these once-rich states to dire poverty.

Cavour, who had started a newspaper called *Il Risorgimento*, meaning Resurgence or Reawakening, knew that Piedmont could not defeat Austria

without a powerful ally which was why he went to the Paris conference to try to win Napoleon III's friendship.

As the great Napoleon's nephew, the French emperor stood for the destruction of the 1815 Settlement and an end to Austrian rule in Italy, where France could again become the dominant influence. Accordingly, he arranged a secret meeting in 1859 with Cavour, at which he promised to send armed help, providing that Austria could be seen to be the aggressor and Piedmont the innocent victim. By sending an ultimatum demanding the disbanding of Piedmont's armed forces, Austria duly obliged and was heavily defeated by the Franco-Piedmontese army at Magenta and Solferino[1] in northern Italy.

In several states, the Italians ousted their dukes and duchesses and voted to join Piedmont-Sardinia in a Northern Italian Kingdom, but Napoleon III, horrified by the bloodshed at Solferino, backed away and concluded an armistice with Austria. He was, however, induced to recognise the new kingdom in return for the cession of Savoy and Nice to France, which Cavour most sorrowfully accepted in 1860.

Italy was still not united, for the Pope, protected by French troops, excommunicated all those who had risen against their overlords; Venetia remained in Austrian hands and the Kingdom of Two Sicilies was only beginning to get its own insurrection under way.

This uprising brought Garibaldi to the fore, the colourful patriot who had fought in South America and come back to Italy to take part in the 1848 revolt. Home from exile in America, he now turned up in Sicily at the head of his One Thousand Redshirts and, in a brilliant campaign, beat the Neapolitan army and crossed over to the mainland. Welcomed like a saviour, he advanced swiftly to Naples where he defeated Francis II and made ready to go on and liberate Rome from papal rule.

Cavour was aghast. Realising than an attack on Rome might provoke an international crisis and undo all that had been gained, he persuaded Victor Emmanuel to lead the Piedmontese army across the Papal States and try to make Garibaldi see reason. The old firebrand was unwilling to give up his plan but, in the end, he resigned his command and retired to the island of Caprera. Plebiscites in the Two Sicilies and all the Papal States, except for Rome itself, called for union with Piedmont and, in February 1861, Victor Emmanuel was proclaimed King of Italy. Four months later, Cavour died, worn out by the strain of ceaseless work, but his dream, save for Rome and Venice, had been realised and Italy was free.

Cavour's death left the new state without the leader it badly needed, for there was a lack of experienced politicians, as well as a good deal of regional jealousy, hostility of republicans towards the monarchy and the Pope's refusal to come to terms with those who had robbed him of his estates. The poverty of the lawless south and the country's lack of coal and iron for industry caused millions of Italians to emigrate to North and South America.

The government took refuge in an aggressive foreign policy and, in 1866,

---

[1] It was at this battle that an observer, a Swiss banker named Henri Dunant, was so moved by the sufferings of the wounded that he started a movement which led to the founding of the Red Cross at Geneva in 1864.

The meeting of Garibaldi (centre) and Victor Emmanuel (right) at Teano, 9 miles north of Naples, on 16 September 1860, when Garibaldi put aside his republicanism and accepted the King. Together they rode in triumph into Naples. Together they had helped to make Italy a nation.

joined Prussia in her war against Austria, during which the Italian army and navy suffered defeats, but Prussia's overall victory allowed Italy to acquire Venice. The Franco-Prussian war of 1870 caused French troops to be withdrawn from Rome and the city was entered by Italian troops on 20 September. In the following year, it became Italy's capital and the Pope, 'the prisoner of the Vatican', shut himself away in his palace, a policy which was followed by his successors until 1929, when Mussolini recognised the Vatican as an independent state.

Attempts to win colonies in Africa met with little success, for the French forestalled the Italians by occupying Tunis (1881), and, after Italy had acquired a protectorate over part of Somaliland, her army suffered a humiliating defeat at the hands of the Ethiopians at Adowa in 1896.

Good progress was made, however, in industry, especially around Turin; Pirelli founded his rubber factory in 1872, Breda set up the Terni steelworks in 1886, naval yards at Pozzuoli were opened in 1885 and government subsidies helped to build the shipping industry, the Navigazione Generale Italiana. From 1883, a start was made to harness rivers to generate electricity; Marconi began his experiments in wireless telegraphy, the first Italian factory for making cars was established in Turin as early as 1895 and, by 1914, Fiat was producing 18 000 cars a year.

GERMANY UNIFIED

Austria's defeat in Italy was due to the alliance between Cavour and Napoleon III and also to the fact that she could no longer look for support (as in Hungary in 1848) from Russia. This was the price Austria had to pay for not helping the Tsar during the Crimean War, when the Austrian government was only too happy to see the Danubian provinces freed from Russian control. The end of that friendship also meant that she had no ally to call upon in her next, and more serious, peck of troubles.

The Congress of Vienna (1815) had decided that the confederation of 39 German states set up by Napoleon should continue to exist as a barrier against France and, in the next 50 years, the Confederation remained under Austrian domination. Prussia, not a member of the Confederation, came to be more and more regarded as the leader of Germany. This spirit was seen in 1848, when German liberals offered a German crown to the King of Prussia, but Frederick William, realising that he would have Austria and Russia about his ears, declined the honour. Nevertheless, the idea of German unity had been born and the states already had their own customs union (the *Zollverein*) and were linked by a new railway system.

The man who created a unified Germany was Otto von Bismark, a Prussian *Junker*, an aristocratic landowner, who ranged himself alongside King William I in his contempt for the milk-and-water ideals of the liberals. In his opinion, what was needed was a policy of 'blood and iron' - war and

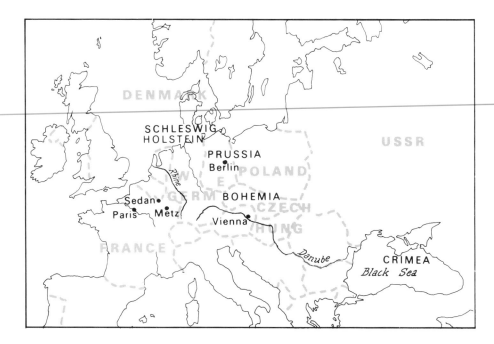

Otto, Prince von Bismark (1815-98), the Prussian statesman, whose aim was to unify Germany under Prussian leadership, which he achieved through defeating Austria and France. After 1871, his policy was to safeguard and consolidate the new Germany, hence the quarrel with William II, who favoured further aggression.

determined action - to overthrow Austrian control. As Prime Minister of Prussia from 1862, this wily realist was prepared to use every artifice in order to bring all the other states under Prussian dominance.

He began by siding with the King against Parliament and, in collaboration with Count von Moltke, the Commander-in-Chief, he built up a powerful army. Next, he persuaded Austria to join in a squalid little war against Denmark over the duchies of Schleswig and Holstein, to which the Danish King had put his claim. Then, after Denmark's inevitable defeat in 1864, he picked a quarrel with Austria over the peace settlement, and, having promised Venetia to Italy and lulled Napoleon III into neutrality by vague promises, he declared war on his ally. In July 1866, the Prussian forces shattered Austria's army at Sadowa in Bohemia (Czechoslovakia) and the war was over in seven weeks. The speed of the entire operation had prevented any alliance between France and Austria and the French viewed the situation with angry dismay: 'It is France who has been defeated at Sadowa', remarked one of their marshals bitterly.

The northern states were now brought together into the North German Confederation under Prussian leadership, with William as President and Bismark as Chancellor. The southern states - Bavaria, Wurtemburg, Baden and Hesse-Darmstadt - held aloof and there was even talk of forming a separate league. Nevertheless, each made a defensive military alliance with Prussia, by which it was agreed that if one of the signatories was attacked, the others would come to its assistance. Hence, all that Bismark had to do was to provoke France into declaring war.

The opportunity arrived in July 1870, when the Spanish throne became vacant. Bismark put forward a German candidate, a Hohenzollern prince, cousin to King William I, who gave his full consent. The French, feeling that they would be encircled, angrily demanded the withdrawal of the Prussian candidate. King William, troubled by this reaction and, at 73, wanting a quiet life, put pressure on the young prince to withdraw his claim. The old King then considered the incident closed. Not so the French. Elated by their triumph, they demanded 'guarantees for the future', which an ambassador presented to William at Ems, where he was taking the waters for his health. The King answered mildly that his cousin's withdrawal was sufficient and, after the meeting, he sent by telegraph an account of what had happened to Bismark in Berlin. The Chancellor and Moltke 'doctored' the Ems Telegram to make it appear that the King had curtly refused an insulting demand. The text was published in the German press and then, mistranslated, in French newspapers, where it appeared more offensive than ever.

Napoleon, whose popularity was at a low ebb, owing to the Mexican fiasco (see p. 333), decided to restore his prestige by putting this upstart state in its place. On 16 July 1870, the ageing sick Emperor declared war on Prussia and placed himself at the head of the French army.

On the other side of the Rhine, the southern states were unanimous in their support for Prussia, whose army outclassed the French as completely and as swiftly as they had dealt with the Austrians. After several lightning victories, they surrounded the main French army at Sedan and, on 2 September, bombarded it into surrender. Among the thousands of prisoners was Napoleon himself.

Sedan marked the end of monarchy in France, for the people declared the Third Republic two days later, and, with passionate courage, made ready to continue the fight. Léon Gambetta, an ardent republican, escaped by balloon from Paris, leaving the encircled capital to raise fresh armies, but his half-trained levies were soon overcome by the Prussians. After suffering the horrors of a four-months' siege, the Parisians opened their gates to the Germans on 28 January 1871.

The Franco-Prussian War was over and Bismark's terms were hard: France was made to hand over the provinces of Alsace and Lorraine (with Lorraine's immense deposits of iron ore), pay a huge indemnity and accept a German army of occupation until it was paid. The victors chose to have the German Empire proclaimed in Louis XIV's Hall of Mirrors at Versailles, where, in the presence of all the German princes, dukes and generals, William I of Prussia accepted the Imperial Crown and the title of German Emperor. The old king was, in fact, far from keen on his new title, but Bismark won him round with the same masterly skill that he deployed in persuading the German states to accept Prussian leadership, Prussian ideas of government, the Prussian Chancellor as Germany's Chancellor, the Prussian capital as Germany's capital and the Prussian belief that loyalty, obedience and discipline were more important than personal freedom.

But for every doubter there were a hundred who greeted these remarkable events with joyous enthusiasm. After centuries of division and weakness, Germany was united at last and through her victories over Austria and France, the strongest military power in the world. Was it any wonder that many should think of themselves as the master race, heirs to a greater destiny and yet more triumphs?

For a time, all went wonderfully well. German industry, enriched by Lorraine's coal and iron, expanded at an enormous rate and, while German goods found their way into the markets of the world, German chemists and inventors produced machines, alloys, plastics, dyes, drugs, weapons and explosives that a booming state demanded. All this while the Iron Chancellor was still at the helm. To protect the German Empire he made the Triple Alliance with Austria and Italy, and, at home, he reacted strongly to opposition from the Catholic Church and the Socialists. Cunning as always, he stole the Socialists' thunder by granting the workers benefits which were only being dreamed about in other countries - sick pay, accident compensation and old-age pensions.

In 1888, the old Emperor died and was succeeded by his son, Frederick III, the husband of Queen Victoria's eldest daughter. When he died after a reign of only three months, the Imperial Crown passed to their 23-year-old son, William II, known to the irreverent British as 'Kaiser Bill'. In 1890, after an almighty quarrel, this truculent young man dismissed Bismark from office and became in effect his own Chancellor, ruling the country in collaboration with personal favourites and the chiefs of the armed forces.

After 'dropping the pilot', as a famous British cartoon put it, William II set Germany on a new course. In his speeches, he constantly stressed Germany's imperial might and the army's special, almost mystical role: 'The soldier and the army, not parliamentary majorities, have welded together the German Empire', he declared. 'My confidence is placed on the army'.

Convinced that Germany was being denied her rightful 'place in the sun', he embarked on a vast programme of military and naval armament. Conscription was stepped up, so that, with every German male spending two or three years in the army, the country could put an enormous number of

Kaiser William or Wilhelm II (1859-1941) on his way to a grand military review at Potsdam in 1913. For over 20 years, he had identified himself with Germany's military and naval growth and by his tactless public utterances had antagonised France, Britain and Russia. To some extent, therefore, he was responsible for the outbreak of war. From 1914 to 1918, he played the part of a war-leader but real decisions were in the hands of the German General Staff.

trained men into the field. But this was not enough. 'I shall never rest', declared the Kaiser, 'until I have raised my navy to the same standard as my army', so Admiral Tirpitz was given the task of building a fleet to rival the British Navy.

This bellicose policy alarmed France and Russia into forming a Dual Alliance, while Great Britain emerged from her so-called 'splendid isolation' to come to an understanding with France called the *Entente Cordiale*. But Kaiser William seemed to go out of his way to give and take offence. He upset the British by siding openly with the Boers in South Africa and he enraged the French by visiting North Africa to announce Germany's 'great and growing interest in Morocco'.

In fairness, there was much to understand in the Kaiser's attitude. He and his countrymen felt that they were being denied the just rewards for their industry and efficiency; they felt encircled by enemies, for they knew that the French were longing for revenge; they feared the Russian monster and hated the smug complacency of the British, who, by some accident of history, had

Siege of Paris during the Franco-Prussian War of 1870-71: Avenue d'Orléans during bombardment. The city held out from 17 September 1870 until 27 January 1871.

been able to help themselves to colonies and a great part of the world's trade. For all his posturing, William was of small importance; it was not he, but the military leaders, men like Helmuth von Moltke[1], the Chief of Staff, and von Tirpitz at the Admiralty, who held the real power in Germany. They and their staffs worked out a master-plan by which both France and Russia would be defeated and, according to that plan, the German war-machine would reach its peak in the summer of 1914.

FRANCE

On 28 January 1871, the city of Paris surrendered to the Prussian army and thereby brought an end to the war which changed the whole balance of power which had existed in Europe since the downfall of the first Napoleon.

News of the armistice was received in the streets of the capital with a mixture of rage and bewilderment, for the working-class population still clung to their belief that defeat might somehow be averted.

They felt betrayed. Napoleon III's abject capitulation at Sedan had been

[1] The Younger, nephew of Count von Moltke, architect of the victories over Austria (1866) and France (1870).

393

Opening of the Paris Exhibition 1867: arrival of the Emperor Napoleon III and Empress Eugénie at the Grand Entrance of a vast glass-and-iron building on the Left Bank where the Eiffel Tower now stands. The great fair lasted seven months, attracting six million visitors from all over the world.

followed by General Bazaine's 'treasonable' surrender at Metz with 175 000 men and, then, during the Siege, General Trochu, commanding 350 000 armed citizens enrolled in the National Guard, had made no determined effort to break out and join forces with Gambetta's army in the provinces. In the besieged city, there had been no food-rationing, except by price, so the black marketeers flourished, the rich had their private suppliers and the poor came near to starving. As most ways of earning a living ceased, the one source of income for thousands of families was the pittance paid each day to the National Guard.

During its last years, Napoleon III's Second Empire had been seething with discontent. Paris, most splendidly rebuilt by Baron Haussmann, seemed to be the very centre of the civilized world, where, at the Great Exhibition of 1867, visitors from less gifted nations could only marvel at the brilliance of French achievements. The city positively glittered with affluence, for, under Napoleon III's régime, industrial production doubled, the railway network quadrupled in size, ship-building flourished and great banking concerns like the Crédit Lyonnais were founded.

Yet, the one class in this get-rich society which seemed to have missed out was the workers. Their wages had risen by only a little and, in Paris, Haussmann's destruction of many of the old slum districts had crowded the poor ever more densely together and had put up rents so high that it was reckoned that half the population lived in desperate poverty.

Although Napoleon had been popular for a time, the hard-core of Parisian radicals had never forgiven him for destroying the Republic they had created in 1848. His opponents included all kinds of Left-wingers, from die-hard Jacobins to Anarchists and Marxists; there was also a great mass of moderates and Republicans, led by Adolphe Thiers, and even a good many monarchists who wanted a Bourbon back on the throne.

Elections held in February 1871 returned a National Assembly in which conservatives outnumbered all the rest by two to one. To the disgust of Paris, only a dozen or so extreme socialists were elected and the leadership of the Assembly went to a man hated as an oppressor of the working-class - Adolphe Thiers, a wily old politician, who was determined to assert the government's authority over the turbulent Parisians.

Realising that the National Guard, retaining its weapons issued during the Siege, represented a major threat, Thiers sent General Lecomte into Paris with some regular troops to recover 200 cannons, of which the National Guard had taken charge. A hostile mob tore the general from his horse and murdered him, whereupon his soldiers retreated, leaving the capital in the hands of excited insurgents.

A Central Committee of the National Guard decided to hold municipal elections which returned a Council dominated by extremists who immediately assumed the title, hallowed by all revolutionaries, of 'Commune de Paris', and took up residence at the Hôtel de Ville. But, although crowds marched about waving red flags and chanting 'Vive la Commune!', the leading Communards had no plan of action nor any clear-cut programme.

Losing valuable time, they held lengthy debates, argued and intrigued among themselves to such an extent that few decisions were taken and no leader emerged with the drive of a Robespierre or Lenin. By the first days of April, Thiers had scraped together an army of 60 000 troops, which, under the command of General MacMahon, began to make probing attacks on the city's outer defences. The National Guard dashed towards the danger points with such enthusiasm that they forgot to bring along the cannons which had been the original cause of the uprising! Undisciplined and badly led, they fell back before the regulars, constantly dismissing their commanders and executing hostages, until, in Bloody Week (21-28 May), as the city went up in flames, they made their last stand behind the barricades of Montmartre.

The carnage was terrible. Droves of prisoners were lined up to be shot and, when the ghastly business was ended, some 25 000 men, women and children had died, more than in any battle against the Prussians, more perhaps than in the whole duration of the Terror.

The failure of the Paris Commune wiped out the leadership of the working-class movement for a generation and ought to have killed all idea of revolution. In fact, it did not. Instead, it created a legend of working-class heroism and martyrdom; it caused Marx to analyse its failure and Lenin to study its course and vow not to make the same mistakes in his own revolution.

During the period between 1871 and 1914, France appeared to recover from her wounds and Paris regained her traditional reputation as the world's centre of intellectual and artistic life. Yet the nation had lost its self-confidence, for it was too easily prone to political scandals like the Dreyfus Affair[1], and to taking umbrage over foreign incidents like the Fashoda Crisis and the German Emperor's visit to Morocco. In truth, the French were acutely conscious of their military and industrial weakness compared with Germany, whose seizure of Alsace-Lorraine remained an open wound and an abiding affront to every patriotic Frenchman.

THE BALKANS, SCANDINAVIA AND IRELAND

During the 19th century, the Ottoman Empire's tyrannical rule in south-east Europe all but disappeared. The basic cause of the Turkish decline was the rise of Slav nationalism, which fired a great revolt of the Serbs in 1804. This was crushed but Greece won her freedom in 1830 and, from then on, the other oppressed peoples set their hearts on the same goal.

They could look for support principally to Russia, since it had long been her policy to win control of the Balkans and this she seemed to have attained by her victory over the Turks in the Russo-Turkish war of 1877-8. But the prospect of Russia increasing her influence in this area and the Middle East so alarmed Disraeli, the British Prime Minister, that he persuaded the rulers of Europe[2] to accept his own proposals. They resulted in independence for

---

[1] A notorious case of injustice which, for more than a decade (1894-1906), divided France into bitterly hostile camps and became an impassioned struggle between Left and Right. It centred about Captain Dreyfus, a Jew, a regular army officer who was falsely accused of passing military secrets to the Germans.

[2] At the Congress of Berlin, 1878.

Serbia, Bulgaria and Rumania (or Romania), while Bosnia and Herzegovina were given the 'protection' of Austria, who annexed them both in 1908.

Meanwhile, nationalism flared up in Turkey, where a revolutionary group called the Young Turks clamoured fiercely for a revival of Turkish power. In face of this threat, Serbia, Bulgaria, Greece and Montenegro formed the Balkan League and, in 1912, defeated their old enemy. Unfortunately, the victors fell out among themselves. Bulgaria attacked Serbia and Greece, but when Rumania and the defeated Turks fell upon the attacker, Bulgaria had to give in and Serbia emerged as the strongest Balkan state. Her burning ambition was to wrest Bosnia from Austria and the Austrians, well aware of the fact, became determined to crush Serbia at the first opportunity.

Far away in northern Europe, Norway gained its independence without violence. From the 14th century, its fortunes had been dependant on other parts of Scandinavia, for, from being united to Sweden, it became a province of Denmark in 1536 and, nearly three centuries later, in 1814, was joined again to Sweden, under Napoleon's ex-marshal, Bernadotte. The union was never a happy one and, in 1905, after the two countries had agreed to separate, the Norwegian parliament chose a Danish prince to be king. He was crowned King Haakon VII in 1906 in Trondheim Cathedral.

Finland, a dependency of Sweden for 500 years, was ceded to Russia in 1809, but retained a measure of freedom until the end of the century, when the Russian government began to tighten its control of Finnish affairs. Taking advantage of the Russian collapse in 1917, the Finns declared their independence and, after a struggle against Russian troops, the country became a republic in 1919.

Denmark, a great Scandinavian power in the 16th century, had its fleet destroyed by the British during the Napoleonic wars and, with the loss of territories to Sweden and (in 1864) to Prussia, the Danes suffered a long period of poverty and distress. However, with the Farmers' Party in office and adoption of intensive farming methods, the country recovered and, by 1914, was a prosperous kingdom ruled by a hereditary monarch and an elected parliament.

The unhappiest country in Europe was probably Ireland, where, after the Battle of the Boyne in 1690 (see p. 245), a Protestant oligarchy passed vindictive anti-Catholic laws and a great part of the population led a miserable existence, their trade restricted and their land taken from them. The poverty of the country was appalling. The French Revolution fired a spirit of revolt and, after the Irish Rebellion of 1798 had been put down, Pitt, the British Prime Minister, became convinced that Ireland must be persuaded to send Members to the Parliament at Westminster. But the Act of Union (1801) was distrusted, all the more so when Pitt's implied promise of Catholic emancipation was frustrated by George III.

In 1846, the potato crop failed and, in the Great Famine that followed, a million men, women and children died of starvation and another million emigrated to America. Paradoxically, food in plenty was being exported from Ireland during this terrible time, but the peasants simply had no money to buy grain, however cheap. Hundreds of thousands of them moved to Lowland Scotland, where they accepted low wages in the iron and ship-building industries rather than stay at home to starve. Their arrival in such

Charles Stewart Parnell (1846-91), the Irish politician, a Protestant, who led the Home Rule party at Westminster and the Land League in Ireland. No extremist, he was absolved from charges of being involved in murder and violence, but his love affair with Kitty O'Shea, wife of an Irish member, lost him the support of Gladstone and his own party. He married Mrs O'Shea but died a few months later.

numbers invariably led to the creation of Catholic areas of poverty and overcrowding, as well as to the passionate rivalry which still exists between the Catholic Irish and the Protestant Scots.

The Irish Question continued to dominate affairs at Westminster for the rest of the century, during which Charles Stewart Parnell became the 'uncrowned King of Ireland' and Gladstone, the Prime Minister, tried in vain to get Parliament to pass his Home Rule Bills. At long last, the Liberal party under Asquith succeeded where Gladstone had failed, and Home Rule was passed in 1914, only to be postponed because of the outbreak of war. For a time there was peace; then, at Easter 1916, a rising occurred in Dublin, which was easily suppressed, because it lacked widespread support. However, the British government foolishly ordered the excution of a few republicans, thereby creating martyrs and a heroic legend. Eamon De Valera, who escaped the firing-squad because he held American citizenship, assumed leadership of the nationalist cause after his release from prison in 1917. When the First World War ended, bitterness had become so intense that for most Irishmen the issue was no longer Home Rule but complete independence.

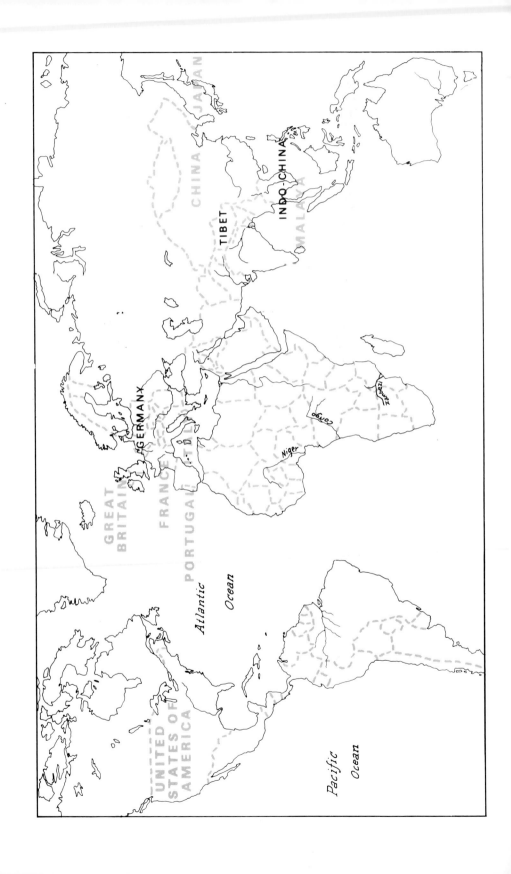

19 The Imperialist Scramble
1800 – 1914

After 1870, Europeans renewed their assaults upon the world's territories and markets. The Industrial Revolution was making rapid headway and all the major countries were becoming interested in finding markets overseas for their goods, though at this stage, a stronger reason for wanting colonies was national pride.

The two new nations, Germany and Italy, wanted to prove that they were every bit as important as Great Britain, while France was anxious to repair her damaged prestige by showing she was still a great power. It was not difficult to select the areas that were still available to Europeans; South America had to be ruled out because of the Monroe Doctrine; Canada, Australasia, and India were firmly in British hands, which left the coast of China, parts of South-East Asia, the Pacific islands and, above all, Africa.

Apart from Egypt and some of the coastal regions, Europeans knew very little about Africa; the interior was unexplored; most geographers thought that the Niger flowed east to join the Nile, whose source was still a mystery, and nothing was known of the courses of the Congo River and the Zambezi. In the early years of the century, a Scotsman, Mungo Park, discovered the source of the Niger and sailed down it to Boussa, where he was drowned in 1806. Others continued his work and, by 1830, the Niger was found to have no connection with the Nile, but to flow into a great delta on the Gulf of Guinea. The French explorer, René Caillé (1799-1838) crossed the Sahara from Sierra Leone to Timbuktu and Heinrich Barth, a German employed by the British government, travelled the Saharan trade routes in the 1850's and published his discoveries, which included information about the Arab slave trade. Between 1841 and his death in Zambia in 1873, David Livingstone, the Scottish missionary, crossed central Africa from Angola to Mozambique, travelled the length of the Zambezi and discovered the Victoria Falls and Lake Nyasa. His books fascinated the public and his disappearance and subsequent 'rescue' by H.M. Stanley, an American journalist sent out to find him, made the world's headlines and convinced Europeans that great opportunities awaited the white man in Africa. This intense interest was not fired solely by human greed, for Livingstone, more than anyone else, awoke people to the horrors of the slave trade and aroused passionate determination

Sir Henry Morton Stanley (1841-1904), born John Rowlands in Wales, went as a lad to America where after many adventures he became a newspaper correspondent. Sent by the *New York Herald* to find David Livingstone in Africa, he won world-fame by doing so and went on to trace the course of the river Congo to the sea. Leopold II of Belgium took up his offer to open up the area and employed Stanley to make treaties with chiefs and to found the Congo Free State. Stanley wrote many books, again became a British citizen and a Liberal M.P.

to bring it to an end and also to send out missionaries to start schools and convert Africans to Christianity.

John Hanning Speke, in company, first, with Richard Burton and, later, with James Grant, explored much of East Africa and tracked the Nile flowing out of Lake Victoria; their work was carried on by H.M. Stanley, a born adventurer, whose explorations included an amazing journey down the Congo River to the Atlantic Ocean. Thanks to these men and the support of learned societies, much of Africa's geography was known to the rest of the world by the last decade of the century.

Until the 1870's, however, only a small part of the continent was under foreign rule. The British had been in South Africa since 1815, had annexed Lagos (Nigeria) in 1861 and established a colony on the Gold Coast (now Ghana) in 1874. The Sultan of Turkey had long been the titular ruler of Egypt and most of North Africa, but his rule was so lax that the kingdoms were practically independent and the Albanian viceroy, Mehemet Ali, an admirer and pupil of Napoleon, had transformed Egypt into a modern state between 1805 and 1848. Napoleon's expedition and de Lesseps's feat in building the Suez Canal (completed in 1869) had given the French a special interest in Egypt, yet, to their chagrin, it was the British who secured control

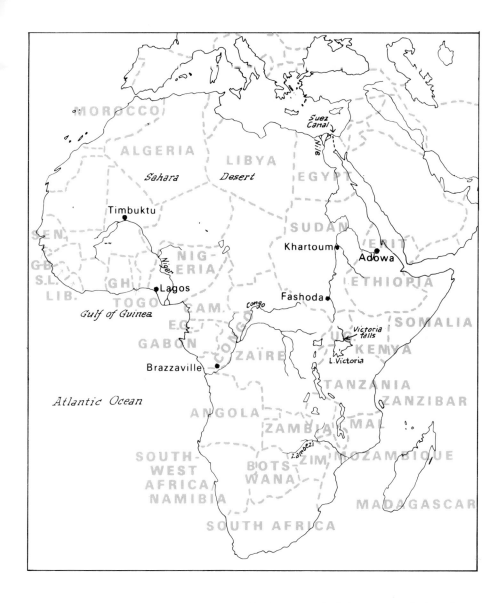

of the Canal, when Benjamin Disraeli, the Prime Minister, astutely bought 40 per cent of the shares in 1874. France had conquered Algeria in the 1830's and had later acquired Senegal, whence her agents pushed inland to the upper reaches of the Niger.

Portugal, the oldest colonial power, still held her widely-separated possessions of Guinea (now Guinea-Bissau), Angola and Mozambique, but colonies in the modern sense hardly existed anywhere and European rule reached only a few miles inland.

The 'scramble for Africa', in which the leading powers rushed to stake claims and to bargain with one another for this or that region, was started by

403

two countries which had not previously shown any interest in the continent. The first was Belgium, whose King, Leopold II, founded the International African Association in 1876 and employed H.M. Stanley to explore the Congo basin and compile a report of its resources. His agents made treaties with African rulers, so that a great part of Central Africa, with its rubber, palm-oil, timber and ivory, came under the personal control of the Belgian king as the Congo Free State (now Zaïre).

This enterprise stirred the French into sending their own agent, Pierre Brazza, to make similar treaties, which secured vast grants of land and resulted in the establishment of the French Congo, with many trading-stations, including Brazzaville. The British government, not for the moment interested in acquiring any more African territory for itself, decided to put a stopper on these activities by making an agreement to give Portugal control of the mouth of the Congo, which would make it difficult for any other country to exploit the interior. France and King Leopold naturally took offence and turned for help to Europe's most powerful statesman, Count Bismark, who proposed a full-dress Conference in Berlin to sort out the various 'spheres of influence.'

By this time, Germany herself was the other newcomer to the African scene, for, between 1883 and 1885, she annexed four considerable territories - South-West Africa (Namibia), Togoland (Togo), Kamerun (Cameroon) and German East Africa (Tanzania). Whether this action was to satisfy a longing for empire or to deflect French hostility in Europe by encouraging ambitions in Africa, it certainly sparked off the scramble that led to the whole continent being shared out among seven European powers.

Meanwhile, there was trouble in Egypt. Since the 1860's, the country had been ruled for the Turkish Sultan by the Khedive Ismail, an energetic reformer, who spent large sums on education and irrigation and, after the opening of the Suez Canal, received financial help from France and Britain. His debts became so enormous that a Franco-British committee was set up to take charge of Egypt's finances, an arrangement which provoked an army revolt, led by an officer named Arabi Pasha. Fearful for the safety of the Canal, France and Britain agreed to act together, but, owing to a domestic crisis, the French backed out and it was left to the British to defeat Arabi in 1882 and to stay on to support the new Khedive and set the country back on its feet.

The Khedive's adviser, Sir Evelyn Baring (afterwards Lord Cromer), became in effect the real ruler of Egypt, which angered the French and was by no means to the liking of Gladstone and his liberal government, since they were opposed to imperialism. When the Khedive appealed for help to deal with a massive revolt in the Sudan inspired by a religious leader called the Mahdi (or Messiah), Gladstone sent General Gordon, a former Governor of the Sudan, to take charge of the withdrawal of the Egyptian garrisons from the rebellious province. However, Gordon, a strange, independent-minded man, disobeyed orders and was killed at Khartoum in 1885. The outcry at the death of a popular hero helped to bring down the Liberals, who were replaced by a Conservative government under Lord Salisbury, at the time when the Imperial Federation League was formed in London and the British people were beginning to pride themselves on 'the Empire on which the sun never sets'.

At the Berlin Conference of 1884, Bismark presided over a gathering of 15 nations (no Africans were present) which recognised the Congo Free State and persuaded Portugal to let it have access to the sea. Resolutions were passed on the slave trade, free trade and various issues; lines were drawn on maps to define 'spheres of influence' and several large inland areas were left blank, as though to intensify the scramble.

The upshot was that France secured the bulk of West and Equatorial Africa, apart from the four British possessions of Gambia, Sierra Leone, the Gold Coast (Ghana) and Nigeria. Later on, she granted part of the French Congo to the German colony of Kamerun in return for being given a free hand in Morocco. To obtain a stepping-stone between her African and Indo-Chinese empires, French troops occupied Madagascar, which was formally annexed in 1896.

Britain's increased share owed rather more at first to the activities of private individuals than the government. Cecil Rhodes formed the British South Africa Company (1889) and was the driving force behind the annexation of Bechuanaland (now Botswana), in order to stop the Portuguese and the Germans moving inland and cutting off the British from their territories to the north. In 1890, Rhodes sent settlers to found Rhodesia (Zimbabwe) and Britain soon took possession of Northern Rhodesia (now Zambia) and Nyasaland (Malawi).

In West Africa, Sir George Goldie's Royal Niger Company (1886) brought under control the territories which later became known, first, as the Niger Coast Protectorate and, later, Nigeria, a state in which there were over 200 ethnic groups, each with its own language. On the other side of the continent, Sir William MacKinnon formed the British East Africa Company (1888) to counter German activity in that region.

With Gladstone gone and Lord Salisbury in office, the British government felt bound to take responsibility for these activities and Salisbury built his African policy round his conviction that Britain must keep control of Egypt and therefore of the Suez Canal, her 'life-line' to India. For this reason, he accepted the huge French expansion in West Africa and came to an agreement with Germany to define the borders of German East Africa and the British territories in that region which were later known as Kenya and

Uganda. He also exchanged the island of Heligoland (annexed from Denmark in 1807), which commanded the sea approach to the Kiel Canal, for the island of Zanzibar (now part of Tanzania) which therefore became a British protectorate in 1890. In the north-east, he fixed the frontier with the newly-claimed Italian colony in Somalia.

After their calamitous defeat at the hands of the Ethiopians, the Italians had to be content with the arid coastal strips of Eritrea and Somalia, until, in 1911, they seized Libya from the decaying Turkish Empire. Spain secured part of Morocco, as well as a stretch of the Atlantic coast and a small piece of equatorial Africa called Spanish Guinea (now Equatorial Guinea).

Thus, by 1914, Africa was divided into 40-odd political units under the control of one or another of the European colonial powers. Only two states remained independent - Ethiopia (or Abyssinia, as it was called for many years), by virtue of the Emperor Menelik's victory over the Italians at Adowa, and Liberia, a small republic in West Africa, founded in 1822 as a home for freed American slaves and precariously surviving on American help and German trading interests. A remarkable feature of Africa's partition was that it was carried out without the rival powers taking up arms against one another, although there was one collision, the Fashoda Incident of 1898, which nearly led to a major war.

The French, who bitterly regretted leaving the British in sole charge of Egypt, sent Commandant Marchand with a small company of soldiers all the way from Gabon in equatorial Africa to Fashoda on the Upper Nile, where he hoisted the French tricolor at a point some 400 miles south of Khartoum. In effect, this would extend French dominions from the Atlantic to the Red Sea.

However, while Marchand was making his 2-year journey, General Kitchener had been slowly moving south from Egypt with an Anglo-Egyptian army, building a railway as he advanced. In September 1898, he reached Khartoum and defeated the Mahdi's successor at the Battle of Omdurman. When he learned of Marchand's presence at Fashoda, he confronted him with overwhelming force and requested him to withdraw, on the grounds that Egypt could not allow a foreign power to control the upper waters of the Nile. For several weeks, France and Britain stood on the brink of war, until France, finding no support from Russia or Germany, withdrew her claim. Sudan thenceforward came under joint British and Egyptian control as the Anglo-Egyptian Sudan.

After the Fashoda Incident and the South African War (in which the Boer republics never got the help from Britain's European rivals which Kruger had expected), the 'scramble' came to an end and interest in Africa suddenly evaporated.

Having secured the prestige of owning colonies and found that, except in

Charge of 21st Lancers at the Battle of Omdurman, 1 September 1898 (painted by Wood-ville). Kitchener's Nile army defeated the forces of the Khalifa to put an end to the Mahdi's state in the Sudan. Serving with 21st Lancers was young Winston Churchill who thus took part in the last classic cavalry charge in British warfare.

British South Africa and the Belgian Congo (Zaïre), there was little readily available wealth to exploit, the powers turned back to their interests in Europe and left Africa to be governed by a handful of officials at the lowest possible cost. Some of the figures are quite astonishing; the British administrator who ruled Nyasaland (Malawi) did so with £10 000 a year and 75 Indian soldiers under one British officer; in Nigeria, Lord Lugard ruled a territory containing about 10 million inhabitants with a staff of 5 administrators and a regiment of the West African Frontier Force, consisting of two or three thousand African soldiers under about 120 European officers. He had a budget of a little over £100 000 a year.

These colonial forces were of course better armed and disciplined than any that might oppose them, but their puny numbers suggest that they were mainly a police force and they hardly support the view that the brutal imperialists kept their power by machine-gunning defenceless Africans. There were many instances when ruthless measures were taken to put down opposition - as happened in the British suppression of the Zulu and Matabele warriors (in South Africa and Rhodesia), of the Ashanti in West Africa and the Nandi of Kenya; in the crushing of Algerian revolts by the French and in the German massacre of the Herrero of South-west Africa. King Leopold's Company exploited the Congolese with such brutality that, when news leaked out, an international outcry compelled the Belgian government to take over the King's private investment in 1908.

In many cases, the newcomers were permitted to extract minerals or occupy land in return for gifts, though they usually failed to realise that this did not give them permanent rights. Treaties were made and a regular system of colonial rule was introduced called *indirect rule*, which meant that chiefs, ranging from local headmen to powerful kings, were given support and kept in power provided they co-operated with the colonial authorities. The chiefs were expected to assist in collecting taxes and to provide men to work on European plantations, in mines and on road-building.

What was the effect of colonial rule on the people of Africa? There were gainers and losers, according to whether they chose to be friends or enemies of the white men. Some chiefs, realising that resistance was hopeless, made agreements which increased their power and enabled them to defeat their own traditional enemies. European missionaries found that starting schools was by far the most effective way of winning converts to the Christian religion and, all over Africa, many Africans gained an education and therefore some of the knowledge and skills of the Europeans. Gold and diamond-mining, extraction of minerals like copper, manganese and chromium, European-style farming, production of rubber, cocoa, coffee, sisal, tea and tobacco, the building of roads, railways, towns and ports required immense numbers of workers who therefore became wage-earning labourers. The new industries caused many Africans to leave their villages and go to work in towns where they learned to mix with people from other tribes, to adapt to different ways of life and to begin to think of themselves, not only as Yoruba or Ibo, as Kikuyu or Luo, but also as Nigerians or Kenyans. African nationalism was born.

European money, machinery and skill were invested primarily to produce profits for Europeans, but, in the long run, they created assets which were to belong to Africans themselves, though whether the European style of life which has emerged in Africa is a good development is open to question.

In some areas - Rhodesia, British and German East Africa, the Portuguese territories and parts of the French and Belgian Congos - many Africans lost the lands they had previously cultivated to state and private companies or to European settlers who took over the best farming land. Many were forced to move to 'designated areas' and others, while left in possession of their own land, were prevented from moving on to what would have been uncultivated, unoccupied areas. However, Europeans never emigrated to Africa in the vast numbers which made their way to America; the British certainly settled in sizeable numbers in the south and in Rhodesia and Kenya; the French built their provincial cities in North Africa, a good-sized community of Portuguese grew up in Angola, but German emigration was always small, the Italian colonies were too arid to support many settlers and some

Kimberley in about 1888: diamond workers searching gravel at De Beers, the South African diamond company formed by Cecil Rhodes who made a fortune out of diamonds first discovered at Kimberley in 1870. Diggers came from all over the world to try their luck in the deposits along the Vaal river.

European countries, like Russia and the Scandinavian nations, sent virtually no emigrants at all. Colonial rule brought a common language, usually English or French, to wide areas of Africa, but there was a fundamental difference between British colonial policy and that of the other European powers. As time went by and particularly after the First World War, the British came to feel that it was their duty to govern their colonies justly, while carrying them forward towards the time when they would be able to stand on their own feet; there was of course a good deal of self-interest in this attitude, but there was also a measure of good will.

The French, Belgians, Italians and Portuguese regarded their colonies as extensions of their own countries and expected that in time their African subjects would become citizens of France, Belgium, Italy and Portugal. This meant that the continental Europeans were never involved, like the British, in arguments about when the time was right for independence, since their Senegalese and Angolans, say, were going to become Frenchmen and Portuguese.

The mistake which all the Europeans made was in thinking that colonial rule would last a very long time. With the spread of western education, Africans were certain to become capable of carrying out industrial and commercial activities for themselves and of ruling themselves again in independent states. No matter whether the official policy was a move towards independence or citizenship, the problem areas were bound to be those in which sizeable numbers of Europeans were resolved to keep their political and economic supremacy.

19th-century imperialism extended beyond Africa. All the peoples of the Pacific Islands came to be ruled by one or another of the colonial powers; the French took control of Indo-China; the British of Malaya and Burma and they also entered Afghanistan and Tibet in order to guard the approaches to India.

For a time, it looked as though China, like Africa, might be shared out among the colonial powers, because the Manchu government became too feeble to resist the leading European countries, Japan and the United States when they demanded slices of territory, ports and trade concessions. However, China's resilience and vast population made that ancient country a very hard nut to crack.

By 1914, the greater part of the inhabited world had come under the control of the 'western world' (i.e. the USA and the leading countries of Western Europe) and was dominated by western ideas, western languages, western industrial methods, western economic and political theories - a dominance that was to be challenged and to some extent overthrown in the second half of the 20th century.

PART FOUR

The Rise of the Super-powers

1 The First World War

The Great War, as it was called for a generation or so, broke out in Europe the beginning of August 1914. Each side, of course, put the blame on the other, the Germans declaring that there was a conspiracy to encircle Germany, while the Allies (France, Russia and Britain) said it was caused by German aggression.

For 20 years, the situation in Europe had been dangerously tense, with Germany growing ever stronger and more pugnacious, France nursing bitter resentment over the loss of Alsace-Lorraine in 1871, Austria bent on taking control of the Balkans, Serbia passionately hostile to Austria and Russia standing by to champion the Slav peoples of south-east Europe. Great Britain, a maritime power, with little interest in continental rivalries, became so alarmed by the growth of Germany's battle-fleet that her government took steps to get on closer terms with France and to make a friendly approach to Russia.

This meant that Europe became divided into two power-blocs - the Triple Alliance of Germany, Austro-Hungary[1] and Italy[2], on the one side, and the Triple Entente of France, Russia and Britain, on the other, with the obvious danger that a quarrel between two countries would bring their partners into the arena.

At a time when nationalism, press scares and belligerent stances were the order of the day, war was probably inevitable. It had always been the way of settling differences, and, after 99 years without a general European war, there may have been a deep longing for excitement and violence. In 1914, no-one had any idea of the horrors of a prolonged war between industrialised powers and it seemed much more heroic to fight for King and Country (almost every country in Europe was a monarchy) than to sit down under injustice or insult. Furthermore, it was widely believed that success in war was the measure of a nation's standing in the world and the supreme test of its manhood.

---

[1] Since 1867, Austria and Hungary had been united under a common monarch, Francis Joseph, and was known as the 'Dual Monarchy'.
[2] Moved by fears of French colonial activity in North Africa, Italy joined the Austro-German alliance in 1882.

412

In this atmosphere, any incident could bring about an explosion and, with a kind of doomed certainty, it occurred on 28 June 1914 in the small town of Sarajevo in Bosnia, a Serbo-Croat province which had been annexed by Austria in 1908. The Archduke Franz Ferdinand, heir to the throne of Austria, was shot dead there by a student, one of a group of young conspirators, and the Austrian government, convinced that the crime had been planned in Serbia, decided that the time had come to crush this vexatious little country.

Having made sure that Germany, her ally, would support her actions, Austria sent an ultimatum to Serbia demanding terms which amounted to total humiliation. Rather surprisingly, Serbia accepted them all but one and

413

the crisis seemed to be over. But Austria, not to be baulked by her prey, declared war on Serbia on 28 July 1914.

This reckless decision provoked a chain reaction. The Tsar Nicholas II felt that national honour compelled Russia to go to Serbia's assistance and he therefore ordered general mobilisation, that is to say, the call-up of millions of conscript soldiers who were to be transported by rail to strategic points decided upon by the General Staff.

Once Russia mobilised, Germany was bound to follow suit, partly to support Austria, her ally, and partly because the German generals believed that Russian preparations for a war were nearing completion. They recognised that war with Russia would mean war with France as well, because the two countries were allies, and they had made their plans to cope with this situation. To avoid fighting on two fronts, they would knock out one of their enemies immediately and this had to be France, because Russia was so vast that it would take much longer to defeat her huge armies and conquer the territory which Germany needed for *lebensraum*, 'living-space', i.e. the areas which imperial Germany (and, later, Nazi Germany) wanted to annex because they were rich in economic resources.

For this design, the Schlieffen Plan had been prepared in 1905 by General von Schlieffen; in essence, it proposed a powerful attack through Belgium to by-pass French frontier defences and a sweep round into France in a great curve that would envelop Paris. Once France was knocked out, the German armies would be speedily transferred east on the railways which had been constructed for that purpose. If the British intervened – and it was not certain that they would do so – the new German Fleet would take care of their navy and, on land, their little army was of no account.

The 'entente' between Britain and France was not a precise military alliance. The British Foreign Secretary never made it clear that his country would fight if France was attacked and, as late as 24 July 1914, was saying that the Austro-Serbian dispute was of no concern to Britain.

In this situation, the French showed remarkable moderation. Assuredly, they feared the Germans and had helped Russia to build factories and railways, but their moves had been essentially defensive and they believed that self-interest would bring Britain to their side.

When Russia mobilised, Germany sent an ultimatum, demanding Russian demobilisation. Knowing that this would leave her defenceless, Russia refused and, on 1 August 1914, Germany declared war. In accordance with the Schlieffen Plan, France had to be defeated first, and therefore, on the morning of 4th August, German troops marched into Belgium.

This calculated disregard of a small country's neutrality brought Britain into the war. Her Liberal government, which included two great war-leaders of the future in David Lloyd-George and Winston Churchill, was more

Belgian refugees on foot and in horse-drawn vehicles seek safety in flight from the German occupation of Brussels, from 20 August 1914. To their eternal credit, the Belgians did not save their skins by giving the Germans free passage; on the contrary, they put up a valiant resistance against impossible odds.

concerned about Irish Home Rule than Balkan squabbles and saw no reason why Britain should get involved. However, in the event, it was not to aid France or to destroy Germany that induced the British to take up arms, but an uprush of sympathy for 'brave little Belgium', whose neutrality they believed they were obliged to defend by virtue of the 1839 Treaty of London, by which all the major European powers, including Prussia, had guaranteed Belgium's perpetual neutrality.

It is possible to understand the reasons why five great powers blundered into a conflict that was to put an end to the political, economic and military dominance of Western Europe, but why did so many other countries join in?

To the surprise of most nations, especially the Germans, the Dominions of the British Empire immediately ranged themselves alongside the country that was supposed to exploit them, and one could only suppose that they were moved by feelings of loyalty or were concerned for their own safety should Britain be defeated.

Italy, ostensibly the ally of the Central Powers (Germany and Austro-Hungary) stayed out for a time, but joined the Allies in 1915, on the promise of territory to be wrested from Austria. Turkey, much courted by the Germans before the war, came in through hatred of Russia and suspicion of British and French ambitions in the Middle East. The USA eventually joined the Allies in 1917, because a German victory would have meant a military dictatorship in Europe; Allied propaganda helped to swing public opinion, and the Germans foolishly persisted in sinking American ships and then made a bid for Mexico's support with the offer of Texas and Arizona. Bulgaria's dislike of the Serbs made her the ally of Germany; Greece was more or less bullied into the Allied camp by France and Britain; Rumania

415

joined the same side in the hope of picking up some easy spoils and Germany declared war on Portugal, because she was giving aid to Allied shipping. Spain had the good sense to stay neutral, as did Switzerland, the Netherlands and the Scandinavian countries. Finally, Japan, Britain's ally since 1902, came in solely to seize Germany's colonial possessions in China and the Pacific.

Nearly everyone greeted the outbreak of war with patriotic enthusiasm and thought that it would soon be over. The cost and the upset to international trade would be so great, they said, that no country would be able to stand a long war; after all, Prussia had beaten Austria and France in a few weeks and, in the past (if one chose to forget the examples of the South in the American Civil War and the Boers in South Africa), governments had usually made peace long before their people were exhausted or ruined.

These expectations proved false. In this war, the main contenders were industrial nations with the capacity to produce and go on producing the supplies of war; all could call up millions of men for the armies, and, if the call-up of these vast numbers caused a drop in food-production and manufactured goods (which it did), civilians had to go short and tighten their belts. Normal economics were thrown overboard, as governments took control of industry, agriculture, wages, prices, manpower and propaganda.

Yet, those who expected a short war were very nearly right. 'Remember, we can be in Paris in a fortnight', the Kaiser had remarked and, in August 1914, when two German armies struck through Belgium, his boast might well have come true. Two events prevented this happening. The Belgians put up an unexpectedly stiff resistance and the Russians mobilised so quickly that Moltke felt obliged to divert troops to meet the Russian threat. As a result, he was unable to put quite enough weight into his right hook; nor did he swing it in a wide enough curve.

When they did get into France, slightly delayed, the Germans were surprised by the fighting quality of the small but highly professional British Expeditionary Force, which checked the enemy advance at Mons. This gave Joffre, the French Commander-in-Chief, time to launch a counter-attack when the Germans made the mistake of turning south-east *across* the defences of Paris, instead of encircling the capital. Paris was saved; the knockout blow was parried and, in the opinion of some experts, Germany had already lost the war.

In September, the Germans pulled back to positions north of the River Aisne and, after desperate Allied resistance around Ypres to save the Channel ports, two vast armies went below ground, into trenches that eventually stretched from the Belgian coast, across northern France to the borders of Switzerland.

Trench warfare was not new. Since the English Civil War, commanders

The Kaiser William II (centre) with his Chief of General Staff, General Helmuth von Moltke, at the Front in 1914 with Prussian officers.

had known that earth was a better defence against artillery-fire than stone or brick, but, hitherto, the occasional use of trenches had not prevented generals exercising all the so-called 'arts' of war, with cavalry attacks, outflanking movements, tactical withdrawals and so on. These became impossible on the Western Front, where huge immovable armies faced one another across 'No Man's Land', a stretch of ground criss-crossed by belts of barbed wire, the American farming invention which became the master defence-weapon of the war.

By the time the war was a few months old, it ought to have been obvious that massed infantry attacks were doomed in the face of an entrenched, determined enemy armed with magazine rifles and machine-guns. Yet it took the generals a long time to accept facts that outraged their ideas of how a war ought to be fought, although, in fairness, the Allied generals, in particular, were under pressure from politicans, newspaper tycoons and civilians to win victories, never mind the cost.

All kinds of efforts were made to break the deadlock. Gunnery experts devised 'creeping barrages' of artillery fire to move just ahead of the advancing infantry, but they were not effective because heavy shell-fire turned muddy ground into a morass, without destroying the barbed wire.

417

Battle of Flanders: British troops go over the top. In 1914, the British army numbered some 150000 men or 6 divisions; Germany mustered 87 divisions. Austria 49 and France 62. Russia mobilised 114 divisions, poorly equipped and short of artillery.

Even if the enemy's front line was captured, there were more lines further back, connected to deep defences which could be reinforced from inexhaustible reserves in the rear. Poison-gas was a dangerous weapon, because the wind might change direction; shells specially designed to destroy barbed wire were tried with only limited success and, to begin with, aeroplanes were used merely for observation.

Early on, commanders had little faith in these contraptions made of wood, wire and canvas; there was a period of air-duels between famous 'aces' and of bombing raids by German *Zeppelins*, but these had little effect on battles on the ground and none on industrial production. However, aeroplanes played an increasingly important part in support of infantry and, by 1918, the British had 22000 aircraft, compared with the 272 of 1914.

Generals on both sides tended to go on believing that the best way to win the war was to break through the opposing defences by frontal assaults and, in the process, kill so many of the enemy that his will to resist would be broken. Casualties were therefore horrific: 250000 Austrians killed and wounded in a month of 1914; 600000 French and German casualties in the five months' Battle of Verdun (1916) and 420000 British casualties in the battles of 1917 known as Passchendaele.

Both sides also tried to win by starving the enemy of vital foods and raw materials. The British, holding virtual command of the seas, instituted a blockade which, in the last year of the war, inflicted such hardship on Germany's civilian population that it was one of the factors which brought about her collapse. The two giant navies met only once, when, in the Battle of Jutland (1916), the Germans had rather the better of a confused engagement, but never again ventured out from behind their protective minefields. Instead, they concentrated on submarine attacks on Allied merchant ships with such effect that they sank over 1000 vessels in three months and, by mid-1917, it was reckoned that Britain's food supply would last for only a matter of weeks. The answer to this threat was to organise the ships into 'convoys', escorted by destroyers equipped with hydrophones and depth charges.

The weapon which finally broke the stalemate on the Western Front was the tank, a British invention first used on the Somme in 1916 without much success, owing to its slowness and the small numbers involved, but those who believed in its potential, managed to keep production going and, eventually, to provide the Allies with an armoured vehicle which could cross broken country and crush barbed-wire entanglements ahead of the advancing infantry. In August 1918, tanks, accompanied by low-flying aircraft, won a victory near Amiens so decisive that it convinced Ludendorff, the German supreme commander, that the war was lost.

Since the autumn of 1914, the Germans had been carrying on the war on two fronts which their generals had said was impossible. Their first task was

A British merchant ship being torpedoed, 1916. This remarkable photograph was actually taken by the commander of a German U-boat.

419

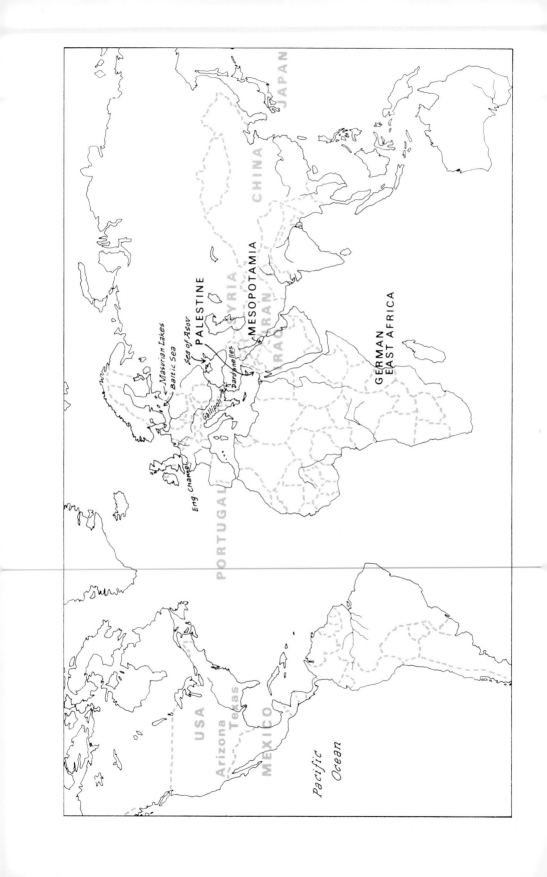

A field hospital in a Russian forest.

to halt the alarming advance of two Russian armies into East Prussia and to do so, they called out of retirement a Hanoverian general named von Hindenburg, who, with Ludendorff, his brilliant young Chief of Staff, won two tremendous victories at Tannenberg and the Masurian Lakes (September 1914). The Russians lost a third-of-a-million men but, further south, they defeated the Austro-Hungarian forces and drove so far into Galicia (southern Poland), that the Germans had to transfer troops from the Western Front to stem the advance of 'the Russian steamroller'.

The war on the Eastern Front was never as static as the grim struggle in northern France; the fighting swayed to and fro over a vast area between the Baltic and the Sea of Azov, where, in plains, marshes, forests and mountains, the Russians, although short of modern weapons, especially field-artillery, fought with the stubborn courage they had shown against Napoleon. Indeed, General Brusilov's brilliant offensive of 1916 saved the Allies from almost certain defeat by compelling the Germans to transfer 35 divisions from the Western Front, but, by the end of that year, the Russians were being pushed back and back eastwards, and, with their government in chaos, towards the collapse and revolution of 1917.

In addition to the two main theatres of war, there were several 'sideshows', three of them undertaken against the Turkish Empire in the hope that success would bring the Balkan states to the Allied side and open the way to an attack on Germany from the south-east. With Turkey knocked

421

A blindfolded Turkish officer being led into the Australian lines at Gallipoli to negotiate a truce for the burial of the dead. In one action the Turks left 3000 dead in mounds in front of the Australian trenches.

out of the war, it would be possible to open the Dardanelles to sea-traffic and supply Russia with the materials her armies needed. In Britain, Winston Churchill pressed hard for this plan, which, if it had been carried out as a combined operation between powerful land and sea forces, must have been successful. As it was, Kitchener did not feel able to release sufficient numbers of troops from France; over-optimism and muddle gave the Turks time to organise their defences and the Allied force, including many from the Australian and New Zealand Army Corps - the ANZACS - which landed on the Gallipoli peninsula, was too small for the task. With the loss of nearly a quarter-of-a-million men killed, wounded or evacuated sick, the Gallipoli Campaign ended in total failure.

The second 'side-show' was an expedition to Mesopotamia to bring under Allied control the countries (and their oil) we now know as Iran and Iraq, while the third campaign was launched from Egypt into Palestine and Syria to support a revolt by the Arabs against their Turkish rulers. There were also some minor actions to mop up German colonies around the globe and a protracted campaign to win German East Africa.

Italy, enticed into the war by Britain and France, fought a stubborn campaign against the Austrians in northern Italy and suffered a defeat at Caporetto (October 1917) so calamitous that troops had to be switched from the Western Front to hold the line. However, the most decisive event of 1917 was the entry into the war of the United States, whose small regular army could make little impact on the terrible struggle that was going on in northern France, but the knowledge that America's vast resources were coming to their aid provided a tremendous uplift to the Allies' morale and a corresponding blow to Germany's dwindling hopes of victory.

The arrival of a powerful ally was all the more welcome in view of Russia's collapse and abandonment of the Eastern Front. Under the best of their generals, the Russian armies had achieved miracles of endurance and valour, but, in 1915, the Tsar had taken the disastrous decision to assume supreme command, leaving direction of home affairs in the hands of his German-born wife, the Tsarina Alexandra, who was herself under the sinister influence of Grigory Rasputin, a drunken 'holyman', whose hypnotic powers were supposed to have cured the Tsarina's only son of haemophilia.

Through his ascendancy over the doting Tsarina, Rasputin turned the imperial government into a farce, dismissing ministers at will and replacing them by his own nominees. Eventually, in December 1916, Rasputin was murdered by a group of nobles, but the damage had been done, for, by that time, the government was totally discredited and, to make matters worse, there were widespread rumours of treachery and of pro-German leanings by the Tsarina and her friends.

Even so, at the beginning of 1917, the huge Russian armies were still fighting strongly and industrial production was in full swing. The trouble was that the workers in the towns were short of food, because their wages had not kept pace with prices; transport was inadequate and the peasants were refusing to produce all the food that was needed. They themselves could not afford the inflated prices of manufactured goods and were demanding that the land of the great estate-owners should be turned over to them.

In March 1917 (February, according to the Russian calendar), strikes and food riots broke out in Petrograd, formerly St Petersburg, The Duma, or parliament, dared to criticise the Tsar and warn him that the situation was serious, whereupon Nicholas dismissed the Duma. At this, many soldiers joined the workers and formed their own *soviets* or workers' councils. The revolt spread like wildfire to become the so-called February Revolution, which compelled the Tsar to abdicate in favour of his brother. But the people, sick of the war and with their age-old grievances now at boiling-point, were determined to have a republic. A provisional government was set up under the leadership of a moderate socialist named Kerensky, who tried to carry out two impossible tasks - to create a democratic state and persuade the soldiers to go on fighting. Meanwhile, a much more dynamic figure was waiting in the wings.

Vladimir Lenin had been living in exile in Switzerland[1], keeping in touch with his Bolshevik comrades, ceaselessly organising control of the trade unions, co-operatives and newspapers and spreading anti-war propaganda. From the German viewpoint, here was the very man to bring about the collapse of Russia's war effort, so, in April 1917, they had him transported from Switzerland across Germany to Petrograd, where a soviet of Marxists was already demanding a share in the government. However, Lenin found that the Bolsheviks were not yet in control and when the government branded them as traitors, he fled in disguise to Finland, where he would find Bolshevik supporters.

The situation in Russia grew worse. The war was going badly and peasant soldiers kept drifting home in thousands, as agitators put it about that the war was being fought only to benefit the ruling class. The people were hungry; bread riots broke out in many towns, and, in country districts, peasants began seizing the landowners' fields.

When General Kornilov, the new army Commander, marched into Petrograd to replace the provisional government by a military one, Kerensky, in a desperate effort to retain his position as premier, had arms issued to Bolshevik bands, known as the Red Guards. They drove Kornilov out and won control of the city; Lenin came back from Finland and, with his friend, the brilliant Trotsky, overthrew Kerensky and, as chairman of the Council of People's Commissars, assumed complete power.

Where others may have been confused or excited by the chaotic state of affairs, Lenin knew exactly what to do. His first actions were to suppress the Mensheviks and Social Revolutionaries, since he intended to share power with no-one; next, he announced the nationalisation of the land and the immediate end of the war.

Germany took full advantage of her good fortune, demanding terms so harsh that even Trotsky could not accept them at first, but Lenin was willing to pay the price for power. It amounted to a great part of western Russia, including the grain-lands of the Ukraine, most of the coal-mines and a third of the Russian population. The Treaty of Brest-Litovsk ended the war on the Eastern Front and enabled Germany to concentrate all her remaining strength against her enemies in the West.

It was now or never. The German military leaders knew that the Dual Monarchy and Turkey were almost exhausted; shortages of food and materials in Germany were becoming acute; Britain had not been starved into surrender and, as the year advanced, vast numbers of fresh American

[1] See page 383

German troops on the Western Front: a patrol defending a ruined house in the environs of Arras.

troops would be arriving in northern France. But there was still a last chance of victory, if it were taken quickly. Russia's collapse allowed the transfer of a million men and thousands of heavy guns to the Western Front, where the knock-out blow was to fall upon the British.

The great German offensive of March 1918 broke through the Allied line in places and forced the British to pull back in a full-scale retreat. Further south, a series of thunderous attacks brought the Germans within reach of Paris, a situation so critical that supreme command was belatedly given to the French general, Foch, who flung in every available unit to save the day. By the time the German advance was halted, their line had developed two vulnerable bulges.

All this time, American troops were arriving in France and beginning to acquit themselves well. In July, Foch felt strong enough to strike at the German bulge on the River Marne, overriding the objections of his colleague, Marshal Pétain, the pessimistic hero of Verdun, and, then, sensing that the miracle of victory might be within his grasp, he ordered a heavy attack on the second, the Amiens bulge, where British and French troops, supported by tanks, forced the Germans to retreat in disorder.

425

Suddenly, after four years of stalemate, the whole front began moving, slowly, ponderously, like an avalanche impelled by the immense weight behind. The Germans could not stop it. Still fighting strongly, they fell back towards their own frontier, as their leaders, realising that they were beaten, tried to end the war as suddenly as they had started it.

On the 4 October 1918, they asked the President of the United States for an armistice. Woodrow Wilson replied that Germany must accept the Fourteen Points, which he had taken upon himself to announce to the world in January 1918, without consulting the Allies who had been fighting for more than three bitter years.

The celebrated Fourteen Points were, briefly, as follows:

1. No more secret treaties.
2. Freedom of the seas, even in wartime.
3. Free trade between nations.
4. Reduction of armaments.
5. Adjustment of colonial claims.
6. Russian territory to be evacuated.
7. Belgium to be freed.
8. Alsace-Lorraine to be returned to France.
9. Italy's frontiers to be adjusted.
10. Peoples of the Austro-Hungarian empire to have the opportunity to govern themselves.
11. Balkan states to be restored and Serbia to have access to the sea.
12. Non-Turks in the Turkish empire to be freed.
13. Poland to be re-created.
14. An association of nations to be formed.

In the Fourteen Points, it was easy to detect Wilson's concern for peace and justice and it was also clear that he believed that the war had been caused by the greed of governments for territory and power and that national minorities should have the right to set up their own independent states, for he had listened sympathetically to the groups of Czechs, Poles, Serbs, Slovaks and others who had been pleading their causes in the USA.

While negotiations took place, Germany's allies collapsed - the Bulgarians on 30 September, the Turks on 31 October and Austria on 3 November, after the Italians had avenged their defeat at Caporetto. Bereft of allies, the German generals became all the more anxious for the government to make peace before their armies had been driven back onto German soil, so that they could claim that they had never been defeated in the field, but had been betrayed by their allies and the civilians at home. In fact, the German people had stood up marvellously well to the strain of war and it was only when their armies were in full retreat that riots broke out in many parts of the country, and workers formed Russian-style 'soviets'.

The end came suddenly. On 7 November, the German armistice delegation was handed the agreed terms: the German army must withdraw behind the Rhine; arms, equipment, submarines and battleships were to be surrendered; the Treaty of Brest-Litovsk was to be annulled. On 9 November, William II and the Crown Prince fled to the Netherlands and the German people, angered that the Kaiser had deserted the army in its hour of defeat, were content to let him go. On that day, a republic was declared in Berlin. On 11 November, the armistice came into force, the guns on the Western Front fell silent and the Great War was over.

A British Sopwith *Camel*, one of the tough manoeuvrable fighter-planes which, in the latter stages of the war, enabled the Allies to overcome the initial inferiority of their aircraft to German planes such as the *Albatros*, *Halberstadt* and *Fokker*. The Sopwith *Camel* was fitted with a machine-gun timed to fire *through* the propeller.

2 Versailles and the Aftermath

The Peace Conference opened at Versailles in January 1919, when representatives from 32 states were present, but not one from Germany. Later, this
enabled the Germans to complain that they were forced to accept a *Diktat*, a
dictated peace, and it helped to create the myth that the Treaty of Versailles
was a harsh, vindictive settlement.

At the Conference, the stage was held at first by the strongest of the
victorious powers, France, Britain, the USA, Japan and Italy. However,
Japan was only concerned with her gains in the Far East and the Italian
Prime Minister withdrew when he found that Italy was not going to receive
all the territories she expected. This left the vital decisions to the 'Big Three'

'The Big Four' at Versailles in 1919: Lloyd George with Orlando, Clemenceau with
Woodrow Wilson.

428

- Woodrow Wilson, the idealistic, self-righteous American President;. Clemenceau, who represented the demands of France for compensation and security, and Lloyd George, who, although out to extract every advantage for Britain, wanted a settlement based on realism rather on mere revenge.

Considering the complexities of their task and the fact that they distrusted one another, the Big Three reached a settlement in a remarkably short time. France recovered Alsace-Lorraine and was to receive the coal output of the Saar for 15 years, as compensation for her own destroyed mines. Instead of being made into a separate state, as France wanted, the Rhineland would remain part of Germany, though occupied by Allied troops for 15 years.

Germany was to lose territory to a resurrected Poland and East Prussia would be cut off from the rest of the Fatherland by a 'Polish Corridor' giving. Poland access to the Baltic. The port of Danzig (Gdansk) became a free (i.e. self-governing) city, three Baltic republics were created - Estonia, Latvia and Lithuania, which, with Finland, received their independence from their former Russian overlords. Union between Germany and Austria was forbidden and Germany's colonies were put into the care of the League of Nations, as 'mandated' territories, i.e. to be held by supervisory powers until they were ready for self-government.

Separate peace treaties were made with Austria, Bulgaria, Hungary and Turkey, which, in the effort to promote justice and self-determination for smaller nations, stored up troubles for the future. The Austro-Hungarian empire was cut to pieces, leaving Austria a small impoverished republic and Hungary, a separate state two-fifths of its former size. The Dual Monarchy's subject peoples had proclaimed their independence during the closing weeks of the war and these were now declared to be the separate states of Czechoslovakia (created out of the old kingdom of Bohemia, with Moravia and a large part of Hungary) and Yugoslavia, which was a much enlarged Serbia. Rumania was rewarded for ending on the winning side with slices of territory at the expense of Hungary and Russia, while Bulgaria, a loser, had to give land to Yugoslavia and Greece.

Woodrow Wilson's ardent belief in self-determination (the right of every people to govern itself) and the fervent nationalism of Czechs, Slavs, Poles and Baltic peoples created a number of small states which would be incapable of defending themselves against a revived Germany or Russia and which, because of the centuries-old mixture of races in Europe, contained their own minorities. Yugoslavia's population, for example, included Serbs, Croats, Slovenes, Magyars, Albanians and Italians; Poland had a great many German, Russian and Polish groups living within its borders and there were large Magyar and German minorities in Rumania. Most dangerous of all, there were 3 million German-speaking people in the Sudetenland, which was added to Czechoslovakia in order to give the new state a defensible frontier.

To make Germany incapable of renewing the war, her army was restricted to 100 000 volunteers, with no tanks, heavy guns or aircraft, and her navy was to have no submarines or warships over 10 000 tons. But, when all was said, Germany had suffered less in terms of losses than France, Britain and Russia; her territory had not been invaded and her people had not suffered occupation or pillage. Compared with many other treaties, notably that of Brest-Litovsk, the Treaty of Versailles was not particularly harsh, but the Germans were outraged.

Their indignation stemmed principally from the humiliation inflicted upon the German representatives, who were marched into the Hall of Mirrors at Versailles and made to sign the treaty which included the hated War Guilt clause, blaming the war on German aggression. To France and Britain, this was a statement of plain fact. After all, they hadn't attacked Serbia or invaded Belgium, but, to the Germans, it was an abominable insult, inserted into the treaty to justify the demand for reparations.

430

The French town of Lens in 1918, after its buildings and coal-mines had been system-matically destroyed by the Germans. It was for this kind of destruction that the French demanded reparations.

The idea that Germany should pay the cost of the war seemed to the French no more than simple justice. France had suffered terribly. Out of a population smaller than Britain's, one-and-a-half million men were killed and several millions wounded; in the north-east, the countryside had been devastated, towns and villages wrecked and hundreds of factories, mines and industrial buildings destroyed or damaged. Belgium, too, had suffered grievously and Great Britain, although her homeland had scarcely been damaged, had lost three-quarters of a million killed and had incurred gigantic debts to the United States in order to pay for the war and to act as banker to the Allies. No one knew what the war had cost Russia, since she was not represented at Versailles and the country was now in the throes of civil war.

So, what must Germany pay? No-one knew. Some estimates were as high as £24 000 million, but, Lloyd George, who realised the folly of setting too high a figure, urged that the amount should be settled later. In the end, the sum was fixed at £6 600 million, an amount far beyond Germany's ability to pay.

In fact, she never did pay it in full. Reparations remained a bone of conten-tion for years and all they did was to nourish the Germans' resentment and fill some of the Allies, notably the British, with feelings of guilt. The French did not share this view and would have been happy to see Germany ruined,

431

but in truth the whole matter of reparations would have been best forgotten and might well have been abandoned if the USA had accepted a proposal to cancel all war debts. But the American view was that those who borrow money, should pay it back. The most imaginative achievement of the settlement, the League of Nations, was largely the creation of Woodrow Wilson, who insisted that the League's Covenant or solemn promise be set at the head of all the peace treaties.

The purpose of the League was to promote international peace. Its members promised to respect one another's territory, to submit disputes to arbitration, to reduce armaments and to abide by the rule of law. In addition to disputes, the League would concern itself with the Mandated Territories, refugees, health, drugs, communications, international justice and conditions of labour.

Here, at last, was an organisation that transcended nationalism and European dominance, for 26 of the original 42 Members were countries outside Europe. For a time, the League was reasonably successful and, in non-political affairs, it achieved a great deal, but, from the start, it had weaknesses that were to prove fatal.

The first and most cruel blow was the absence of the United States, for, on Wilson's return to America, he was faced by a hostile Congress, which had made up its mind to turn its back on Europe. Russia, too, was absent from the League, as she had been from the peace conference, and Germany was not admitted until 1926. Hence, the League was only a league of *some* nations and, in the absence of the United States, came to have the air of an Anglo-French alliance. It could succeed only as long as its members respected the Covenant but, when they refused to do so, it had no effective way of making them obey the rules.

---

[1] In politics, the terms 'right' and 'left' came into use because, in most European parliaments, members holding progressive views sat on the left of the semi-circular chamber (as seen from the president's chair), while those holding conservative views sat on the right. Hence, liberals, socialists, communists and revolutionaries are said to be 'left' or 'left-wing', and moderates, conservatives, Fascists and, usually, militarists, are said to belong to the 'right'. Even communist states have their 'Left Opposition' and 'Right Opposition (or Deviation)'.

3 Post-war Upheavals

EUROPE

While the Peace Conference was still in session at Versailles, fighting broke out in various parts of Europe. The Baltic republics, Estonia and Latvia, had to fend off invading forces of Bolsheviks and Germans; the Czechs seized some valuable territory claimed by the Poles, who compensated themselves by attacking Russia. Led by Marshal Pilsudski, their army pushed the Polish frontier 200 miles to the east and they also grabbed a slice of territory belonging to Lithuania.

Hungary's government was overthrown by a Communist uprising which was soon defeated by right-wing[1] forces under Admiral Horthy, at about the time when a Rumanian army invaded the country and captured Budapest.

Kemal Ataturk (centre) at the battle of Gallipoli, where he began the career which was to bring him leadership of Turkey, and to be considered its saviour.

Under pressure from the Allies, the Rumanians withdrew in 1920, loaded with booty, leaving the Hungarians to cope with their poverty and immense losses of territory and population.

THE NEAR EAST

By the Treaty of Sèvres (1920), Turkey was to keep Constantinople but to lose part of Anatolia and all the Arab lands of the Ottoman Turkish Empire. The Greeks, eager to take advantage of their old enemy's downfall, invaded western Anatolia in order to create a Greek province around Smyrna (now Izmir) where many Greeks had lived for centuries. The infuriated Turks rose to arms under General Mustafa Kemal, who had already overthrown the Sultan. In three campaigns of 1920-2, he defeated the Greeks and captured Smyrna, a victory which persuaded the Allies to allow Turkey to have a new treaty in place of the old one. Kemal agreed to abandon claims to the Arab lands in return for retaining all Turkish territory and he insisted on a million Greeks leaving Anatolia for Greece.

After this dramatic victory, Kemal, who added Ataturk ('Father of the Turks') to his name, set to work to modernise his country. He introduced Western-style education, European dress and votes for women, abolished polygamy and decreed that Islam was no longer the state religion. These measures, known as Kemalism, laid the foundations of a modern national state, but, ruthless dictator as he was, Kemal could not carry all his people along with him and, when he died in 1938, Turkey was by no means wholly westernised.

THE MIDDLE EAST

A similar course of events took place in Persia, where the nationalists were led by an army officer by the name of Reza Khan, who overthrew the government and put through a programme similar to that of Kemal Ataturk.

Anglo-Egyptian troops move in to stop a Wafdist riot in Cairo. Violence broke out when the Wafd leaders were deported to Malta.

He then deposed the Shah and had himself elected Reza Shah Pahlavi, with dictatorial powers to introduce industrial growth and Western ideas. In 1935, the Shah changed the country's name to its ancient name of Iran and his régime, in spite of its corruption and repression, brought great benefits to the people, at least to those in the towns, though, as in Turkey, there remained an obstinate nucleus of resistance to modernisation.

In the 1920's, Middle East oil was not an important issue, for it only represented a tiny percentage of world production, so, although the Anglo-Persian Oil Company had been granted a concession, Britain made no effort to stay on in Iran. Her interests in the Arab lands of the former Ottoman Empire seemed much more important.

Five new states had emerged - Syria and the Lebanon as French mandates; Transjordan, Iraq (formerly Mesopotamia) and Palestine as British mandates. The French drove out Faisal, the King of Syria (1920) and, after stiff resistance by the Arabs, the country became a republic, with France retaining control of foreign policy, the army and finance. The Lebanon was given a similar constitution.

Britain pursued a somewhat different line, arranging for Emir Abdullah

436

ibn Hussein to rule Transjordan under British supervision, while, in Iraq, Emir Faisal, the deposed King of Syria, became king (1921-33), with a British High Commissioner holding a large measure of control, which was gradually relaxed until the mandate ended in 1932, by which time Iraq had developed into an independent, though not very stable, state.

Since 1914, large numbers of British troops had been stationed in Egypt to safeguard the Suez Canal and the route to India. The continued occupation of their country was naturally resented by many Egyptians who formed the *Wafd* or Nationalist Party to demand independence and a seat at the Peace Conference. When its leaders were deported in 1919, the Wafd led a major revolt which was put down by British troops, but the unrest persisted until, in 1922, the British government decided to grant a kind of semi-independence in which Egypt was given a constitution and a parliament. Sultan Fuad became King Fuad 1, British interests were to be safeguarded and they continued to rule the Sudan. This arrangement by no means satisfied the Wafd, because the British army remained in occupation and there were arguments about the use of Nile water to irrigate the Sudan. However, by 1929, the British agreed to return the Sudan to Anglo-Egyptian joint control.

If Britain's difficulties in Egypt were of her own making, she found herself landed with an intractable problem in Palestine. For centuries, this small country had been a province of the Ottoman Empire, with a largely Arab population - in 1919, there were some 700 000 Arabs and only about 60 000 Jews - but, since the founding of the Zionist movement[1] in 1897, Jews had been constantly arriving and settling in what they felt was their national homeland. During the war, the British government issued the Balfour Declaration of 1917, which, partly out of genuine sympathy for the Jews and partly to win support in the USA, stated

> 'His Majesty's Government view with favour the establishment in Palestine of a National Home for the Jewish people, and will use their best endeavours to facilitate the achievement of this object, it being clearly understood that nothing shall be done which may prejudice the civil and religious rights of existing non-Jewish communities . . .'

Thus, when Britain took charge of Palestine on behalf of the League of Nations, she was expected by Jews all over the world to keep her word. Unfortunately, the Arabs had not been consulted and, worse, when during the war they were encouraged to rebel against their Turkish overlords, they believed that they would be given all the Turkish provinces, including

---

[1] Launched by Theodor Herzl, a Hungarian Jew, 'to secure for the Jewish people a home in Palestine guaranteed by public law.'

Palestine. To establish a Jewish National Home, while at the same time protecting the position and rights of the resident population, was an impossible undertaking, which could only lead to accusations of bad faith.

Throughout the inter-war years, Jewish immigrants continued to enter Palestine, so that, by 1936, nearly one-third of the total population was Jewish. The newcomers, aided by largely American funds, quickly established themselves as a vigorous community which was deeply resented by the Palestinian Arabs. Disorders broke out, with widespread terrorism, and both sides laid the blame on Britain. A plan was put forward to divide the country into Jewish and Muslim areas, but this was hotly opposed and, as the 1930's advanced, the position worsened, because the sinister policies of Nazi Germany brought more and more refugees to the land which both Jews and Arabs regarded as their own.

IRELAND

Nearer home, Britain had to try to find a solution to the 'Irish Question'. In the 1918 British General Election, 73 Irish seats had been won by the Sinn Fein ('Ourselves Alone') republican party, led by Eamon De Valera, who,

Easter Rising 1916: a street barricade in Dublin, where the Irish Volunteers occupied the General Post Office and proclaimed the birth of the Irish Republic. The rising lasted less than a week, for it had little public support until the authorities foolishly executed the leaders.

instead of going to the Westminster Parliament, London, made themselves into an Irish parliament in Dublin and declared the republic. The British were not prepared to go beyond Home Rule and fighting broke out between the Irish Republican Army (the IRA) and the Royal Irish Constabulary, reinforced by a force of demobilised soldiers known as the 'Black and Tans', whose brutality aroused bitter resentment.

A truce was called and some of the Irish leaders, but not De Valera, accepted the Peace Treaty of December 1921, which made Ireland a self-governing Dominion of the British Empire, with the name of the Irish Free State. The Treaty also laid down that 6 largely Protestant counties of Ulster should remain part of the United Kingdom, with 13 M.P.s at Westminster and their own parliament at Stormont Castle, Belfast.

Those who accepted partition did so in the belief that it was only a temporary arrangement, but De Valera and his republican followers took up arms against the pro-Treaty government. Irish patriots who had served together against the English then fought one another with far greater bitterness until, after more than a year of murderous fighting, the new Government forced De Valera to call off the resistance and retire from the scene.

He was soon back in politics, forming his own party called Fianna Fáil

('Soldiers of Destiny') and, in the election of 1932, he came to power as president (prime minister) of the executive council. At once, he set about improving Ireland's economic position and breaking all links with the United Kingdom.

During the Second World War the country, renamed Eire, stayed neutral and, afterwards, although De Valera was defeated in 1948, his opponents completed one of his most cherished aims by taking the Republic of Ireland, as it now became, out of the British Commonwealth. With one of those belated gestures of generosity which Britain makes from time to time, Clement Attlee, the Prime Minister, insisted that Irish citizens were not to be regarded as aliens but were to enjoy the same rights in Britain as formerly.

There still remained the deadly problem of Northern Ireland. Partition had remained a grievous disappointment to all the nationalists, for, instead of time bringing tolerance and understanding, the prospect of unity seemed farther off than ever. There were several reasons for this. Over the years, the Protestants of the 6 counties, some two-thirds of the population, had consolidated their control of business, employment and elections to an extent that made them dread any possibility of becoming themselves a minority in a united Ireland. The extremist Orangemen had never relaxed the age-old feud with the Catholics and, in any case, the North and the South had been taking such different paths since 1921 that Partition seemed to have become a permanent fact. In the post-1945 era, for example, Northern Ireland's industry and agriculture became merged with the British and, as the measures of the Welfare State were introduced into the North, its education, health and social services left the South further behind.

To those who still longed passionately for a united Ireland, it looked as though two possible solutions existed. One was the use of force, but the IRA, although sporadically active, was now a banned organisation which appealed to no-one except the most extremist republicans. In any case, the Irish government came out strongly against the use of force, because it would inevitably create more hatred than it could remove. A much more positive solution was to end Partition through a policy of co-operation between North and South, bearing in mind that the Northerner, even if he called himself a Loyalist, was an Irishman, who always thought of himself as an Irishman.

Hence, when the prime ministers of the two Irelands paid visits to one another for friendly talks early in 1965, it looked as if conciliation was beginning to win the day. Alas for such hopes, the Reverend Ian Paisley put himself at the head of a Protestant group totally opposed to such a policy and, in a general election, won an uncomfortably large number of votes. Meanwhile, another, mainly Catholic, movement arose - the Civil Rights

Association - which ignored the Partition Issue in order to concentrate on discrimination against Catholics in local elections, housing and jobs.

In January 1969, a march by Civil Rights supporters from Belfast to Londonderry (Derry to all nationalists) was ambushed by Unionist supporters. Attacks also took place on Catholics in Belfast and when disorders between the rival religious groups became too violent for the RUC. (Royal Ulster Constabulary) to control, the Northern Ireland Prime Minister asked the British government to send in troops who were welcomed as protectors by the Catholic population.

The Stormont government hurried through reforms to the voting system and abolished the 'B Specials', the Protestant auxiliary police force. But it was too late. Extremists on both sides had taken charge; the disorders grew worse and, predictably, the IRA entered the fray with the avowed intention of severing all of Northern Ireland's connection with Britain, while the Ulster Volunteer Force (UVF) was set up to maintain Protestant supremacy. Ten years later, after hundreds of murders and millions of pounds' worth of damage, a solution to the Irish Question seemed farther off than in 1921.

RUSSIA

When, at a bitter price, Lenin bought peace with Germany in March 1918, he had only got rid of Russia's main enemy. Civil war broke out, in which the Bolshevik forces, the Reds, were opposed by the anti-revolutionary White Russians, an ill-assorted mass of army officers, royalists, liberals and socialists of various hues whom Lenin despised. In fighting that ranged from Petrograd (Leningrad after 1924) across Siberia to Vladivostok, the White Russians put four armies in the field and were supported by an army-corps of Czech ex-prisoners of war and some battalions of British, French, American and Japanese troops.

The Allies, furious at what they considered Russia's treachery, intervened in the hope of overthrowing the Bolsheviks, who were urging workers in the West to rise against their capitalist governments. But the numbers of Allied troops were too small to have any effect on the civil war, except to create lasting resentment of foreigners' attempt to overthrow the Russian people's cause.

The peasants supported Lenin because he had given them the land and they knew that victory for the White Russians would mean the return of the landowners. Brilliantly led by Trotsky, they fought so stubbornly that, by 1920, the White armies were beaten and the Allied troops withdrawn from Russian soil.

The Bolsheviks had won, but, in the bitter struggle, their leaders had created a one-party police state more tyrannical than the Tsarist régime had

Lenin and Stalin speaking to Red Guards in the Smolny, 1917. Lenin rewarded Stalin for his loyalty and only later came to distrust him. He died before he could bring about Stalin's downfall.

ever been. To some extent, this was understandable, because the country had been so shattered by revolution and years of war that industrial production, cereal production, railway stock and numbers of livestock were only a fraction of the 1913 level. During the civil war, peasants and workers had accepted 'war communism', whereby the Bolsheviks impounded food to feed the towns and took over factories and workshops for the state, but, when peace brought no freedom or improvement of their lot, the peasants refused to produce more than they needed for their own use.

Lenin therefore devised the New Economic Policy (NEP) to conciliate the people by allowing the peasants to sell surplus food for profit and returning many small factories to private ownership. This watered-down communism benefited the peasants more than the urban workers, but did not bring about the desired growth in industrial output.

Meanwhile, the Bolsheviks, who had set up the Comintern (Communist International) to found Marxist parties throughout the world, had been disappointed by its results. Communist risings in Hungary and Germany were defeated and, while practically every European country had its own communist party dedicated to revolution, most of them were small, for the majority of workers gave their votes to non-revolutionary socialist parties which were nearly as scared of communism as were the capitalist employers.

Lenin's death in 1924 brought a decisive change in the direction of Bolshevik Russia (which had been re-named the Union of Soviet Socialist Republics - the USSR or the Soviet Union), because, from the group of top Party officials jostling for power, there emerged Josef Stalin, a man less brilliantly gifted than either Lenin or Trotsky, but equally ruthless. As General Secretary of the Party, he controlled the appointment of all full-time officials to posts throughout the country and, using this power to make himself supreme, he got rid of every rival, including Trotsky himself, and brought the whole Soviet Union under his own iron rule.

Nothing was allowed to stand in the way of industrial advance. The NEP was cast aside and 5 million *kulaks* (prosperous peasants) were killed or transported in order to impose collective farming on the countryside and produce food for the workers in the towns. From 1928 onwards, two Five Year Plans were instituted to build factories, new cities and power stations and, since machines, tractors and modern weapons were more important than consumer goods, the people were forced to work for little reward. There was even a fall in real wages, but, by 1938, 80 per cent of industrial production came from plant built during the period of the Five Year Plans. Russia was an autocratic state, ruled by its sombre dictator and the dreaded Cheka or secret police, but it was again a great power.

GERMANY

The German republic which came into existence after the Kaiser's abdication in 1918, was a liberal democracy, with an elected president and a National Assembly at Weimar, a university city about 200 kilometres southwest of Berlin. From the outset, the Weimar government was beset by enemies to the left and the right[1] who wanted to overthrow the new democratic constitution.

Communist risings in Berlin and in the Ruhr mining districts were put down with the aid of the regular army, and a right-wing revolt (1920), led by a monarchist named Kapp and General Ludendorff, collapsed as the result of a general strike by the trade unions.

While their government was struggling to survive, the German people were feeling the effects of war shortages and the Allied blockade. Food and fuel were scarce, malnutrition was widespread and, to add to their troubles, the Germans received the report of the reparations Commission that they must pay huge sums to the Allies. After half-hearted attempts to comply, they declared they could not pay, whereupon, in January 1923, Poincaré, the French premier, ordered the French army to march into the Ruhr, the major

[1] See footnote on page 432

443

Chaos and hunger in Berlin where shops were plundered during the period of German inflation and the army had to be called in to maintain order.

coal- and steel-producing region of Germany, to take for themselves the reparations which the French and the Belgians believed the Germans could pay if they were made to do so. British protests that the ruin of Germany would harm the whole continent were dismissed as soft-headed nonsense and Poincaré expressed his country's view when he remarked that no-one would ever get anything out of Germany except by force.

The German workers resisted the occupation of the Ruhr with strikes and sabotage and their government decided to evade their debts by inflating the currency so recklessly that money ceased to be worth the paper it was printed on. Whereas 20 marks had been equal to £1, the rate of exchange rocketed to 22 000 million marks to the pound and practically everyone on fixed incomes became destitute.

This calamitous state of affairs had to be ended and a new Chancellor, Gustav Stresemann, called off the sabotage campaign in the Ruhr and agreed to resume payment of reparations. The Americans, interested in reparations because much of the cash would be passed on to them, produced the Dawes Plan in 1924, which allowed Germany to pay in accordance with her industrial recovery year by year and this was to be aided by massive American loans. The French withdrew their troops from the Ruhr and, when France, Belgium, Britain, Germany and Italy signed the Locarno Pact in 1925, recognising the frontiers between Germany and her western

French cavalry enters Essen, in the Ruhr, January 1923.

neighbours, Europe seemed to have taken a great stride forwards towards stability. However, there were elements in Germany working for the overthrow of the Weimar Republic.

One of the consequences of the occupation of the Ruhr was the arrival on the political scene of Adolf Hitler. In November 1923, this obscure ex-corporal, who had become one of the leaders of the National Socialist Party (the Nazis) in Munich, organised the so-called 'Beer Hall Putsch', when he and General Ludendorff led a march through the streets to proclaim a nationalist government. A few police bullets scattered the marchers and Hitler was arrested and sentenced to five years in prison. His trial gave him a platform from which, thanks to the newspapers, he was able to address the nation and, after his release in less than a year, he was allowed to resume his self-appointed mission to build up a party that would restore Germany's 'greatness'.

A different type of nationalist (or patriot) was the veteran war-hero, Field Marshal von Hindenburg, whose election as President in 1925 gave heart to militarists and all who hated the Treaty of Versailles. Under his presidency, Germany stepped up her secret re-armament, training picked men to be the officers of the future, carrying out research into modern weapons, using civil airfields and flying clubs to recreate a German Air Force and arranging for Germans to take part in tank and aircraft training on Russian soil. This

445

became possible after Germany and Russia signed the Treaty of Rapallo in 1922, renouncing war compensation and agreeing to co-operate in diplomatic and commercial affairs. The two countries had much in common; both hated the new Poland, both were re-building their shattered economies and both felt that they were shunned and distrusted by the rest of Europe. The alliance improved Germany's international status and in 1926 she was admitted to membership of the League of Nations.

4 The Twenties

THE USA

The USA did very well out of the war. As the country which made the Allied victory possible, her prestige was immense and Woodrow Wilson was received in Paris like a Messiah. American casualties had been light and overall gains in wealth enormous, for, through supplying the Allies with food and munitions, the United States changed from being a debtor country, as she had been in 1914, to a creditor country. Her industry was so booming that, by the 1920's, America was producing more than half the world's manufactured goods and this abundance gave her citizens standards of living never dreamed of in any other continent.

Charlie Chaplin and Jackie Coogan in *The Kid*, 1921. The London comedian had gone to America before the War to make his name with Fred Karno and the Keystone company, with whom he adopted his bowler hat, baggy trousers and flat-footed walk. By 1919, he was the best-known and most easily-recognised actor in the world.

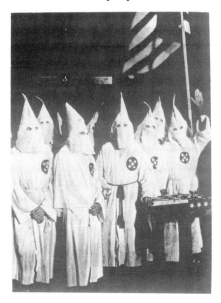

Ku Klux Klan recruits taking oath at an initiation ceremony at Baltimore, Maryland, 1923. Started in Tennessee in 1865, the original Ku Klux Klan soon died out, but was revived in 1915 for a few years and again revived in 1945 as a terrorist organisation.

Charles Lindbergh with the *Spirit of St Louis* - the plane in which he made the first solo crossing of the Atlantic in 1927. He flew from New York to Paris in 33 hours.

As prices went down and wages went up, Americans became the first people to regard luxuries like motor-cars and radios as necessities. Theirs was the homeland of skyscrapers, hire-purchase, the motion picture industry, jazz, department stores and impeccable plumbing. It was also the homeland of Prohibition, that futile ban on alcohol which produced a decade of gangsterism, and of the Ku Klux Klan, which harried Jews and Catholics, as well as blacks.

There was a paradox in post-war America's attitude to Europe. Having saved democracy, the USA turned its back on Versailles, shut the door on immigrants, put up tariffs in order to keep foreign goods out and insisted on repayment of war-debts. Yet huge private loans poured into Europe and also into Canada, Latin America and Asia.

EUROPE

Europe certainly needed help to recover from war damage and dislocation of trade. The economic unity of the Dual Monarchy had gone and the new states were trying to survive by putting high customs duties on imported goods. This hampered trade and so did the absence of Russia from the business world, while Germany, the most important industrial country in Europe, was suffering from inflation and the burden of reparations.

Britain, formerly so rich and powerful, was very much in the doldrums, because, after a brief post-war boom, there occurred a sharp rise in unemployment and disorders which, in places, were not far short of riots. Part of the trouble was that the government felt obliged to honour Britain's debts to the USA, irrespective of whether her own European debtors paid up, but a far bigger reason for her difficulties was that world demand for British coal, iron, steel, ships and railway-engines had declined and, with rising tariffs, it was difficult to sell manufactured goods abroad. In an age that was turning to oil, electricity and mass-production, Britain was falling behind her competitors.

A new political force arose in the Labour Party, which actually became the Government for a short while in 1924, but a right-wing Government was soon back in office when the country was almost brought to a stand-still by the 1926 General Strike. It was soon over and its failure humiliated the workers and weakened the Trade Union movement for 20 years, but there was virtually no violence and most of the strikers went back to work at the behest of their leaders.

General Strike, May 1926: armoured cars escorting a food convoy through Oxford Circus to Hyde Park, London, for distribution.

Benito Mussolini (1883-1945), the Italian dictator, 'Il Duce', wearing the black-shirt Fascist uniform, addresses a people's rally in his usual melodramatic style.

In Central Europe, economic distress, alien minorities and fear of communism caused nearly all the new states - Czechoslovakia was the shining exception - to turn, sooner or later, to 'strong men'. They included Pilsudski in Poland, Admiral Horthy in Hungary, King Alexander in Yugoslavia, army officers in Greece and dictators in the new Baltic states.

Dictatorship, in the evil form of Fascism, also took hold in Italy, where communist agitation, poverty and unemployment reduced the country to a state of turmoil. While the government dithered, Benito Mussolini, a one-time Socialist, formed the *Fasci di Combattimento* (combat groups) to beat up communists, socialists, strikers and town officials. These tactics brought new recruits to the Fascists - police, army officers, magistrates, industrialists and all who were scared of left-wing politics.

By 1922, Mussolini had supporters all over Italy and he ordered his Fascists in Milan to make the 'March on Rome' to demand strong government. This was no more than a bluff, but the government turned feebly to King Victor Emmanuel III, who, possibly fearing for his throne, invited Mussolini to be Prime Minister.

450

The posturing bully soon obtained powers to crush all opposition in parliament and outside. Taking his cue from the Bolsheviks, he welded the Fascist gangs into an élite which controlled local government, the press, radio, education and trade unions. He retained the King, cabinet and parliament as a facade, but the real executive was the Fascist Grand Council and he himself held absolute power as *Il Duce*, the leader.

Mussolini certainly injected a new energy and discipline into the country; he tackled unemployment with a programme of public works, encouraged the farmers and gave state aid to industry. Although his régime was fundamentally gimcrack and he could not solve Italy's economic problems, Mussolini's bravado impressed a great many people in Europe, including Hitler - and Winston Churchill, for a time!

Others followed the example he set. Fascist parties arose in France and Britain, without becoming much more than a nuisance, but, in Spain, a general, Primo de Rivera, overthrew parliament and later the king, and established himself as a dictator, the forerunner of Franco. In Portugal, General Carmona took charge of the 1910 republic with Dr Salazar as his financial minister, the man who was later to rule the country from 1932-68.

Although France did not abandon democracy, it suffered from an electoral system which gave rise to more than a dozen political parties, endless jobbery and governments which lasted about six months. This tended to create cynicism at home and to lower French prestige abroad. The Ruhr occupation was a costly fiasco and, with a vast reconstruction programme to pay for, France got into serious financial difficulties, which brought Poincaré back into office, with emergency powers to rule by decree. Helped by increased industrial output and better conditions of trade, France (like Britain in the same period) enjoyed a brief spell of stability between 1926 and 1929.

THE FAR EAST

Japan experienced an economic boom during the war, when, free from Western interference, she was able to seize the German ports in China, to exploit the markets of South-East Asia and build factories on the Chinese mainland. The Allies placed orders for Japanese ships and munitions, causing steel and the textile production to expand at an enormous rate, thanks to coal from Manchuria and iron-ore from China and Malaya.

Confident of its power, the Japanese government in 1915 presented China with Twenty-one Demands, which were intended to turn China into a Japanese protectorate. Britain and the USA made diplomatic protests and Chinese patriots were infuriated, but there was little they could do while their country was so weak. Their anger became all the fiercer when they learned that the Versailles peace settlement had awarded the province of

Shantung, previously leased to Germany, to Japan and there flared up a violent student revolt, known as the 'May 4th Movement' of 1919, which demanded a boycott of Japanese goods and rejection of European interference.

Since the 1911 Revolution, Sun Yat-sen had established himself in the

southern city of Canton, where he formed the Kuomintang or People's National Party, and tried to expand his limited power with the aid of Russian advisers and an uneasy alliance with the newly-formed Chinese Communist Party, whose members included a young librarian, named Mao Tse-tung.

But vast areas of the country were untouched by the Revolution which had swept away the imperial régime and the Confucian ideals that had held the country together for 2000 years. Japan controlled some of the northern territories; guerilla bands roamed the countryside and military despots ruled whole provinces as independent war-lords. The peasants, apparently unmoved by revolutionary ideas, continued to till the soil in passive misery, their lives made increasingly wretched by war, famine and a shortage of land caused by the steadily increasing population.

Sun Yat-sen died in 1925 and was succeeded by his brother-in-law, Chiang Kai-shek, a trained military man from the landowner class, who was determined to defeat the warlords and unite China under a strong government. With his allies from the Right and the Left, he made steady progress and brought huge areas into control, but the Nationalists and the Communists were fighting for different ideals and Chiang Kai-shek and his close supporters in the Kuomintang were horrified to find that the Communists were letting the peasants take over land in the provinces freed from warlords.

Mao Tse-Tung on the Long March, the epic 13 000 km journey from Kiangi province in the south to the north-west of China and back to Shensi, which the Communists undertook in order to escape annihilation by Chiang Kai-Shek's Nationalists. Thousands perished on the year-long march, but it confirmed Mao's position as heroic leader.

In 1926, Chiang launched a savage offensive against the Communists, killing hundreds of their leaders and forcing the survivors to flee to the mountainous south, where Mao Tse-tung formed the Red Army. Chiang responded with what he called his Bandit Extermination Campaigns, a long drawn-out series of operations which compelled the Communists to abandon their southern base and seek safety in the remote socialist-controlled Shensi province, hundreds of miles away in central China. The Long March of 1934, when 100 000 men, women and children endured a year-long trek across mountains and deserts, became an epic of heroic courage in the Communist annals. Less than one-third survived and, for the time being, it seemed as if the Kuomintang had triumphed. But the Red Army still existed and Mao Tse-tung had won the peasants' allegiance

Away to the south of China, communist ideas began to penetrate the infant nationalist movements directed against the colonial powers. In Vietnam, then part of Indo-China, a young Marxist, named Ho Chi Minh, was actively arousing opposition to the French rulers of his country and, in the East Indies, where the Dutch had to suppress Communist revolts in Java and Sumatra, the leading nationalist was Ahmed Sukarno, destined to become President of a united Indonesia after the Second World War.

LATIN AMERICA

On the other side of the world, the 20 independent republics of Latin America possessed a widely-shared culture and a common colonial past. A sparse population, huge areas of jungle and mountains and an absence of cheap or free land to lure men into the interior gave rise to a number of great coastal cities - Rio de Janeiro, Buenos Aires, São Paulo, Montevideo, Santiago, Lima, Caracas - in which as many as one-third or a quarter of the entire population might live, most of them in slums, since poverty was endemic and wealth concentrated into a few hands. In the countryside, most of the land was divided into great estates (*haciendas*) owned by absentee landowners, yet peasant grievances produced only one rural revolt leading to a full-scale revolution - in Mexico in 1911, when the dictator, Porfirio Diaz, was overthrown.

Most of the states had some of the apparatus of democracy - political parties, parliaments and secret ballots - but, even in the most advanced countries, Argentina and Chile, real political power was still in the hands of the great landowners. In Cuba, Venezuela and Peru, students took the lead in organising opposition to the dictatorships set up in the 1920's. Communist ideas and the influence of the Russian Revolution filtered through, but made little headway, as yet, and the student movements and a certain amount of reforming zeal among young army officers in Brazil and Chile were the main expressions of discontent.

Since independence in the 19th century, the republics had relied a great deal on foreign capital to develop their industries and communications. Formerly, Britain had been the leading investor, but, after the war, when most of the Western European countries were much poorer, the USA became the dominant financial power. Primary products, such as beef and wheat in Argentina, coffee and cotton in Brazil and Colombia, sugar in Cuba, rubber in Brazil (until about 1920 when South-East Asian plantations ruined that industry), were grown for export and there was increasing mineral production - nitrates and copper in Chile, Bolivian tin, Venezuelan and Mexican oil - all depending heavily on American finance.

THE DEPRESSION WORLDWIDE

In the United States, business, apart from farming, was still booming and millions of dollars were being lent abroad. There was plenty more for gambling on the Stock Exchange, which became a sort of obsession for thousands of Americans, a game in which shares always went up, so everyone was a winner and no-one could lose - until the bubble burst.

One day, in October 1929, in Wall Street, home of the New York Stock Exchange, someone big sold a lot of shares. Rumours went around and more people began to sell. Panic set in; everyone wanted to sell but suddenly there were no buyers and all those wonderful share certificates were practically worthless. Borrowers were ruined; hundreds of banks went bankrupt and business houses and factories closed their doors.

America's real wealth was unchanged. The mines, oil-wells, cattle ranches, automobile plants and steel foundries were still there, but, for some mysterious reason, confidence and buying-power had collapsed. As people spent less, unemployment rose, so that America's 1.5 million unemployed in 1929 became 5 million a year later and 15 million in 1932.

Reverberations of the Wall Street Crash spread round the world, bringing disaster to countries whose fragile economies were too closely linked to America's to be able to stand the shock of the loans drying up and creditors wanting their money back. Once the flow of dollars stopped, the underlying weakness of the world's economy came to the surface; it was overproduction of food and raw materials. During the war, farmers and plantation owners in many countries had increased their output, but, by the mid-twenties, as European agriculture returned to pre-war levels, there was a world glut of foodstuffs. Prices came down, so farmers tried to recoup by growing bigger crops, which only increased the surplus and brought prices lower still. Besides food, there was also overproduction of rubber, copper, zinc, silver, cotton and coal.

Since the primary producers got less for their grain, meat and minerals, they bought less from the manufacturing countries, who, in hope of protecting their own products, put up tariff walls to keep out foreign goods. So, as trade declined, unemployment grew and grew, like a monstrous fungus no-one could control.

Mass-unemployment meant under-consumption, because the man without work could only afford the bare necessities of life, which led to the tragic absurdity of millions of people being ill-clad and undernourished, while textile factories were closed and farmers were burning crops and dumping wheat and coffee into the sea.

Britain had 3 million unemployed by 1931, Germany more than 6 million, Italy about 3 million and France, less dependent on exports and industry, probably one-and-a-half million, because, in a country of small farmers, unemployed city workers simply went to live with relations in the country. Central Europe became poverty-stricken; half of Japan's factories were closed; nearly a third of Australia's work force was unemployed in 1933 and New Zealand, which tried to solve its problems by putting more men on the land, had riots in Auckland. Just about the only countries which did well in the 1930's were Southern Rhodesia (Zimbabwe) and South Africa, because they produced a commodity whose price actually went up - gold.

In Latin America, the Depression provided opportunities for the military to intervene everywhere, except in Mexico. Not even Argentina was exempt; the most highly developed of all Latin American countries had been ruled since 1914 by the Radical Party, but popular discontent and a disastrous drop in exports brought the Argentinian army to power. But the senior officers represented conservative interests, so little social change took place until 1943, when some extreme nationalists in the army, among them Colonel Peron, took control.

A military coup in Brazil ushered in the 15 years' dictatorship of Vargas, whose forceful rule earned him a good deal of popular support, whereas, in Chile, a right-wing dictatorship's harsh treatment of urban workers prompted a Popular Front alliance of liberals, socialists and communists, which won the 1938 elections. In the aftermath of the Chaco War (1932-5), between Bolivia and Paraguay, Bolivia's defeat gave rise to a military Nazi-style regime, and Paraguay also succumbed to the rule of its army officers.

In the smaller, less industrialised countries, the economic crisis strengthened the hold of the landed classes and prevented any improvement in the living standards of the poor. Mexico, however, was the exception, for President Cardenas tackled discontent by distributing land to the peasants and nationalising the oil industry. Here, as in several Latin countries, the Depression actually stimulated efforts to start home-based industries, so that, by 1939, industrial production in Mexico, Chile, Colombia and Brazil almost doubled.

5 The Road to Disaster

In most countries of the world, governments tackled the Depression in the same way - by cutting public spending and putting tariffs on foreign goods; even Britain, the home of Free Trade, followed this policy, although a system of 'Imperial Preference' was arranged for countries within the Empire.

However, in spite of the fact that the so-called remedies - spending-cuts and protection - made things worse than they would have been, recovery was beginning to stir from about 1933. This was partly due to the low prices of raw materials; in Britain for example, industries such as chemicals, rayon, radio, electrical goods, cars and building, began to flourish and unemployment came down to about 2 million in 1935. The old industrial areas of coal-mining and ship-building were still in a bad way, but, in southern Britain, where most of the new industries were located, workers enjoyed a higher standard of living than ever before.

THE USA

In the United States, recovery took a more dramatic course, after the election in 1932 of a Democratic President, Franklin D. Roosevelt. On taking office, he promised to give the American people a 'New Deal' and, through his buoyant personality and gift of finding words that appealed directly to the ordinary citizen, he created an atmosphere of optimism and positive thinking.

In essence, Roosevelt's New Deal meant spending instead of cutting down - spending public money in order to create work and get business flowing again. At unprecedented speed, he had Congress pass laws to reform banking, to improve unemployment relief, to aid farming and industry and put an end to Prohibition. Huge government loans were made for houses, roads, bridges, parks and dams; vast projects were carried out, the most celebrated being that by the Tennessee Valley Authority, which was formed to tackle destitution in a great area stretching across half-a-dozen states where 3 million people were living in poverty.

In a country devoted to rugged capitalism, many Americans were deeply angered by higher taxes and controls on free enterprise, which smacked of socialism. But the rescue work succeeded - or partially so - for business and industry did pick up and Americans got some of their confidence back, although there were still 8 to 9 million Americans out of work in 1939.

THE FAR EAST

It was not altogether surprising that Japan, which, like Italy and Germany, had had little experience of democracy should turn (like them) to violence as a way out of economic difficulty.

Japan's economy was shattered by the Depression and when exports of manufactured goods fell by two-thirds, it seemed vitally important to expand business on the mainland of Asia. Since 1905, the Japanese had invested heavily in Manchuria on the mainland of northern China, but, by this time, their presence there was increasingly resented by the Chinese, so, in 1931, the Japanese made an armed take-over of the entire province. Re-naming it Manchukuo, they turned it into a puppet state, with the last of the Manchus on the throne.

On China's behalf, Chiang Kai-shek appealed to the League of Nations, which passed a resolution deploring Japan's behaviour, but did nothing more, so the aggression went unchecked and more Japanese troops entered the country to prepare for the next attack on Chinese sovereignty.

It came in 1937, when a major war broke out that was to ravage China for the next 11 years and to lead eventually to the triumph of Mao and the Communists. Early on, the prospect of Japanese victory alarmed Stalin into advising Mao to come to terms with Chiang Kai-shek and fight alongside the Nationalists. This he did, but for a long time the combined Chinese forces failed to halt what seemed to be the invincible advance of Japanese armies across all the northern and coastal areas. However, China is a vast country. It absorbed armies, munitions and money like a sponge. The resistance of its people, inured to centuries of hardship, proved to be indestructible and it was in a desperate attempt to solve the problems of the China War that Japan attacked the American fleet in Pearl Harbor in 1941.

The invasion of Manchuria was a mortal blow to the League of Nations, and much blame fell upon the member-states, especially Britain, because she and the USA were the only powers with strong naval forces in the Far East. But, in truth, it was difficult to see what could be done to deter Japan from embarking on the war or to make her stop once it had started. In any case, China was a long way off and, with the Depression and the pugnacious behaviour of Germany and Italy, there was enough to worry about nearer home.

EUROPE

The Depression brought Germany to the verge of ruin. Her dollar-aided recovery came crashing down and, by 1931, more than 6 million Germans were out of work. The government tottered, no party could command a majority in the Reichstag and Hitler and his Nazis began to come into their own. In 1928, they had only 12 seats, but in 1932, when 230 of Hitler's followers were elected, their ranting leader had become a major power in the land.

Hitler's appeal to the German people cut across all social classes, from street thugs to worried civil servants, to rich industrialists, for this evil man, so commonplace in appearance, was an inspired orator who had a mesmeric effect upon all who listened to his outpourings. In a torrent of speeches, he promised everything: revenge, recovery, glory. He and the Nazi Party would make Germany great again, purify the country from inferior races and those traitors who had stabbed her in the back, solve unemployment, scrap reparations, tear up the Treaty of Versailles and restore the German people to their rightful place as the Master Race. With the Fascist obsession with strength and national glory Hitler proclaimed himself the *Führer* (leader), demanding total obedience from the entire nation and, later, an oath of personal loyalty from every member of the armed forces. Much more vile was his fanatical hatred of the Jews and his absurd theory of the racial superiority of Germans who were said to be pure-blooded 'Aryans'.

This heady nonsense and a mistaken belief by right-wing leaders that they could use Hitler to confound the growing Communist Party and discard him later on, brought the 34-year-old Austrian to power. In 1933, Hitler became Chancellor of Germany. At once he demanded and obtained powers to draft laws without reference to the Reichstag, which was the end of the Weimar Republic and of the Germans' brief acquaintance with democracy.

Nazis, appointed to key positions, took control of all aspects of German society, from local government to press, radio, art and education. Like the Bolsheviks, they used terror as a calculated weapon to overcome opposition and they kept the whole country in a fever of excitement to maintain the impression that things were happening, that Germany was on the march. Vast rallies were held, with all the panoply of banners, uniforms and militaristic pomp, at which Hitler, the Führer, poured out his messages of hate and patriotic exultation. Germany's children were systematically drilled to swallow the Nazi idealogy (and even to betray their own parents) and, in defiance of Versailles, a colossal programme of re-armament was started, thus bringing work and good wages to millions who had been unemployed. Was it any wonder that, in a plebiscite, 89.9 per cent of the German people gave their approval to Adolf Hitler?

The Nazis set out to win the allegiance of the young in order to provide the basis for the 1000-year Reich. These pictures illustrate the mesmeric attraction of Nazism for the German people, especially the young. Above left: Hitler with child mascot. Above right: youth on parade, Nuremberg. Below: torchlight procession, Berlin.

461

These developments were viewed with dismay by the democracies and, indeed, by Russia, too. Hitler or no Hitler, Germany was bound to be a problem, for she had not been destroyed in 1918 and, as she revived, she would surely demand revision of the peace settlement and, through her population and industrial power, dominate central Europe and overshadow France. In 1919, the Allies had hoped that the creation of the Weimar Republic would transform Germany into a liberal democracy, but, when economic depression revived the old aggressive nationalism, the question for those who cared about peace was what could be done to contain Germany.

The one-time Allies were in poor shape. France, with most to fear, looked to the new states of eastern Europe, but they were too weak to be of much help; Russia, now an unpredictable dictatorship, would be of little use as an ally, since her armies would have to cross Poland, which the Poles would never permit; the USA was no help either, for, although Roosevelt was aware of the dangers of isolation, Americans wanted to have no more truck with Europe and with people who didn't pay their debts. As for the British, they naively believed in the League of Nations, disarmament and an end to

When Sir Oswald Mosley, founder of the British Union of Fascists, proposed a march through the East End of London in October 1936, thousands of people gathered to protest. This photograph shows demonstrators fleeing as police arrive to break down a barricade they have erected. In Cable Street, Stepney, the East Enders broke up the last of Mosley's Fascist marches.

The Dictators: Mussolini, giving the Fascist salute, and Hitler stand shoulder to shoulder during a march past in Munich, September 1937.

war, which made them militarily too weak to deter anyone who threatened the peace, so the French built the Maginot Line, a vast system of fortifications to make their eastern frontier impregnable. This extended through Alsace and Lorraine but not along the frontier with Belgium which was regarded as a neutral country.

Meanwhile, Mussolini's longing for glory and an African colony caused him to send an army to invade Ethiopia (1935), where even his incompetent generals could not fail to overcome adversaries armed with spears and obsolete guns. This aggression put France and Britain in an embarrassing position, because, as leading powers in the League, they had to take some action, yet they wanted to keep Italy on their side of the fence against Germany. In the end, their feeble protests failed to stop the aggression and threw the offended Mussolini into Hitler's arms. The exultant dictators signed a treaty of friendship and Italy joined the Anti-Comintern Pact (or Axis), which Germany and Japan formed in November 1936 to oppose Communism.

Worse still, the Ethiopian campaign gave Hitler his own triumph. Taking advantage of the distracted atmosphere, he sent German troops into the Rhineland to occupy the 'demilitarized' zone where their presence was forbidden by the Treaty of Versailles. The French, with their Polish and Czech allies and, possibly a couple of British divisions, could have annihilated the then puny German army, but the gamble came off, because, when the others hung back, France was not prepared to act alone. Once again, nothing happened to deflate Hitler's ego or to hearten those who wanted to believe in collective security.

The spotlight now fell on Spain, where, in 1936, a civil war broke out between the left-wing Republican government (the Spanish monarch had left the country in 1931) and forces of the right, called 'Nationalists', led by General Franco. The Spaniards were not allowed to fight out their quarrel among themselves, for the civil war came to be seen as a conflict between Fascism and Communism, in which Hitler and Mussolini sent lavish help to Franco and tried out their tanks and aerial bombing techniques, while Stalin (who at this time was engaged in 'purging' the Red Army and wiping out half the officer corps) gave limited assistance to the Republicans.

An International Brigade, in which socialists from many countries served, also supported the 'Republicans', but, after three years of vicious warfare

Spanish Civil War: last stand in Irun, September 1936, by a Republican sniper as he takes aim from a ruined farmhouse at advancing Nationalist rebels.

464

German troops cross the Czech border into the Sudetenland, 3 October 1938, following the Munich Agreement. In the following March, Hitler ordered the take-over of the rest of Czechoslovakia; German tanks entered Prague and to mark the occasion the Führer spent one night in the Czech capital.

which cost half-a-million lives, the Nationalists captured Madrid and Franco assumed absolute power. Europe's third Fascist dictator, he was to outlast both the others and to die nearly 40 years later, still Head of State and still reviled by socialists the world over.

The Spanish Civil War was of immense significance, because it convinced Hitler that the democracies had neither the will nor the means to resist aggression. In Britain, Winston Churchill was thundering out prophecies of disaster, but hardly anyone paid attention to a politician who was generally regarded as a war-mongering imperialist. The country wanted peace and there were plenty of people who believed that the sensible thing to do was to appease the Germans by remedying what was thought to be the injustice of Versailles.

Hence, when Hitler annexed Austria in 1938 to achieve the *Anschluss*, or union, which had been forbidden by the Treaty, Britain did not support French protests. After all, Austria, like the Rhineland, had a German-speaking population and it was natural for them to want to be united. But Czechoslovakia now lay exposed to the aggressor and there were 3 million Germans living in that part of the country called the Sudetenland. Their presence made it easy for Sudeten Nazis to make an outcry about Czech 'persecution'.

Hitler had always seen Austria and Czechoslovakia as the essential core of his German Empire. On the first page of *Mein Kampf*, he had written, 'German Austria must return to the German Motherland'; Czechoslovakia, Poland, White (western) Russia and the Ukraine were also needed to give Germany her longed-for *lebensraum* or living space.

This time, it really looked as if the powers would stand up to Hitler. Czechoslovakia was a democracy created by the Treaty of Versailles; it possessed a fine army, an alliance with France and a pact with Soviet Russia. Moreover, France said she would fight if Czechoslovakia were attacked and Stalin proposed an alliance with the Western powers. But Neville Chamberlain, the British prime minister, knew better. In his opinion, they should solve the problem by peaceful discussion.

Accordingly, at Munich, in September 1938, Hitler, Mussolini and the French and British prime ministers (no Czech or Russian was present) agreed that the Sudetenland should be handed over to Germany. Betrayed by her friends, Czechoslovakia was now doomed and, 6 months later, when German tanks overran the rest of the country, no-one lifted a finger to help her.

This outrage convinced Chamberlain that something must be done, so, with French backing, he gave Poland a guarantee of support and, rather warily, opened talks with Russia. This was surely enough to bring Hitler to his senses? Then the bombshell exploded. On 24 August 1939, the world learnt with horrified disbelief that Germany and Russia had signed a non-aggression pact and, almost immediately, that Hitler was demanding the port of Danzig (Gdansk) and the Polish Corridor.

One absolute certainty in international affairs had seemed to be the undying enmity between Germany and Russia, yet here was Stalin making a pact with Hitler, who had never concealed his hatred of Communism and contempt for the Slav race. Undoubtedly, Stalin was playing for time against the attack from the west which he always feared. Any faith he might have had in France or Britain had disappeared after the Munich Agreement; therefore, he would agree to a partition of Poland, which would push Russia's frontiers some distance to the west, grab the Baltic States and get ready to face the expected onslaught. For Hitler, the Pact meant that he could deal with Poland without the spectre of war on two fronts, because he was confident that France and Britain would abandon their guarantee to Poland, as they had abandoned Czechoslovakia.

6 An Overall View of the Second World War

On 1 September 1939, German armoured divisions invaded Poland and, two days later, to the 'stunned surprise', it was said, of the Nazi leaders, France and Britain honoured their guarantee to Poland and declared war on Germany.

The Second World War was in many ways a revival of the First, being fought by pretty well the same contestants for much the same reasons. For the Germans, it was a war to assert their superiority and rectify the injustice of Versailles; while the Allies fought to prevent the German domination of Europe, having been driven to the point of overcoming their reluctance and cowardice by Hitler's broken promises and acts of aggression.

The second war differed from the first in a number of ways. In the first place, it was much wider-spread, being fought right across Europe and, significantly, into Germany itself; major campaigns took place in North Africa, China and all over South-East Asia, from the Philippines, Burma, Indonesia and Malaya to the north coast of Australia and, at sea, naval actions were fought by fleets, submarines and surface raiders across all the oceans of the world. To a greater extent than in 1914-18, it was 'total war', involving civilian populations, whose homes, factories, and food supplies were targets for attack; so was their morale, which was ceaselessly assailed by propaganda (radio became a major weapon), bombing, mass-executions and reprisals.

There were differences in the actual fighting, for, generally speaking, the stalemate of trench warfare did not occur, owing to the tactical use of tanks and aircraft. The Germans, who had absorbed the lessons of the First World War better than their opponents, made great use of the 'blitzkrieg', or lightning war, which consisted of violent bombing attacks on the enemy's communications and key-positions, followed by the advance of powerful tank columns, which crashed through defences and penetrated deep into enemy territory. Motorised infantry accompanied these armoured spearheads and poured through gaps to fan outwards and mop up the broken forces of the enemy.

Early on, these tactics enabled the Germans to overrun Poland, the Netherlands and France with astonishing speed, but they were less successful

467

later on. The Russians (attacked in 1941 by their 1939 ally) possessed the numbers, the determination and, above all, the space to cope with blitzkreig tactics, because, even when they suffered defeats and losses of territory, they could fall back and back, lengthening the German communications and drawing their enemy farther from his supply bases. Eventually, when it became possible to form a defensive front, there occurred slogging matches like those of the First World War and the casualties were correspondingly high. At least 4 million Russian soldiers were killed and 2 million Germans, whereas the British, who did not have much of this kind of fighting, suffered but a third of their 1914-18 losses.

Aircraft were infinitely more important in this war; to the extent that victory was not possible without air superiority. Yet both sides exaggerated the importance of the bomber and Britain and Germany delivered innumerable raids on each other's cities without decisively affecting the course of the war. In the end, the war had to be won on the ground and at sea, and it was there that aircraft played a crucial part in support of armies, warships and landing-craft.

The obvious exception to this theory was the case of Japan, which was bombed into surrender while her armies were still undefeated. But, by that time, the atomic bomb had a destructive power which previously existed only in people's imaginations.

The Germans had not been able to rebuild the great fleet of 1914, so there was never the prospect of another Battle of Jutland, unless the Germans could acquire the French warships in 1940. When this seemed likely to happen, the British navy promptly put them out of action, to the lasting anger of the entire French nation. However, apart from a few surface-raiders, the main threat to Allied sea communications came from submarines. An outstanding development in naval warfare was the use of aircraft-carriers, in which the Japanese were initially so far ahead of their contemporaries that they gained a series of whirlwind victories in 1941.

The war was more mechanised and scientific than any previous conflict. German scientists devised magnetic mines, 'V.1' flying bombs, and 'V.2' supersonic rockets, while the British invention of radar gave them the lead in tracking aircraft, guiding bombers to targets and enabling ships to locate the enemy. In addition, British and American scientists (some of them refugees from Nazi Germany) worked together to produce the atomic bombs which caused Japan's surrender in 1945. More humanely, medical science, advanced surgery and production of the drug penicillin saved countless lives which otherwise would have been lost.

The key commodity of the war was oil and much of the Allied and German strategy was directed towards defending or obtaining oil supplies.

The failure of the Germans to win the oil fields of the Caucasus and the Middle East was a major factor in their defeat.

Throughout history, cruelty and war have been inseparable and this war was no exception. Ill-treatment and murder of prisoners, enslavement of workers and destruction of cities of no military importance had occurred in earlier wars, if not on such a scale, but there was no precedent for the treatment meted out by Hitler's criminals to the inmates of concentration camps nor for the extermination of millions of Jews in gas-chambers. People in the democracies felt all along that, to some extent, they were fighting a moral war, but it was not until 1945, when Belsen, Auschwitz and other horror-camps revealed their ghastly secrets, that the world fully realised the true nature of the Nazi régime.

7   The Second World War

The blitzkreig overwhelmed Poland in a matter of days and, before the Germans could take the entire country, Stalin stepped in to grab his half. To improve Russia's defences, he also seized the Baltic states of Estonia, Latvia and Lithuania, and invaded Finland.

With the French and British armies almost totally inactive in northern France, nothing much happened for 6 months, until, on 9 April 1940, the Germans launched a series of attacks so brilliantly successful that, by June, they seemed to have won the war. Sweden remained neutral, but Denmark and Norway were swiftly occupied and there followed the invasion of the Netherlands and Belgium and a drive on into France which by-passed the now-useless Maginot Line and divided the Allied armies. In the face of overwhelmingly superior armour and air-power, French resistance collapsed even more abjectly than in 1870; Paris was captured and, on 22 June, France signed an armistice, accepting total defeat. The government moved to Vichy, with Marshal Pétain, the one-time hero of Verdun, as Head of State, a pathetic old man, whose aim was to lessen his country's suffering by co-operating with the Germans. The one Frenchman of note willing to carry on the fight was General de Gaulle, who escaped to England and took command of the 'Free French'.

Meanwhile, to avoid encirclement, the British army had made for Dunkirk, where more than 300 000 troops were embarked for England, leaving their arms and equipment behind. By this time, Chamberlain's place as Prime Minister had been taken by Winston Churchill, because, in spite of his chequered career, he was the one man acceptable to all political parties. The hour produced the man. In frequent radio addresses to the nation, Churchill rallied the people and called forth qualities of courage and unity they hardly knew they possessed. Even so, their brave determination and the support of all the Dominions, except Eire, would have been in vain had it not been for the narrow stretch of the English Channel, which the Germans would have to cross in order to gain their final victory in the West.

No sea invasion could succeed without command of the air and, through August and September 1940, a great air battle, called the Battle of Britain, was fought over southern England between the Luftwaffe (German Air

Blitz on London: a London street after an air raid in September 1940.

'Scramble!' Fighter pilots made a dash for their aircraft during the Battle of Britain. The command 'Scramble!' meant 'Take off to meet enemy aircraft' (whose approach was detected by radiolocation - Radar - and Observer Corps posts).

472

Force) and the Royal Air Force. It ended with the Luftwaffe's defeat, when it could no longer afford its losses in day operations, though it was still able to mount a prolonged campaign of night bombing.

The Battle of Britain, fought by a few thousand airmen and technicians, changed the whole direction of the war, because Hitler called off the invasion and decided to attack Russia. His reasons for doing so may have been anxiety about Russia's policy of moving her frontiers forward, but it seems more likely that the conquest of Russia was always uppermost in his mind. Not only would it expunge Communism from the face of Europe, but it would give Germany the living-space, minerals and oil which the 'master race' required. Moreover, the Red Army's poor showing against the Finns convinced Hitler that victory would be as swift as it had been in the West and would show the obstinate British that it was pointless to carry on the war.

Preliminary to the great attack, Hitler compelled Rumania, Hungary and Bulgaria to join the Axis alliance and, in the spring of 1941, launched the blitzkreig against Yugoslavia and Greece. British troops there, and in Crete, were driven out, though they did well in North Africa against Mussolini's legions and also liberated Ethiopia. By this time, however, Hitler was riding high and, with almost every country in Europe in his grip, he felt able to spare one of his finest generals, Rommel, for the North African 'side show'. Commanding the German Afrika Korps, Rommel took control from the dispirited Italians and forced the British to fall back to the Egyptian frontier.

Peasants fleeing before the German advance into Russia. By December 1941, 70 million people were living under German rule in occupied Russia. Millions were deported for slave labour, millions arbitrarily executed.

Near Kiev, July 1941. German troops move eastwards at the start of 'Operation Barbarossa'. By the evening of the first day, forward units of the German armies were already far inside Soviet territory.

'Operation Barbarossa', the invasion of Russia, was launched on 22 June 1941, when colossal German forces began the attack in three main thrusts: north-east, through the Baltic states, towards Leningrad; in the centre, towards Moscow and south-east, through Kiev, across the Ukraine. There was also a drive from Rumania towards Odessa on the Black Sea.

For several weeks, the Germans advanced in spectacular fashion, inflicting one defeat after another upon the retreating Russians, but, by mid-August, the offensive began to slow down, as supply lines lengthened and the Russians showed no signs of cracking. In December, they halted the Germans 30 miles short of Moscow and both sides dug in for the winter. Hitler had not quite achieved the swift knock-out, but, in 5 months, his armies had advanced 700 miles and had inflicted such damage that it seemed unlikely Russia could survive another campaign in the spring.

At the beginning of the war, Britain had to pay dollars for American war materials and carry them in her own ships, but, early in 1941, when the money had run out, the United States agreed to provide Lease-Lend Aid, or supplies without payment. This was very much the work of President Roosevelt, who formed a close understanding with Churchill, whom he met at sea, so that, together, they could draw up the Atlantic Charter, stating their reasons for opposing tyranny and their hopes for the post-war world. All this was not far short of an alliance, but it would have been difficult for Roosevelt to draw his people into the war in Europe had not Japan's attack been followed four days later by Hitler's declaration of war on the United States.

This act of supreme folly brought America's vast resources to bear against Germany at the time when Russia was still fighting strongly. However long it might take, Germany's defeat was now certain.

THE FAR EAST

Meanwhile, Japan's war with China had been going on for four years and the Chinese people, in spite of tremendous suffering, were still unconquered. Supplies of arms reached them along the Burma Road and through French Indo-China, but the French government was in no position to resist when the Japanese occupied Indo-China in July 1941. At this, the United States, which had long been sympathetic towards China and was becoming increasingly anxious about Japanese ambitions in South-East Asia, stopped all trade with Japan, a critical blow to that country's overstrained economy.

But in South-East Asia there were vast riches, most of them belonging to Britain and the Netherlands, who could do little to defend their colonial possessions. It would be easy to conquer Malaya and the Dutch East Indies and acquire their oil, rubber, tin and other products, provided the USA did not interfere. Yet the United States was certain to see such action as a threat to American power and influence in the whole Pacific area, so much so that her leading military and naval officers regarded Japan as a potential enemy to a far greater extent than Germany. The key to war in this area was naval supremacy and the Japanese High Command, headed by General Tojo, decided to seize it by delivering a devastating blow against American sea-power.

On 7 December 1941, a strong force of Japanese carrier-borne aircraft made a surprise attack on the American fleet at Pearl Harbor, the American naval base on one of the Hawaiian islands in the mid-Pacific, inflicting such damage that it gave the Japanese the supremacy they desired.

This brilliantly executed victory was followed by a series of triumphs even more spectacular than those of the Germans in 1940, as the American naval bases of Guam and Wake were taken, followed by Hong Kong, Singapore, Malaya, the Dutch East Indies, the Philippines, Burma and New Guinea.

Japanese attack on Pearl Harbor, December 1941. The Japanese carrier-based aircraft sank and damaged 19 vessels: seven battleships out of the US fleet strength of eight were sunk or put out of action and nearly 5000 Americans were killed or wounded in the two-hour attack.

476

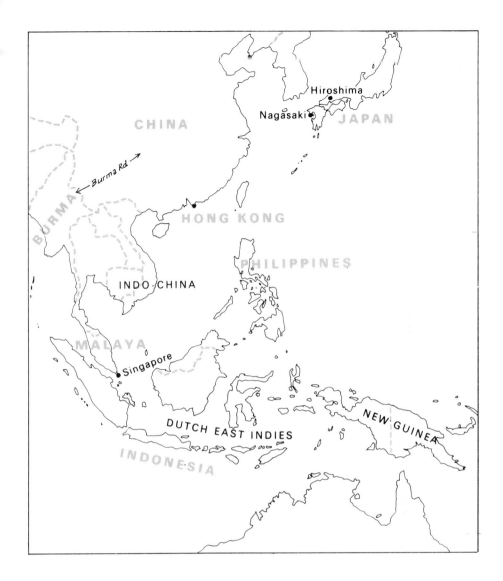

Everywhere, as they overcame the forces of the colonial powers, the Japanese proved themselves to be ruthless efficient fighters, but the Americans, whose hurt pride made them all the more determined, soon struck back, winning two great naval battles (the Coral Sea and Midway Island), which tipped the balance of sea-power back in America's favour. But there was still a long hard slog ahead, as the Americans attacked Japanese merchant-shipping, carrying precious raw materials to Japan from the newly-conquered territories, and, with the Australians, captured island after island in a bitterly-fought campaign to get within striking distance of Japan itself.

1942 proved to be a momentous year. It began with Axis triumphs on all fronts - in Russia, where Hitler, who had taken supreme command, launched

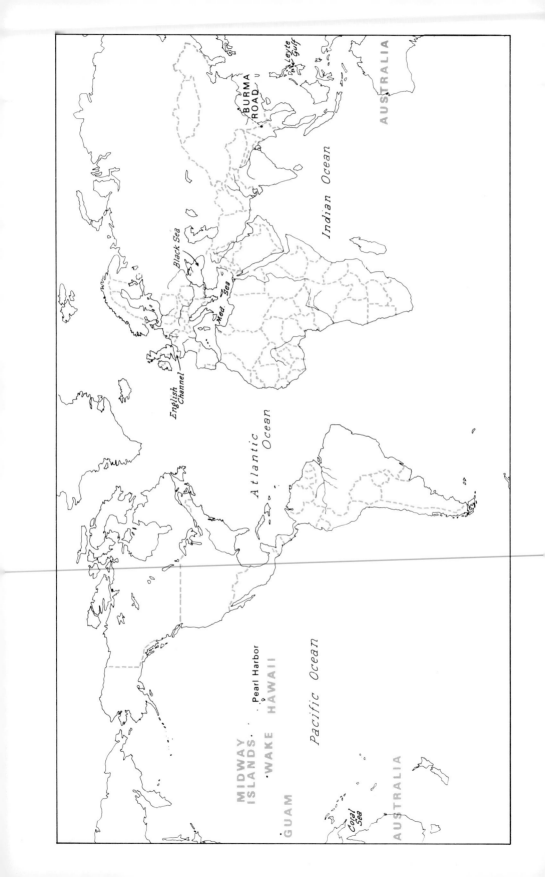

a terrific drive into the south-east; in the Pacific, in North Africa and in the Atlantic, where German submarines sank several million tons of shipping. Yet, by the end of that year, four great battles had turned the tide in the Allies' favour. The Battle of Midway Island changed the situation in the Pacific; in North Africa, the British under General Montgomery defeated the Germans and Italians at El Alamein, near Alexandria in Egypt, and joined forces with Anglo-American armies which had landed in French North Africa. In November, at Stalingrad (now Volgograd) on the Volga, the Russians isolated a German army and practically annihilated it. This disaster compelled the Germans to pull back some 200 miles and thenceforward they were always on the defensive. They had lost hundreds of thousands of their best troops, Leningrad was still uncaptured and Germany itself was under heavy bombardment by the British Royal Air Force. The fourth victory was won on the Atlantic Ocean, where Allied naval and air forces managed to reduce the submarine menace to a level which enabled the Allies to receive American supplies crucial to the next phase of the war.

EUROPE

From the United States' entry into the war, Roosevelt had agreed to give priority to the defeat of Germany, but, in spite of Russian reproaches, a landing in France was not possible until 1944, simply because the necessary landing craft and special equipment did not exist. For that reason, and also to hearten resistance movements in Yugoslavia and Greece, the armies of North Africa were launched against Italy in 1943. The Italians soon caved in and Mussolini was overthrown, but, in spite of his problems in Russia, Hitler poured troops into Italy and denied the Allies the easy victory they had expected.

When the long-awaited landing on the coast of Normandy in northern France took place on 6 June 1944, the Germans were caught off guard, so that, by the time they recovered, a firm beachhead had been established, from which American and British troops, under the overall command of an American general, Dwight Eisenhower, fought their way inland against an obdurate defence. In August, they liberated Paris, where General de Gaulle received a rapturous welcome, and another successful landing took place in the south of France; Brussels and Antwerp were relieved in September and, with the Germans in retreat on three fronts, it looked as though the war must be over by the end of the year.

By this time, the Russians were advancing across Poland and into Rumania, Bulgaria, Yugoslavia and Hungary, where local communists came out to greet them. As each country was liberated, it found itself in the grip of a puppet government subservient to Moscow, and Greece would have gone the same way, but for the arrival of British forces in October.

The Germans, putting up an astounding resistance everywhere, were now in a hopeless situation, because Hitler, wounded in an assassination attempt and now almost certainly insane, was determined to drag his country down to ruin. The misguided Allied policy of 'unconditional surrender' ruled out the chances of his overthrow and of a group of senior commanders asking for armistice terms. Throwing his reserves into a great counter-attack in the Ardennes region of north-eastern France, Hitler delayed the entry of American and British armies into Germany by several weeks, so that it was March before they were across the Rhine, racing on in hope of reaching Berlin before the Russians. Roosevelt was dying; American policy was to avoid offending Stalin and therefore the Anglo-American forces were halted on the Elbe, leaving the field clear for the Russians to enter Vienna on 12 April, Berlin on about a fortnight later and Prague soon afterwards.

On 30 April, Hitler committed suicide in his headquarters beneath the ruins of Berlin and, during the next few days, the German armies surrendered. The war in Europe ended on 7 May 1945.

British soldiers driving liberated Hungarian officers in an American jeep, Osnabruck, 5 April 1945.

Hiroshima: an aerial view showing the complete devastation after the explosion of the first atomic bomb, dropped from an American B29 Super-Fortress bomber on 6 August 1945. The official estimate of 306 000 casualties is now considered much too low.

THE FAR EAST

It took a little longer to finish off the conflict in the Far East. From October, the Japanese government knew that it must be defeated, because, in Leyte Gulf, the greatest sea-battle of the war, the Americans defeated the Japanese navy so heavily that the Philippines were lost and, with them, control of the sea routes to the Dutch East Indies and the oil that was the life-blood of the Imperial Fleet. On land, a British army, fighting a brilliant campaign in atrocious conditions, was well on the way to liberating Burma, and American aid was again reaching Chiang Kai-shek in China.

In the summer of 1945, when American bombers were pounding the Japanese cities, everyone realised that a sea-borne invasion would be immensely costly, since the Japanese would put up a suicidal resistance in defence of their homeland and Emperor. The American President, Harry S. Truman, therefore decided, with Churchill's assent, to use a weapon of such destructive force that invasion would be unnecessary.

Accordingly, on 6 and 9 August, two atomic bombs were dropped upon the cities of Hiroshima and Nagasaki with such appalling effects that the Emperor ordered his soldiers everywhere to lay down their arms. On 2 September 1945, the Japanese government surrendered and, six years after Hitler had invaded Poland, the Second World War came to its end.

8 An Uneasy Peace

During the war, three meetings took place between the leaders of the United States, Britain and the USSR - at Tehran, Iran, in 1943, Yalta, on the Black Sea coast, February 1945, and Potsdam, August 1945, by which time Roosevelt had been succeeded by Truman and Churchill replaced by Clement Attlee. All along there were deep differences beneath the cordial surface. Britain was concerned about Poland, but Stalin, now in possession of that country, was not going to let the anti-communist Poles form a government; Roosevelt, who admired Churchill, nevertheless thought he was an unrepentant old imperialist, whose policies would be a bigger danger in the post-war world than Russian communism; he reckoned that he and Stalin could settle affairs amicably.

At Potsdam, Attlee and his Foreign Secretary, Ernest Bevin, tried to impress the Americans with a sense of danger at Russia's new-style imperialism, but without much success. Perhaps it was too early to discern that the war fought to save Europe from Nazism had ended by delivering half the continent into the grip of a communist tyranny. Germany lay in ruins; France and Italy had been defeated; Britain was exhausted, and all the other countries, except the neutrals, were trying to recover from the demoralisation of defeat and occupation. In this chaotic situation, there was one man, Josef Stalin, who knew exactly where he was going. His armies had taken every capital in Central Europe and he saw to it that each had a government acceptable to Moscow.

Russian officials built up communist parties, sometimes in alliance with other parties; opponents were rounded up and liquidated; the right of people to choose a government, as promised in the Atlantic Charter, was ignored, so that, by 1948, Poland, Bulgaria, Rumania, Hungary, Czechoslovakia and Albania all had communist governments. So, too, had Yugoslavia, but its leader, Tito, was a national hero and no puppet of the Soviet state.

Germany, with no government at the end of the war, was divided into four zones, administered by Britain, the USA, France and Russia. The Western Allies followed similar policies and were generally agreed that Germany must be helped to get back on her feet. Not so the Russians. Understandably,

'The Big Three' meet in Tehran, November 1943. Left to right: Marshal Stalin, President Roosevelt and Mr Churchill. The conference established a close relationship between Roosevelt and Stalin. In his concern for the future of Poland and the British Empire, Churchill was the odd man out.

Churchill on tour, 1945. In the General Election campaign, the great war-leader was greeted everywhere with enthusiasm. Yet the British electorate rejected his party and voted instead for the Beveridge Plan (Social Security) and nationalisation. Hence, the Labour Party won a sweeping victory.

their idea was to strip their zone bare of industrial equipment, as 'reparations' for the damage done inside Russia, and there developed an argument so intense about currency and access to Berlin (which was in the Russian zone, but also divided between the powers into four sectors), that the Allies amalgamated their zones into the Federal Republic of Germany (West Germany) and the Russians organised the German Democratic Republic (East Germany).

From 1949, the two states, one a capitalist democracy, the other a communist satellite, glared at each other across a fortified border and all hope of a united Germany vanished for the forseeable future. In Churchill's words, an 'Iron Curtain' had come down across Europe and nothing could be done, short of the USA employing the atomic bomb, for the countries which had fallen into Russia's grasp.

In truth, the loser of the war was not just Germany, but Europe itself. Almost every country was impoverished; the empires of Britain, France, Belgium and the Netherlands were about to crumple and the continent which for long had been the greatest force in world history had destroyed its own supremacy. From 1945, the European Age was over and thenceforward the world would be dominated by two non-European giants, the United States and the USSR. Perhaps, with their populations, resources and dynamism (for they are really much alike), this was bound to happen and the war only accelerated their advance. At all events, a third giant, China, would soon be coming up behind them.

For a time, Britain was regarded as one of the Big Three. Her solitary stand in 1940, her people's tenacity and the immensity of their war effort gave Britain enormous prestige. Yet the cost of two great wars, the mobilisation of all her resources and the sale of overseas assets had reduced her strength so greatly that she was no longer in a position to play the role of a great power. Furthermore, the very fact that she had emerged victorious seemed to inhibit her people from making the intense efforts which marked the recovery of countries which had suffered defeat and occupation.

This was seen when France put forward a plan to pool French and West German coal and steel resources. Belgium, the Netherlands, Luxemburg and Italy agreed to join in an association called the European Coal and Steel Community (1952), which developed into the European Economic Community (EEC) or Common Market. But Britain, suspicious of foreign ways and concerned about Commonwealth links, stayed aloof[1] and missed the economic upsurge which the original Common Market members so evidently enjoyed.

France, for a time apparently broken by her wartime disasters and the

---

[1] Britain was admitted to membership in 1973.

humiliating surrenders of Indo China and Algeria, came bouncing back in the 1960's under de Gaulle's positive leadership, when she became the dominant force in the EEC. Like France, the Netherlands had suffered crushing burdens imposed by the Germans and she, too, had to accept the loss of an empire, but, thanks to the discovery of natural gas and the development of one of the world's greatest oil-refineries, her economic recovery was complete. Belgium prospered from a wide range of manufacturing industries and also through Brussels becoming the administrative capital of the EEC, while Italy made marked industrial progress, at least in the north. Norway's reconstruction based mainly on hydro-electric, metal and forestry industries, produced excellent results and the discovery of North Sea oil promised even greater prosperity in the future. It was possibly for this reason that the Norwegians decided not to join the EEC.

Of all the states of Western Europe, West Germany's recovery was the most remarkable. In 1945, she was separated from her eastern half, many of her cities lay in ruins and her leaders were universally condemned for their crimes against humanity. Twenty years later, thanks partly to American aid but greatly to the German people's discipline and hard work, Germany had achieved her 'economic miracle' and was once again one of the most powerful industrial countries in the world.

Within the framework of the EEC, France and West Germany, enemies for so long, became the leading powers and achieved a remarkable rapport when Giscard d'Estaing and Helmut Schmidt were heads of government in these two countries. This photograph shows them in discussion in 1978, by which time Britain was a member of the EEC and even provided the EEC President, Roy Jenkins, seen standing in the background.

The United Nations Organisation took over from the League of Nations the role of international forum. Its members included all the major powers and were representative of most parts of the world. The Preparatory Commission that met in San Francisco in 1945 had 51 representatives, of whom those in the photograph are a cross-section: remarkably, the Soviet representative, Andrei Gromyko, was still prominent in Foreign Affairs 40 years later.

THE UNITED NATIONS ORGANISATION

The aim to replace the League of Nations by a new organisation was fulfilled in 1945 at San Francisco, when the representatives from 51 nations met to draw up the United Nations Charter. From the start, one great defect of the old League was remedied, for the United States and Russia became members and, as if to emphasise that American isolation was dead, the permanent headquarters of the United Nations was set up in New York. All the member states were represented with one vote each in the General Assembly, in which debates took place and resolutions were passed, in front, as it were, of a world audience. There was a permanent staff, the Secretariat, headed by the Secretary-General, whose post gave him a high moral standing.

The Security Council was to be responsible for keeping the peace and for asking member states to supply armed forces should these be needed. Of the 11 members, 5 were permanent - those from the United States, Britain, France, Russia and China (then Nationalist China). Each of the permanent members was given the right of 'veto', i.e. to prevent any action by the Security Council and, although the veto did not prevent the General Assembly debating an issue, in practice, it came to be used as a weapon of rivalry, especially by the Soviet Union.

Like the old League, the United Nations Organisation has been in some ways a disappointment, simply because there is no way to make powerful nations work together unless they want to. Its principal value is perhaps as a forum for discussion and as an organisation whose agencies carry out a great deal of work to improve the world's agriculture, finances, health, education and child-care.

A Food and Agriculture Organization (FAO) expert shows two Ivory Coast farmers how an irrigation system works in an area where the rainy season is followed by drought. The FAO helps many Third World countries with advice on such matters as crop yields, pest control, livestock and food storage.

9 The Cold War

EUROPE

In 1945, there was much good will towards the Russian people. Everyone admired their courage and recognised that the Red Army had played the major role in destroying Hitler's war machine. In a new era of peace and understanding, the Russian leaders would surely put away their old fears and suspicions.

But Stalin could not believe there was no danger of attack from the West. As a lifelong communist, he regarded capitalism as an inefficient system which always solved its difficulties by making war. Hence his retention of huge armed forces, his distrust of his recent allies, and determination to press on with the production of a Russian nuclear bomb.

It did not take the Americans or the British Labour government long to realise that their benevolence had been sadly misguided, as Stalin installed Soviet-sponsored governments in Central Europe and retained troops in China and Iran, while protesting volubly about British forces in Greece and Indonesia (where they were awaiting the return of the Dutch).

It was the situation in Greece which convinced the Americans that they would have to adopt a policy of 'containing' Russia. In October 1944, the arrival of British troops in Athens had helped to frustrate a communist take-over, but, after a royalist government took office in 1946, civil war broke out in which communists were provided with arms via the neighbouring Balkan states. Britain, unable to afford the cost of the operations, revealed that she was no longer a world power by asking the United Nations to take over the commitment, whereupon President Truman came to the recue with massive military and economic aid to the Greek government.

The 'Truman Doctrine' of helping 'free peoples' to resist armed minorities and outside pressure was also applied to Turkey. Then came the huge programme known as the Marshall Plan[1] or, in full, the *Organisation for European Economic Co-operation* (OEEC). It offered assistance, usually in the form of dollars, to all European countries so that they could build

---

[1] Named after George Marshall, a top general of the US Army, who became Secretary of State.

factories and get production going, for the theory was that Communism would be less likely to flourish when people were busy and prosperous than when they were suffering hunger and injustice.

Russia and its satellite states refused Marshall Aid and, when the Czech government appeared to hesitate, a coup d'état in Prague promptly took Czechoslovakia into the communist camp. Elsewhere, the Plan was so successful that the Americans developed their 'Point Four' programme of aid to underdeveloped countries outside Europe, which spurred Russia into devising her own Molotov Plan or Comecon (Council for Mutual Economic Assistance) to win support by offers of aid to satellites and uncommitted nations.

The next step in the struggle which became known as 'the Cold War', was an attempt by the Russians to drive the other powers out of Berlin by blocking all the land routes from West Germany. This crisis was foiled by an

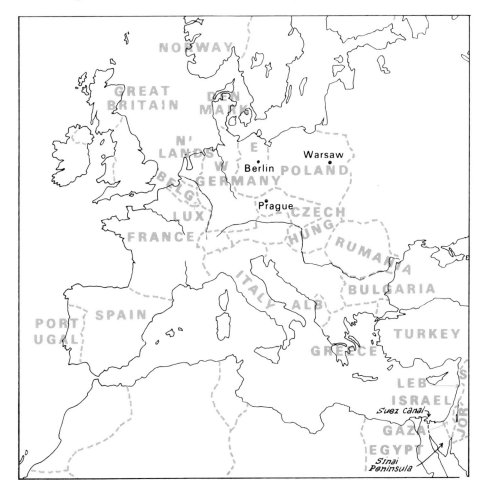

Berlin, December 1961: East German soldiers line the Friedrichstrasse at the sector border, while workmen complete the new reinforced wall barring the border. The Allied crossing was reduced to a small gap in the wall, sealing East Berlin off even more completely from Western Europe.

Allied airlift, after which the Russians built a massive wall across the city to prevent all communication between their zone and the zones of the capitalist enemy.

Short of actually firing guns, the two giants were now at war with one another, enlisting allies and making every use of the weapons of propaganda, espionage and bribery. In response to this alarming development, some of the smaller fry - Britain, France, Belgium, the Netherlands and Luxembourg - formed the Western Union, pledging themselves to unite against aggression. This led to a wider pact, called NATO (North Atlantic Treaty Organisation), when, in 1949, the five Western Union countries were joined by the USA, Canada, Italy, Portugal, Iceland, Denmark and Norway. Two years later, Greece and Turkey became members. Franco was too much hated by some of the democracies for Spain to be invited, but the United States signed a separate treaty with the General and obtained bases in Spain.

The OEEC and NATO were created to confront communism in Europe and, since neither would be effective without a strong West Germany, the American, British and French zones were amalgamated in 1949 to form the Federal Republic of West Germany, with a parliamentary democracy and a Christian Democrat as Chancellor. The new republic was allowed to re-arm and, in 1955, West Germany became a member of NATO.

Russia's reply on the propaganda front was to revive the pre-war

Comintern (see page 442) as the Cominform (Communist Information Bureau) to organise opposition to 'American Imperialism' and to undermine the Marshall Plan by fomenting unrest in western countries. To counter NATO, Russia created the Warsaw Treaty Organisation (1955), also known as the Warsaw Pact, for defence of the Soviet bloc. Its members were the USSR, East Germany, Poland, Czechoslovakia, Hungary, Bulgaria, Rumania and Albania.

THE FAR EAST

The Cold War became a global struggle which shifted to the Far East, where Japan's defeat had not brought peace to China. Allied governments had long recognised Chiang Kai-shek as the country's rightful leader and, when the United Nations was founded, Nationalist China became one of the permanent members of the Security Council. But, by this time, the Kuomintang was a corrupt, inefficient organisation, whose appeal to the Chinese people, in particular to the peasants, was far less than that of the Communists, who had brought peace and order to the areas they held during the war years.

In 1946, Mao Tse-tung's armies began to move south against Nationalist forces lavishly supplied with American equipment, but without the will to carry on the fight. Whole divisions surrendered to the Communists and, in 1949, Chiang withdrew to the island of Formosa (Taiwan), where, with the remnant of the Kuomintang, he kept up the pretence of being head of the government of China. On the mainland, Mao Tse-tung proclaimed the People's Republic of China.

The triumph of Communism in the land containing a quarter of the world's population seemed to have provided Russia with a colossal success and the Americans with a corresponding defeat. They refused to recognise the People's Republic, went on supporting Chiang and soon found themselves involved in a strange and perilous war - strange, because the USA was never officially at war with Russia or China and perilous, because it could have developed into the Third World War.

The battle-ground was Korea, a peninsula of north-eastern China, which had been ruled by Japan since 1910. With Japan's defeat in 1945, Russian troops moved in from the north and Americans from the south. By agreement, the two zones were divided by the 38th parallel of latitude, so that North Korea came to have a communist régime, while South Korea, nominally under United Nations' supervision (in practice, American) elected a right-wing government under a petty dictator. After numerous border incidents, North Korean forces invaded South Korea in June 1950 and captured Seoul, the capital.

This attack, which was almost certainly engineered by Stalin, since Mao

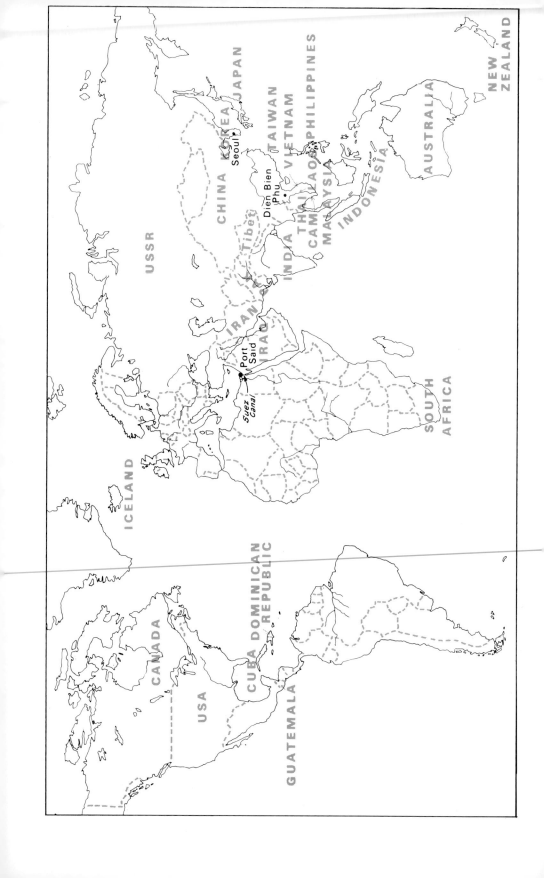

Seaborne landing at Inchon, September 1950: American marines are seen landing from their assault craft 200 miles behind North Korean lines, after warships and aircraft have bombarded coastal defences. This daring manoeuvre was the first counter-offensive by the UN forces.

had little influence in the area at this time, was condemned by the Security Council, which asked member states of the United Nations to send armed assistance to South Korea. There was no Soviet veto since the Russian delegate had walked out in protest against communist China's exclusion from membership.

Sixteen non-communist countries sent units to serve in Korea, but half the ground forces (South Koreans made up the rest) and nearly all the equipment and aircraft were American. Led by the American general, Douglas MacArthur[1], they drove the North Koreans back across the 38th parallel and on towards the Chinese border, as though to unite the whole of Korea, but, at this point, Mao Tse-tung intervened. A 'volunteer' Chinese army forced the Americans to retreat, whereupon MacArthur, concerned only for the military situation, proposed bombing raids on Chinese bases inside China. Realising the danger from such action, President Truman dismissed MacArthur from his command in April 1951 and proposed a cease-fire. A weary struggle went on around the 38th parallel for two years, until an armistice was signed to bring the Korean War to an end.

Thus, at the cost of a devastated and still divided country and some 3 million Korean lives, the second great crisis of the Cold War ended with the

[1] A brilliant soldier, who, as Supreme Commander of the Allied Powers had been ruling Japan since 1945 with almost unlimited authority.

Americans committed to containing communism anywhere in the world.

Towards that end, Congress voted billions of dollars to strengthen Western Europe's defences and America's own armed forces; Japan was given a course of education for democracy, vast amounts of aid to rebuild her economy and a treaty of friendship that turned the former enemy into a cherished ally. Meanwhile, the countries of Latin America were awarded an agreement called OAS (Organisation of American States, 1948), which provided security in the event of an attack on any American state. Unfortunately, the 'good neighbour' policy of giving material aid to these poorer countries was nullified by the support which the United States gave to any anti-communist leader, no matter that he might be a brutal dictator like Trujillo of the Dominican Republic, Ubico of Guatemala or Batista of Cuba.

Something also had to be done in South-East Asia, where Indo-China might well become another Korea. During the Japanese occupation, a nationalist movement led by the communist revolutionary, Ho Chi Minh, made such headway that, when the French returned in 1945, they were unable to re-impose their authority in the north-east of the country, which the nationalists called by the pre-colonial name of Vietnam. A gruelling jungle war broke out, in which Ho Chi Minh's guerillas received help from communist China and the USA gave more than a billion dollars' worth of military aid to the French. In 1954, after a disastrous defeat at Dien Bien Phu, the French gave up the struggle and Indo-China became the separate states of Laos, Cambodia and Vietnam, each of which had been an independent and ancient kingdom prior to the arrival of the French in the 1860's. The last of these was divided into North Vietnam, under communist rule, and South Vietnam, a republic, supported by the United States. This was the Korean situation over again and the outcome was to be even worse for American policy.

For the moment, however, steps were taken to create another anti-communist defence, called SEATO (South-East Asia Treaty Organisation, 1954). Its members, the USA, Britain, France, Australia, New Zealand, the Philippines, Pakistan and Thailand, agreed to take joint action against aggression, although, in practice, SEATO was never as strong as NATO. This was largely because none of the members, apart from the USA and Thailand cared very much about Indo-China. France had had enough; Britain was more concerned about defeating communist guerillas in Malaya; Pakistan came in to win American support in her quarrels with India and Australia and New Zealand were there because they had become allies of the USA, since it was obvious that they could no longer look to Britain for protection.

A notable absentee from SEATO was Indonesia, whose nationalist forces had defeated the Dutch in their attempt to re-establish colonial rule. The

USA, opposed as always to old-fashioned European imperialism, used the lever of the Marshall Aid to persuade the Netherlands to recognise Indonesia's independence. Sukarno, the flamboyant President, created a large army, expelled all Dutch citizens, and, by his reckless extravagance, well-nigh ruined the country's economy. His nationalising of foreign enterprises and the advance of PKI (Indonesian Communist Party), which he was thought to support, brought him into collision with two giant American oil companies, whose influence and an army coup were enough to bring about his overthrow. His successor reversed Sukarno's policies and launched a campaign against the communists in which at least a million people were killed.

THE MIDDLE EAST

The policy of containing communism also brought the Americans into the Middle East, which had long been the preserve of Britain and France. Tired of being the whipping-boy of both the Jews and the Arabs, Britain withdrew her troops from Palestine in 1948, whereupon Ben Gurion, the Jewish leader, proclaimed the Republic of Israel, whose soldiers swiftly won the first of their wars against the forces of the Arab League (Egypt, Iraq, Jordan, Lebanon and Syria) and seized more territory than had been allotted to the new state by the United Nations in 1947, when a special UN commission recommended partition.

Jerusalem, the city sacred to Jews, Christians and Muslims, suffered discord, warfare and partition as the Republic of Israel established itself. Western Jerusalem became the Israeli capital in 1950 and the whole city came under Israeli rule after the war of 1967.

The Israeli triumph ensured the undying hostility of the Arab world and the exodus of three-quarters-of-a-million Arabs, who fled from the occupied areas of what was for many years their traditional homeland to eke out a miserable existence in refugee camps in Gaza, Jordan and Syria. Not only did the Palestinian Arabs pose an economic and a moral problem, but they were to provide recruits for the Palestine Liberation Army, dedicated to destroying the state of Israel.

This development put the Americans in a tricky position, because, while they were deeply committed to supporting Israel, they were anxious to avoid antagonising the Arabs and endangering their own access to Middle East oil. Further east, radical nationalists in Iran thrust the young Shah aside in 1951 and nationalised the Anglo-Iranian Oil Company, but they got the country into such financial straits that the Russians seemed likely to step in. So the United States government switched the military aid already provided to the Iranian government to the Shah, enabling him to take control of the country. The Russians were therefore kept out and the British oil monopoly was broken – an outcome that was doubly satisfying to the USA.

Although they seldom saw eye to eye with the British in the Middle East, the Americans did support Britain's formation of the Baghdad Pact (1955),

Mr Krishna Menon (left), India's delegate at the London Conference of August 1956 which failed to resolve the Suez crisis, discusses the affair with Colonel Nasser. Anglo-French paratroops landed at Port Said on 5 November and, on the very next day, Britain and France agreed to a cease-fire!

496

with Turkey, Iran, Iraq and Pakistan, which Dulles, the US Secretary of State, called 'a solid band of resistance against the Soviet Union'. It may have been so, but in other parts of the Middle East, the Arab countries presented anything but a solid front, for there were long-standing feuds between various states and two of them, Syria and Egypt, were already receiving Soviet aid and Iraq was to do so, after a revolution overthrew the monarchy in 1958.

The 'special relationship' that was supposed to exist between the Americans and British was severely shaken by the dramatic events which occurred in Egypt in 1956. There, the continued presence of British advisers and troops was resented by Egyptian army officers who engineered the revolt of 1952, which deposed King Farouk and, two years later, brought Colonel Nasser to power. The ablest Egyptian statesman since Mehemet Ali, Nasser introduced many reforms to alleviate poverty and he took on the leadership of the Arab world in its hatred of Israel. He also sent help to the Algerian rebels against French colonial rule and accepted Russian military and economic aid to Egypt.

In an attempt to woo Nasser away from Russia, Britain proposed an Anglo-American loan to finance the building of the Aswan Dam, a vast irrigation project that would increase food production. The offer was accepted, but Nasser's friendship with various communist states so offended the Americans that they backed out, whereupon Nasser announced that he would nationalise the Suez Canal Company (owned mainly by Britain and France) and pay for the Dam out of its profits.

The upshot was the Suez Crisis of 1956. Israeli troops invaded Sinai, defeated the Egyptian army and captured masses of Russian equipment; British aircraft bombed Egyptian aerodromes and Anglo-French forces landed at Port Said and prepared to move down the Canal, which the Egyptians had already blocked with sunken ships.

This piece of old-fashioned imperialism created an uproar in the United Nations, where the world was diverted by the spectacle of American and Russian delegates joining together to condemn an act of naked aggression. President Eisenhower was furious that anything should have taken place anywhere without his permission; the Russians issued threats and world opinion was so scathingly hostile that Britain and France withdrew their forces and retired from the scene to reflect upon the immense damage they had done to Western democracy and their own prestige.

Although he had suffered a crushing military defeat in the Sinai Peninsula, Nasser was now a popular hero and Israel had won a major victory over her principal enemy, but an indirect consequence of the Suez affair was the total subjugation of Hungary to Russia.

497

Hungary's last battle for freedom, November 1956: Russian soldiers in Budapest watch while an officer advances menacingly on the photographer.

By this time, Stalin was dead. The tyrant who created modern Russia died in 1953 and was succeeded, after some jostling for power, by Nikita Kruschev, who gave the impression of being a less menacing personality and actually criticised some of his late master's misdeeds. In a programme of 'de-Stalinisation', Kruschev had millions of prisoners released from labour camps, reduced the power of the secret police and allowed a few more goods into the shops. This promise of better times had its effect in several of the Iron Curtain countries and, in Hungary, the people dared to demand the withdrawal of Russian occupation troops. This was too much for Kruschev. If one country broke away, the rest of the satellites would demand independence and the whole Soviet security system would be in danger of collapse. In November 1956, taking advantage of UNO's preoccupation with Suez, he ordered Russian tanks into Budapest where the uprising was crushed with vengeful brutality.

10 Cold War II: Co-existence or Confrontation?

If one could forget Hungary and the treatment that was dealt out to the disobedient Poles, Kruschev seemed to be altogether milder and more co-operative than Stalin. He talked about 'peaceful co-existence' with the West, and, unlike Stalin, he left Russia and went about the world, meeting the heads of governments and cracking jokes with workers like some jovial old man of the people.

But it was only a surface thaw. Although the Chinese denounced the Russians for going soft and betraying true Marxist-Leninist teachings, Soviet aid was still being given to any state or party which opposed American influence and Americans continued to support anti-communists in Asia, the Middle East and Latin America.

By means of secret agents and reconnaissance planes, each side kept a ceaseless watch on the other, but, in August 1957, the American nation was stupefied to learn that the Russians had put 'Sputnik', a rocket-launched satellite, into space. The implications were terrifyingly obvious. Similar rockets could carry atomic warheads, and these could fall on American cities, without warning, for the radar defences had suddenly become obsolete. The 'Space Age' had arrived and, with it, the need to concentrate vast resources upon producing space-craft and intercontinental ballistic missiles so powerful that they would deter the other side from using its own equally powerful missiles!

It was the siting of missile-bases a mere 90 miles from the United States which produced the next crisis. In 1958, on the island of Cuba, a revolution, led by a young lawyer named Fidel Castro, overthrew the dictatorship of Fulgencia Batista, whose hateful régime had been propped up for more than a decade by American business interests. In order to improve the lot of the peasants, Castro nationalised the land and seized American property without compensation. When the American government retaliated by refusing to buy Cuba's main crop, sugar, Castro turned for help to the Russians, who supplied him with money, tractors, oil and technical advisers. They also brought in some highly dangerous equipment.

In October 1962, an American spy-plane spotted missile-sites and rocket launch-pads on the island, whereupon the new US President, John F.

Kennedy, at 43 the youngest in American history, ordered a naval blockade of Cuba to stop any missiles arriving. He then told Russia that the sites must be dismantled. Kruschev at first denied that there were any missile-sites and then declared that the Russian ships would go through to Cuba. The United States government ordered rockets to be made ready to fire at Russia and for several days, the world stood on the brink of a nuclear war.

Fortunately, both leaders drew back. Each realised the enormity of power which he held in his hand; talks were started and an agreement was reached that the ships would turn back, the sites would be flattened and the United States would not interfere in Cuban affairs. A special telephone link - a 'hot line' - was installed between Washington and Moscow, so that the two leaders could talk to each other direct in the event of another confrontation. In the following year, the USA, the Soviet Union and Britain signed a Test Ban Treaty, agreeing to stop all tests of nuclear devices in the atmosphere and thereby limit the spread of such weapons.

The Cuban crisis convinced Kennedy and the United States government that they must stand firm against communism in areas where they believed they had a right to act. One of these was Vietnam. Since the French withdrawal of 1954, the North had been ruled by Ho Chi Minh and the

John F. Kennedy (1917-63), President of the USA, whose youth and enthusiasm endeared him to millions in America and abroad. Here seemed to be a man whose liberal ideals could bridge the gulf between East and West and change the world by helping underprivileged people everywhere. In practice, he failed to persuade Congress to accept some important domestic reforms, but in foreign affairs he surmounted the Cuban crisis, concluded the Nuclear Test Ban Treaty and was working earnestly for international peace and co-operation. However, at the time of his murder, he had deeply involved the USA in Vietnam.

South Vietnam, October 1966: a US First Cavalry trooper covers his fellows as they float a wounded comrade to safety in a native boat following a pitched engagement between the Cavalry and the Communist 610th Division.

South by Ngo Dinh Diem, a corrupt Catholic politician, whose position in a mainly Buddhist country, infiltrated by thousands of communist guerillas from the North (the Vietcong), would have been hopeless but for American support. As the Vietcong successes multiplied, Kennedy increased the number of American 'military advisers' and provided funds to build houses, schools and hospitals for the South. But many of the South Vietnamese, whether from fear of the communists among them or from a desire to see their country freed from foreign influence, were not to be won over.

In November 1963, Kennedy was assassinated in Dallas, Texas, and his successor, Lyndon B. Johnson, followed Kennedy's policy, but on a far greater scale. The force of 'military advisers' became an American army more than half-a-million strong, which, with at least the same number of South Vietnamese troops, fought a long bitter war against an elusive enemy, furnished with military supplies from China and the Soviet Union, while between 1964 and 1969 the US Air Force dropped more bombs on North Vietnam than all the air forces had dropped on Europe in the Second World War. But, in vain. This was a conflict which the Americans could not win, because they never had the whole-hearted allegiance of the South and, latterly, as the casualties mounted and the horrors increased, a great part of the American nation became passionately opposed to the war.

Heavy street fighting in Hue, South Vietnam, February 1968: US marines were airlifted to Hue to recover it from Vietcong troops who had been holding the central part of the ancient city.

Highway I, South Vietnam, December 1975: South Vietnamese fleeing before the advancing Communist troops. By now, the final stage of this tragic conflict was being fought between the Vietnamese themselves and the sole hope for many of the losers was to try to escape abroad with the 'Boat People'.

502

From 1969, therefore, the task of the President who succeeded Johnson – Richard Nixon – was to find a way to withdraw the American forces without seeming to leave the South in the lurch. His solution was to arm, feed and clothe a Vietnamese army so large that eventually it would include about half the adult male population of the South. After long negotiation and the spread of fighting into Laos and Cambodia, the USA and the two Vietnams agreed on a cease-fire in January 1973.

Nixon promised to come to the rescue of the South if the North violated the settlement; American troops left the country, and, two years later, when the South Vietnamese government was still trying to subdue an internal revolutionary movement, the North Vietnamese launched their final attack. No help came from America. Saigon fell in April 1975 and the long agony of the Vietnam war ended with total victory for the communists. The sole consolation for the West was that the Cold War seemed to have become less intense, as it gave way to 'détente' – a lessening of the strained relationship which had existed for so long between Russia and the USA. Both were still furnishing their clients with financial aid and weapons, but neither had quite the same grip on his own bloc.

France, for instance, under de Gaulle, refused to go on accepting American leadership, but much more surprising was the split between Russia and China which broke the unity of the communist world. It became public from about 1960, after Kruschev's denunciations of Stalin had offended the little state of Albania, for the Chinese supported the Albanian view that Stalin had been a true Marxist, whereas Kruschev was a 'deviationist', a turncoat who renounced the orthodox communist view that war between East and West was inevitable. So, when Russian aid was withdrawn from Albania, the Chinese sent a limited amount of help and, when China and India had their shooting war on the Indo-Tibetan border, Russia supplied India with military equipment. There were also some territorial disputes and clashes between Russian and Chinese frontier guards.

The fact was that China was becoming stronger and more confident. She regarded herself as the only true Marxist state; her Five Year Plans had greatly raised industrial production and, in 1964, she announced that her scientists had exploded a nuclear bomb. As in Russia, Communist Party officials controlled and directed the economy and every aspect of life.

This was by no means pleasing to Mao Tse-tung. The veteran leader wanted China to live by the communist ideal of a society run by the workers, not by a bureaucratic élite, and, in 1966, he launched the 'Great Proletarian Cultural Revolution' to sweep opposition aside. He appealed to young party loyalists to form themselves into companies of Red Guards and, armed with copies of the 'little red book' of *Thoughts of Chairman Mao*, to travel the length and breadth of the land and purge China of wrong thinking and to make party officials, teachers and civic authorities stand trial and confess their errors.

With Mao raised to the level of God, revolutionary committees took over from the Party, and, for three years, China was convulsed by its 'Cultural Revolution', which dislocated government, industry and education to such an extent that Mao himself realised that this kind of fanaticism had gone too far. In 1969, he called on the army to suppress the Red Guards and restore order. The revered leader went on to complete the turn-about with a startling change in foreign policy, no less than a reconciliation with the USA and Japan.

The split in the communist world had not escaped the Americans' notice and, in 1971, the United States government dropped its long-standing opposition to communist China's membership of the United Nations and bowed to Mao's insistence that Nationalist China (still in Taiwan) should be expelled. In the following year, Nixon became the first American President to visit China and he went on to Moscow for talks with Brezhnev, the successor to Kruschev, who, in these more lenient times, had been allowed to retire to the country.

Edwin E. Aldrin Junior walking on the moon, a photograph taken by his fellow-US-astronaut, Neil Armstrong. With Michael Collins, they had lifted off from Cape Kennedy in *Apollo II* on 16 July 1969 to land 4 days later on the moon in the Lunar Module whose leg can be seen in the picture. After 21 hours, they rejoined Collins in *Apollo II*.

Détente was helped forward by the astonishing feats of scientists and astronauts in their exploration of Space. As already mentioned, Russia took the lead in 1957, when 'Sputnik' went into orbit and, four years later, a Russian became the first man to travel in space. He was soon followed by an American and, in 1969, after intensive research, there occurred what still seems the greatest triumph of 20th-century technology, the landing on the Moon by two American astronauts, whose first hestitant steps were watched by millions of television viewers in their own homes.

After the apparently impossible had been achieved, both countries went on putting robot craft into space to survey the planets and increase man's knowledge of the universe. No other country could afford the colossal cost of space exploration which had as much to do with prestige and military power as with scientific investigation. The 'space race' was of course part of the arms race and it provided both the giant-powers with knowledge of how to annihilate each other and indeed to destroy life on earth.

This understanding of their fearsome capacity resulted in the two rivals getting together to see if it was possible to limit the spread of nuclear weapons. In 1969, they signed the Nuclear Non-proliferation Treaty and persuaded most of the countries of the world to agree not to manufacture atomic bombs, but it was a major weakness of the Treaty that France and China did not sign it, nor, indeed, did Israel, Egypt, Japan, or South Africa. Discussions known as SALT (Strategic Arms Limitation Talks) also took place to find a way to cut back on the development of missiles, because even the two super-powers were beginning to feel the strain of the arms race. Intercontinental ballistic missiles and anti-missile systems were staggeringly expensive and, with the conquest of space and the use of satellites to observe rival countries, it was time to pause and think about putting on the brakes. In their discussions, Nixon and the Russian leaders also got round to minor agreements on space research, pollution and an increase in trade between their countries.

Thus, by the 1970's, tension was easing in Europe and greater causes for anxiety lay in the distrust between Russia and China and in the conflict between Israel and the Arab world.

11 The End of the Old Empires

The Cold War, dominating world history for 30 years, brought many benefits to needy countries, especially the under-developed ones, which have became known as the 'Third World'. Both superpowers handed out aid to their adherents and did their utmost to win over the uncommitted nations with friendly gestures and offers of support. Soviet-American rivalry also played an important part in the break-up of empires, for both the giants were hostile to the old imperialism, particularly the Americans. Brought up on the story of their own war of independence, they felt duty-bound to criticise the European colonial powers and put pressure on them to relinquish their overseas possessions.

During the Second World War, France, Belgium and the Netherlands were occupied by Germany and therefore their governments were unable to maintain authority over their colonies. Indo-China, the East Indies, Burma and Malaya were overrun by the Japanese, whose rapid victories ruined the Europeans' prestige and destroyed the legend of their invincibility. Moreover, during the absence of their former rulers, most of the colonies developed nationalist movements, with leaders like Sukarno and Ho Chi Minh, who had no intention of backing down when the war was over.

As we have seen, the Dutch tried to recover their possessions but, after a long struggle, were forced to accept Indonesia's independence. The French, too, made great efforts to hold on to Indo-China but, even with American backing, they had to admit defeat.

NORTH AFRICA

The French army was determined not to do so in Algeria, because it was considered a part of France and had more than a million French settlers -colons - who owned the best land and ran the country. Opposed to them, a comparatively small number of Algerian nationalists formed the FLN (Front de Libération Nationale) and raised an army which, with support from other Arab countries, engaged the French forces in a savage conflict which lasted 7 years and brought France itself to the verge of civil war. In 1958, the army generals organised a revolt which compelled the Paris government to turn to

General de Gaulle (1890-1970) broadcasting to the French people after he had achieved the difficult task of ending the Algerian war. Throughout his career, he worked to make France strong and independent in world affairs, an aim which caused him to insist on changes in the EEC which favoured France. He was adamant in opposing Britain's entry.

the one man who could save the situation - General de Gaulle, because he stood above politics and was acceptable to the army. But the generals mistook their man. As President of the Fifth Republic, de Gaulle used his power to bring the disastrous war to an end and, in spite of attempts to kill him and overthrow the government, Algeria was granted self-government in 1962. Since Tunisia, Morocco and Mauritania had already attained freedom, the whole of French North Africa was now independent.

Spain allowed the colony of Spanish Sahara to be partitioned between Morocco and Mauritania, a French possession which had opted for independence in 1960. The Spanish government's action was partly in order to win Arab support for its claim on Gibraltar, whose population had voted overwhelmingly to retain its British connection.

There was no question of Italy recovering Libya, her North African colony which had been the battlefield of the desert armies. It became an impoverished monarchy, until the discovery of oil brought wealth and a military coup (1969), led by a young officer named Gadafy. As head of state, Gadafy adopted a policy of inflexible hostility to Israel and a readiness to finance terrorism in various parts of the world.

INDIA

With a Labour government in office from 1945, the British showed a readiness to divest themselves of empire that would have surprised Roosevelt if he had been alive to witness it. Remarkably, they began with India, the most valuable and, for generations, the most cherished of all their possessions.

For more than a century, India had been ruled by a handful of officials and soldiers, who, for the most part, succeeded in bringing order and justice to a vast country where chaos had reigned after the break-up of Mogul power. The British always intended to grant self-government and hoped that India would become a Dominion, like Canada and Australia, but, as happened in other parts of the Empire, there was no agreement about *when* the Indians would be ready to rule themselves. Indeed, many of the British dismissed the aims of the nationalists as no more than fanciful notions, an attitude that was hurtful to educated Indians well aware of their country's cultural past.

After the First World War, the first real steps were taken towards Dominion status when Indians were given control of some aspects of

Mahatma (Mohandas K.) Gandhi (1869-1948) as a young barrister in South Africa where for 20 years he campaigned for justice for the Asian immigrants. In 1914, he returned to India to take the lead in opposing the British *raj* through non-co-operation and civil disobedience. His saintly way of life, concern for the poor and the Untouchables, and his desire for harmony between Hindus and Muslims won millions of followers, but there were many who ignored or opposed his teachings.

509

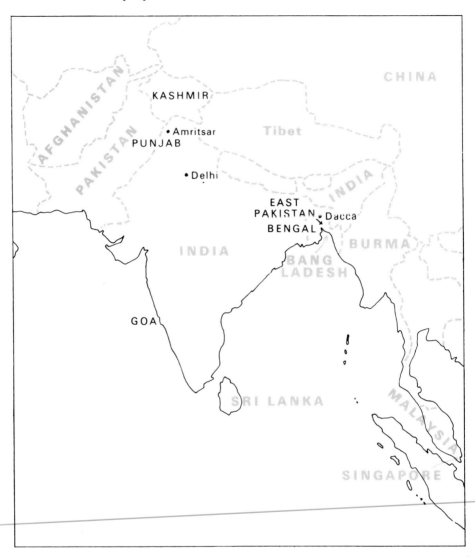

government, such as agriculture and education. By this time, the atmosphere had been profoundly changed by a war in which the Russian, German, Austrian and Ottoman empires had been overthrown, and the USA had proclaimed the principle of national self-determination. The Indian National Congress, now led by the saintly Mahatma Gandhi, objected to the introduction of some repressive security laws and organised a programme of civil disobedience. In spite of Gandhi's appeal for non-violence, riots broke out, in which some Europeans were killed and there occurred the tragic folly of Amritsar, in April 1919, when a British general ordered his men to fire upon an unarmed crowd refusing to disperse. Nearly 400 civilians were killed and any chances of Indian co-operation became even less after Gandhi and Nehru, his chief assistant, were arrested and sent to prison.

However, efforts by both sides to promote goodwill went on slowly, until, in 1935, the provinces were given self-government, so that the Viceroy retained control only of defence and foreign affairs. Unfortunately, by this time, hostility between Hindus and Muslims was causing communal riots and bloodshed; Congress had become to all intents and purposes a Hindu organisation and the Muslim League was putting forward the idea of a separate Muslim state.

In 1942, after the fall of Singapore, the British government sent a mission to India to promise complete self-government after the war in return for Indian help, but Gandhi and Jinnah, the Muslim leader, demanded immediate independence. This was refused and the British continued to rule India. As it happened, only a few Indians went over to the Japanese and the Indian Army fought extremely well in Burma and Africa, so that, in 1946, the British government offered to redeem its promise made four years earlier.

It was easier to talk about self-government than to accept it. One difficulty was the position of some 500 semi-independent princes, whose states

Gandhi with Pandit Jawaharlal Nehru (1889-1964), President of the All India Congress, at Bombay in 1946. More practical and active in Congress politics than Gandhi, Nehru was always his lieutenant and devoted supporter; he disagreed with him on important issues such as industrialisation, but never for a moment disputed the Mahatma's leadership.

comprised about one-third of the sub-continent, but, far worse, was the implacable hatred between Hindus and Muslims. The latter were the minority, but there were nevertheless 70 million of them and, while the politicians argued interminably, the country was disintegrating into chaos and bloodshed.

Suddenly, in February 1947, Attlee, the British Prime Minister, threw out a challenge to bring both parties to their senses. He set a time limit by which the British would leave, thereby forcing the Indians to find a speedy solution to their differences. It had to be partition. India's unity was broken and, on 15 April 1947, the separate states of India and Pakistan came into existence, both free and equal Dominions of the Commonwealth.

The cost of partition was enormous, for, as soon as the British relinquished their rule, Hindus and Muslims let themselves go in a frenzy of slaughter, in which about half-a-million people lost their lives. In the Punjab, as many as 11 million panic-stricken refugees fled across the dividing line, roughly half each way, to find safety among their own people. Even worse for the future outlook, Pakistan consisted of two widely separated parts and there was Kashmir, precious to both sides, with a mainly Muslim population and a Hindu ruler who chose union with India.

One of the countless victims of intolerance was Gandhi himself, who had done his utmost to bring violence to an end. In New Delhi, he was assassinated by one of the Hindu fanatics who detested his expressed love for Muslims and Untouchables, the lowest hereditary class in Hindu society.

Fortunately for India, Nehru, the first Prime Minister, was to prove himself one of the world's foremost statesmen, who, while exerting a moderating influence in international affairs and keeping India uncommitted to either America or Russia, tried to modernise his country and improve the people's living standards. In his 17 years of office, Nehru achieved a great deal; a series of Five Year Plans put through a vast expansion of heavy industry; steps were taken to improve education, to try to abolish the caste system, to reduce privilege and give civil rights to women and Untouchables; almost alone of the Third World countries which gained independence, India remained a parliamentary democracy.

Yet India resisted change more than any other of the developing nations. Traditions of Hindu society, the caste system and the fact that, in spite of industrialisation, the majority of Indians were illiterate peasants, living in villages and cultivating the land in much the same way as their forefathers, made progress difficult. By far the greatest problem was the growth of population, which almost doubled in 30 years after the war, to reach 590 million in 1975. Economic growth could not keep pace with such a rise; the new industries could not provide enough jobs and the land did not produce sufficient food to feed the people, so that a predominantly agricultural country had to spend precious resources on buying imported food and, in famine years, thousands of Indians starved to death.

Nehru's policy of peaceful co-existence with all other nations was not always consistent, for he approved the armed seizure of the tiny Portuguese state of Goa and, like all Indians, he resented the existence of Pakistan and was ready to use force to keep Kashmir out of Pakistani hands. Then, in 1962, a dispute about the frontier between India and China led to fighting and a humiliating defeat for India.

After Nehru's death in 1964, his daughter, Mrs Indira Gandhi, came to the fore as a popular leader, who defied the more conservative elements in the Congress Party and won a commanding victory at the polls in 1971. After that, in spite of accusations of corrupt practices and a period when she ruled by decree, censoring the press and imprisoning her critics, Mrs Gandhi remained the most forceful personality in Indian politics. Her popularity with the masses enabled her to survive many tribulations, including a crisis in India's relations with Pakistan.

From independence, Pakistan had to face enormous difficulties. The new country was much weaker than its neighbour; it was divided geographically into two widely separated parts, whose peoples differed from one another in language, writing, culture and racial characteristics. The Bengalis of East Pakistan, poor and extremely numerous, had little in common, apart from religion, with the militaristic Punjabis of West Pakistan. Jinnah, the ablest leader, died soon after independence and, with no-one else respected by both parts of the state, there followed a decade of disorder with an army officer, General Ayub Khan, taking control as a 'strong' President, who was in effect a dictator. From 1958-69, Khan's policy was aimed at military survival against India and economic advance, including land reform, but the failure of the 1965 invasion of Kashmir and a general lack of progress caused the army to replace him with another general, who restored parliamentary elections. These revealed how deeply divided the country really was, for East Pakistan voted overwhelmingly for separation, while West Pakistan wanted a united Pakistan and sent an army to put an end to the Bengali break-away. During the fighting, millions of terrified refugees fled across the border into India, creating a problem which Mrs Gandhi's government 'solved' by ordering the well-equipped Indian army to invade East Pakistan (1971). Dacca, the capital, was captured in a matter of days, the Pakistani forces surrendered, a new independent state called Bangladesh ('Bengali land') was proclaimed and Jinnah's dream of a united Muslim Pakistan fell into ruins.

Thus, within 30 years of independence from British rule, the Indian sub-continent was divided into three hostile states: Pakistan, which in 1977, reverted to rule by a military dictator and, with Russian designs on Afghanistan, stood in the front line of the West's defences against Soviet expansion; Bangladesh, a desperately poor, over-populated country, which also accepted rule by army officers, and India, a democracy, whose leaders made much of their peaceful non-aligned policies, yet who had acted aggressively against neighbouring states and had made a treaty of friendship with the Soviet Union in return for the materials of war.

TROPICAL AFRICA

Decolonisation - the granting of independence by the imperial powers - presented more problems in Africa than in Asia, where, as we have seen, India and Pakistan became independent in 1947. Ceylon, re-named Sri Lanka, and Burma followed suit in 1948, Indonesia in 1949 and Malaya, after the defeat of a communist guerilla movement, in 1957. The French had by then withdrawn from Indo-China and, in the Middle East and North Africa, a whole group of states - Syria, Lebanon, Libya, Tunisia, Morocco and the Sudan - divested themselves of their colonial past without much difficulty.

This was largely due to the fact that most of these countries had educated leaders and centuries-old traditions of civilisation. In short, they were capable of governing themselves as modern nations, but the situation appeared to be quite different in the tropical countries of Africa.

The colonies which had been formed in the 19th century with little regard to tribal areas or even to geography, mostly had low standards of living, little formal education, poor communications and little sense of national unity. Some countries possessed great mineral wealth, but, generally speaking, arable land was neither plentiful nor especially fertile and the Europeans' main interest was to produce 'cash crops', such as cocoa, coffee, tobacco, groundnuts and rubber, for export. Not much was done to improve food production for the Africans' own needs and colonial governments tended to leave education to missionary societies, whose schools could cater for only a minority of children, although there were a few outstanding secondary schools, which became training grounds for Africa's future leaders. Tropical African society was composed of tribes, whose rivalries and differences in language and culture made it difficult to see how they would work peaceably together after they gained independence. However, two of the much maligned colonial powers, Britain and France, did take some positive steps to guide their colonies along the road to self-government and, after the Second World War, Britain's Colonial Development scheme provided millions of pounds to improve agriculture, to combat pests like the tse-tse fly and to build roads, factories, schools and colleges. Even so, there were bound to be arguments about the pace of political change and some African leaders, like Nkrumah, Kenyatta and Banda, were put in prison for the same kind of activities which had landed Gandhi and Nehru in Indian jails.

Julius Nyerere (left) and Kwame Nkrumah, two of Africa's best-known political leaders, meet at Accra, Ghana, in 1961, when President Nkrumah was beginning to wield authoritarian power and Nyerere had not yet become President of Tanzania. Perhaps it was this visit that decided him to adopt less flamboyant policies in his own country.

In the British colony of Kenya, where there was a relatively large white settler population, a liberation movement called Mau Mau waged a terrorist campaign from 1952-6 which was put down by regular troops and, as already mentioned, the French *colons* in Algeria fought a much more prolonged war against the nationalists.

In 1955, there were only 5 independent African states, but, once having made up their minds to go, Britain, France and Belgium departed with such speed that, by 1970, there were more than 40 independent states and the days of white minority rule in the rest of Africa seemed to be numbered. The Gold Coast and British Togoland combined to form Ghana (a name derived from the ancient and somewhat distant kingdom of Ghana), which was the first colony in tropical Africa to become independent, when it did so in 1957. It seemed to be an ideal choice, for this was a country with good farming land, valuable mineral deposits, a thriving cocoa industry and an articulate leader, Kwame Nkrumah, who became the elected Prime Minister.

Ghana's freedom boosted the hopes of nationalists in other territories and, between 1960 and 1964, Britain granted self-rule to Nigeria, Sierra Leone, Tanganyika (which, with Zanzibar, became Tanzania), Uganda, Kenya, Nyasaland (Malawi) and Northern Rhodesia (Zambia). Where there were only a few white settlers, the hand-over usually went smoothly, with expressions of goodwill, promises of continued aid and Commonwealth membership, but things were more difficult in colonies with a large white minority, owning most of the property and the best land, and claiming that it was they who had developed the country. For a time, Britain tried to shelve this problem by supporting the idea of federations - Kenya, Tanganyika and Uganda in one, the two Rhodesias and Nyasaland in another - in which the whites would retain political power, but when these collapsed in the face of demands for majority rule, the British settlers, like the Algerian *colons*, found themselves abandoned by their own kin.

In Northern Rhodesia, elections were held which brought to power the African leader, Kenneth Kaunda who in 1964 became the first president of his country, an independent republic re-named Zambia. Events took a similar course in Nyasaland, which achieved independence in the same year under the name of Malawi, with Hastings Banda, an African doctor, as prime minister.

Committed to giving priority to black interests, Britain denied independence to Southern Rhodesia, where only a few Africans had a vote, so, in 1965, the White Rhodesians' Prime Minister, Ian Smith, made a unilateral declaration of independence (UDI), which invoked the wrath of the United Nations and demands by black African states for armed intervention, which Britain refused. With help from South Africa, the 'illegal' régime held out for 14 years, but, in the end, as should have been evident from the start, black majority rule had to be granted in a country where Africans outnumbered whites by more than 25 to 1, and which was renamed the Republic of Zimbabwe.

The French took much the same view as the British, feeling that, once they had lost Algeria, there was no point in hanging on to less valuable colonies. French Guinea, following Ghana's example, demanded and received independence as Guinea in 1958, which led to French West Africa and French Equatorial Africa dissolving into 12 separate states - Ivory Coast, Upper Volta, Niger, Chad, Central African Republic, Gabon, Cameroon, Mali, Dahomey (later called Benin), Guinea, Senegal, Congo People's Republic - and Madagascar became the Malagasy Republic.

In 1960, the Belgians, unnerved by outbreaks of violence, quit the Congo (Zaïre) so hurriedly that the country collapsed into a state of blood-thirsty chaos, which became civil war when the copper-rich province of Katanga broke away to try to become a separate state. A strong UN force was brought in and, by 1965, sufficient order had been established for an elected government to take office. It was at once dismissed by the chief of the army, who, declaring himself to be both President and Prime Minister, assumed dictatorial power.

Lubumbashi (formerly Elisabethville), Zaïre, 1961: white mercenaries serving under Moise Tshombe, leader of Katanga's breakaway. Later, as premier of Zaïre, Tshombe used drastic measures to combat a serious rebellion; he was dismissed in 1965 and Colonel Mobutu assumed supreme power.

The one country which shared none of the sudden enthusiasm for African independence was Portugal, the oldest of the colonial powers, but a poor country which derived a good deal of benefit from its colonies.

Its Fascist government, headed by Dr Salazar, had nothing to fear from public opinion in its repression of black nationalists nor, as it happened, from the United States, which turned a blind eye to what was going on in Mozambique and Angola, because Portugal's naval bases were essential to NATO. Hence, while most of Africa was achieving self-government in the 1960's, Portugal maintained white rule in its colonies with the aid of a powerful armed force. However, nationalist organisations, armed and supported by neighbouring black states, gradually exerted such pressure on Mozambique and Angola that the Portuguese could no longer afford the cost of what was amounting to full-scale war. Salazar's successor was overthrown in 1974 by an army revolt and the new government withdrew its white settlers and granted full independence to Mozambique, Angola and Guinea-Bissau.

By this time, it was becoming clear that self-rule by Africans was not going to mean Western-style parliamentary democracy and that the hoped-for unity and strength of the new Africa was an illusion. The colonial powers had given the African peoples little training in Western political skills - they had hardly had time to do so - and, in many places, the tribe was the focus of

517

loyalty, not the nation. After the Congo (Zaïre) disaster, a similar tragedy occurred in Nigeria, the largest and most heavily populated British colony in Africa.

With over 50 million inhabitants, valuable minerals, oil and some 40 years of progress towards self-government, Nigeria's future looked promising when independence was granted in 1960. But this vast geographical area had no real unity. As in most African states, there were many peoples, the principal ones being Hausa in the North, proud semi-nomadic traders living under the rule of Muslim emirs, the Yorubas of the Western Region, farmers and craftsmen, and the Ibos of the Eastern Region, talented busy people whose industriousness was disliked by the other peoples.

The constitution was a federal one, with regional governments and a central government, whose first prime minister, Balewa, was a Hausa. From the outset, there was discontent, with allegations of corruption and the Yorubas and Ibos complaining that Hausas were getting all the best jobs. In 1966, the central government was overthrown by an army coup in which Balewa was assassinated and Colonel Gowon assumed power and the task of trying to put an end to the wholesale killing of Ibos in regions outside their own tribal lands. In 1967, after the Ibos had declared their own Eastern Region the separate state of Biafra, civil war broke out, which lasted for nearly three years and took a dreadful toll of life, from the fighting, starvation and disease. Overwhelmed by superior forces, the Biafrans surrendered in January 1970, but the expected annihilation of the Ibo people did not occur. Instead, Gowon did his utmost to bring about reconciliation, so that, within a remarkably short time, Nigeria, almost alone among African states, moved into a healthy economic position.

However, the crushing of Biafra, coming so soon after the civil war in the former Belgian Congo (Zaïre), pointed a grim warning to the dangers of tribalism. Where the continent desperately needed peaceful development, there was all too often bitter rivalry leading to political upheavals in which the coup, a swift seizure of power, usually by the army, became the accepted solution to a country's difficulties. Gowon himself was deposed by the military élite which had brought him to power, and, much earlier, in 1966, Nkrumah, Ghana's 'Founder of the Nation', was overthrown while he was visiting China. His reckless extravagance and dictatorial style of government brought about the downfall of this gifted man who had been so full of ideas for his country's advance. His dilemma was the dilemma of all the Third World leaders: how to eradicate poverty and raise the people's standard of living without the vast sums of capital needed for irrigation, agricultural reform and industrial development.

Another country which suffered the growing pains of nationhood was Uganda, where tribal and regional rivalries caused Obote, the Prime

Jomo Kenyatta (1889-1978) arriving at London Airport in 1962: a Kikuyu, educated at the London School of Economics, he returned to Africa when over 50 to become president of KANU (Kenya African National Union). He spent several years in prison for managing the Mau Mau movement and, on his release, took over leadership of his country's affairs. In 1964, he became Kenya's first president, when it became a republic within the Commonwealth.

Minister, to assume absolute power and, in 1971, he, like Nkrumah, was deposed while out of the country, by a military coup. Its leader, General Idi Amin, a brutal mountebank, crushed all potential opposition, expelled the 40 000 strong Asian community and aroused such fear and hatred that, in 1979, he himself was overthrown by a liberation movement from Tanzania.

A happier state of affairs prevailed in Kenya, where Jomo Kenyatta provided firm leadership, without resorting to the tyranny of Nkrumah or Amin. The country possessed few natural resources and there were tribal jealousies and prosperous Asian and European communities, which accounted for the introduction of one-party rule and a policy of Africanisation. A hero-figure, who inspired the same kind of respect as Tito in Yugoslavia, Kenyatta adopted the role of a benevolent dictator, guiding his people along like a wise old father, to enable Kenya to avoid financial and political anarchy.

Another outstanding leader was Julius Nyerere, who, as President of Tanzania, gave his country - one of the poorest in Africa - many years of stable government. He, too, instituted one-party rule, because his aim was to build a socialist state by means of extensive nationalisation, self-help and village projects. He wanted to create a country which would be different from the Russian industrial state and, in keeping with passionate belief in equality, a total contrast to South Africa.

THE CARIBBEAN

Across the Atlantic, in the Caribbean Sea, the islands came under European dominance from the time of Columbus (1492). The large Spanish islands of Cuba, Haiti and the Dominican Republic (Hispaniola), and Puerto Rico had become self-governing by the 20th century, when they suffered much turbulence and corruption which resulted in American intervention, until Cuba broke away in 1953.

The British islands lay scattered and the problem of granting independence seemed to be chiefly one of size. In 1958, Britain brought about the Federation of the West Indies, in the hope that it would exist as an independent unit. However, some of the larger islands felt that they were being saddled with small backward islands which would be a drain on their resources. Jamaica and Trinidad therefore withdrew and were at once granted independence. The Federation was dissolved in 1962: St Kitts, Nevis and Anguilla were formed into an independent group; Barbados became independent in 1966 and Britain devised a scheme whereby the rest of the small islands became Associated States, having internal self-government, but leaving defence and foreign policy to Britain. North of the West Indies proper, the

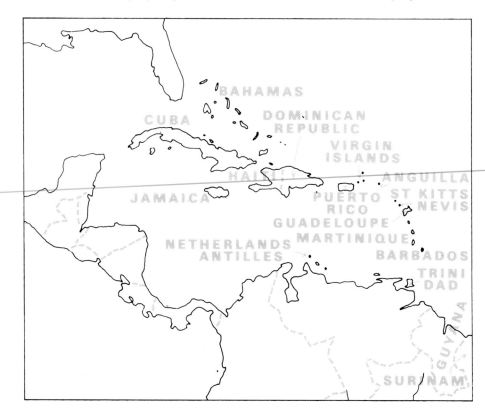

Caribbean political leaders round the Conference table in London, 1956, when Mr Norman Manley (Jamaica), Dr Eric Williams (Trinidad and Tobago) and Sir Grantley Adams (Barbados) played prominent parts in the creation of the short-lived West Indian Federation. It was defunct by 1961.

Bahamas had a British governor until 1973, when they became independent. Although not free from racial and economic problems, the ex-British states managed to retain a reasonable calm.

In 1917 the United States bought the Virgin Islands, formerly the Danish West Indies, from Denmark and they became a USA territory, while, in 1946, the French possessions, Guadeloupe and Martinique, were each granted the status of a *département* of France. The Netherlands Antilles, consisting of 6 small islands in Dutch control since the 17th century, were given domestic self-rule in 1954, while remaining part of the Kingdom of Netherlands. On the mainland of South America, Surinam (formerly Netherlands Guiana) became a self-governing part of that kingdom until 1975, when it was granted independence.

In 1968, the former British West Indian islands created the Caribbean Free Trade Area, which was joined by Guyana (formerly British Guiana), the South American mainland state formed in 1966. Like many emergent nations, Guyana favoured Marxist policies and, to the disapproval of the USA, made friendly approaches to Cuba.

521

SOUTH AFRICA

By the end of the 1970's, the one part of Africa where black nationalism had not triumphed was South Africa, which had become a Dominion of the British Empire in 1910. At that time, about one third of the white inhabitants were British, nearly all the rest being Boers of Dutch descent, who had long since severed any connection with the Netherlands. The entire white population was outnumbered four to one by Africans, mainly Bantu of various tribes and there were two other large groups of non-whites, the 'Coloureds' of mixed descent and Asians from the Indian sub-continent, whose forbears had come to work in the sugar plantations of Natal during the last part of the 19th century.

From 1910, the government was dominated by Boers, the first prime ministers being Botha (to 1919) and Smuts, both of them heroes of the South African War, but afterwards firm supporters of the British connection, so that they took South Africa into the First World War on the Allied side. This attitude was not pleasing to the Afrikaaner (Boer) Nationalists, who came to power in 1924, under Hertzog.

The Nationalists never relented from their belief that white Europeans were the master race, destined to govern black people and to rule the land

The dreary reality of apartheid: a bridge over railway lines has separated passageways for blacks and whites.

which belonged to them, they said, because their ancestors had been there before the Bantu and had created its farms, cities and industries.

When the South African parliament voted by a narrow majority in 1939 to join the war against Hitler's Germany, Hertzog relinquished the leadership to Smuts, who became recognised as a major statesman of the world, a keen supporter of the Commonwealth and the United Nations. The fact of their own prime minister being on friendly terms with people who accepted the idea of racial equality was highly offensive to the Boers and, in the 1948 election, the Nationalist Party, led by Dr Malan, came to power pledged to maintain white supremacy and a policy called 'apartheid'.

Apartheid meant segregation of the races, though its defenders said it merely meant 'separate development', whereby the blacks and the whites would have their own territories, towns and ways of life. In practice, apartheid deprived non-whites of civil liberties, such as the right to vote, to form trade unions, to go about freely, to marry someone of a different race, to attend major schools and universities, to dwell or run businesses in areas reserved for whites - and those areas amounted to more than 80 per cent of South Africa. In this society, the Africans were kept at a great disadvantage because so much less money was spent on their education and welfare than on those of the whites. The police were given far-ranging powers and the 1950 Suppression of Communism Act enabled the authorities to use harsh measures against those who spoke out against this oppressive system - and they included many white liberals and Christians.

A central feature of apartheid was the creation of eight reserves or *bantustans*, as 'homelands' for black South Africans in which they would eventually be allowed to govern themselves. Blacks could be forcibly moved to a bantustan from a 'white area', but, since the bantustans comprised only 14 per cent of the country and were so poor and arid that they could not possibly become self-supporting, blacks had to find employment as migrant workers in the towns and factories of the white areas.

Resistance to the Nationalists was almost impossible in a police state, but the Africans adopted Gandhi's tactics of civil disobedience against the pass laws requiring them to carry identity cards. On one such occasion, in 1960, at Sharpeville in Transvaal, the police opened fire, killing 67 Africans and wounding many more. This incident outraged world opinion, without shaking the South African government or stopping the flow of foreign investment into the country's industries, which produced such economic growth based chiefly on mineral resources and cheap African labour, that, by the mid-1960's, white South Africans had the highest income per head of any people in the world. The United Nations, the communist states and the Organisation of African Unity (founded by African states in 1963) all condemned apartheid and called for economic sanctions against South

Africa, but, while Britain's Labour government might refuse to sell arms, France was ready to do so and there were plenty of countries, including some of the black states, prepared to trade with the white supremacists. Protest largely took the form of cancelling sporting tours and expelling South Africa from the Olympic Games.

An issue that invoked condemnation by the International Court of Justice of the United Nations was South Africa's continued presence in Namibia, the territory which was formerly called German South-West Africa. In 1920, by the terms of the Treaty of Versailles, it was entrusted to South Africa as a mandate of the League of Nations to be prepared for independence. After the Second World War, South Africa declined to enter into a new trusteeship agreement required by the United Nations or to withdraw its administration. This decision provoked African resentment in Namibia, with strikes, disorders and guerilla attacks from Angola and Zambia. The South African government stated that it accepted the principle that the territory should attain independence and, in 1975, began talks with various ethnic groups, but SWAPO (South West Africa People's Organisation) denounced this development on the grounds that the talks were not being held with properly-elected representatives. As a result, the National Assembly of 1979, whose election was organised by the South Africans, appeared to stand little chance of establishing stability and freedom in Namibia.

By the late 1970's, the situation in South Africa was considerably changed by a drop in the price of gold and huge rises in oil prices; far more dangerous was the situation in Namibia, the independence of the former Portuguese colonies and of Southern Rhodesia (Zimbabwe), because this made South Africa vulnerable for the first time to armed attack from states bordering her northern frontier. Could a country, however rich and well-armed, whose ruling class numbered less than 5 million whites, survive for long against world-wide hostility?

12 Latin America in Search of a Future

The Great Depression produced an era of violence in Latin America, as military cliques and populist dictators seized power and revolutions became commonplace. During the Second World War, when the continent was cut off from sources of foreign goods, there was further industrialisation, which drew hundreds of thousands of peasants into the cities. But governments did little to see that the great profits brought benefits to the workers; furthermore, the population was increasing faster than economic growth, so that the gulf widened between the wealthy few and the hungry masses. In these circumstances, people looked in various directions for solutions to their problems: to strong leaders and military take-overs, to Marxism, Christian Democrat parties and 'popular fronts' of left-wing groups.

In Argentina, Juan Perón, who had been one of the leaders of an earlier

Juan Perón and his wife Eva ('Evita') at Buenos Aires in 1948, when their social and economic policies seemed to be working well. Eva's looks and personality held tremendous appeal to the masses; she had genuine gifts as a political leader and Perón's career went steadily downhill after her early death in 1952.

military coup, was elected President in 1946 and, for nearly 10 years, he ruled the country with the kind of flair which had made Mussolini (whom he admired) so popular in Italy. His power rested upon the support of the army, the labour unions and the masses of peasants who had flooded into Buenos Aires. By redistributing some of Argentina's wealth, he raised the workers' living standards and his attacks on foreign business interests appealed to nationalists. But the economy was not strong enough to stand the strain of his social welfare programme and, as his dictatorship became more extreme, he lost the support of the Church, the middle-class and the army, until, isolated, he was overthrown in 1955 and forced into exile in Spain.

The Perón legend - *Peronismo* - lived on, for the working-class remembered him as the only leader who had ever helped them and the extreme right longed for a return to his fascist measures. So, in 1973, he was back in office, only to die a year later, without having done anything to solve his country's problems. Once again, the armed forces took charge and yet another general was sworn in as President.

Meanwhile, Bolivia had a revolution in 1952, which gave land reform to the peasants; Guatemala's revolutionary government was overthrown in 1954 by right-wing rebels aided by the CIA, (Central Intelligence Agency of the USA); Venezuela, growing rich from its oil, had a revolution in 1958 which actually produced a democratic constitution, and Brazil embarked upon an expansionist programme which produced inflation and chronic discontent. Peru, whose dependence on aid from the USA was resented by left-wing groups, came to be ruled by a pro-American military junta.

In 1959, occurred the Cuban Revolution, which made a far greater impact than any of the other upheavals, for, as we have seen, it brought the world to the brink of nuclear disaster. Further, its leader, Castro, became convinced that it was Cuba's mission to keep 'continuous revolution' going and to free Latin America from economic servitude.

In the 1960's, Cuban-inspired guerilla movements occurred in Bolivia, Peru, Venezuela and Guatemala, usually with the aim of winning over rural areas to some kind of peasant communism. The results were disappointing because the rural poor tended to be apathetic and the revolutionaries turned instead to urban terrorism.

Cuba, a small island, heavily dependent upon its sugar crop, could not have survived, much less interfered in other countries, without support from the USSR, whose leaders undoubtedly considered the money to be well spent, since the actual amount must have been minuscule compared with the billions of dollars which the USA continued to pour into Latin America. Moreover, Castro's education programme was designed to train the scientists and technicians who would be needed throughout South America when successful revolutions took place, as Cubans believed they must.

Moscow, May 1963: obviously dressed by different tailors - but full of mutual regard - are Fidel Castro, the President of Cuba, and Nikita Kruschev, the Soviet leader, seen together at Kruschev's out-of-town house, near Moscow.

Ernesto, 'Che', Guevara, the Argentine writer, guerrilla leader and cult-hero of the revolutionary Left everywhere, played a leading role in the Cuban revolution which overthrew Batista. Castro rewarded him with an important post in the new government, but Guevara slipped away to organise guerrilla warfare in Bolivia. During a clash with US-trained forces in 1967, he was captured and shot.

527

One country, however, which still had some leanings towards democracy was Chile, where, in 1970, probably for the first time in history, a communist government was legally *elected*, without revolution or civil war. A coalition of left-wing groups called Popular Unity won the election and brought into office, as President, a thorough-going Marxist named Salvador Allende, who did not hesitate to nationalise banks, businesses and the copper industry and to redistribute the land.

These measures aroused the wrath of the USA and, by scaring away investment, made it difficult for Allende to carry out major schemes to abolish poverty. His parliamentary majority was precarious, and he was frustrated by middle-class opposition on one side and by revolutionary extremists on the other. In 1973, the Popular Unity government was destroyed by the armed forces and Allende died by murder or suicide.

If the Cuban Revolution gave impetus to revolutionary movements, it also spurred the rise of Christian Democrat parties in the continent which has the largest concentration of Roman Catholics in the world. The Church remained strongly anti-communist, but showed signs that it was moving away from its traditional conservative attitude to support policies aimed at reducing poverty and illiteracy.

The Cuban Revolution also prompted the setting up of various trade organisations. The *Alliance for Progress*, for example, was founded in 1961 as a partnership between the USA and Latin American countries; most of the finance came from Washington, where Americans believed that the Alliance would create prosperity, as the best defence against left-wing revolution. In fact, things did not quite work out as the planners expected, for, while the money was welcome, Latin American people went on resenting United States dominance; indeed, the very fact that the USA detested communism tended to make communism popular!

Nevertheless, it was recognised that co-operation between the states must increase if the gap between Latin America and the developed world was to be narrowed. After 150 years of independence, many of its problems seemed no nearer solution, yet the continent possessed enormous potential riches and its own distinctive contribution to music, architecture, literature, sport and race relations. The danger was that Latin America would succumb to extremism of the Right or Left: the hope was that it would offer an example to the rest of the Third World.

13 The Oil-rich Middle East

Three happenings in the Middle East which made a major impact on world affairs, were the withdrawal of French and British influence, the creation of the state of Israel and the rise of the oil states.

The decade after 1945 saw the end of French and British control of countries which had formerly been part of the Ottoman Empire: Syria, Lebanon, Iraq, Palestine and Jordan. During this phase, Britain also agreed to depart from the Sudan and the Canal Zone of Egypt. There followed the Suez Crisis of 1956, a feeble attempt by two European powers to re-assert their dominance and it ended in failure, with the United States and the Soviet Union poised to step into their shoes and win over 'clients' with offers of help. Israel could not survive without American support and Egypt and Syria needed Russian arms and technical aid against Israel. Turkey, Pakistan, Iran

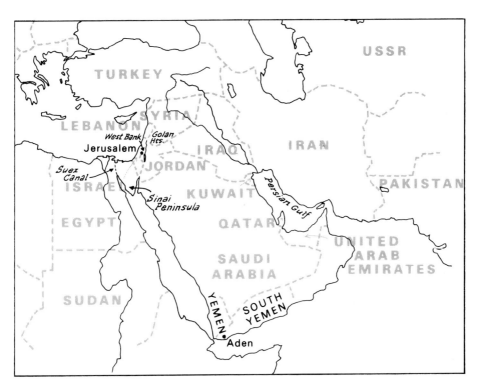

and Iraq (for a time) joined the Baghdad Pact as part of the Western defence system against communism.

With the Canal, India and Singapore (which became self-governing in 1959) gone, Britain realised that there was no longer any point in keeping up a 'presence' east of Suez and, therefore, in the 1960's, British troops began to be withdrawn from various positions along the fringes of Arabia - Kuwait, Aden, South Yemen, Qatar on the Persian Gulf and the United Arab Emirates (formerly known as the Trucial States).

By this time, Israel had won the wars of 1948 and 1956 and, in spite of Arab trade boycotts, was making great economic progress. But a Palestine nationalist organisation called *El Fatah* mounted guerilla attacks on Israeli settlements, which were answered by reprisal raids on refugee bases in Jordan and the Lebanon. In 1967, Nasser, in a new bid for Arab leadership, called for an Islamic holy war to wipe Israel off the map, whereupon the Israelis got their blow in first, destroying the Egyptian airforce on the ground and capturing the whole of Sinai, the Old City of Jerusalem, the West Bank of the Jordan and the Golan Heights on the Syrian border. The Six-Day War, as it was called, enlarged Israel and raised the Israelis' morale, but it solved no problems. The Arab states still refused to recognise the existence of Israel and the Palestinians were as determined as ever to go on fighting. So much so that the PLO (Palestine Liberation Organisation, formed in 1964) became a major force in politics, gathering world-wide support and, eventually, representation in the UN Assembly.

Nasser died in 1970 and was succeeded by Anwar Sadat, a more subtle politician, who realised that Egypt, with a fast-growing population and widespread poverty, could not afford to go on piling up debts to Russia for the supply of arms, but must not lose face with the rest of the Arab world. Having tried vainly to persuade Israel to withdraw from occupied territory, perhaps through exasperation with the Russians' domineering attitude, he ordered all the Soviet 'advisers' to leave the country, and took the gamble of ordering a sudden attack on Israeli positions in Sinai on 6 October 1973, at the time of the Jewish festival of Yom Kippur. Syria and Iraq, also armed with Russian weapons, made a simultaneous assault on the Golan Heights, but the Israelis, fighting with the knowledge that defeat would mean national extinction, beat their enemies back within a fortnight.

Although the Yom Kippur War resulted in stalemate, there was a glimmer of hope in that both sides showed signs of wanting to find a peaceful solution, provided that Egypt and Syria could recover their lost territories, Israel could have her existence recognised and some way could be found to placate the Palestinians. The chances of the super-powers being drawn into the conflict were all too real, so there was almost universal applause for Sadat, when he went to Jerusalem to meet Israeli leaders and to issue a joint

Egypt's President Anwar Sadat received the Nobel Peace Prize, together with Israel's Prime Minister Menachem Begin, for their efforts to bring peace between their countries. This photograph of March 1979 shows them in Washington after signing the peace treaty. Sadat was assassinated in 1981 by Egyptian army officers who hated his policies.

declaration of 'No more war'. The difficulties that lay ahead were underlined when a group of Arab states, including Syria, Saudi Arabia, Iraq, Libya and Algeria, totally condemned Sadat's peace moves and the PLO leader told Arabs everywhere to take 'a stronger grip on your guns'. At this, the Israelis became less co-operative and a new hard-line government rejected any idea of withdrawal from the lands conquered in 1967.

The American President took an active part in encouraging the peace talks because, behind the West's concern to calm down this explosive part of the world, lay an acute anxiety about Middle East oil. Prior to the Second World War, the oil wells of Rumania, Mexico, Venezuela, Texas and California had supplied a good part of the needs of developed countries, but the enormous increase in consumption of oil for road transport, aircraft and industry after 1945 led to exploitation of oil resources in the countries of the Persian Gulf. In 1974, Iran's production was 30 times greater than in 1945, Saudi Arabia's 140 times greater, and, in less than 20 years, the tiny state of Kuwait became one of the world's biggest producers. Western oil companies, mainly British and American, held most of the oil concessions, but, as the independent countries grew stronger, they changed the terms of the

Two Arabs in traditional dress on the sand dunes of Abu Dhabi: beyond them one of the oil installations which produce the fabulous wealth of this tiny state, one of the United Arab Emirates on the shore of the Persian Gulf. Besides oil, Abu Dhabi possesses some of the largest reserves of natural gas in the world.

532

Sanandaj, north-west Iran, March 1979: a Kurd watches tensely, as gunmen on guard follow his gaze, during intermittent shooting in the city. Kurdistan is a mountainous region in parts of Iran, Iraq, Turkey and the USSR and the Kurds fought bitterly for independence against, first, the Turks and, until 1975, against Iraq.

concessions (or put an end to them), so that they held control and received far greater royalties.

The ruling élite of the oil-producing countries became not only fabulously rich, but immensely powerful, as it became obvious that they could threaten the very livelihoods of the United States, Japan and Western Europe. They set up OAPEC (Organisation of Arab Petroleum Exporting Countries) to advance their interests, and, when the Yom Kippur War broke out in 1973, they used oil as a political weapon to threaten countries sympathetic to Israel. By the late 1970's, they had raised the price of oil so high that it became a major factor in the world's economic recession.

But, if the Arab countries were united in their oil policy and hatred of Israel, they were divided among themselves on many issues. There were political differences, in that some of the states, notably Egypt, Iraq and Libya, had strong republican régimes, which were disliked by the kings of Saudi Arabia, Jordan and the rulers of smaller Arab states, who had no love for the modernisation programmes of Arab socialism. In the republics, there were differences between Marxists and orthodox Muslims, which made it difficult

533

for Syria and Iraq (both on close terms with the USSR) to get on with Egypt, whose Soviet advisors had been dismissed; in the Lebanon, hostility between the Christian and Muslim halves of the population led to a civil war in which the PLO took a hand. Warlike Kurds in the north of Iraq kept up a long-running battle for independence; rival nationalist groups fought each other in South Yemen, while in the adjoining state of the Yemen, republicans supported by Egypt defeated royalists supported by Saudi Arabia.

Though not Arab, Iran typified the instability of the Middle East. The Shah Pahlavi, who was restored to power in 1951, ruled like an enlightened despot, trying to drag his 30 million subjects from their medieval lot into the 20th century by forcing them to accept land reform, public health schemes, industrialisation and social uplift. Like any despot, he oppressed those who opposed his policy: Shi'ite (strict Muslim) religious leaders, traditionalists and communists, who detested his western ideas, personal wealth and pro-USA stance. In 1979, he was overthrown and driven into exile by a revolution, whose fanatical leader, the aged Ayatollah Khomeini, proclaimed an Islamic Republic. As in the French and Russian revolutions and in many ex-colonies of the world, it looked as if the people, in getting rid of one tyrant, had landed themselves with a worse tyranny.

Tehran, March 1980: Iran's strong man, Ayatollah Khomeini, addressing Muslim students still holding 52 American hostages, in a meeting at his residence in north Tehran. Ayatollah Khomeini said, 'Our hostage taking proved to the poor countries of the world that the great devils (USA) can be defeated.'

534

14 Today's World

The world in the last quarter of the 20th century is a world in which changes have been swifter and more dramatic than those which occurred in earlier historical periods. Since 1900, an unparalleled increase in wealth has been brought about by industry's greatly increased productivity, based, since the Second World War, on new technologies. In the United States, for example, industry produced sufficient wealth, if it were divided equally, to give every person an income of $ 770 in 1938, but, by 1975, this figure had risen to over $ 6500. In the post-war years, industrial growth in West Germany and Italy rose by more than 5 per cent a year, compared with about 2 per cent in Britain, while Japan, with a growth rate of 9.8 per cent per annum in the 1960's, became the world's third industrial power.

Increased industrial production of course meant more goods. In 1975, there was one car and one television set for every two persons in the USA, but, in India, there was one car to more than 500 persons and a television set to every 2000. More important, the developed countries had far and away the preponderance of the world's tractors, combine-harvesters, power-stations, universities, research laboratories and hospitals. In fact, by 1970, one-sixth of the world's population enjoyed 70 per cent of its real wealth.

Even in the western world, millions of people were ill-clad and undernourished in 1900 because their wages were low; in the 1930's, because they were out of work, but, by the 1970's, poverty as it existed in those earlier years, had disappeared.

Most people in developed countries have achieved immensely higher standards of living, that is to say, they are better fed, clothed and housed than ever before in history; they have more leisure, live longer, are less prone to disease and are better cared for in sickness, old age and misfortune than their ancestors would have believed possible. These improvements in the lives of ordinary people have come about through social idealism, private enterprise, trade union agitation, and state legislation.

Bismark's Germany led the way in the 1880's with workers' insurance schemes against sickness, accident and old age; New Zealand was not far behind with various liberal measures, including the Old Age Pension Act and, in Britain, Lloyd George's 1911 National Insurance Act introduced unemployment benefit. From these beginnings stemmed the modern Welfare

State, which provides citizens with education, medical care, housing and pensions. It varies, of course, in scope. In some countries, such as Britain, Sweden and most communist states, its benefits are well-nigh comprehensive; in others, like Canada, Australia and the USA, there is more emphasis on voluntary contributions, private health insurance and home-ownership, while in Italy and Japan, great industrial firms finance their workers' benefits. To a greater or lesser degree, almost all of the affluent countries accept the principle of the state caring for its citizens' welfare.

As we survey social and political changes in our century, no problem seems more serious than population increase. In 1830, there were about 1000 million persons in the world, a figure reached after centuries of slow

increase; in 1930, there were 2000 million and, 50 years later, over 4000 million. In short, the *rate of increase* is increasing, so that the world's population may well double again in the next 30 years.

The causes are clear. It is not a case of rising birth-rates, for they are falling, even in India, but of more babies surviving infancy and of more adults living longer. This is because people eat more and better food; their homes and clothes are cleaner; public health and medical care have greatly improved and scientists have discovered how to control killer-diseases, such as malaria, smallpox, tuberculosis and cholera. In England, a male citizen in 1850 could expect to live to be about 40 (less in industrial areas), but, by 1970, he was likely to reach 69 and a woman 75. In India, although male 'life expectancy' was only 42, the death rate had been halved since 1920.

This tremendous increase in population is by no means evenly spread, for, in Europe and North America, populations are rising only slowly, at barely 1 per cent a year, whereas, in Asia, they are growing very fast: in India, for example, at 2.6 a year. Hence, by 1980, more than half the worlds' people were Asians, living on about one-fifth of the earth's surface; they numbered 595 out of every 1000 persons alive, compared with 179 Europeans, 108 Africans, 75 North Americans, 55 Latin Americans and only 5 Australians and New Zealanders.

Part of the reason why the fastest growing populations live in the world's poorest countries is because, in an agricultural society, more children mean more hands to work the family's land and to keep the parents in old age. So, in India, peasants tend to ignore the government's attempts to encourage birth-control, whereas, in rich industrial countries, people choose to limit their families in order to enjoy more leisure and a higher standard of living. Nor is India's population growth the fastest, for there are higher rates in Sri Lanka, Taiwan, Indonesia and some of the countries of Africa, Latin America and the Middle East.

It used to be generally assumed that the poor states would expand their

Africans who fled their villages under the pressure of war found shelter only in this municipal rubbish dump in Harare (formerly Salisbury), Zimbabwe, an example of the plight of destitute peasants the world over.

food production and industry and gradually catch up with the developed countries. But over-population means there is less food and resources to go round; it brings unemployment, land shortage, overworking of poor soil and shanty-town squalor. Poor countries lack the capital to build factories and start industries or to educate their people in technical skills and modern farming methods. The gap between the rich and poor world grows wider.

Considering the colossal rise in population, farming has done remarkably well to produce enough food for most of the world's people. This has been achieved through scientific research into fertilisers, pesticides, better strains of plants and animals – and, of course, through mechanisation. Here, again, it is the developed countries which have been able to do best, because they possess the wealth to increase wealth. Some of them help Third World countries with food, loans and technical advice, and the United Nations and organisations like OXFAM take aid to famine regions. Yet relief schemes, however worthy, cannot solve the long-term problem of there being too many people on earth.

One fear is that poverty and its accompanying sense of injustice may lead to political upheavals, even to revolution and war. There is already the example of Bangladesh and might not China try to expand into the USSR's underpopulated lands, for the reason that Japan occupied Manchuria in the 1930's i.e. for trade and investment? Mass-emigration, which actually reduced poverty-stricken Ireland's population in the 19th century, became a feature of the post-Second World War period, when, in addition to exodus from areas of famine and natural disaster such as there had always been, millions of Eastern Europeans fled to the West, Hindus and Muslims sought safety in India or Pakistan, many Jews made their way to Israel, while Turks, Greeks, Italians and Algerians found jobs in the richer states of Western Europe. Countries with a tradition of European settlement, like Australia, Canada and Argentina accepted large numbers of immigrants, though some did not admit non-Whites. The USA relaxed its pre-war restrictions on immigration and, after the Commonwealth Citizenship Act of 1947, the British government encouraged West Indians and Asians to settle in the UK, so that, by the mid-1970's, upwards of 2 million immigrants and their children were living in London and the industrial areas of Britain.

A natural consequence of population increase has been the growth of urbanisation. There are now more than 60 cities in the world with over 2 million inhabitants; some, like Tokyo, New York and Paris, are the capitals of rich countries, but many others, such as Bombay, Jakarta, Bogota and Cairo are situated in poor countries of the Third World. In every type of country, rich or poor, capitalist or communist, the proportion of people living in towns and cities has increased at an unprecedented rate. This is partly because jobs in factories, offices, shops, public services and so on are to

In the latter part of the 20th century, there is increasing concern about the effects of industrial pollution and about the wastefulness of many industrial practices. The Lacq research station in south-west France is one centre where scientists seek to remedy the situation by their work on plastics, pollution, insulation and medicine.

be found in towns, whereas highly-mechanised farming needs very few workers, only 3 or 4 out of every 100 workers in England and the USA. In South-East Asia, by contrast, 80 per cent of all workers are employed on the land. Yet there, as in Africa and Latin America, towns and cities are still growing rapidly.

The difference is that, in most of the Third World countries, the rural population has not fallen. In fact, it goes on rising, causing unemployed peasants to migrate to the cities to eke out a miserable existence in shacks and hovels clustered about the outskirts. Even where architects have designed a dream city, Brasilia, the new capital of Brazil, no-one has been able to prevent the growth of its slum shanty-town.

Up until the Industrial Revolution, man's pursuit of progress made little impact on the natural world, apart from cutting down forests, and barely 200 years have passed since he began to scar the countryside with slag heaps, quarries and tall chimneys.

Coal smoke polluted the atmosphere of 19th-century cities and created the dense fogs of Charles Dickens' day, but modern industry produces much more harmful waste, which is got rid of by being pumped into rivers, dispersed as fumes over the land or into the sea. Poisonous discharges kill fish and wildlife; deposits such as cyanide and radio-active waste threaten human life perhaps for generations; nuclear explosions, chemical fertilisers and pesticides upset the balance of nature and 'smog', a deadly mixture of smoke and exhaust gases from motor vehicles, makes life so unpleasant in cities like Tokyo and Los Angeles that people take to wearing masks as a protection against lung disease.

Most countries are taking belated steps to reduce pollution and protect the environment; these steps include production of smokeless fuels, better engine design, noise reduction, agreements to ban the dumping of dangerous waste into the seas, protection of wildlife and fisheries, recycling of waste material, cleaning up rivers, creating 'green belts' and national parks. The difficulties are immense, because of the demands of industry and people's desire for ever-higher standards of living. Some governments refuse to stop testing nuclear weapons or cutting down forests or killing whales; as yet, no-one seems likely to abandon, or even reduce, motor transport and travel by aeroplane. Poor countries cannot be expected to forgo industrial development or to pay much attention to the views of those who have themselves been responsible for so much pollution and waste.

Besides being anxious about pollution and the prospect of nuclear destruction, people have come to realise that mankind is trying to get from the material world more resources than there are in it. Indeed, experts can already predict dates by which some of those resources, particularly oil, will have run out.

541

However, the position is not hopeless, for there are signs that the great powers recognise the need to conserve the earth's riches and to reach international agreements which may even require a certain amount of sacrifice of their own interests. In this connection, it is significant that the Third World may hold the whip-hand, because it possesses so many of the minerals required by modern industry, and a number of countries, encouraged by the success of the oil-producing states (OPEC, the Organisation of Petroleum Exporting Countries, founded in 1961 to include non-Arab as well as Arab countries), have got together to control their output. Over 80 per cent of the world's copper, for instance, comes from Zaïre, Zambia, Peru and Chile - just four countries, which decided to cut production in the 1970's. Bauxite comes principally from Algeria, Ghana, Guinea, Senegal and Guyana; tin chiefly from Nigeria, Zaïre, Thailand, Malaysia, Indonesia and Bolivia and mercury from Nigeria, Mexico and Algeria. Councils and associations have been formed to reduce the supply of these primary products, and also of phosphates, coffee, cocoa, natural rubber and bananas, in order to force up prices and give the poorer countries a bigger share of the world's wealth.

In Western societies, there were for a great many years three groups of people who were treated as inferior beings. They generally worked in menial occupations for low pay or none at all and they had next to no say in how society was run. They were, of course, women, negroes and young people, all of whom have asserted themselves in recent times.

Women were the first to do so. Thanks partly to the French Revolution, they won some important civil rights during the 19th century, such as the right to own property after marriage, but, generally speaking, they had to wait a long time for political rights. In Britain, the Suffragette campaign of protest came to an abrupt end in 1914, but, after the war, women over 30 were given the vote, though it was 1928 before the age was reduced to 21, the same as men. In the USA, only 11 states had granted votes to women by 1914 (Wyoming as early as 1869), but, like the British parliament, Congress yielded to pressure in 1920.

Women's suffrage has been granted at different times in different countries; for example, New Zealand in 1893, Norway in 1912, France in 1944 and Switzerland in 1971, while, in totalitarian countries, such as USSR and Cuba, much is made of women having exactly the same rights as men. However, as it became clear that the right to vote was only a step towards real equality, there arose in the more sophisticated countries, like the USA, Britain and France, Women's Liberation movements which campaigned, not so much for new laws, as for changed attitudes towards the position of women in society, especially in industry and the home.

They have had considerable success, though it has made no impact, so far,

Birmingham, Alabama, May 1963: the Rev. Martin Luther King announces that he and other Negro leaders are calling a halt to anti-segregation mass demonstrations because they believe honest attempts are being made to settle racial differences. King was awarded the Nobel Peace Prize in the following year, which brought him world-wide respect, but his insistence on non-violence was to be rejected by militant blacks.

upon the lives of countless millions of women in Asia and Africa. Even in Arab countries, where girls may now attend universities, they are expected to behave in keeping with the traditions of the male-dominated Islamic society.

Negroes in the USA formed a socially inferior class ever since the days of slavery and their status of second-class citizens hardly changed during the century following upon the Civil War, until, in the 1960's, there arose a strong protest movement to put an end to racial discrimination. Its leader, Martin Luther King, became a national figure, whose Christian faith and passionate sincerity helped to convince President Kennedy that Congress must pass a Civil Rights Act to remove discrimination. When it failed to do so, Luther King's plea for non-violence fell, like Gandhi's in India, on deaf ears and savage riots occurred in the run-down areas of northern cities, such as Chicago, Newark and Detroit. A movement known as Black Power rejected the idea of integration into a white-dominated society and Luther King himself was shot dead in Tennessee in 1968, still condemning violence and the 'racism in reverse' of black separatists.

There followed a decade of reduced militancy, as school segregation was ended, many black students entered universities and negroes were elected to Congress and state legislatures. But the death of Luther King seemed to have removed the one man capable of bringing harmony to race relations in the USA.

In some ways, the position of the West Indians in Britain was different. As Commonwealth citizens, they came of their own free will from their Caribbean islands to find work, usually in factories and public transport, and, in a country which still possessed a liberal tradition and a high level of respect for law and order, a great many of them settled down uneventfully in some of the poorer districts of London and Midlands towns. Difficulties arose with the arrival of a generation of British-born youngsters, who, as full-employment faded, became increasingly alienated from a society which seemed to condemn them to unemployment, bad housing and police harassment. That they did not help themselves by resorting to violence and petty crime only underlined the need for government action to avert conflict in a land which was only beginning to realise that it had become a multi-racial society with problems which refused to go away.

The third of the three formerly-docile groups to make their presence felt were the young. For long bound to conform to the adult's world by lack of money and the traditional disciplines of home and school, teenagers (the word itself was new) and students discovered in the 1960's that plentiful jobs, student grants and the widespread collapse of established values gave them all kinds of heady freedoms and their own exclusive 'pop-culture'.

Protest began at universities, where students felt they should have more say in the running of their colleges, and flowed on to much wider political

Multi-racial Britain 1981: a mixed racial group in London's East End.

May 1968: following an appeal by the trades unions, 100 000 workers demonstrate in Paris. The student with a banner seated on her companions' shoulders recalls Delacroix's painting of Liberty in the July Revolution of 1830 (see page 323).

issues, in particular, Nuclear Disarmament and the Vietnam War. A revolutionary movement, known as the New Left, which rejected party politics for direct action, made many converts in the universities and 1968 became the year of student revolution in the USA, West Germany, Japan,

Northern Ireland, where young people have been drawn into taking part in street violence. Here, in a 'Christian' community, the lad has bottle bombs lined up behind the parapet.

France, Italy and Britain. Anti-war and radical demonstrations led to clashes with police and the military, in which some students were arrested, injured and actually killed. Japanese students were particularly militant, perhaps because Japanese life was strongly authoritarian, but the 'student revolution' reached its climax in Paris, where many Parisians and French workers supported the students in their battles against the police; barricades went up in the streets, the Sorbonne (the university) was occupied, the city's Latin Quarter and a number of factories were taken over in a violent defiance of authority.

De Gaulle's government was badly shaken, but the movement petered out and, by the early 1970's, student revolution seemed to have died down. However, in some countries, such as China, Iran and Egypt, students remained a powerful force in politics and there were groups of young people, particularly in West Germany and Italy, who carried out acts of terrorism and continued to revere revolutionary heroes such as Lenin, Ho Chi Minh, Rosa Luxembourg, co-leader of a Berlin revolt of 1919, and Che Guevara, the friend of Castro, a legendary figure who was killed in Bolivia in 1966.

To say that we live in an age of violence is only to repeat what man has been saying throughout the centuries. The history of a nation is all too often an account of the wars it has fought and lasting peace, so ardently prayed for, has always seemed to be an unattainable dream. For millions of people, the

First World War was 'the war to end war', but, as we know, it led directly to a conflict which in many ways was even more barbarous.

Since 1945, major wars have taken place in Korea, Vietnam, Algeria, India, Uganda, Nigeria, Zaïre and the Middle East; lesser, but still terrible, outbreaks of killing have occurred all over the world, even in smaller countries like Cyprus and El Salvador. Arab-Israeli raids and counter-raids are almost daily occurrences; so are the murders and explosions in Northern Ireland. In West Germany, Italy, the USA and many developed nations, no less than in the Third World countries, the urban guerilla, the hi-jacker, the political assassin have become familiar figures - terrorists to their enemies, freedom-fighters to their friends.

Wars and political violence are matched by civil disorders that were practically unknown a few years ago. The dangers of city life in, say, 18th-century London seemed to have been put an end to by street-lighting and regular police forces, but, by the 1970's, many cities in the USA and Europe were unsafe after dark and, in some places, even in daylight. 'Mugging', hooliganism, vandalism and acts of senseless cruelty seemed to have become everyday features of a world which, paradoxically, cared greatly about human rights and social welfare.

Perhaps the world's problems would be solved by science and technology. Science was the new God, mysterious and all-powerful. After all, it had created the 'second Industrial Revolution' of the 20th century, with its entirely new electrical and chemical industries, the marvels of radar and jet-propulsion, of nuclear reactors and space-exploration, of transistors, computers, silicon chips, anti-biotics, plastic surgery and heart transplants. This second Industrial Revolution, though, was different from the first one, because, instead of creating vast numbers of jobs, its aim was to achieve maximum production with the minimum number of workers. It was an exciting and, at the same time, an alarming period in which to live, but, with man's astounding capacity to master his environment, he could still look forward with hope.

Index

Page references to illustration captions appear in **heavy type**

Index

Index